# ISTHMIA

—

## VOLUME III

## TERRACOTTA LAMPS

# ISTHMIA

EXCAVATIONS BY THE UNIVERSITY OF CHICAGO

UNDER THE AUSPICES OF

THE AMERICAN SCHOOL OF CLASSICAL STUDIES AT ATHENS

VOLUME III

## TERRACOTTA LAMPS

BY

OSCAR BRONEER

AMERICAN SCHOOL OF CLASSICAL STUDIES AT ATHENS
PRINCETON, NEW JERSEY
1977

PUBLISHED WITH THE AID OF A GRANT FROM THE OLD DOMINION FOUNDATION

**Library of Congress Cataloging in Publication Data** (Revised)

Broneer, Oscar Theodore, 1894–
  Isthmia.

  Includes indexes.
  CONTENTS: v. 1. Temple of Poseidon. 2. Topo-
graphy and architecture. 3. Terracotta lamps.
  1. Isthmia, Greece-Antiquities. 2. Excavation
(Archaeology)—Greece—Isthmia. I. Title.
DF261.I85B76         938'.7         76-362971

PRINTED IN GERMANY *at* J. J. AUGUSTIN, GLÜCKSTADT

# PREFACE

This third volume of the Isthmia series is the last that I shall author. It would not have been possible to bring this to completion but for the help I have received from several assistants. For, although I have written or dictated the text in its entirety and am solely to be blamed for its shortcomings, others have contributed so much and so importantly that the work is in a real sense the result of co-operative efforts. It is, therefore, both a pleasure and a deep-felt obligation to record here the names and contributions of each of those who have made it possible for this volume to appear at the present time.

The drawings for Plates 1–13 are all the work of Jean Carpenter, who also made the final arrangements and collages of the Plates of photographs 14–40. By an oversight the drawing of catalogue number **1** was left as a pencil sketch and was later inked by Stella Bouzaki. Marcia W. Langdon, the chief photographer, generously volunteered her services, and used her technical knowledge and skill to give the photographs the best possible quality. After her departure from Greece, our veteran photographer, Emile Seraf, was called in to make photographs of a few lamps which had been omitted earlier.

We began work on this volume in 1972 and continued with some interruptions until the summer of 1975. Because of gradual impairment of my eyesight during those four years I became increasingly dependent on the help of younger persons. At the very first division of the lamps into related groups or types, and at various later stages of the work, Georgia Kefala (now Mrs. Belitsi) rendered valuable assistance. After this preliminary disposition of the material, I dictated the description and measurements of all the lamps that were originally included in the inventory. Maria Mitchell and Jeanne Marty (now Mrs. Peppers) made the first rough copy of the manuscript at my dictation. Thereupon, Anna Manzoni, who stayed in Corinth for a longer period, made extensive contribution toward the work. We visited a number of museums in northwest Greece and the Peloponnesos and made notes of the collections of lamps. Miss Manzoni undertook the very laborious task of searching through all the baskets of pottery for lamp fragments which had been considered too small to be entered in the original inventory. For this time-consuming work she was successful in enlisting the help of some of her friends who were visitors in Corinth. The vastly increased number of items resulting from this process entailed further refinements of the classification with consequent retyping of the manuscript. After Miss Manzoni's departure I obtained the services of Carol Stewart (now Mrs. Harward), who continued the work through the fall of 1973 and the first five months of 1974; but she too had to leave before the manuscript was finished. She made the preliminary disposition of the photographs for the plates, retyped most of the manuscript and made the tedious compilations of the Concordance. For ten months during the final stages I had the part-time assistance of Julie Boegehold, who compiled the records that went into the chapter on Provenance and Distribution of Types. Through her expert handling and the complete retyping of the manuscript errors were detected and eliminated, and the text received its final revision. Mrs. Boegehold also undertook the tedious job of checking for the last time the two sets of numbers (inventory and catalogue) against each other, verified all references, and compiled the bibliographical list.

The manuscript was completed and submitted to the Editor in June, 1975. By the time the first proof sheets had appeared I was no longer able to see to do the proofreading. By that time I had been fortunate enough to obtain the able part-time assistance of Kathleen Slane Wright. She carried out the arduous tasks of reading proof and compiling the index.

To these assistants, and more especially to my wife, Lula Logan Broneer, I would further record my sense of gratitude for endurance of considerable hardship caused by the idiosyncracies and irritability of a scholar under pressure to bring a major, often tedious, task to completion.

This sketch of the contributions of my assistants is far from complete, but it will convey a picture of the very large part played by each in the making of the volume. To enable me to engage their services and to meet other expenses incurred in preparation of the volume, I received a grant from the Andrew W. Mellon Foundation (Old Dominion Foundation), and it gives me great pleasure to express to the Trustees of that Foundation and to its president, Nathan M. Pusey, my sincere thanks.

Throughout the work of excavation at Isthmia and during preparation for its final publication, I have enjoyed the facilities of the American School of Classical Studies, and I wish to record my indebtedness to the past and present directors of the School and of the Corinth Excavations. The Greek Archaeological Service, through its directors, ephors, and epimelites, has offered much courtesy and helpfulness since the beginning of the excavations; with reference to this volume of the Isthmia publications, I am particularly grateful for access to study collections of lamps both in Athens and in the provinces.

Others to whom I am indebted for help in connection with my work on *Isthmia* III are mentioned in the text and notes throughout the volume. The many references to *Agora* IV and VII show how much I have depended on the work of their authors, Richard H. Howland and Judith Perlzweig Binder, for the dating of the lamps from Isthmia.

To the Editor, Marian H. McAllister, I am deeply indebted for advice and numerous courtesies throughout the work on the manuscript and the printing of the book. She also compiled and added to the volume the catalogue-to-inventory concordances, which entailed work far beyond that of ordinary editing.

It was my purpose from the very beginning to make the volume on the lamps complementary to *Isthmia* I and II which deal with topographical and architectural matters of the site. Other scholars are now at work on—or will soon be engaged in—the study of other movable finds: inscriptions, sculpture, pottery, terracotta figurines, metal objects, coins, etc. These I trust will be finished and be added to the series without undue delay, as funds become available for publication. The funds, originally provided for volumes I and II, came from donations obtained through the efforts of Professor Charles H. Morgan, and now form a revolving fund through which we hope it will be possible to finance the publication of this and all subsequent volumes of the Isthmia series.

During my study in preparation of this volume, the lamps from Isthmia, like most of the antiquities from that site, were housed first in the Old Museum, and later in the basement of the New Museum, at Ancient Corinth. They have now been transferred to the storeroom of the new Isthmia museum where they are still arranged in the order in which they appear in this book. A few of the more significant pieces are now on display in the showcases of the museum.

As of June 1, 1976, Elizabeth R. Gebhard will succeed me in charge of the work at Isthmia. She will have full responsibility for installations, exhibition and all further publication of the finds from the University of Chicago excavations at Isthmia.

ANCIENT CORINTH, GREECE                                          OSCAR BRONEER
March, 1976

# CONTENTS

# CONTENTS

# LIST OF ILLUSTRATIONS

# SELECT BIBLIOGRAPHY AND ABBREVIATIONS

The books and articles listed below are only those to which references are made in this volume. The earlier literature on lamps—prior to 1930—can be found in my book on terracotta lamps from Corinth, *Corinth* IV, ii, pp. 300–304. More recent books are listed in the select bibliographies of *The Athenian Agora* IV, 1958 and VII, 1961. The most complete bibliography, up-to-date to 1955, appears in Bernhard, *Lampki Starożytne*, Warsaw, 1955.

*Agora* = *The Athenian Agora, Results of Excavations Conducted by the American School of Classical Studies at Athens*
  IV. Richard H. Howland, *Greek Lamps and their Survivals*, Princeton, 1958
  V. Henry S. Robinson, *Pottery of the Roman Period, Chronology*, Princeton, 1959
  VI. Clairève Grandjouan, *Terracottas and Plastic Lamps of the Roman Period*, Princeton, 1961
  VII. Judith Perlzweig (Binder), *Lamps of the Roman Period*, Princeton, 1961
*A.J.A.* = *American Journal of Archaeology*
*Archaeological Reports* 18 = H. W. Catling, "Archaeology in Greece," *Archaeological Reports for 1971–72*(No. 18), p. 8
*Argos* = Anne Bovon, *Lampes d'Argos, Études péloponnésiennes* V, Paris, 1966
Bailey = Donald M. Bailey, "Lamps in the Victoria and Albert Museum," *Opus. Athen.* 6, 1965, pp. 1–83.
*B.C.H.* = *Bulletin de correspondance hellénique*
Bernhard = Maria Ludwika Bernhard, *Lampki Starożytne*, Warsaw, 1955
Bieber, Margarete, *The Sculpture of the Hellenistic Age*, New York, 1955
Bovon, see *Argos*
Brants = Johanna Brants, *Antieke Terra-Cotta Lampen, Uit het Rijksmuseum van Oudheden te Leiden*, Leiden, 1913
Broneer, Oscar, "A Late Type of Wheel-made Lamps from Corinth," *A.J.A.* 31, 1927, pp. 329–337
  "A Calyx-Krater by Exekias," *Hesperia* 6, 1937, pp. 469–486
  "Excavations at Isthmia, Third Campaign, 1955–1956," *Hesperia* 27, 1958, pp. 1–37
  "Excavations at Isthmia, Fourth Campaign, 1957–1958," *Hesperia* 28, 1959, pp. 298–343

  "Excavations at Isthmia, 1959–1961," *Hesperia* 31, 1962, pp. 1–25
  "Paul and the Pagan Cults at Isthmia," *H.T.R.* 64, 1971, pp. 169–187
Broneer, see also *Corinth* IV, ii; *Corinth* X; *Isthmia* I; *Isthmia* II
Bruneau = Philippe Bruneau, *Délos, Exploration archéologique de Délos*, XXVI, *Les Lampes*, Paris, 1965
Bruneau, P., "Lampes corinthiennes," *B.C.H.* 95, 1971, pp. 437–501
*B.S.A.* = *Annual of the British School of Archaeology at Athens*
Cardaillac = Fernand de Cardaillac, *Lampes antiques découvertes dans l'Afrique du Nord*, Tarbes, 1922
Caskey, John L., "Objects from a Well at Isthmia," *Hesperia* 29, 1960, pp. 168–176
Clement, Paul, Δελτίον 26, 1971, Χρονικά (publ. 1974), pp. 100–111
*Corinth* = *Corinth, Results of Excavations Conducted by the American School of Classical Studies at Athens*
  IV, ii. O. Broneer, *Terracotta Lamps*, Cambridge, Mass., 1930
  VII, iii. G. Roger Edwards, *Corinthian Hellenistic Pottery*, Princeton, 1975
  X. O. Broneer, *The Odeum*, Cambridge, Mass., 1932
Dakaris, Soterios, «'Ανασκαφὴ εἰς τὸ Νεκρομαντεῖον τοῦ 'Αχέροντος», Πρακτικά, 1961 (Athens, 1964), pp. 108–119
*Délos* XXVI, see Bruneau
Δελτίον = 'Αρχαιολογικὸν Δελτίον
Deneauve = Jean Deneauve, *Lampes de Carthage*, Paris, 1969
Deonna, Waldemar, "Les lampes antiques trouvées à Délos," *B.C.H.* 32, 1908, pp. 133–136
Edwards, see *Corinth* VII, iii
Fremersdorf = Fritz Fremersdorf, *Römische Bildlampen*, Bonn and Leipzig, 1922
Furtwängler = Adolf Furtwängler, *Die Sammlung Sabouroff* I, Berlin, 1883–1887
Gebhard, Elizabeth, *The Theater at Isthmia*, Chicago, 1973
Graham, A. J. *et al.*, "An Attic Country House below the Cave of Pan at Vari," *B.S.A.* 68, 1973, pp. 355–452
Grandjouan, see *Agora* VI

Haken = Roman Haken, "Roman Lamps in the Prague National Museum and in other Czechoslovak Collections," *Acta Musei Nationalis Prague*, Series A, XII, Prague, 1958

Heres = Gerald Heres, *Die punischen und griechischen Tonlampen der staatlichen Museen zu Berlin*, Berlin, 1969

*Hesperia* = *Hesperia*, Journal of the American School of Classical Studies at Athens

Howland, see *Agora* IV

*H.T.R.* = *Harvard Theological Review*

Iconomu = C. Iconomu, *Oraite Greco-Romane*, Dobrogea, Romania, 1967

*Isthmia* = *Isthmia, Excavations by the University of Chicago under the Auspices of the American School of Classical Studies at Athens*
> I. O. Broneer, *The Temple of Poseidon*, Princeton, 1971
> II. O. Broneer, *Topography and Architecture*, Princeton, 1973

Iványi = Dóra Iványi, *Die pannonischen Lampen*, Budapest, 1935

*Jahrb.* = *Jahrbuch des deutschen archäologischen Instituts*

Kardara, Chrysoula, "Dyeing and Weaving Works at Isthmia," *A.J.A.* 65, 1961, pp. 261–266

Kübler = Karl Kübler, "Zum Formwandel in der spätantiken attischen Tonplastik," *Jahrb.* 67, 1952, pp. 99–145

Lepikowna = Wilhelmina Lepikowna, *Lampa Starżytna*, Lwów, 1938

Lerat = L. Lerat, *Lampes antiques, Catalogue des Collections Archéologiques de Besançon*, Paris, 1954

Loeschcke = Siegfried Loeschcke, *Lampen aus Vindonissa*, Zürich, 1919

Menzel = Heinz Menzel, *Antike Lampen im römisch-germanischen Zentralmuseum zu Mainz*, Mainz, 1969

Mercando = Liliana Mercando, *Lucerne greche e romane dell'Antiquarium Communale*, Roma, 1962

Mikulčić, Ivan, "The West Cemetery: Excavations in 1965," *Studies in the Antiquities of Stobi* I, 1973, pp. 61–92

Nilsson, Martin P., "Lampen und Kerzen im Kult der Antike," *Opus. Arch.* 6, 1950, pp. 96–111

Oleiro = J. M. Bairrão Oleiro, *Museu Machado de Castro: Catálogo de lucernas romanas*, Coimbra, 1952

*Opus. Arch.* = *Opuscula Archaeologica*

*Opus. Athen.* = *Opuscula Atheniensia*

Perdrizet, P., *Fouilles de Delphes*, V, *Monuments figurés*, Paris, 1908

Πρακτικά = Πρακτικὰ τῆς ἐν Ἀθήναις Ἀρχαιολογικῆς Ἑταιρίας

Perlzweig, see *Agora* VII

Robinson, Henry S., "A Sanctuary and Cemetery in Western Corinth," *Hesperia* 38, 1969, pp. 1–35

Robinson, see also *Agora* V

Shear, T. Leslie, Jr., "The Athenian Agora: Excavations of 1972," *Hesperia* 42, 1973, pp. 359–407

Siebert, Gérard, "Lampes corinthiennes et imitations au Musée National d'Athènes," *B.C.H.* 90, 1966, pp. 472–513

Szent. = Tihamér Szentléleky, *Ancient Lamps*, Amsterdam, 1969

Vegas = Mercedes Vegas, *Novaesium* II: *Die Römischen Lampen*, Berlin, 1966

Vermaseren, Maarten J., "The Legend of Attis in Greek and Roman Art," *Études préliminaires aux religions orientales dans l'empire romain* IX, Leiden, 1966

Walters = Henry B. Walters, *Catalogue of the Greek and Roman Lamps in the British Museum*, London, 1914

Weinberg, Saul S., "A Cross-section of Corinthian Antiquities," *Hesperia* 17, 1948, pp. 197–241

Wiseman, James, "Excavations in Corinth, the Gymnasium Area, 1967–1968," *Hesperia* 38, 1969, pp. 64–106
> "The Gymnasium Area at Corinth, 1969–1970," *Hesperia* 41, 1972, pp. 1–42
> "A Trans-Isthmian Fortification Wall," *Hesperia* 32, 1963, pp. 248–275

# INTRODUCTORY COMMENTS

The terracotta lamps discovered in the Sanctuary of Poseidon at Isthmia follow in the main the typology established for the more representative collection from Corinth itself.[1] There are, however, some important differences that will justify the appearance of a separate volume on lamps in the series of Isthmia publications. Apart from some material differences, which will appear in the description of the several types, the majority of the lamps from Isthmia served a different purpose. Whereas the utilitarian functions of lamps predominated in the commercial metropolis of Corinth, a large percentage of the lamps from Isthmia were integrated with the cult apparatus of the gods. This aspect is reflected in the relative frequency of certain types and in the creation of new types.[2]

The collection as a whole is of limited value for lychnology as such. The number of types is too small for that purpose; in fact several types are represented only by minor fragments or by none at all. The lamps from Isthmia are important rather as material documents for the history and significance of the site. More than other portable objects from the excavation, the lamps can be used as index to the chronology and purpose of the various monuments and the activities they housed. That being the case, it seems useful to have a complete list of all recognizable lamp fragments with their provenance, so as to make it possible to determine in which part of the Sanctuary the several types had been in use at any given time in the history of the site. Small fragments, so long as their type can be recognized, tell their story in this respect as effectively as whole lamps. For this reason we searched through all the thousands of excavation boxes filled with pottery sherds and removed the lamp fragments, which we then numbered separately. By this time-consuming process we more than doubled the number of inventoried items in the original list of lamps. Most of the added pieces are by themselves insignificant fragments, many of which would normally have been discarded, together with such sherds of pottery as are not considered useful as material for dating. It did not seem necessary, however, to burden the catalogue with description of such minor fragments; only their type, date, and provenance are important, and such data can be found with the help of the section on Provenance and Distribution of Types, pp. 84–91.

It is regrettably true that over most of the Sanctuary there was little reliable stratification, because the soil that covered the ancient surface was so shallow that the plow of modern tillers had reached down through the fill and left scratches on the ancient stones and hardpan underneath. Since this would naturally result in totally mixed deposits, it may seem to render the records of provenance all but useless. That is not the case, however. Even where no undisturbed fill could be isolated, the proportion of sherds of the several lamp types has a bearing on the nature of the monuments concerned. Although fragments of lamps may wander far and wide, they rarely migrate in groups of one type; the overwhelming majority tend to remain close to the place where the lamps had originally been used.

---

[1] Oscar Broneer, *Corinth*, IV, ii, *Terracotta Lamps*, Cambridge, Mass., 1930, henceforth referred to as *Corinth* IV, ii.

[2] It must be recognized that any division into types is arbitrary, hardly more than a convenient device for making references. For example, the Greek and Hellenistic lamps from Corinth (*Corinth* IV, ii) are grouped into 18 types; the lamps from the Athenian Agora (*Agora* IV), which cover approximately the same length of time, 7th to 2nd century B.C., have been divided into 48 types with many more subtypes and variants. The author of the *Lamps of the Roman Period* (*Agora* VII) dispensed with typology altogether. She grouped her material into two large divisions: "Imported Lamps" and "Attic Lamps." The Attic lamps of the 3rd and 4th centuries, comprising about three fifths of the total number, she "grouped according to representation or pattern on the disc." For a discussion of the usefulness or disadvantages of a typological arrangement, see her book, *Agora* VII, pp. 1–2; and cf. *Corinth* IV, ii, p. ii.

The several areas from which the lamps and lamp fragments were collected in our excavation are of limited extent. That makes it all the more likely that the lamp fragments from the mixed fill indicate the approximate vicinity of their original use. For example, if a specific sector produced predominantly lamps of Hellenistic types, we should certainly be justified in concluding that such an area was not to any great extent occupied before the period of Alexander the Great or after the destruction of Corinth by Mummius in the year 146 B.C. Thus the lamp fragments culled from totally mixed deposits cast their own light on chronology and the use and nature of the several cult places within the Isthmian Sanctuary.

It would be impractical to create a new classification based on the lamps from Isthmia. The typology in this volume follows that of *Corinth* IV, ii, with some modifications. When necessary the types have been divided into subtypes; and one new group, the most numerous of all, has been added. Since there is no equivalent type among the lamps from Corinth, this group is here designated merely as Palaimonion Lamps and is further divided into types and subtypes. I am conscious of the fact that my old typology does not cover all the known types from Greece, not even all the types subsequently found at Corinth. Furthermore, a few of the items from Isthmia, apart from the Palaimonion lamps, do not readily fit into the old typology. But *Corinth* IV, ii, which has been used for a long time, has set a pattern, and it would be confusing to propose a new series of types with different numbers. When the lamps discovered at Corinth since 1929 are published, a new classification will have to be made.

Since my publication of *Corinth* IV, ii, more than forty-five years ago, several important studies of ancient lamps have appeared, the principal ones of which are listed in the bibliography. These have not only added many new types but have refined and perfected the chronology. This has been made possible through better excavation technique and more accurate recording than was the practice more than half a century ago, when most of the lamps included in *Corinth* IV, ii were discovered.

The lamps from Isthmia fall into four large groups, distinguished chronologically and, in a lesser degree, by provenance. Necessarily they overlap to a great extent. The first group, Types I–VII D, consists of Classical Greek lamps from the 6th to mid-4th century B.C. Most of these were probably used in the Temple and cult of Poseidon. They come chiefly from the area of the Temple of Poseidon, from the Temple dumps to the north and east of the Temple, and from the Large Circular Pit. By comparison with later types, they are not numerous. Most of them would have been brought by temple personnel and worshipers, not as votive objects in a strict sense, but for illumination. Many of the later lamps were doubtless used in the same way, but some may have been intended primarily as dedications. There is no strict distinction between the two uses.

The second group, Types VII E–XIV, consists of Hellenistic types, mostly of the 3rd and 2nd centuries B.C. Some of them were found at various points in the temenos of Poseidon, but by far the greatest number came from the Rachi, the occupation of which covers the two centuries represented by this group.[3] The buildings with which they are associated were mostly of an industrial nature, and the lamps had obviously been used purely for illumination.

At Isthmia as at Corinth we must assume a hiatus of more than a century, from 146 to 44 B.C., i.e. the time that Corinth was virtually nonexistent. This situation accounts for the nearly total absence of late Hellenistic lamps, such as Types XIV, XV, XVIII[4] and XIX. Actually the rebuilding of the Isthmian Sanctuary on a large scale seems to have been delayed till well into the first half of the 1st century after Christ. With the reactivation of the cult of Poseidon in the time of Augustus and the return of the Isthmian Games to their original site,[5] a new era began that extended through nearly three centuries. This period is represented by the third large division of lamps from Isthmia, by far the most important group, both because of their overwhelmingly large number and the purpose they served. The vast

---

[3] For the date of the commercial activities on the Rachi, see Chrysoula Kardara, *A.J.A.* 65, 1961, pp. 261–266; *Isthmia* II, p. 64, note 72.

[4] On Type XVIII and the reason for its scarcity at Corinth, see *Corinth* IV, ii, pp. 61–66.

[5] See below, footnote 23.

majority of lamps in that group came from the Palaimonion. They comprise the common forms of imported relief lamps, Types XXII–XXV, the locally produced wheelmade lamps of Type XVII, the Palaimonion lamps, and the later and less numerous but artistically superior Corinthian lamps of Type XXVII.[6] No less than 771 lamps of this period are of Type XVI, and this number includes very many small fragments that have been added largely for the sake of statistics. Type XVI, however, is exceeded in numerical frequency by the Palaimonion lamps, of which there are 1221 whole lamps and inventoried fragments. More than half of the lamps from Isthmia belong to these two types. The Palaimonion lamps are all but unknown elsewhere in Greece.[7] Even at Corinth itself, so far as I am aware, this type is missing. It is a cult vessel in a strict sense, which probably came into existence in response to a specific need during the nightly ceremonies in the worship of Palaimon. Many Palaimonion lamps, especially the later varieties, came from undisturbed fill of the sacrificial pits.[8] They occurred in great numbers throughout the Palaimonion area, and at all depths, from the level of the Early Stadium floor all the way to the modern surface. The most common type of portable lamps that appeared in the same context is Type XVI, which has much in common with the Palaimonion lamps. Both types were cast on the wheel and lack decoration; and both must have been mass-produced, perhaps in the same shops, and sold to worshipers at very little cost. It is obvious that they are products of a local Corinthian lamp industry, but no factory has yet been found in which they were made.

The fourth group, Types XXVIII–XXXIII, is a heterogeneous lot of late Roman and Early Christian lamps. A few belong to the 3rd century after Christ, but most of them are of the 4th, 5th, and 6th centuries. By far the greater number of them belong to Type XXVIII. They were found thinly scattered over the whole terrain; only in the Theater were they relatively numerous. They belong for the most part to the period of destruction, when the buildings of the Sanctuary had fallen into disrepair and later when they were finally pulled down to furnish material for the fortifications.[9] Most of them are of Athenian manufacture, others are Corinthian, and a few seem to be Argive. Many have pagan representations on the discus, but lamps with Christian symbols are numerous. Some belong to the specifically Christian type, Corinth XXXI, which originated at North African sites, but only a very few fragments are genuine imports. The Sicilian lamps of Type XXXII are represented by several fragments, and all but a few of those appear to be of local make.

The latest of the lamps from Isthmia, Types XXVIII–XXXIII, all come within the framework of the Classical tradition. The glazed lamps of later Byzantine times, Corinth Types XXXV–XXXVII, are totally lacking. The Isthmian Sanctuary ceased to exist after the construction of the trans-Isthmian fortification in the Early Christian period, which was repaired and rebuilt under the Emperor Justinian.

The lamps included in this publication, however, do not show the whole range of the lampmakers' products found at Isthmia. The excavations carried on since 1967 by the University of California at Los Angeles (UCLA), chiefly in areas outside the temenos of Poseidon and the Palaimonion, are to be published later. They have brought to light many lamps, most of them belonging to the fourth group, and among them are specimens of unconventional forms that appear to have come from some as yet unidentified shrine.[10]

[6] See below, under Palaimonion Lamps, pp. 35–52, and the chapter on Provenance and Distribution of Types, pp. 84–91.

[7] Recently a group of lamps of related shape have come to light in the Athenian Agora, together with pottery of the 5th century B.C. They have a central tube with two oil-holes near the bottom (two are pictured in Plate 38a, b courtesy of T. Leslie Shear, Jr.). They differ from the Palaimonion lamps chiefly by the addition of a handle and by the superior quality of the material. See T. Leslie Shear, Jr., *Hesperia* 42, 1973, p. 365, and pl. 67, t. It is unlikely that the makers of the Palaimonion lamp can have had knowledge of the Athenian lamps produced some five centuries earlier. It is of interest, however, that both groups would seem to have been used in hero cults.

[8] These pits, their contents and chronology, are discussed in *Isthmia* II, pp. 100–104, especially note 8.

[9] This destruction now seems to have taken place—or at least begun—at the end of the 4th century of our era rather than, as was formerly assumed, in the time of Justinian. Evidence for the earlier date came from the UCLA excavations conducted by Paul Clement since 1967; see *Isthmia* II, p. 2 and note 5; and *Archaeological Reports* 18, p. 8.

[10] See Paul Clement, Δελτίον 26, 1971, Χρονικά (publ. 1974), p. 108, pls. 90, 91.

# TYPOLOGY AND CATALOGUE

The measurements that appear in the catalogue are given in meters as follows: L(ength) includes nozzle, but not the handle; D(iameter) is used for the early handmade and the wheelmade lamps, and also for the early Roman moldmade relief lamps;[11] W(idth) for all other moldmade lamps. H(eight) does not include the handle, which is often lacking and when found usually projects above the level of the top. Measurements based partly on restoration or estimate are placed within parentheses. Dimensions that cannot be estimated with accuracy are sometimes preceded by *ca*. Right and left sides are determined by holding the lamp face up with the nozzle toward the holder, as indicated in the photographs, Plates 14 to 37.

The provenance shows the area or particular monuments in or at which the lamp was discovered. In some instances, as in the Large Circular Pit, the depth is also given. In the few cases where no provenance is indicated, the information is missing, either because the lamp came from outside the excavations or because the records in such instances are incomplete. See further the chapter on Provenance and Distribution of Types, pp. 84–91.

## CLASSICAL GREEK LAMPS, TYPES I—VII D

### TYPE I. 1–12.

The earliest lamps from Isthmia correspond closely to those of Corinth Type I. There is considerable variation within the type. The rim in particular shows the rudimentary formations that were later accentuated and became the distinguishable features of the several types. The nozzle too varies a great deal. Only one lamp, **3**, has an unbridged nozzle. Of all the lamps of Type I that have the rear half preserved only one, **2**, lacks the handle. Both the vertical band handle and the horizontal handle occur. The earlier specimens of the type have no raised base. The clay varies from a coarse, brick-red variety, exemplified by **2**, to a fine levigated clay of the local pale yellow variety. Some, particularly the earlier lamps within this type, are unglazed; others preserve a thin dull glaze.

The date of Type I is the 6th century B.C. It is conceivable that the earliest specimens, **1** and **2**, go back to the very end of the 7th century, and the type may have lasted on into the early years of the 5th century. Eight of the twelve lamps of this type came from the Large Circular Pit, whose contents date from the end of the 7th to the second half of the 5th century B.C.[12] The dates given in the catalogue are based chiefly on parallels from the Athenian Agora.

**1.** IP 2524 + IP 5776. Pl. 1. From Large Circular Pit, depth 17.42–18.50 m.

L. (including handle) *ca*. 0.11; W. *ca*. 0.075; H. 0.031.

Two non-joining fragments of an early lamp of peculiar shape. Very heavy fabric; gray core with dull red surface, unglazed. Parts of the rim and shoulder are preserved; nozzle and handle are largely missing. Enough of the handle remains to show that it was of a broad, vertical type extending from the inner edge of the rim almost to the base. The body was quadrangular, but with a rounded back and curving shoulder. The rim, which is flat on top, makes a rather sharp angle with the side. Probably of local make.

---

[11] The later moldmade lamps are rarely perfectly circular; hence the width W. (= greatest width) is given rather than the diameter.

[12] In the preliminary excavation reports (*Hesperia* 28, 1959, p. 303; 31, 1962, p. 2), I proposed an earlier date for the filling of the Large Circular Pit. Further study of the material has shown that some, though very few, pottery fragments belong to the second half of the 5th century B.C. See *Isthmia* II, Appendix I, pp. 135–136. The final study of the pottery from the pit has not yet been completed.

For the shape compare boat-shaped lamp, *Corinth* IV, ii, no. 43, and p. 35, fig. 17. A triangular lamp from the Athenian Agora, though different in shape, belongs to the same category of early lamps of heavy fabric and peculiar shape. Howland, *Agora* IV, p. 20, very plausibly characterizes this as "one of the earliest examples extant—being the first after the Mycenaean period and the subsequent dark Geometric epoch." The same might pertain to the lamp from Isthmia; no more definite date can be proposed.

**2.** IP 2526. Pls. 1, 14. From Large Circular Pit, depth 17.42–18.50 m.
H. 0.032.
Right half and nozzle missing. Coarse, red clay with dark gray core. Probably handmade. Front part blackened by fire. Rim and base form obtuse angles with the sides. Probably from the beginning of the 6th century B.C.
For the profile, cf. *Corinth* IV, ii, p. 32, fig. 14, no. 2 and see *Agora* IV, pls. 1, 29, no. 9. The Athens lamp is restored with an unbridged nozzle.

**3.** IP 1017. Pls. 1, 14. From Palaimonion.
L. 0.106; D. 0.087; H. (0.035).
Much restored, no part of bottom preserved. Red clay; black glaze on end of nozzle, rim and handle. Rim set off from curving sides, with top of rim slanting toward the inside. Short unbridged nozzle; horizontal handle.
The profile resembles *Agora* IV, Type 6 A, pls. 2 and 30, nos. 41, 42, dated *ca.* 550 B.C., but the Isthmia lamp is probably earlier.

**4.** IP 4011. Pl. 14. From Temple of Poseidon.
Small fragment from rear of lamp preserving base of handle and part of rim and side. Buff clay, probably Corinthian; dull black glaze on both interior and exterior surfaces. Broad flat handle, extending straight out (downward on Plate 1), not forming loop. Narrow rim projecting slightly toward the outside, an early ancestor to the rim of Type II. Sides form a uniform curve toward the bottom.
Cf. *Corinth* IV, ii, pl. I, no. 15. This type of horizontal handle occurs on several unpublished lamps from Corinth; it is not found on lamps from the Athenian Agora. For the profile, cf. *Agora* IV, no. 67, dated by context to the "second quarter of 6th century B.C."

**5.** IP 2445. Pls. 1, 14. From Large Circular Pit, depth 15.65–19.70 m.
L. 0.091; D. 0.053; H. 0.022.
Handle and part of nozzle restored. Pale buff clay; slight traces of grayish wash. Curving sides, no rim; vertical loop handle; long nozzle with large wick-hole; flat base. Handmade with indications of paring on sides and nozzle. From the end of the 6th or beginning of the 5th century B.C.

Among the published lamps from Corinth there are no very close parallels, but one fragment of such a lamp, CL 3959, was found in 1939 in a well that had been filled up in the early years of the 5th century B.C. It may be a mere coincidence that the type is so poorly represented at Corinth itself, but it is rather remarkable in view of the comparatively large number (5) found at Isthmia. The shape is similar to *Agora* IV, Type 15, pls. 4 and 32, no. 86, which, as the author suggests, is probably an import from Corinth. This is likely, and it is clear that the lamps from Isthmia, **5–8**, are of local make. They were found at about the same depth in the Large Circular Pit. Another almost complete example came from the 1970 excavations carried on by the UCLA expedition (Clement, Δελτίον 26, Χρονικά, p. 106, pl. 84, d). It came from the fill between the two parallel retaining walls of the Earlier Stadium. Since the lamp belongs to "the turn from the 6th to the 5th century B.C.," it is likely to have found its way there from the Archaic Stadium; the stone packing of that building is preserved close to the later walls.

**6.** IP 2322. Pl. 14. From Large Circular Pit, depth 19.35–19.45 m.
H. 0.021.
Only front part, including the nozzle, preserved. Ash-gray surface with reddish core; no glaze. Nozzle widens toward the end. Handmade; indications of paring on the nozzle.
Shape and date like **5**.

**7.** IP 2442. From Large Circular Pit, depth 15.65–19.70 m.
H. 0.023.
End of nozzle and rear half of body missing. Reddish gray clay with many white spots that seem to be particles of lime, and darker core. No glaze or wash preserved. Handmade.
Shape and date like **5**.

**8.** IP 5774. From Large Circular Pit, depth 17.80 m.
Small fragment. Reddish buff clay, inside stained dark gray, perhaps from the oil.
Same shape and date as **5**.

**9.** IP 2251. Pls. 1, 14. From Theater Cave, West Chamber.
L. 0.0765; D. 0.056; H. 0.026.
Handle and bridge of nozzle missing. Buff clay, dull gray glaze with a tinge of brown covering whole lamp inside and outside. Side and rim make uniform curve. Horizontal handle; nozzle probably bridged. Raised base, slightly concave underneath.
This is probably the latest lamp of Type I. Of the published lamps from Corinth, *Corinth* IV, ii, pl. I,

no. 35, and p. 32, fig. 14, profile 10, comes closest to the lamp from Isthmia. There are no good parallels from Athens among the lamps with a bridged nozzle. Of those with unbridged nozzle, *Agora* IV, Type 5, pls. 2 and 30, nos. 31–33, resemble our **9** in profile. It is conceivable, though unlikely, that the nozzle on **9** was unbridged. The edges on both sides show break. Athens Type 5 has been dated in the "second quarter into fourth quarter of the 6th century B.C." A single lamp of Type 8, no. 56, which was attached to a circular base, resembles Isthmia **9**. It is dated to "the end of the 6th or early 5th century B.C."

**10.** IP 2451. Pls. 1, 14. From Large Circular Pit, depth 15.65–19.70 m.

Handle, nozzle and parts of body missing. Buff clay, dull black glaze covering whole lamp except part of base. Rim continues the uniform curve of the sides, then dips down slightly to form a shallow depression between the outer part and the up-turned inner edge. Vertical loop handle, short bridged nozzle, nearly flat base.

The quality of clay and glaze bespeak Corinthian manufacture, and there are some fragmentary examples of the shape among the unpublished lamps from Corinth. For the profile, cf. *Agora* IV, Type 5, pls. 2 and 30, no. 37, dated from "second quarter into fourth quarter of 6th century B.C."

**11.** IP 5022. From Temenos, East End.

Small fragment from rear of lamp. Light red clay; reddish brown glaze. Narrow rim with the edge turned up, curving side.

Shape probably much the same as **10**, but smaller.

**12.** IP 2056. Pls. 1, 14. From Large Circular Pit, depth 15.50–15.70 m.

D. (0.098); H. 0.027.

Tip of nozzle and part of rim missing. Pale yellow clay; traces of black glaze on the inside. Narrow rim, slanting toward inside and projecting slightly over curving edge of body. Raised base, deeply concave underneath. The break in the rear is at the point where a vertical handle would have been attached, and the possibility must be admitted that such a handle existed at a somewhat higher level than usual. If that is correct, it would have been an unlooped handle like that on **4**, but narrower. That kind of handle seems to be a Corinthian peculiarity. Cf. *Corinth* IV, ii, pl. I, no. 15. Isthmia lamp **12**, like **4**, is a predecessor of Type II, but differs from all the lamps of that type in the narrow rim and the profile of the base. This kind of base begins to appear in Type VI and becomes prominent in Type VII.

The profile resembles that of *Agora* IV, pl. 2, no. 45, which also had a raised base but was flat underneath. This is dated by context to the end of the 6th century B.C.

## TYPE II. **13–27.**

In the course of the 6th century B.C., lampmaking in Greece progressed from a stage of experimentation, as shown in Type I, to assured craftsmanship, and by the end of the century several types had evolved that held their shapes for more than a century. The leading centers in this process were Corinth and Athens. In the beginning, Corinth held the lead and some early types apparently originated there, but the Corinthian clay was inferior in quality and the glaze tended to peel off. By the middle of the century the products of Athenian lampmakers had reached a state of perfection that left their Corinthian competitors far behind. The Athenian lamps soon came to be preferred to the local products, which became progressively more imitative.

Type II comprises a readily distinguishable lot with broad rim inclining inward and projecting on the outside beyond the line of the walls. As the type developed, the rim became wider so as to decrease the central opening. None of the lamps of Type II from Isthmia had a handle. The nozzle, which is preserved in only two cases, is short and the wick-hole encroaches upon the rim. Only one example, **20**, had a low raised base; on the others the bottom is slightly concave underneath, and in some instances it forms a conical projection on the inside. Two of the lamps of this type, **13** and **27**, are of Corinthian make, but most of them are Attic, as is evident from the hard, red clay, and smooth black glaze. In some instances the glaze is red, almost the color of the clay, but shifting to darker red and black in spots. On many of the Attic lamps the rim has an inner stripe of lighter black or slightly reddish color. Howland has explained this as the result of stacking in the kiln. That is probably correct, but it may have been done purposely to obtain differences in color.[13] The circle formed by this inner band of lighter color is not always concentric with the outer or inner edge of the rim, and this would seem to indicate that the two colors were produced by stacking. The glaze covers the rim and nozzle and usually the inside bottom, but not the underside of the rim. The rest of the lamp, i.e. the walls and the bottom, have a thin slip or wash of nearly the same color as the clay. It was applied only on the outer edge of the bottom, the inner concave part being left without such wash.

[13] *Agora* IV, p. 32. As so often happens, what eventually became an element of decoration probably began accidentally as the result of technical improvements necessitated by use. For the method of stacking lamps in the oven, see Fremersdorf, pp. 71–76, figs. 72–74.

All but three of the lamps of Type II came from the Large Circular Pit, which contained pottery from the 7th to the 5th century B.C.[14] Type II is predominantly of the 6th century B.C., though it may have continued into the first two decades of the 5th century. It corresponds in general to *Agora* IV, Type 16, the earliest examples of which, 16 A, are Corinthian. According to Howland, *Agora* IV, p. 31, the type was first exported to Athens from Corinth and was later imitated by Athenian lampmakers. After the Athenian products reached the Corinthian market, they served as models for the Corinthian producers. This being the development of the type, it is likely that the best of the Corinthian examples from Isthmia, e.g. **13**, is earlier than the Attic lamps of the type.

**13.** IP 2443. Pls. 1, 14. From Large Circular Pit, depth 15.65–19.70 m.

Fragment preserving left half of rim and base of nozzle. Yellow clay, Corinthian; traces of glaze on rim, with thin lines in concentric bands of slightly different color at outer and inner edges.

Cf. *Corinth* IV, ii, pl. I, no. 53. A similar lamp fragment was found in 1973 in the Corinthian Agora with a black-figure Band Cup of *ca.* 525 B.C., but the lamp may be earlier. Two lamps of this kind from the Athenian Agora, *Agora* IV, pp. 30–31, nos. 92 and 93, have been dated in "the early 6th century B.C. and well into the third quarter of the century."

**14.** IP 1578. Pls. 1, 14. From Large Circular Pit, depth 4.55 m.

D. 0.0905; H. 0.020.

Nozzle and front part missing. Bright red clay with slightly darker wash on unglazed parts; red glaze with streaks of black covering rim and outside. Attic. The rim is comparatively narrow as on **13**, and the lamp is thus to be placed among the early Attic lamps of Type II.

Cf. *Corinth* IV, ii, p. 32, fig. 14, no. 12, and Pl. I, no. 52; *Agora* IV, Type 16 B, pl. 32, nos. 94 and 96; *Argos*, planche A, pl. 1, no. 12.

**15.** IP 1534. Pls. 1, 14. From Large Circular Pit, depth 4.80–5.25 m.

L. 0.1085; D. 0.087; H. 0.0215.

Partly restored but all dimensions preserved. Dull red clay with traces of slip on unglazed parts; black glaze on rim, nozzle and part of inside, tending to flake. Attic.

See references under **14**.

**16.** IP 2446. Pls. 1, 14. From Large Circular Pit, depth 15.65–19.70 m.

D. 0.081; H. 0.021.

Fragmentary. Red, slightly mealy clay; poor red and dark brown glaze, covering rim and part of inside. Probably Attic.

**17.** IP 2452. Pls. 1, 14. From Large Circular Pit, depth 15.65–19.70 m.

D. 0.084; H. 0.020.

Most of nozzle and rear part missing. Red clay with slightly darker wash on unglazed parts; black glaze covering rim and most of the inside. Attic.

**18.** IP 2525. Pls. 1, 14. From Large Circular Pit, depth 17.42–18.50 m.

H. 0.019.

Right half preserved. Red clay with slightly darker wash on unglazed parts; good black glaze on outer edge of rim, reddish tinge on inner half. Attic. The outer edge of the inner circle is not concentric with the outer edge of the black part.

**19.** IP 2376. Pls. 1, 14. From Large Circular Pit, depth 18.75 m.

L. 0.102; D. 0.084; H. 0.021.

Completely preserved except for a small fracture at the outer edge of the rim. Red clay with slightly darker wash on unglazed parts; fine black glaze covering rim, inside, and nozzle. Inner part of rim slightly lighter black with reddish tinge. Attic. Very broad, flat rim with correspondingly small opening and nearly vertical sides merging gradually into slightly concave base. Short nozzle with wick-hole encroaching upon rim. This shows the final development of Type II. *Ca.* 500 B.C.

Cf. *Agora* IV, pls. 4 and 32, no. 100.

**20.** IP 3489 a and b. From Northeast Area.

Fragment preserving part of rim with edge of wick-hole. Red clay with slightly darker wash on unglazed parts; good black glaze on rim and part of inside. Attic. Very broad rim, much like that of **19**.

**21.** IP 2453. Pl. 14. From Large Circular Pit, depth 15.65–19.70 m.

D. 0.087; H. 0.022.

Composed of many fragments, preserving parts of rim with edge of wick-hole, sides and bottom. Red clay with slightly darker wash on unglazed parts; fine black glaze on rim and most of inside. Evidence of stacking visible on rim. Attic.

Shape and date like **19**.

**22.** IP 1743. From Large Circular Pit, depth 10.65–12.30 m.

[14] See footnote 12.

H. 0.0225.

Fragment preserving part of rim and edge of wick-hole. Bright red clay with slightly darker wash on unglazed parts; black glaze on rim and nozzle, not on inside. Attic.

**23.** IP 5768. From Large Circular Pit, depth *ca.* 17.80 m.

Small fragment preserving parts of nozzle, rim and side. Light red clay, probably Attic; brown and black glaze covering the inside of nozzle and rim, the remainder covered with a thin wash of the same color as the clay.

**24.** IP 5008. From Temenos, East End.

Small fragment preserving part of rim and side. Light red clay, probably Attic; black glaze. Rim narrow with only slight projection toward the outside.

**25.** IP 5769. From Large Circular Pit, depth *ca.* 17.80 m.

Small fragment of rim and side. Light red clay, probably Attic; black glaze partly worn off.

**26.** IP 5897. From Temenos, East End.

Small fragment of rim and side. Light red clay; brown glaze, applied on the inside and in concentric lines on the outer and inner edges of the rim, which turns up slightly. *Ca.* middle of 6th century B.C.

Cf. *Corinth* IV, ii, p. 32, fig. 11, and p. 133, no. 45; *Agora* IV, nos. 71 and 72.

**27.** IP 4618. From Large Circular Pit, depth 15.20–15.40 m.

Small fragment of rim and side. Pale buff Corinthian clay, no glaze preserved. Rather narrow rim with wide projection toward the outside.

## TYPE III. 28–35.

Examples of Type III from Isthmia are not numerous; only one whole lamp and seven fragments can be recognized as belonging to this type. The rim, which does not project on the outside, is narrower than the rim on Type II, and the central opening is correspondingly larger. One lamp, **28**, had no handle; another, **32**, had a horizontal handle. On one fragment, **30**, the top of the rim and nozzle are covered with black glaze, and apparently the inside bottom was similarly glazed; others are glazed all over. The clay in some instances is the typical red Attic variety; other fragments, e.g. **31–33**, may be of local make. The fabric of the latter is reddish buff or ash gray; and the glaze, which seems to have covered the whole lamp, is a dull dark brown and black variety of rather good quality. Types II, III, and IV are closely related in general shape and also in date. They are mostly 6th century lamps, but late examples of the three types come down into the 5th century B.C.

Type III corresponds to Athens Type 19, *Agora* IV, pp. 39–42, which the author dates from "the last quarter of 6th century B.C. to *ca.* 480." This agrees well enough with the date I proposed for Type III of the Corinthian lamps, *Corinth* IV, ii, p. 39.

**28.** IP 3938. Pls. 1, 15. From Temenos, East End.
   L. 0.089; D. 0.066; H. 0.022.

Complete. Red clay; red and dark brown glaze. Rather broad nozzle with large wick-hole which does not encroach upon the horizontal rim. No base, but the center rises on the inside to a conical projection.

The closest parallel from Athens is *Agora* IV, Type 16 B, pls. 4 and 32, no. 94, dated in the last quarter of the 6th century B.C.; it is there classed with the lamps of Corinth Type II. The rim on the Athens lamp is not encroached upon by the wick-hole and it has a very slight projection toward the outside. These are characteristic features of Type III. Our **28** is very similar to a lamp of Corinthian make from Nemea, illustrated in *Corinth* IV, ii, p. 39, fig. 18.

**29.** IP 2636. Pl. 1. From Northeast Cave.
   H. 0.018.

Nozzle and part of rim and side preserved. Dark red clay; black glaze on the nozzle and inside, the rest is unglazed. Attic. Angular profile, narrow, nearly horizontal rim, and the wick-hole does not encroach upon it. The base is flat underneath. In profile, the sides converge toward the bottom and form an obtuse angle with the flat underside. Near the top, just below the rim, there is a double groove, giving the false impression that the rim projects as in Type II.

**30.** IP 1798. Pl. 15. From Large Circular Pit, depth 15.05–15.25 m.

Fragment preserving left side of rim and part of nozzle. Red clay; black glaze covering rim, nozzle and part of inside. Attic.

**31.** IP 1308. Pl. 15. From Large Circular Pit, depth 0.00–1.00 m.

Fragment, preserving most of nozzle and part of rim. Reddish gray clay, dull dark brown and black glaze. Curving side forming sharp angle with the rim, short broad nozzle with the wick-hole encroaching only slightly upon the rim. The rim makes no projection toward the outside.

**32.** IP 5045. Pls. 1, 15. From West Roman Cistern.
   L. *ca.* 0.10; H. 0.026.

Right half preserved, including part of nozzle and attachment of handle. Light red clay; dull mottled black and brown glaze covering all the surfaces of the lamp. Horizontal band handle; raised base, slightly concave underneath.

**33.** IP 4794. From Palaimonion, northeast of Temple, 1.25–1.05 m. above stadium floor.

Small fragment of rim and side. Ash-gray clay; dull black glaze.

**34.** IP 5775. From Large Circular Pit, depth 17.80 m.

Small fragment of side and rim. Reddish buff clay, slight trace of brown glaze. Probably Corinthian.

**35.** IP 5435. From Large Circular Pit, depth 1.25–1.50 m.

Small fragment preserving parts of nozzle, rim and side. Dull gray clay; black glaze.

## TYPE IV. 36–74.

The origin of Type IV is to be traced to some later examples of Type I, e.g. **9** and **10**. The characteristic feature is the uniform curve of the sides, which merge into the slightly in-curving rim without any kind of demarcation between the rim and the side. The rim varies in width, and the narrower rim is usually found on early examples of the type, but this is not always the case. There is also a gradual evolution of the nozzle, from the short broad type with large wick-hole, e.g. **36**, to the long narrow kind with the wick-hole well removed from the outer circumference of the body, as on **58**. The length and shape of the nozzle forms the best criterion for the comparative dates of individual lamps. Most of the lamps had a handle, and both the vertical and the horizontal forms occur. The base is usually low and flat underneath, and some have no raised base. The type had a long period of use; its gradual evolution resulted in the emergence of three subtypes.

TYPE IV A. **36–42.**

The lamps of this variety have a low flat body with rounded sides and a short nozzle, as in Types I–III. Some, probably of the earlier specimens, have no base, the others have a slightly raised base. A single specimen, **42**, which certainly comes late in the series, had a horizontal handle. On none of the others is a handle present, but only three have the rear half preserved. The glaze covers the top, except for a reserved band which divides the inner part of the rim from the outer part. In one case, **36**, a broad band at the inner part of the rim is reserved; in the others the reserved stripe is narrow. On one late specimen, **42**, there is no reserved band, but the inner part of the rim is a bright red, contrasting sharply with the darker color of the rest of the lamp. This may, as in the case of Type II, have resulted from stacking, but is probably intentional. All the lamps of this subtype appear to be Attic.

**36.** IP 2523. Pls. 2, 15. From Theater Cave.

D. *ca.* 0.102.

Nozzle and several adjoining fragments from rim of rather large lamp. Red clay; black glaze on rim and inside bottom; broad reserved band on inner edge of rim. Attic.

Cf. *Agora* IV, Type 21 A, no. 157 (500–480 B.C.).

**37.** IP 2454. Pls. 2, 15. From Large Circular Pit, depth 15.65–19.70 m.

H. 0.022.

Left half and most of nozzle missing. Small piece from left half of rim belongs to this lamp, but does not join. Red clay; light brown glaze on rim, nozzle and inside. The base is not raised but is slightly concave with small depression in the center. Probably Attic.

For the profile see *Agora* IV, Type 21 A, pl. 6, nos. 157 and 160, which, however, differ from our **37** in other respects. They date from the late 6th or early 5th century B.C. The published lamps from Corinth offer no close parallel.

**38.** IP 2373. Pls. 2, 15. From Large Circular Pit, depth 17.42–17.80 m.

H. 0.021.

Fragment; front half preserved. Red clay with traces of slightly darker wash on unglazed parts; black and reddish brown glaze. Down-turned rim, forming uniform curve with rounded sides; short nozzle, raised base, slightly concave underneath. On the rim is a reserved band separating the darker glaze on the outside from the reddish brown glaze at the inner edge. This probably did not result accidentally from stacking, since the two halves of the rim are separated by the reserved stripe. Attic.

For the profile see *Agora* IV, Type 21 C Prime, pl. 6, no. 178; Type 21 B, no. 165 (490–460 B.C.).

**39.** IP 2450. Pl. 15. From Large Circular Pit, depth 15.65–19.70 m.

L. 0.097; D. 0.079; H. 0.022.

Fragment preserving nozzle, part of rim, and most of the bottom. Red clay with darker wash on unglazed parts; rather dull black and dark brown glaze on nozzle, rim and inside. Reserved stripe dividing rim into two bands. Raised base, slightly concave underneath. Probably Attic.

**40.** IP 2527. From Large Circular Pit, depth 17.42–18.50 m.

Rim fragment with part of wick-hole preserved. Reddish gray clay; brown glaze.

**41.** IP 2444. Pl. 15. From Large Circular Pit, depth 15.65–19.70 m.

Nozzle and part of rim of large lamp like **36**. Reddish buff clay; black glaze with reserved band on rim. Broad, blunt-ended nozzle.

**42.** IP 2315. Pls. 2, 15. From Large Circular Pit, depth 18.20 m.

L. (0.091); D. 0.075; H. 0.020.

Nozzle and handle restored. Red clay; black and red glaze. Broad band of red around the opening; on the sides the glaze varies between the two colors. Rounded sides and broad rim; horizontal handle, raised base, nearly flat underneath. Probably Attic.

Cf. *Agora* IV, Type 21 B, no. 165 (*ca.* 490–460 B.C.).

TYPE IV B. **43–73.**

The lamps of Type IV B correspond fairly closely to Corinth IV and Athens 21, A–D. They have rounded sides, merging into the rim, which is not set off in any way from the sides. Most of them had a handle, vertical on the earlier specimens and horizontal on the later. The nozzle on the earlier lamps of the type is short, but in most cases the wick-hole does not encroach on the rim. One exception is the miniature lamp, **59**, on which the large wick-hole comes partly within the outer edge of the rim. The later lamps, **48, 49, 57, 58**, have longer nozzles with the wick-hole well removed from the outer circumference of the body of the lamp. In general, the shape of the nozzle is the best indicator of relative date.

The earlier specimens have no raised base; on the later, as on the lamps of Type IV A, the base is raised and slightly concave underneath. Among the 31 whole lamps and fragments of Type IV B, only a few, **50, 51, 58, 65, 72, 73**, appear to be of Attic clay; the others are either Corinthian or from some unknown center. The locally made lamps, some of which appear to be earlier than the imported ones, have a dull black or dark brown glaze that covers the whole surface inside and outside.

The great variation in the shape and the length of the nozzle shows that Type IV B covers a long period of time, from the end of the 6th century B.C. into the 4th.

**43.** IP 2317. Pls. 2, 15. From Large Circular Pit, depth 18.85 m.

L. 0.093; D. 0.072; H. 0.029.

Handle partly restored. Reddish buff clay; dull black and brown glaze covering all but the bottom. Curving sides merging into rather flat rim. No raised base, flat bottom. Short nozzle with large wick-hole encroaching only slightly upon the rim. Vertical band handle. Probably Corinthian.

This and the two following lamps have no exact parallels from the Athenian Agora, and none among the published lamps from Corinth. A fragmentary lamp of this shape from Argos, no. 29, Bovon dates to the beginning of the 5th century B.C. This agrees well with the date of the three Isthmia lamps which came from the Large Circular Pit, the contents of which are mainly from the first half of the 5th century and earlier. The profile and the shape of the nozzle point to a date at the end of the 6th century B.C. or the beginning of the 5th.

**44.** IP 2375. Pls. 2, 15. From Large Circular Pit, depth 19.35 m.

L. (0.084); D. 0.065; H. 0.0185.

Nozzle and handle restored. Buff clay; dull black glaze. Shape as in **43**, but with wider rim and correspondingly smaller opening in the center. Slightly concave underneath. Probably local fabric.

For date and references, see **43**.

**45.** IP 1569. From Large Circular Pit, depth 1.25–1.50 m.

D. (0.077); H. 0.0195.

Tip of nozzle and rear half of body missing. Buff clay; dull black glaze covering the whole lamp. Nozzle and bottom trimmed by paring. Probably a local product.

Shape and date like that of **43**.

**46.** IP 5438. From Temenos, South Side.

Small fragment preserving parts of rim, side and handle. Light red clay; dull brown glaze apparently covering the whole lamp. Horizontal handle. Probably local product.

**47.** IP 2447. Pl. 2. From Large Circular Pit, depth 15.65–15.70 m.

D. 0.0655; H. 0.019.

Nozzle and handle broken away. Red clay; dull red and light brown glaze covering the whole lamp. Sides curving uniformly and merging with slightly overhanging rim. Small horizontal handle, very low base, slightly concave underneath. Probably a local product.

Cf. *Agora* IV, Type 21 B, pls. 6, 34, no. 165 (490–460 B.C.).

**48.** IP 2572. Pls. 2, 15. From Sacred Glen.

L. (0.086); D. 0.0665.

Handle, tip of nozzle and all lower part missing. Reddish buff clay; black glaze covering all parts.

Horizontal handle and rather long nozzle with wick-hole well removed from outer edge of rim. Probably not Attic.

For the shape see *Corinth* IV, ii, pl. II, nos. 71, 82; *Agora* IV, Types 21 C, no. 176, and 21 C Prime, no. 177 (dated in the "last quarter of the 5th century B.C. and well into the early years of the 4th century"). The Isthmia lamp, which shows a later development of the type, is probably not earlier than the middle of the 4th century B.C. Cf. also *Argos*, nos. 58, 60.

**49.** IP 1160. Pl. 15. From North Temenos Dump.

Nozzle and part of rim preserved. Red clay; black glaze shifting to brown in spots. Shape similar to **48** and date probably the same.

**50.** IP 1318. From Large Circular Pit, depth 1.30 m.

Fragment of rim and attachment of handle. Reddish gray clay; good black glaze. On the rim is a broad band, also painted black but set off from the rim with slightly duller glaze. This could have resulted from stacking. Attic. Probably second half of 5th century B.C.

**51.** IP 1323. Pl. 15. From Large Circular Pit, depth 0.60 m.

Nozzle and part of rim preserved. Grayish brown clay; good black glaze, apparently covering the whole lamp. Very short nozzle and edge of rim turned down. Probably Attic.

The profile and nozzle are rather similar to Athens Type 21 B, no. 168, found in a well with contents dated to 430–420 B.C. The upper two meters in the Large Circular Pit, where this fragment was found, contained mixed fill of Greek and Roman times; hence there is no evidence from stratification that has a bearing on the date.

**52.** IP 6110. From East Propylon.
   D. 0.063; H. 0.025.

Nozzle, most of handle, and rear part of body missing. Buff clay; dull black glaze largely peeled off. The glaze originally covered the whole lamp. Horizontal handle, raised base. Local fabric.

For shape and date see **48**.

**53.** IP 4182. From Sacred Glen.
   H. 0.0295.

Fragment. Buff clay; black glaze which appears to have covered the entire lamp. Horizontal band handle, no raised base. Local product.

Date, *ca.* middle of 4th century B.C.

**54.** IP 5836. From North Temenos Dump.
   H. 0.021.

Fragment from front part of lamp. Light red clay with dull mottled black and brown glaze that covered all parts. Horizontal handle, raised base. Local fabric.

Date, second half of 5th century B.C.

**55.** IP 4223. From Temenos, East End.

Small fragment preserving part of rim, side and nozzle. Light red clay; dull light brown and darkish brown glaze. Probably local fabric.

**56.** IP 4355. From Temenos, South Side.

Small fragment preserving parts of nozzle, rim and side. Reddish buff clay; dull brown glaze. Local fabric.

**57.** IP 5046. From Sacred Glen.

Nozzle, part of rim and side preserved. Light red clay; dull black glaze. Probably local fabric.

**58.** IP 716. Pls. 2, 15. From Rachi, South Slope Cistern.
   D. 0.060; H. 0.027.

Only front half of lamp preserved. Brick-red clay; black glaze shifting to brown in spots, covering inside and outside. Curving sides with heavy rim sloping inward. Rather long nozzle with small wick-hole. No raised base, but slightly concave underneath. It probably had a handle, not indicated in section, Plate 2. Probably Attic.

The long nozzle and small central opening indicate late date, probably second half of the 4th century B.C., but the absence of a raised base is peculiar for this date. The pottery from the Cistern is dated mainly in the second half of the 4th century B.C. and first half of the 3rd.

**59.** IP 370. Pls. 2, 15. From outside the excavated area.
   L. 0.051; D. 0.041; H. 0.014.

Miniature lamp, complete. Buff clay; traces of dull brown glaze. Probably local product. No handle. Side and rim merging; short nozzle with large wick-hole; flat base, slightly raised, but not clearly set off from side.

The date is probably late 6th or early 5th century B.C. There are no close parallels from the Athenian Agora. See *Corinth* IV, ii, p. 137, fig. 61, which, however, is later, as shown by the longer nozzle.

**60.** IP 4046. From Sacred Glen.

Fragment of small multiple lamp attached to circular base; part of base attachment preserved. Dull gray clay; no glaze extant. Local make.

For probable date see **59**.

**61.** IP 1322. Pls. 2, 15. From Large Circular Pit, depth 0.60 m.
   H. 0.020.

Fragment preserving nozzle and parts of rim and base. Reddish gray clay; black glaze that tends to peel off. Nozzle very short, but wick-hole does not encroach upon the rim. Curving sides merging gradually into narrow rim. Slightly raised base, concave underneath and unglazed.

Cf. *Agora* IV, Type 21 B, no. 165 (490–460 B.C.).

**62.** IP 3954. From Sacred Glen.

Attachment of horizontal handle and part of nozzle preserved. Red-buff clay; light brown glaze. Probably local fabric.

**63.** IP 4158. From Sacred Glen.

Fragment preserving part of nozzle, rim and side. Light red clay; dull brown glaze. Probably local fabric.

**64.** IP 5894. From Large Circular Pit.

H. 0.0245.

Fragment preserving parts of nozzle, rim, side, and raised base. Reddish gray clay; dull black glaze. Probably local.

**65.** IP 4181. From Sacred Glen.

Fragment from top of nozzle and rim. Red clay; reddish brown glaze covering entire lamp. This may be of Attic make.

**66.** IP 3928. Pl. 15. From Temenos, East End.

D. 0.073; H. 0.027.

Handle, nozzle and part of right side missing. Light red clay; dull brown glaze. Horizontal band handle;

raised, slightly concave base, set off from sides by shallow groove. Probably local fabric.

For shape cf. **47**, but **66** is later, early 4th century B.C.

**67.** IP 4155. From Sacred Glen.

Fragment from right half of lamp. Attachment of horizontal handle preserved. Pale yellow clay; traces of black glaze. Local fabric.

**68.** IP 4267. From Theater Drain.

Fragment. Light buff clay, Corinthian; traces of black glaze. Horizontal band handle. Possibly same lamp as **69**.

**69.** IP 4268. From Theater Drain, abandoned about the middle of the 4th century B.C.

Parts of nozzle, rim and side preserved. Buff clay; black glaze, largely peeled off. Local fabric.

**70.** IP 4012. From Temple of Poseidon.

Lower part of lamp preserved. Light red clay; dull brown glaze; probably local make.

**71.** IP 5896. From East Propylon.

Small fragment of rim. Reddish gray clay; good black glaze. Attic.

**72.** IP 5767. From Large Circular Pit, depth 17.80 m.

Small fragment of rim and side. Light red clay; good black glaze. Attic.

**73.** IP 6158. From Rachi Well, depth 1.60–10.60 m.

Small fragment of nozzle. Red clay; black glaze. Probably Attic.

TYPE IV C. **74.**

The single lamp of Type IV C, **74**, differs from the other lamps of Type IV by the presence of a central tube, which projects slightly above the level of the rim. Because of the form of rim, this specimen is here listed as a subtype of Type IV.

**74.** IP 2318. Pls. 2, 15. From Large Circular Pit, depth 18.00 m.

L. 0.099; D. 0.082; H. 0.0215.

Almost complete. Red clay with slightly darker wash on unglazed parts. Dull black and purplish glaze on rim, nozzle and inside. On the rim are three bands

of black glaze, separated by a narrow reserved band and a somewhat broader purple stripe. No raised base; the bottom curves concavely and forms an open tube in the center. Probably Attic.

Cf. *Agora* IV, Type 22 A, no. 193 (500–460 B.C.).

TYPE V. **75–84.**

There are four nearly whole lamps and several fragments of Type V. They are distinguished by rounded sides and slightly raised band on the rim surrounding the central opening. Two of the completely preserved lamps, **75** and **81**, are without handle; two others, **76** and **83**, had a horizontal handle of which only the attachments remain. None has a raised base. Two of the lamps and some fragments are Attic; a fourth lamp, **81**, completely preserved, is of local clay and is covered with a very thin gray wash, slightly darker than the clay.

The distinguishing feature of the type is the raised inner edge of the rim. One specimen, **76**, which may be slightly later than **75**, has a raised band that is very narrow and set off from the rest of the rim with a reserved stripe. The latest variety of this type, **83**, is transitional to the 4th century lamps of Type VII. It has a much longer nozzle than the others, and, unlike them, it has a raised base, concave underneath. The glaze, which is of good quality but less glossy than that of the common Attic lamps, apparently covered the whole lamp both on the inside and on the outside. The clay, a light red variety that tends to flake, might be Corinthian.

Type V corresponds to Athens Type 20, which, according to *Agora* IV, p. 43, is to be dated in "the first half of the 5th century B.C. (both before and after the Persian wars) into the 460's." Such a date is likely for the earlier lamps of this type from Isthmia, **75–81**, and **84**, all but one of which are of Attic make. All came from the Large Circular Pit. The single example, **83**, with long nozzle and raised base, is very much later. It is grouped with this type because of the shape of the rim.

**75.** IP 2448. Pls. 2, 16. From Large Circular Pit, depth 15.65–19.70 m.
L. 0.103; D. 0.079; H. 0.0205.
Somewhat restored. Red clay; good black glaze on nozzle, rim, and inside. Side forming uniform curve; rim with raised band round central opening. Short nozzle with wick-hole mostly outside outer circle of the body. Concave underneath, no raised base. Attic.
Very similar to *Agora* IV, Type 20, no. 149 (500–480 B.C.).

**76.** IP 2374. Pls. 2, 16. From Large Circular Pit, depth 19.50 m.
L. *ca.* 0.082; D. 0.065; H. 0.020.
Nozzle and handle restored. Red clay, with brown slip on unglazed parts; black glaze with streaks of red. Curving side merging with rim, narrow raised lip around central opening, separated from rim by reserved band produced by scraping. Wick-hole encroaching upon rim; horizontal handle. Concavity on bottom rising to point in the center. Attic.
The closest parallel from the Athenian Agora is *Agora* IV, Type 20, no. 152 (500–480 B.C.).

**77.** IP 5766. From Large Circular Pit, depth 15.80–19.75 m.
Fragment of rim and side. Light red clay; good black glaze. Reserved stripe at outer edge of raised band. Attic.
Very similar to **75** and of about the same date.

**78.** IP 5770. From Large Circular Pit, depth 15.80–19.75 m.
Tiny fragment from rim and side. Gray clay, perhaps darkened by fire; good black glaze. Attic.

**79.** IP 5771. From Large Circular Pit, depth 15.80–19.75 m.
Small fragment from rim and side, preserving attachment of horizontal handle. Light gray clay; good black glaze. Attic.
Profile as in *Agora* IV, pl. 5, no. 153 (500–480 B.C.).

**80.** IP 2449. Pl. 16. From Large Circular Pit, depth 15.65–19.70 m.
Fragment from rim and side. Red clay, somewhat mealy; red glaze on rim, shifting to black in spots. Probably Attic.

**81.** IP 1327. Pls. 2, 16. From Large Circular Pit, depth 6.25 m.
L. 0.092; D. 0.074; H. 0.019.
Complete. Low flat body with rounded sides, raised rim around central opening; no raised base but underside concave. Greenish buff clay; traces of thin brown glaze, like that of Type IV B, **43** and **44**. Probably Corinthian.
It is very similar in profile to *Agora* IV, Type 20, no. 152 (500–480 B.C.) which, however, has a horizontal handle.

**82.** IP 5437. From Large Circular Pit, depth 0.00–12.00 m.
Fragment from rim, side and attachment of horizontal handle. Ash-gray clay; dull black glaze. Probably of local make.

**83.** IP 431. Pls. 2, 16. From manhole to reservoir at west end of South Stoa.
L. 0.090; D. 0.063; H. 0.028.
Handle restored. Reddish buff clay; black glaze tending to peel off, but originally covering the whole lamp. Rounded sides set off from rim by groove; rather long nozzle; horizontal handle. Raised base, concave. This might be of local manufacture.
Cf. *Agora* IV, Type 24 A, nos. 245, 246 (*ca.* 430–420 B.C.), but our **83** is later, probably early 4th century B.C.

**84.** IP 5772. From Large Circular Pit, depth 15.80–19.75 m.
Small piece of lamp like **75**, but with no reserved band. Light red clay; good black glaze. Attic.

## TYPE VI. 85–88.

The lamps of Types I–V belong, with few exceptions, to the 6th and 5th centuries B.C. They had probably been used chiefly in the Temple of Poseidon; most of them, in fact, coincide in date with the existence of the Archaic Temple, destroyed by fire *ca.* 475–470 B.C. The Classical Temple was built, or at least begun, in the

460's.[15] Whether it was finished during a single period of construction or after some interruption it is not possible to determine from the evidence at hand. The interior arrangement was altered, presumably before the end of the 5th century. Then in 390 B.C. fire destroyed so much of the interior that the temple had to be largely rebuilt, apparently on the original plan and with the use of much of the earlier material. From the period of some three quarters of a century between the construction of the later temple and the fire in 390, we have relatively few lamps. With Type VI we reach the 4th century B.C. and thenceforth the lamps become more numerous.

There are only four fragmentary examples of Type VI. They show the evolution from the earlier flat, open type to the smaller, but deeper, lamps of the 4th century and later. In these the central opening has decreased, leaving a hole only large enough for the pouring of the oil. Two lamps of Type VI, **85** and **86**, both Attic, have nearly vertical sides and broad, flat rims sloping toward the central opening. The nozzle is comparatively long and the wick-hole well removed from the outer edge of the rim. They had broad horizontal band handles and raised bases. The fabric is the typical red clay of Attic pottery, and a lustrous black glaze covers the lamps, both inside and outside, except on the underside of the raised base. The other two examples, **87** and **88**, which are of local make, have no handle.

By Athenian parallels, Type VI is to be dated in the first half of the 4th century, probably toward the end of the first quarter or beginning of the second. The two lamps **87** and **88**, from the Rachi, are more likely to be dated in the second half of that century.

**85.** IP 373. Pls. 2, 16. From Papatheodorou Well (Sacred Glen); found with two lamps of Type VII (**109** and **126**).
L. 0.093; D. 0.063; H. 0.036.
Handle, part of right side and end of nozzle missing. Red clay; glossy black glaze covering all but the underside of the base, and the inner half of the rim, which has reddish brown glaze. Attic. Almost vertical sides making a slightly acute angle with the rim which slopes down at the inner edge. Long nozzle with small wick-hole; broad horizontal handle; low base slightly concave underneath.
Cf. *Agora* IV, Type 23 C, no. 228 ("first and especially second quarter of the 4th century B.C.").

**86.** IP 2751. Pls. 2, 16. From Northeast Area, Roman Cistern.
H. 0.036.
Fragment preserving parts of rim, nozzle, attachment of the handle and base. Red clay; black glaze tending to peel off. Nearly vertical sides, with flat rim sloping toward the inside. Long nozzle with narrow hole for the wick; large horizontal band handle; raised base, unglazed underneath. Attic.
Cf. *Agora* IV, Type 23 C, no. 230 ("second quarter of 4th century B.C.").

**87.** IP 6057 + IP 6159. Pls. 2, 16. From Rachi Well, depth 10.60–12.50 m.

L. (0.088); D. 0.0605; H. 0.033.
Tip of nozzle and part of bottom missing. Buff clay; poor black glaze, largely peeled off. Corinthian. No handle; raised base, slightly concave underneath.
A lamp from Corinth of Type VI, *Corinth* IV, ii, pl. III, no. 112, is very similar to our **87** and **88**. There are no good parallels from the Athenian Agora for the two Corinthian specimens. The profile, however, is much like that of *Agora* IV, Type 24 C, pl. 9, no. 258, which is probably Attic, dated in the early part of the 4th century B.C. The Isthmia lamps **87** and **88**, which came from the Rachi, are later, second half of 4th century B.C. Chronologically they would be classed with Type VII, but because they lack the groove that sets off the rim from the side, they belong with the somewhat earlier Attic examples of Type VI, **85** and **86**.

**88.** IP 6139 + IP 6186. Pl. 16. From Rachi, South Cistern; Rachi Well, depth 8.50–8.65 m.
H. 0.030.
End of nozzle and left half of body missing. Pale buff clay; no glaze preserved. The sides incline toward the top. There was no raised base, but only a small part of the underside remains.
For date and parallels see **87**.

## SMALLER PIECES. 89–108.

These twenty fragments, that seem to belong to Types I–VI, are too small to merit individual description.

| | | | |
|---|---|---|---|
| **89.** IP 2529. | **94.** IP 4027. | **99.** IP 5915. | **104.** IP 6163. |
| **90.** IP 251. | **95.** IP 5620. | **100.** IP 2528. | **105.** IP 4437. |
| **91.** IP 2323. | **96.** IP 6122. | **101.** IP 5773. | **106.** IP 4359. |
| **92.** IP 4535. | **97.** IP 5627. | **102.** IP 4051. | **107.** IP 3508. |
| **93.** IP 4431. | **98.** IP 1329. | **103.** IP 4101. | **108.** IP 4215 b, c. |

[15] For the several epochs of the Classical Temple, see *Isthmia* I, pp. 101–103.

## TYPE VII. 109–202.

In the second half of the 4th century and throughout the 3rd century B.C. the most common lamp from Isthmia and Corinth is Type VII. It comprises more lamps than any of the previous types and almost all of them fall within that period of one and a half centuries. The type shows the development from the 5th century lamps, with flat, open body, short nozzle and narrow rim. As the type evolved, it tended to become more globular, and finally in the later examples of the type it took on a lower, watch-shaped body. The nozzle is long and the wick-hole comparatively small. On most of the earlier examples, the sides are not vertical, but show a perceptible inward inclination toward the top. In the later varieties, they form an almost uniform curve in section. The distinguishing feature is the rim, set off from the sides with a prominent groove, which in all the earlier specimens is reserved. After the whole body had been glazed, the color in the groove was scratched away. Nearly all the lamps of Type VII have a raised base, higher in the earlier varieties and deeply concave underneath. Within the type there are six subtypes, distinguished by shape, color of the clay, and glaze.

TYPE VII A. **109.**

There is only one lamp of this variety from Isthmia. It is slightly larger than the others and it is the only one of the type with a horizontal band handle. Although the handle is missing, the two ends attached to the body show that it was bow-shaped, as in *Agora* IV, pl. 38, nos. 267–269. The Isthmia lamp **109** was found together with **126** and some pottery and other objects at unrecorded depth in an ancient well on the property of the late Nikolaos Papatheodorou, west of the Sanctuary of Poseidon. The lamp was published by John L. Caskey and dated by him about the middle of the 4th century B.C. (*Hesperia* 29, 1960, pl. 56, no. 12).

**109.** IP 371. Pls. 3, 16. From Papatheodorou Well[16] (Sacred Glen).
L. 0.104; D. 0.071; H. 0.042.
Red clay; good black glaze. Flat, bow-shaped handle, now missing, except for the two ends. Long pointed nozzle. Sides sloping inward and gradually merging with the top. The rim is set off by reserved groove. Raised base, concave underneath. Attic.

The profile is similar to *Agora* IV, Type 25 A, no. 269, found in a cistern filled up at the end of the 4th century B.C. Isthmia lamp **109** may, of course, be somewhat earlier, but the last quarter of 4th century agrees with the evidence from the Rachi, where several lamps of Corinth Type VII B were discovered.

TYPE VII B. **110–118.**

The lamps of this variety appear to be all of Attic make. They differ from VII A in being somewhat smaller with a tendency toward the globular shape. The glaze covers the whole lamp, both inside and outside, except for the reserved groove, and the underside is also glazed. None of these lamps has a handle or side knob. Date: late 4th century B.C.

**110.** IP 787. Pls. 3, 16. From Rachi Well, depth *ca.* 20 m.
D. 0.062; H. 0.040.
Rear half missing. Red clay; good black glaze covering whole lamp except the bottom of the base. Curving sides, set off from rim by reserved groove. Rather long nozzle; raised base, concave underneath. Attic.
Cf. *Corinth* IV, ii, pl. III, no. 120; and *Agora* IV, Type 25 A, no. 272 (340–310 B.C.).

**111.** IP 6109. From Rachi Well, depth 12.50 m.
H. 0.415.
Red Attic clay; good black glaze. Rim set off by reserved groove. Rather high concave base.
Shape and date as **110.**

**112.** IP 5440. From Rachi, South Cistern.
Fragment of front portion of lamp. Red Attic clay; good black glaze. Reserved groove.

Profile as in *Agora* IV, Type 25 A, no. 272 (340–310 B.C.).

**113.** IP 452. Pls. 3, 16. From Rachi Well, depth 9.90 m.
L. (0.097); D. 0.061; H. 0.041.
Tip of nozzle restored. Red clay; black and red glaze covering whole lamp, even underneath the base. Nearly straight sides set off from rim by prominent groove, which had been covered with glaze that was later scraped away. This is shown by some irregular scratches on the rim. Long nozzle with small wick-hole, restored with too pointed an end; no handle. Raised base, with double concavity underneath. Attic.
Cf. *Corinth* IV, ii, pl. III, no. 116, and *Agora* IV, Type 25 A, no. 272, found in a well, *ca.* 340–310 B.C.

**114.** IP 446. Pl. 16. From Rachi Well, depth 14.27– 15.90 m.
L. (0.089); D. 0.058; H. 0.040.

---

[16] The well was dug by the owner and no record was kept of the depth at which the objects were found.

Tip of nozzle restored. Reddish gray clay; black glaze, largely peeled off, but underside left unglazed. Glaze on rim better preserved than elsewhere. Sides make uniform curve, set off from rim by broad reserved groove. Raised base, concave. Long nozzle with small wick-hole. Probably Attic.

Approximately same date as **113**.

**115.** IP 544. Pl. 16. From Rachi Well, depth 12.00 m.
L. (0.097); D. 0.063; H. 0.041.

Nozzle restored. Red clay; black glaze, which tends to peel off, but no glaze on underside of base. Long nozzle, should be less pointed than shown in restoration. No handle; reserved groove around rim; raised base, concave. Probably Attic.

For date see under **113**.

**116.** IP 802. Pls. 3, 16. From Rachi, South Cistern.
L. (0.095); D. 0.061; H. 0.037.

End of nozzle and small part of base restored. Pale red clay; black glaze tending to peel off, covering the whole lamp, even on the bottom. Rounded sides set off by reserved groove round the rim. Rather high base with deep concavity underneath.

Very nearly the same shape as **113**, but perhaps slightly later in date.

**117.** IP 3959. Pl. 16. Chance find.
D. 0.060; H. 0.039.

Complete, except for tip of nozzle. Red clay; poor black glaze. Reserved groove separating rim from shoulder. Raised base with double concavity, as in **113**. Probably Attic.

**118.** IP 6130. From Rachi Well, depth 14.20–15.20 m.

Fragment from front part of lamp. Reddish gray clay; black glaze. Probably Attic.

TYPE VII C. **119–125.**

The lamps of VII C are made of the typical pale yellow Corinthian clay. Some retain faint traces of a very thin glaze, but in most instances it is impossible to tell whether the lamp was originally glazed or unglazed. The shape is much the same as in VII B. All the complete lamps lack handle and side knob. One example, however, **121**, the top of which is missing, has an attachment on the right side, which seems to indicate that it is part of a side knob. In all other cases, Type VII D–F, the knob is on the left side as you hold the lamp with the nozzle toward you.

Type VII C resembles *Agora* IV, Type 25 A Prime, e.g. nos. 296 and 298, which in Athens occur in contexts from just before and well into the 3rd century. This date agrees with the evidence from Isthmia. Several of the Isthmian lamps came from the Rachi, the industrial establishments of which belong to that period.[17]

**119.** IP 1316. Pls. 3, 17. From Southwest Reservoir, depth 5.65 m.
L. 0.098; D. 0.063; H. 0.0365.

Tip of nozzle and part of right side restored. Pale buff clay, probably Corinthian; no glaze preserved. Sides less curving than in Type VII B, and sharply set off from the top. Rim surrounded by groove. Nozzle as in most lamps of Type VII, but probably a little less pointed than the restoration shows. Low base, concave underneath. For correct shape see Plate 17, **121**.

Very similar to *Agora* IV, Type 25 A Prime, pls. 10, 38, no. 296, dated *ca.* 300 B.C.

**120.** IP 5044. Pl. 17. From Northwest Reservoir.
D. 0.067; H. 0.0375.

Most of nozzle and small part of rim missing. Pale yellow Corinthian clay; slight traces of black glaze. For shape and date see **119**.

**121.** IP 3015. Pl. 17. From Rachi Well, depth 8.70–8.80 m.
L. 0.096; D. 0.063.

Top missing. Pale yellow clay; slight traces of glaze on the inside of nozzle only. The nozzle, which is here original, shows the correct shape for the other lamps of Type VII C, on which the nozzles have been restored. The small excrescence on the right side shown in photograph, Plate 17, must be part of a side knob, which here, by exception, is on the right side.

**122.** IP 478. Pl. 17. From Rachi Well, depth 8.70–8.80 m.
L. (0.097); D. 0.057; H. 0.032.

Tip of nozzle restored. Pale buff clay. No glaze preserved on the outside except slight traces in groove between body and base; dull gray surface on the inside may be discoloration from the oil. Sides make almost uniform curve, sharply set off from top. Wide rim surrounded by groove, nozzle as restored is too pointed; raised base, slightly concave underneath. Corinthian.

**123.** IP 2573. Pls. 3, 17. From Sacred Glen.
L. 0.086; D. 0.0535; H. 0.030.

Small break at tip of nozzle, otherwise complete. Reddish buff clay. No glaze preserved, but on the

---

[17] Chrysoula Kardara, *A.J.A.* 65, 1961, p. 263, dates the settlements and the dye works on the Rachi to 360–240 B.C.

surface is a slip of slightly lighter color than the clay. Curving sides sloping in at the top. Nozzle as in **121**. Raised base, concave underneath. Corinthian.

Cf. *Corinth* IV, ii, nos. 126 and 128. The profile resembles *Agora* IV, Type 24 C Prime, no. 261 ("first half of 4th century B.C."), but the Isthmia lamp is probably later.

**124.** IP 444. Pl. 17. From Rachi.

Nozzle, part of body, and most of rim preserved. Reddish gray clay; traces of brown on inside; the rest of the surface unglazed, except on tip of nozzle.

Shape as in **123**.

TYPE VII D. **126–132**.

Of the seven examples of this subtype, only one, **126**, is completely preserved. All appear to be of Attic manufacture. They differ from Type VII B chiefly in the presence of a side knob, always on the left side. When the lamp is held in the right hand, the index finger fits into the curved knob. In most cases the knob is pierced. Perhaps a string was sometimes inserted in the hole so that the lamp could be suspended when not in use, but the primary use of the knob must have been to provide a secure grip on the lamp.[18] The body is small and tends toward globular shape. The lamps are as a rule unglazed on the underside, but on **129** the bottom has been glazed. All but **132** are glazed. The corresponding type in Athens is *Agora* IV, Type 25 B, which is there dated "second half of the 4th century B.C. into first quarter of 3rd century."

**126.** IP 372. Pls. 3, 17. From Papatheodorou Well (Sacred Glen).

L. 0.090; D. 0.057; H. 0.037.

Completely preserved. Red clay; mottled red and black glaze which tends to flake off. Long nozzle, with rather broad rounded end. Curving sides set off from the rim by deep groove; pierced side knob. Raised base, concave and unglazed underneath.

Cf. *Agora* IV, Type 25 B, no. 311. Our **126** is probably not much later than 350 B.C.; see Caskey, *Hesperia* 29, 1960, p. 173, pl. 56, no. 13.

**127.** IP 455. Pls. 3, 17. From Rachi, South Cistern.

L. 0.087; D. (0.061); H. 0.044.

Part of right side and tip of side knob restored. Reddish brown clay; dull black glaze. Curving sides set off from rim by broad groove which has been scraped after glaze was applied. Perforated side knob. Round-ended nozzle. Raised base, concave and unglazed underneath. Probably Attic.

Cf. *Agora* IV, Type 25 B, no. 310 (from well filled up *ca.* 300–275 B.C.).

**128.** IP 3524. Pl. 17. From Temenos, East End.

D. 0.059; H. 0.035.

Nozzle and front half of lamp missing. Red clay; black and reddish brown glaze. Rounded side set off by groove at outer edge of rim. Perforated side knob. Raised base, concave and unglazed underneath.

Shape like *Agora* IV, Type 25 B, no. 307.

**125.** IP 619. Pls. 3, 17. From Rachi.

L. (0.087); D. 0.057; H. 0.036.

Tip of nozzle restored a little too pointed. Pale buff clay; slight traces of dull, grayish black glaze. Sides tapering toward the top. Nozzle less sharply set off from body than in the other lamps of this subtype. Low base, nearly flat underneath.

There is no close parallel from the Athenian Agora for the profile of this lamp, which probably comes rather late in the series.

**129.** IP 754. Pl. 3. From Rachi, South Cistern, at bottom.

H. 0.0355.

Fragmentary. Red clay; black glaze, covering also underside of base. Broad rim set off from side by narrow, reserved groove. Perforated knob on left side. Raised base, concave.

Cf. *Agora* IV, no. 308.

**130.** IP 6137 a and b. Pl. 17 (IP 6137b). From Rachi, South Cistern.

Two non-joining fragments preserving parts of nozzle, rim, and unpierced side knob. Reddish buff clay; black glaze. Double reserved groove. Probably Attic.

Cf. *Corinth* IV, ii, p. 140, no. 115, fig. 64.

**131.** IP 5777. From Sacred Glen, Well.

Small fragment preserving pierced side knob. Light red clay; black and red glaze. Probably Attic.

**132.** IP 714. Pls. 3, 17. From Rachi, South Cistern.

L. 0.080; D. 0.0555; H. 0.0335.

Part of left side restored. Red clay; traces of black glaze at tip of nozzle and inside. Uniformly curving sides merging into the top. Narrow rim set off by groove. Raised base, concave underneath and rising into a high conical projection on the inside. The left side has been restored without side knob, but this is probably incorrect and the lamp would thus belong to Type VII D.

Cf. *Agora* IV, Type 25 B Prime, nos. 334–336 (275–225 B.C.).

[18] On the purpose of the side knob see *Corinth* IV, ii, pp. 6–7, 13, 51. In *Agora* IV, p. 72, the author explains the knob— or lug—as a device for suspension, but such use could pertain only to lamps with pierced lug, which, as the author points out, are as a rule earlier. In later lamps of this kind the knob is commonly solid, but is usually so shaped as to fit the tip of the finger when the lamp is held in the right hand. The knob may well have served the double purpose.

# HELLENISTIC LAMPS, TYPES VII E – XIV

There was no abrupt break in development between the Classical lamps antedating the period of Alexander the Great and those of later times, nor is the term Hellenistic to be understood in a strictly chronological sense. Type VII, which made its appearance shortly before the middle of the 4th century, continued through the 3rd century and thus forms the bridge between the two eras. The transition is, nevertheless, real. The Athenian lamps, recognizable by the distinct Attic red clay and good-quality glaze, dominated the Corinthian lamp market down to the middle of the 4th century B.C. Most lamps of subtypes VII A, B, and D are Attic, and the locally made lamps, especially Type VII C, are imitations of the Attic models. As we approach the 3rd century, this situation changes. All, or nearly all, the lamps of Type VII E and F, as well as those of C, are of non-Attic origin, most of them Corinthian products. At the same time there is a change in shape, from the rather tall form with high base to the flatter watch-shaped varieties, often with a low base or with no base at all. These changes, however, do not come at the same time on all the varieties, and even within a given subtype the evolution is not consistent.

TYPE VII E. **133–137.**

This variety of Type VII differs from VII D by being somewhat flatter on top, and the groove separating the side from the rim is not reserved. All, with the possible exception of **136** and **137**, appear to be of local make, and all with the left side preserved have side knobs. These lamps have a poor thin glaze which generally covered the whole lamp. One example, **137**, the body of which has the same shape as that of the others, instead of having a low base is set on a high stem. The lower part of the stem has been restored, so that the exact height and shape are uncertain.

**133.** IP 56. Pls. 3, 17. From Rachi.
L. 0.086; D. 0.0565; H. 0.032.
Completely preserved. Light gray clay; poor, dull black glaze, largely peeled off. Rounded sides and groove round the rim. Nozzle more pointed than on VII D. Perforated side knob. No raised base, but concave underneath. Corinthian.

This being a local product, there is no very close parallel from the Athenian Agora. The profile of rim and body is nearly like that of *Agora* IV, Type 25 B Prime, no. 336, but that has a raised base rising to a high conical interior bottom. The date of **133** is probably about the same as that of no. 336 from Athens (275–225 B.C.).

**134.** IP 210. Pls. 3, 17. From Rachi.
D. 0.060; H. 0.032.
Nozzle missing. Buff clay with slightly reddish core; poor brown glaze, largely peeled off. Rounded sides and shallow groove setting off the rim. Solid side knob. Low raised base, completely flat underneath. Local Corinthian product.

There is no close parallel from Athens. The Isthmia lamp, both because of its provenance and the quality of glaze and fabric, is not likely to be later than the first half of the 3rd century B.C.

**135.** IP 213. Pls. 3, 17. From Rachi.
L. 0.0905; D. 0.060.
Lower part missing. Buff clay; dull brown glaze tending to rub off. On the inside, only the wick-hole is glazed. Sides converging toward the rim, which is set off by a shallow groove, not reserved. Rather long nozzle; small unperforated side knob. Probably local product.

Date, about the middle of the 3rd century B.C. Cf. *Argos*, pl. 2, no. 71.

**136.** IP 553a. Pl. 17. From Rachi Well, depth 5.70 m.
H. 0.034.
Fragment preserving parts of top and bottom. Red clay; red and light brown glaze on outside, dark brown on inside. Broad rim set off with groove which is covered with glaze. Raised base, concave. Possibly Attic.

**137.** IP 447. Pls. 3, 17. From Rachi.
L. (0.085); D. 0.058; restored H. (including stem) 0.15 m.
Nozzle and lower part of stem restored. Red clay; light brown glaze, partly peeled off. Sides inclining toward top and curving gradually into rim, which is set off by groove. Solid side knob. Body attached to solid stem, which tapers toward the top. Possibly Attic.

For the profile of the body and rim cf. **135.** Stemmed lamps of various types occur at most sites. See below, Type X, **219,** and cf. *Corinth* IV, ii, p. 49, fig. 24, from National Museum, Athens; *Agora* IV, nos. 312 and 611. Several stemmed lamps from Delos have been published by Philippe Bruneau, *Délos* XXVI, nos. 137, 236, 264, 312, 1599.

TYPE VII F. **138–146.**

Type VII F comprises nine lamps and fragments, all made of the typical blister ware,[19] which probably originated in Corinth. They are somewhat broader and lower than the other subtypes of Type VII. Those with the left side preserved had a pierced side knob and low base, concave underneath. Two are made of dark, almost gray clay; the others are of lighter color, but the difference is probably due to the firing. In most cases there is no obvious glaze, but in the firing the surface has received a different color from that in the core of the clay. Others, e.g. **138, 139,** have what appears to be a thin glaze or slip. Richard Howland (*Agora* IV, p. 91) also observed that "ordinary glaze was not used." He explains the difference in color as due to "a thin wash or slip of gray or orange pink that is used inside and outside, but not constantly."

Type VII F is probably Corinthian, as Howland, *op. cit.*, pp. 91–92, Type 28 A, hesitatingly suggests. It is to be dated in the early decades of the 3rd century B.C. Cf. Saul Weinberg, *Hesperia* 17, 1948, pp. 230, 235, 239, F 11. Among the published lamps from Argos there is at least one fragment that appears to be of blister ware, *Argos*, pl. 3, no. 118.

**138.** IP 486. Pls. 3, 17. From Rachi, Cistern with Pier.
L. 0.0975; D. 0.062; H. 0.029.

Small part of right side restored. Reddish gray clay; dull black glaze covering all the lamp. Curving sides set off from rim by shallow groove. Perforated side knob. Slightly raised base, concave underneath.

Cf. *Agora* IV, Type 28 A, no. 397, from a "well, lower filling, 300–275 B.C."

**139.** IP 246. Pls. 3, 17. From Rachi.
L. (0.103); D. 0.0675; H. 0.028.

End of nozzle and parts of body restored. Red clay; dull black and brown surfacing over the whole lamp. Rather flat top, with rim set off from curving side by shallow groove. Perforated side knob. Low raised base, concave underneath.

For the date see **138.**

**140.** IP 272. Pl. 17. From Rachi.

Top of lamp preserved. Dark gray core, orange-pink surface. Shallow groove sets off rim from side. Side knob perforated, but plug of clay left in the hole.

**141.** IP 720. Pl. 17. From Rachi, South Cistern.
D. (0.066); H. 0.039.

Red clay with dark gray core; no glaze. Rounded sides and groove round the rim. Slightly raised base, concave underneath.

**142.** IP 271. From Rachi.

Part of top and side knob of small lamp. Gray clay with orange-pink surface; unglazed. Perforated side knob; shallow groove around central opening.

**143.** IP 6063. From Rachi, South Cistern.

Fragment of rim and side, preserving pierced side knob. Red clay, grayish brown surface.

**144.** IP 6115. From Rachi.

Two non-joining fragments from top and bottom of lamp. Thin-walled red clay; mottled red and brown surface.

**145.** IP 6062. From Rachi Cistern.

Fragment of rim and side, preserving pierced side knob. Unglazed blister ware with gray core, orange-pink surface.

**146.** IP 5891. From North Temenos Dump.

Fragment preserving part of rim and side with perforated side knob. Ash-gray clay, orange-pink surface.

## FRAGMENTS OF TYPE VII, UNCERTAIN SUBTYPE. **147–202.**

These fragments do not preserve the side knob and cannot be arranged according to subtype. Many have the typical Attic clay and glaze, others are of blister ware or other local fabric.

| | | | |
|---|---|---|---|
| **147.** IP 6267. | **151.** IP 4047 (Pl. 17). | **155.** IP 5490. | **159.** IP 6276. |
| **148.** IP 6132. | **152.** IP 5443. | **156.** IP 4103. | **160.** IP 6127. |
| **149.** IP 6134. | **153.** IP 3955. | **157.** IP 4189. | **161.** IP 6242. |
| **150.** IP 6175. | **154.** IP 5430. | **158.** IP 6018. | **162.** IP 3966 (Pl. 17). |

[19] The term "blister ware" is applied to a ceramic product that was made in Corinth, and exported from there to other parts of Greece. Possibly ceramic factories elsewhere in Greece also produced blister ware, but Corinth appears to have been the chief center of its production for three centuries, from 450 B.C. till the destruction of the city under Mummius in 146 B.C. It is a hard, brittle ware, usually with many small air pockets within the fabric; it is from these that this type of pottery received its name. It was used for a variety of vases long before lamps of this fabric came into the market. The *locus classicus* on this product is found in Edward's recent publication, *Corinth* VII, iii, pp. 274–281. I am greatly indebted to the author and to Marian McAllister for sending me page proof of his chapter on Blister Ware while that volume was still in the press.

| | | | |
|---|---|---|---|
| **163.** IP 4173. | **173.** IP 6092. | **183.** IP 743. | **193.** IP 4316. |
| **164.** IP 6185 a. | **174.** IP 4325. | **184.** IP 2519. | **194.** IP 5442. |
| **165.** IP 4100. | **175.** IP 6135. | **185.** IP 5007. | **195.** IP 4357. |
| **166.** IP 3014. | **176.** IP 4146. | **186.** IP 6108. | **196.** IP 5886. |
| **167.** IP 6277. | **177.** IP 6273. | **187.** IP 4156. | **197.** IP 5416. |
| **168.** IP 6161. | **178.** IP 3957. | **188.** IP 5397. | **198.** IP 4345. |
| **169.** IP 6081. | **179.** IP 3507. | **189.** IP 4188. | **199.** IP 5638. |
| **170.** IP 4205. | **180.** IP 553 b. | **190.** IP 6166. | **200.** IP 4232. |
| **171.** IP 5441. | **181.** IP 368. | **191.** IP 5436. | **201.** IP 594. |
| **172.** IP 6064. | **182.** IP 318. | **192.** IP 6089. | **202.** IP 3963. |

## TYPE IX. 203–214.

There are no recognizable examples from Isthmia of the rather rare Type VIII. Type IX consists of comparatively large, flat lamps with double-convex body and side knob. On none of the existing lamps is a handle preserved, and it is unlikely that any of them had one. The side knob is rarely pierced, and a solid knob can have served no other purpose than to make it easier to hold the lamp. There are two variations within the type.

TYPE IX A. 203–210.

The lamps of IX A are made of red or reddish buff clay, and are covered with glaze of a dark brown or, less commonly, black color. Though probably of Attic make, none has the glossy finish of earlier Attic lamps. All but one, **205**, have high base, deeply concave underneath, some with double concavity, formed by "a little raised disc" (see *Agora* IV, p. 96).

Type IX A corresponds to *Agora* IV, Type 29 A and B. Howland comments on the "lagynos type of profile" and suggests that lamps of this shape may have been produced in the same shops as some lagynoi. He dates the type in the "last quarter of the 4th century B.C. and well into the second quarter of the 3rd century." Since all our lamps of this type came from the Rachi, such a date agrees well with the evidence from Isthmia.

**203.** IP 273. Pls. 4, 18. From Rachi.
L. (0.095); D. 0.071; H. 0.035.
Tip of nozzle and rear part of body restored. Red clay; dull black glaze all over, except in the groove round the filling-hole where the glaze has been scraped away. Double-convex body with blunt angle between the two halves. Short pointed nozzle. Solid side knob. Raised base with deep concavity and disc.
Cf. *Agora* IV, Type 29 B, no. 416 ("early 3rd century B.C.").

**204.** IP 274. Pls. 4, 18. From Rachi.
L. (0.10); D. 0.072; H. 0.039.
Partly restored. Grayish brown clay; dark brown and black glaze all over. Double-convex body with rather sharp angle between the two halves. Reserved groove round the opening. Narrow nozzle with flat top extending from the wick-hole all the way to the groove. Perforated side knob. High raised base, with deep concavity and disc.
Same date as **203**.

**205.** IP 483. Pls. 4, 18. From Rachi, House of Orestadas.[20]
L. (0.097); D. 0.068; H. 0.030.

Rear part restored. Light reddish clay; brown and black glaze covering the whole surface. Double-convex body. Prominent groove, not reserved, round central opening. Rather narrow nozzle with shoulders merging neatly into the body; suture between body and nozzle clearly visible. Solid side knob. No raised base, concave underneath.
Cf. *Corinth* IV, ii, p. 32, fig. 14, profile 38, and p. 144, no. 150. The profile of the body resembles *Agora* IV, Type 29 B, no. 415 ("first quarter and into second quarter of 3rd century B.C."). The absence of a raised base is found both on earlier lamps, *Agora* IV, Type 30 A, nos. 417, 418 ("late 5th century and well into first half of 4th century"), and on *Agora* IV, Type 28 B, nos. 404, 405 ("early to late years of 3rd century B.C., but primarily in first half of century").

**206.** IP 555. From Rachi, South Cistern.
Only part of top preserved. Red clay; black glaze all over, except for reserved groove around central opening.

**207.** IP 445. Pls. 4, 18. From Rachi.
L. (0.092); D. 0.0655; H. 0.028.

[20] The House of Orestadas is so named from a large vessel with the name of Orestadas incised on the rim. See *Hesperia* 27, 1958, p. 32, pl. 14, b. The vessel was made to serve as a beehive, as was then recognized by Professor Demetrios Pallas; *A.J.A.* 65, 1961, pp. 264–265. The identification has since been confirmed by the discovery of similar vessels at several sites in Attica; *B.S.A.* 68, 1973, pp. 391–452.

Right side, part of base, and tip of nozzle restored. Red clay; reddish brown glaze all over. Double-convex body with rather sharp angle between upper and lower halves. Large, perforated side knob. Raised base, concave underneath.

Cf. *Agora* IV, Type 29 A, no. 410 ("first quarter of 3rd century B.C.").

**208.** IP 270. From Rachi.

Small fragment from forepart of lamp. Reddish buff clay; red and brown glaze all over, except on the bottom of the base. Double-convex body; raised base, deeply

concave, with disc in center. Side knob apparently perforated, but mostly missing.

**209.** IP 6061. From Rachi, South Cistern.

Bottom and part of side preserved. Grayish clay; dark brown glaze both outside and inside. Deeply concave raised base with disc.

**210.** IP 6191. From Rachi.

Bottom and part of side preserved. Red clay; black and brown glaze on inner and outer surfaces. Double-convex body as in **204**. Raised, concave base with disc.

TYPE IX B. **211–214.**

The lamps of Type IX B have the same general shape as those of IX A, but they show further development of the type. They have either a very low base or none. The fabric is the local pale buff variety without glaze, or with the glaze almost entirely peeled off. One fragmentary example, **214**, which has been grouped with this subtype, is of the typical blister ware, with dark gray core and pink and gray surface without glaze. It is not entirely clear whether this lamp should be classed as IX B or with Type XI, which is a local imitation of Type IX A. Type IX B is to be dated in the 3rd century B.C., mostly before the middle of the century.

**211.** IP 554. Pls. 4, 18. From Rachi, Cistern.
L. 0.085; D. (0.065); H. 0.025.

Right side restored. Pinkish buff clay, covered with pale yellow wash; no glaze. Rounded side without sharp division between the two halves. Groove close to central opening. Small nozzle, solid side knob. Low raised base, concave underneath.

Its closest parallels are *Corinth* IV, ii, no. 142, pl. IV, and *Agora* IV, Type 28 B, nos. 401–403 (300–275 B.C.).

**212.** IP 719. Pls. 4, 18. From Rachi, South Cistern.
L. (0.0965); D. 0.0675; H. 0.033.

Part of right side and nozzle restored. Buff clay; mottled black and brown glaze, largely peeled off. Double-convex body with the top and bottom halves not very sharply set off. Double groove round central opening; side knob partly restored, probably unperforated. Low base, concave.

Date, 3rd century B.C. This would go best with *Agora* IV, Type 29 A, e.g. no. 412, but there is no very close parallel among the lamps from the Athenian Agora.

**213.** IP 697. From Rachi, Cistern.
D. 0.0675.

Top and nozzle missing. Buff clay; no glaze extant. Rounded sides. Side knob apparently solid. No raised base, concave bottom underneath.

**214.** IP 593. Pls. 4, 18. From Rachi, Orestadas Section.
H. 0.0335; D. 0.0685.

Left side of top and part of nozzle missing. Dark gray clay with orange-pink surface; blister ware. Concave bottom, but no raised base.

Cf. *Corinth* IV, ii, pl. IV, no. 146. For description of blister ware see above, note 19; and *Agora* IV, pp. 91–93, under Types 28 A and B.

UNCLASSIFIED HELLENISTIC LAMPS. **215–217.**

For the following three lamps there is no corresponding type among the published and unpublished lamps from Corinth. They are listed here after Type IX because of their date, which is based chiefly on their provenance. The only thing that the three lamps have in common is the central tube, which in the case of the miniature lamp **217**—if it is a lamp—is solid. The central tube occurs on earlier types, e.g. Type IV, **74**; and on lamps from Corinth it appears early on Type I (*Corinth* IV, ii, pl. I, nos. 7, 11). Among the lamps from Athens it is found on several types, chronologically separated by centuries.

**215.** IP 284. Pls. 4, 18. From Rachi.
L. 0.148; D. 0.111; H. (not including central socket) 0.048.

Large lamp with three nozzles, somewhat restored. Brick-red clay; light brown glaze with streaks of darker brown. Sides curving into nearly horizontal rim with slightly rising inner edge. Three long nozzles with

wick-holes far removed from the rim. High base ring, central tube extending well above the rim, but top broken away. It was probably intended to be set on a standard or suspended.

Lamps with multiple nozzles occur in several different types at all periods. See *Agora* IV, nos. 170, 191, etc. In the Museum in Ioannina there is a lamp almost identical in shape to our **215**. It came from the Nekromanteion at Ephyra and was published by Soterios Dakaris in Πρακτικά, 1961 (Athens 1964), pl. 70 and p. 113. A photograph, kindly furnished by Professor Dakaris, is shown in Plate 38, c. A similar lamp without the central tube is published in *Délos* XXVI, pl. 8, no. 1598. The author, Philippe Bruneau (p. 30), dates the group to which this lamp belongs in the second half of the 2nd century and the beginning of the 1st century B.C. It is unlikely that Isthmia **215** is much later than the middle of the 3rd century B.C.

**216.** IP 3964. Pls. 4, 18. From Northwest Reservoir.
Fragment of miniature lamp preserving only the lower part and central tube. Light red clay; poor black glaze largely flaked off. Raised base. Central socket, full height preserved, probably extended up to level of the rim, which is broken away.

Lamps of the Hellenistic period with central tube and single nozzle are common in Athens. See *Agora* IV, Types 27 A–D, pls. 13, 14, 40.

**217.** IP 4154. From Sacred Glen.
Small fragment from bottom of miniature vessel, probably a lamp like **216**, but with solid tube. Pinkish buff clay; no glaze.

## TYPE X. 218–226.

The lamps of Type X are rather small, without handle, and with no proper rim, the top being continuous with the curving sides. There is only a slight indication of a groove very close to the filling-hole. The nozzle is either rounded at the end or roughly triangular, with a mere suggestion of flukes, and there is no side knob. Most of the lamps are made of the typical buff or light gray clay of Corinth; the clay of others is light red or ash gray. Some preserve traces of glaze. A raised base is either absent or very low. One lamp of Type X, **219**, was set on a tall, solid stand, of which only the attachment remains.

Type X is probably Corinthian. Among the published lamps from Athens there is none of quite the same shape. Although rare at other sites, the type is fairly common at Corinth; no less than 16 examples are among the published lamps, and there are many unpublished examples. There is little difference in shape between Type X and the very rare Type XVII, but the latter is more closely related to Type XVI B by the nature of its clay and the total absence of glaze.

For the date of Type X from Corinth, I suggested that it "began to be produced in the second half of the 3rd century, and continued in use into the 2nd century B.C." This is still the most likely date. It is obviously pre-destruction, i.e. prior to 146 B.C., and since it occurs in relatively large numbers it would have been in vogue through several decades. The still more common Type XI must have come into use while Type X was in the market, and for a time the two types were produced simultaneously. Contemporary lamps from Athens, *Agora* IV, Types 33 A and B, and 34 A and B, are characterized as "Poor Relations."

**218.** IP 1009. Pls. 4, 18. From manhole to Southwest Reservoir.
D. 0.056; H. 0.028.
End of nozzle is missing. Pale buff clay; traces of thin, light brown glaze. Rounded body with no rim, but with a groove close to the edge of the central opening. Slightly raised base, flat underneath.

Probably middle of 3rd century B.C. The manhole to the Southwest Reservoir, where **218** and **222** were found, contained fragments of Megarian bowls but no Roman pottery (see *Isthmia* II, p. 29). This date is suggested by the provenance of **219**, which has much the same shape, but is set on a stem.

**219.** IP 718. Pls. 4, 18. From Rachi, Cistern.
L. (0.072); D. 0.050.
Stemmed lamp with tip of nozzle and part of right side restored. The stem is broken off below its attachment to the body. Light gray clay; brown and black glaze all over. Rounded side with shallow groove close to central opening. Rather short nozzle.

Since **219** came from the Rachi, it is unlikely to be later than about 240 B.C.[21]

**220.** IP 2604. From Northeast Area.
Nozzle. Red clay; brown glaze on the outside and on parts of the inside. Nozzle had bluntly triangular end, slightly wider than at the base, suggesting rudimentary flukes.

**221.** IP 5487 a. Pl. 18. From Temenos, west end of South Side.
L. 0.074; H. 0.029.
Right half preserved, including complete nozzle. Ash-gray clay, thin black glaze or wash. No raised base. End of nozzle rounded and slightly wider than at the base.

When the South Stoa was constructed in the 2nd century after Christ, the fill of the manhole to the Southwest Reservoir was partly removed, because the original ground level was higher than the floor of the stoa. Thus it is likely that the lamp **221**, and also **223** and

[21] See above, footnote 17.

**224**, had come from the upper fill of the manhole. See under **218**, and cf. *Isthmia* II, p. 28.

**222.** IP 6179. From manhole to Southwest Reservoir.
Fragment of nozzle, rim and side. Light gray clay; thin, dark gray glaze.

**223.** IP 5488. From Temenos, west end of South Side.
Nozzle, wider at the end than at the base. Reddish gray clay; thin, dark brown glaze. See above under **221**.

**224.** IP 4291. From Temenos, west end of South Side.
Fragment of rim and side. Light red clay, glazed a somewhat darker red on inner and outer surfaces.

**225.** IP 5875. Pl. 18. From East Propylon Area.
Nozzle. Light red clay; mottled brown and red glaze, much scratched. End of nozzle rounded and wider than base to form rudimentary flukes.

**226.** IP 4050. From Temenos, East End.
Nozzle. Pale red clay; thin brown glaze. End of nozzle bluntly rounded.

## TYPE XI. 227–276.

Of Type XI there are 50 inventoried items, but only two lamps are sufficiently well preserved to show the complete shape. The body is somewhat like that of Type IX, with angular profile and a rather long nozzle, narrower at the end than at the base. All the lamps of this type have vertical loop handles and side knobs. The latter is sometimes pierced, more often solid and rather small. Since all the lamps have handles, the knob has degenerated into a meaningless feature copied from earlier types, VII D and IX. All the lamps and fragments of this type, with one or two doubtful exceptions, are of the typical blister ware: very thin fabric, either dark gray or mottled gray and pink on the surface and usually dark gray in the core. None of the fragments has any obvious traces of glaze, but difference in color between the surface and the biscuit sometimes gives the appearance of glaze. Many of the lamps show marks of paring, especially at the nozzle. All the fragments that preserve part of the bottom have a low base, concave underneath.

Type XI is of local make, the most popular type of lamp at Corinth in the 3rd century B.C. The blister ware occurs in Athens, chiefly in Type 28 A and B, the lamps of which are dated from the last quarter of the 4th century B.C. till near the end of the 3rd century. The author of *Agora* IV (p. 92) concludes hesitatingly that the fabric may be Corinthian. But *Agora* IV, Type 28 A had a different profile from that of our Type XI, which corresponds more nearly to *Agora* IV, Type 29 A, of the same date, but of Athenian manufacture. Type XI occurs frequently at Argos (*Argos*, p. 29 and nos. 125–135), where some of the examples appear to be of Corinthian make. Though it may have been imitated elsewhere, the blister ware was a predominantly Corinthian product.[22]

Of the 50 lamps and fragments of Type XI, 44 came from the Rachi and 2 from the Southwest Reservoir. They are to be dated between 325 and 240 B.C., and rather from the end than the beginning of that period. There is no obvious development in shape within the type, but the relatively large number of fragments indicates that the type endured for a considerable time, through the second and third quarters of the 3rd century B.C.

**227.** IP 208. Pls. 4, 19. From Rachi.
L. (0.098); D. 0.067; H. 0.027.
Handle and tip of nozzle restored. Dark gray clay with the surface in some spots of lighter color; no glaze. Blister ware. Double-convex body. Two shallow grooves close to filling-hole. Perforated side knob, vertical handle. Slightly raised base, concave underneath.

**228.** IP 209. Pls. 4, 19. From Rachi.
L. 0.082; D. 0.054; H. 0.023.
Handle restored. Pinkish gray clay with gray and orange surface; no glaze. Blister ware. Double-convex body. Solid side knob and vertical handle. Small groove close to central opening. Slightly raised base, concave underneath.

**229.** IP 596. From Rachi Well, depth 1.68 m.
H. 0.025.
Fragment. Red and gray clay with mostly orange-red surface. Blister ware. Perforated side knob; vertical handle. Traces of groove setting off sides from the top. Low raised base, slightly concave.

**230.** IP 2635. From Northeast Area.
Fragment from top. Reddish clay with gray core; unglazed. Blister ware. Loop handle, mostly missing. Double-convex body with groove close to filling-hole.

**231.** IP 269. From Rachi.
H. 0.031.
Nozzle and part of top preserved. Red clay with dark gray and reddish surface. Blister ware. Signs of paring under nozzle.

[22] See above, footnote 19.

**232.** IP 592. From Rachi, South Cistern.

Base and most of nozzle preserved. Red clay with dark brown surface. Blister ware. Slightly raised base, concave underneath. Marks of paring on nozzle.

**233.** IP 556. From Rachi, South Cistern.

Nozzle and part of bottom preserved. Dark gray clay with pinkish surface; no real glaze, but on the base and neck are streaks of darker color. Blister ware. Slightly raised base, concave. Indications of paring on nozzle.

**234.** IP 254. From Rachi.

H. 0.029.

Nozzle, parts of right side and base preserved. Red clay; no glaze. Blister ware.

**235.** IP 1150. From Rachi.

Nozzle and part of top preserved. Dark gray clay with pinkish surface; no glaze. Blister ware.

**236–276.** In addition to the nine items described above, there are 41 inventoried fragments of Type XI, making this the most numerous type of Hellenistic lamp.

| | | | |
|---|---|---|---|
| **236.** IP 590. | **247.** IP 6105. | **258.** IP 4340. | **269.** IP 6180. |
| **237.** IP 207. | **248.** IP 6274. | **259.** IP 6192 a. | **270.** IP 6111 a, b. |
| **238.** IP 637. | **249.** IP 6177. | **260.** IP 6114. | **271.** IP 6173. |
| **239.** IP 265. | **250.** IP 6178 a, b. | **261.** IP 6060. | **272.** IP 6192 b. |
| **240.** IP 267. | **251.** IP 6195. | **262.** IP 4341. | **273.** IP 6183 a–c. |
| **241.** IP 54. | **252.** IP 6059. | **263.** IP 6269. | **274.** IP 4183. |
| **242.** IP 55. | **253.** IP 6194. | **264.** IP 6131. | **275.** IP 6120 a, b. |
| **243.** IP 599. | **254.** IP 5918. | **265.** IP 6268. | **276.** IP 4049 a–d. |
| **244.** IP 268. | **255.** IP 6104. | **266.** IP 4264. | |
| **245.** IP 245. | **256.** IP 6082. | **267.** IP 6106. | |
| **246.** IP 266. | **257.** IP 6093. | **268.** IP 6174. | |

## SMALLER PIECES. 277–335.

There are in addition 59 insignificant fragments which, so far as they can be recognized, are parts of Hellenistic Lamps, Types VII–XI. They are of importance only because of their provenance: no less than 22 came from the Rachi, and 14 from the Southwest Reservoir.

| | | | |
|---|---|---|---|
| **277.** IP 6168. | **292.** IP 5024. | **307.** IP 4833. | **322.** IP 5489. |
| **278.** IP 5887. | **293.** IP 6278. | **308.** IP 4343. | **323.** IP 5025. |
| **279.** IP 6102. | **294.** IP 6017. | **309.** IP 6046. | **324.** IP 6182. |
| **280.** IP 6275. | **295.** IP 6079. | **310.** IP 5644. | **325.** IP 5431. |
| **281.** IP 6272. | **296.** IP 6080. | **311.** IP 6181. | **326.** IP 4215 a. |
| **282.** IP 4114. | **297.** IP 6016. | **312.** IP 4020. | **327.** IP 6162. |
| **283.** IP 6020. | **298.** IP 6138. | **313.** IP 4342. | **328.** IP 6157 a, b. |
| **284.** IP 6113. | **299.** IP 6193. | **314.** IP 5639. | **329.** IP 6107 a, b. |
| **285.** IP 6270. | **300.** IP 6280. | **315.** IP 6167. | **330.** IP 4166 a, b. |
| **286.** IP 5487 b. | **301.** IP 5491. | **316.** IP 4290. | **331.** IP 6160. |
| **287.** IP 4338. | **302.** IP 4259. | **317.** IP 5812. | **332.** IP 4069. |
| **288.** IP 6172. | **303.** IP 5415. | **318.** IP 6185 b. | **333.** IP 5439. |
| **289.** IP 6084. | **304.** IP 6126. | **319.** IP 4346. | **334.** IP 4347. |
| **290.** IP 4292. | **305.** IP 4029. | **320.** IP 4344. | **335.** IP 4339. |
| **291.** IP 6137 c. | **306.** IP 6271. | **321.** IP 6241. | |

## TYPE XII. 336, 337.

There are only two lamps from Isthmia that can be classed as Corinth Type XII. As Howland observed in connection with the related lamps in Athens (*Agora* IV, Type 33 A, p. 101), this is an amorphous group of lamps, also characterized as "Poor Relations." The distinguishing feature is the depressed top, which resulted in a raised edge that served as a catch to prevent the oil, when it was poured in, from spilling over the side. The lamps have a low base usually flat underneath. One example, **336**, had a vertical handle; the other, **337**, had none.

There are no side knobs on the lamps of this type from Isthmia or Corinth. **337** is of particular interest because it is an early ancestor of the later ubiquitous Type XVI. Type XII is well represented at Argos (*Argos*, nos. 148–157). Clay and glaze differ so much among lamps of this type that it would be hazardous to assign a particular center for their manufacture. They were probably made locally both at Corinth and Athens, and perhaps at Argos as well. By Athenian evidence, they are to be dated in "the last quarter of 3rd century B.C., into third quarter of 2nd century." A further development of the type in Athens is classed as Type 43 B, which seems to be of the same date.

**336.** IP 914. Pls. 4, 19. From Palaimonion, close to Stadium floor.
  D. 0.063; H. 0.031.

Handle and nozzle missing. Light red clay; poor brown glaze. Sides sharply converging toward top. Depressed top with slightly raised edge round central opening. Vertical handle. Low base, flat underneath.

The profile resembles that of *Agora* IV, Type 34 B, pl. 16, no. 452, but that lamp had a side knob.

**337.** IP 57. Pls. 4, 19. From North Temenos Dump.
  L. (0.0935); D. 0.067; H. 0.033.

Tip of nozzle restored. Light red clay; poor black glaze with pockmarks all over. The sides converge toward the top and just below the rim is a shallow groove. Depressed top, no side knob. Slightly raised base, flat underneath. This late example of Hellenistic wheelmade lamps is a forerunner of the much later Type XVI.

The profile is very much like that of *Agora* IV, Type 35 A Prime, pl. 43, no. 472, which has a side knob. The Athens type has been dated in the last quarter of the 2nd century and into the first quarter of the 1st century B.C. Inasmuch as that is the time when Corinth and the Isthmian Sanctuary had ceased to operate, our **337** should be dated in the first half of the 2nd century, in any case before 146 B.C.

## TYPE XIV. **338.**

There is only a single specimen of Type XIV, which was never very common. It is of importance chiefly as a precursor of Type XVI. It has a convex top, surrounded by the high edge of the rim. This feature, as in Type XII, served to prevent spilling when the oil was poured. Four small holes in the depression between the rim and the convex top permitted the oil to run down into the infundibulum. A loop handle made separately was attached to the rim. The nozzle too was made as a separate piece, and added before the final trimming of the top on the wheel. The base is flat underneath. In the lamp from Isthmia, the fabric is ash gray and covered with a black metallic glaze.

Howland dates the type, his 39, to the "late 2nd century into 1st century B.C." There is really only one lamp from Athens, *Agora* IV, no. 517; the other two lamps listed under Type 39 belong to Corinth Type X. The Corinth collection contains two good examples of Type XIV, one published in *Corinth* IV, ii, pl. V, no. 193. The second (Pl. 40, g) is an unpublished lamp (L 4468), much restored, which is made of light red clay and covered with dark brown and black glaze of excellent quality. This was found in a manhole with pottery from the middle of the 2nd century B.C. Though almost identical in shape with our **338**, and with *Corinth* IV, ii, no. 193, and *Agora* IV, no. 517, the fabric of the unpublished Corinth lamp points to Hellenistic connections of earlier date. It seems likely that the Isthmia lamp **338** belongs to the period of the later Ephesos lamps, Type XIX, which is not represented at Isthmia, though fairly common at Corinth. They were imported to Corinth from Asia Minor during the early decades of the Roman Colony and perhaps earlier (see *Corinth* IV, ii, p. 70). It is no accident that they are absent at Isthmia, where the rebuilding of the Sanctuary was deferred to the early years of the Christian era (see *Isthmia* II, pp. 67–68). At Athens, where the Ephesos lamps are common, the importation of lamps from Asia Minor began about 125 B.C. (*Agora* IV, p. 166), and continued into the 1st century after Christ. In the early decades of that century the Athenian lampmakers produced imitations (*Agora* IV, Type 49 B) of the imported lamps. The ash-gray clay and black metallic glaze of our **338** is similar to that used for the Ephesos lamps. One unpublished lamp from Corinth (L 4120, Pl. 40, f), which is to be dated by context to the late 1st century B.C., is an early form of Type XVI, but has the same clay and glaze as the Ephesos lamps and Isthmia **338**. These examples tend to show that **338** was made at Corinth in the second half of the 1st century B.C., probably near the middle of the century. There are very few specimens of this kind from Corinth (see *Corinth* IV, ii, p. 57 and below, pp. 26–27); all are early examples of Type XVI. They seem to belong to the early years of the 1st century after Christ, when the more decorative Italian relief lamps were brought to the Corinthian market. It was then that the Isthmian Games were returned to Corinthian management and held at Isthmia.[23] The Ephesos lamps, no longer imported to Corinth in large numbers, were being replaced by relief lamps from Italy, and the locally made Type XVI was coming into use.

[23] The date of the restoration (7 B.C.–A.D. 3) is discussed in *Isthmia* II, p. 67, note 2; and Broneer, *H.T.R.* 64, 1971, p. 169.

**338.** IP 3927. Pls. 4, 19. From Temenos, North Side. D. 0.0625; H. 0.032.

Handle and end of nozzle missing. Ash-gray clay; dark gray, almost black glaze which tends to peel off. The top is convex, with a rather large filling-hole in the center and four smaller holes at the edges. The raised rim flares out and forms a channel round the convex top. The four smaller holes were made to permit the oil collecting in the channel to run back into the infundibulum. Slightly raised base, flat underneath.

Cf. *Corinth* IV, ii, pl. V, no. 193. See also *Agora* IV, pls. 19, 45, no. 517, the handle and nozzle of which have been restored; *Délos* XXVI, pl. 6, no. 319.

# LAMPS OF ROMAN IMPERIAL TIMES, TYPES XVI—XVII

No lamps of Types XIII and XV have come to light at Isthmia; and the same is true of Types XVIII and XIX. These are the types in common use elsewhere during the century 146–44 B.C., when Corinth was largely unpopulated and certainly did not exist as an industrial center. After the establishment of the Roman colony by Julius Caesar, the rebuilding of the city and its ancient shrines naturally took precedence over the restoration of the Isthmian Sanctuary. At Corinth there are inscriptions, as well as buildings, not to mention many kinds of portable antiquities, that can be dated to the last half of the 1st century B.C. At Isthmia, however, the reconstruction proceeded at a slower pace. The Isthmian Games had been taken over by the Sikyonians and were probably held at Sikyon itself. Excavations in the Isthmian Sanctuary have produced no evidence of reconstruction before the closing years of Augustus' reign; indeed most of the buildings appear to have been left in their dilapidated condition until the time of Claudius. Since the types of Corinth lamps missing at Isthmia were in use during the last half of the 2nd century B.C. and throughout the 1st century B.C., their absence offers additional testimony to the neglect and virtual abandonment of the Isthmian Sanctuary during those 150 years.

## TYPE XVI. 339–1108.

No less than 771, nearly one fourth of the inventoried lamps from Isthmia, belong to Type XVI. They were found in different parts of the Sanctuary, frequently in the same context as the imported relief lamps, Types XXII–XXV. By far the largest number came from the Palaimonion. That Type XVI is a local Corinthian product was demonstrated in my study of the lamps from Corinth,[24] and the surprisingly large number from the Isthmia excavations corroborate this conclusion. This is the latest type of wheelmade lamp found at Corinth. It belongs to the period when Corinth imported its more elegant lamps from the outside, first from Asia Minor and later from Italy. Type XVI, however, owes little to the imported types; its development can be traced back to the wheelmade lamps of earlier times.

It is now possible, with the help of lamps found at Isthmia and at Corinth since *Corinth* IV, ii was published, to follow the gradual evolution of Type XVI. The origin of the type goes back to some lamps of Hellenistic times, Types IX–XII, which show connection with lamps of the 4th century B.C. (Type VII). These, in turn, had evolved from the 5th century lamps. Thus Type XVI comes at the end of a long process of evolution that harks back to the very beginning of Greek lampmaking. The more immediate predecessors are Types XII and XIV, which are poorly represented at Isthmia. Their relation to Type XVI has been pointed out above, p. 25. There is little difference between the lamp **338** of Type XIV and earlier lamps of Type XVI, except for the fabric and the small holes on the top. But clay and glaze tie **338**, which seems to be of Corinthian make, to the later Hellenistic types, more particularly to the Ephesos lamps, Type XIX, which do not occur at Isthmia. That type, as has been shown in *Agora* IV, pp. 166–170, was very common in Athens from the last quarter of the 2nd century B.C. into the first quarter of the 1st century after Christ. That is exactly the time when the Isthmian Sanctuary was virtually abandoned. Other lamps of the same rare kind as **338** have been found in Corinth (*Corinth* IV, ii, no. 193). An unpublished lamp in the Corinth collection (L 4468, Pl. 40, g) has the same shape as Isthmia **338**, but is of different fabric. The nozzle had a bluntly triangular end with rudimentary flukes, much like the nozzle

---

[24] One lamp of Type XVI, **497**, has been crushed out of shape in the firing. See also *Corinth* IV, ii, p. 57, and Broneer, *A.J.A* 31, 1927, pp. 329–337.

of another early lamp of Type XVI from Corinth (*Corinth* IV, ii, p. 57, fig. 25, no. 287). The clay is light red and the glaze a semi-lustrous black. It does not seem to be Corinthian but may be of Athenian manufacture. There is another unpublished lamp (L 4120, Pl. 40, f) from Corinth that has the shape of the early specimens of Type XVI, with nearly vertical sides and the corner between the body and the flat bottom beveled. The fabric—ash-gray clay, dark gray, metallic glaze—is like that used for the Ephesos lamps, Type XIX.

One other lamp from Corinth (L-72-17, Pl. 40, e) is of importance for our study of the origin of Type XVI. It was found in the recent excavations carried on by Professor Henry S. Robinson, north of the Archaic Temple.[25] The shape is very much like that of the other lamp from Corinth (L 4120), with almost vertical sides and beveled corner at the bottom. But, unlike the other lamps of this type, it has a solid knob on the left side, like that on Types IX and XI. The clay is light red, and orange-red glaze has been applied by dipping. The upper part of the lamp, including nozzle and handle, is glazed, but the base and lower part of the body are left unglazed. The lower edge of the glazed part is irregular and shows the run of the glaze (Pl. 40, e). This too is very likely of Corinthian manufacture, an early link between the Hellenistic lamps and Type XVI.[26]

Though unpretentious in form and virtually without decoration, a Type XVI lamp is as serviceable as any lamp in the catalogue, lacking none of the features that make the lamp useful as an instrument of illumination. The ample loop handle makes it easy to hold and carry; the concave top surrounded with a raised rim makes filling simple and prevents spilling; the sturdy nozzle has a wick-hole deep enough for the wick to reach the bottom and just large enough to produce an adequate flame; the base is wide enough to assure a stable position when the lamp is put down. These lamps, found in such quantities in the Palaimonion, seem to have been intended chiefly for use at a single occasion, i.e. at the festival of Palaimon, after which they could be thrown away or perhaps offered as votive objects to the hero.

The method of manufacture of Type XVI is readily detected from a study of the lamps. In the first step the lampmaker cast a vessel in the shape of a small tumbler; then, while this was still turning on the wheel, he folded in the edges so as to produce a flat top sloping gently towards the center. In so doing he pressed the top down sufficiently to form a raised outer edge. The filling-hole in the center resulted from this process of folding down the sides; it was not, as is the case with most of the molded lamps, produced with a tubular instrument as a last step in the process. After he had shaped the body he added the handle and nozzle. To form the nozzle the lampmaker shaped a short, roughly cylindrical piece of clay with straight ends; then he flattened one end, so as to make it thinner than the other. In so doing he created the broad blunt-ended nozzle with the corners projecting. After he had attached this solid piece of clay to the side of the lamp, he took a tubular instrument of the desired diameter, *ca.* 0.012 m., and pushed it through the nozzle and the side of the body into the interior, and as he pulled it out he removed a cylindrical piece of clay of the size of the wick-hole. In many of the lamps of this type the tubular instrument has left its mark on the bottom of the infundibulum. All this probably took place while the lamp was still attached to the wheel. When he was ready to remove the lamp he inserted a string between the lamp and the wheel and pulled it tight, probably while the wheel was still turning slowly. This process left a series of rough concentric circles or loops on the bottom, which were nearly always left without subsequent trimming. For the handle the lampmaker produced a strip of clay which he then attached, one end just below the rim and the other at the lower edge, a little above the base. This he probably did after he had removed the lamp from the wheel; while it was still fastened to the wheel it would have been difficult to attach the lower end of the handle so close to the bottom. Most handles have the edges slightly raised, so as to produce a shallow furrow through the middle.

The lamps of Type XVI are of fairly uniform size, but there are some exceptions. The larger lamps from Isthmia have a diameter of *ca.* 0.063 m., and there are some as little as 0.050 m. in diameter. Among the lamps from Corinth there are a few with two or three nozzles. One large lamp has two nozzles,[27] one opposite the other, and a large opening on the discus through which extends a vertical handle with a loop at the top, its lower end attached to the bottom of the infundibulum. In some cases two or more lamps of Type XVI were attached to the rim of a standard, usually surmounted by a third lamp of the same kind or by some other feature.[28]

The lamps of Type XVI fall into two groups, differentiated chiefly by the presence or absence of surface coating. The first and smaller group consists of 139 lamps that show traces of color on the surface different from

[25] I am indebted to Mr. Robinson for permission to publish photographs of the lamp and to Rebecca Robinson, who was in charge of the area, for information about the circumstances of discovery. Unfortunately the context of the fill gives no indication of the date of the lamp.

[26] Such a lamp from southern Italy, now in Berlin, is published in Heres, pl. 7, no. 76. It too has a knob on the side, handle, and nozzle with straight end.

[27] See Pl. 40, h (Corinth L 4207), and cf. *Corinth* IV, ii, pl. V, no. 285.

[28] *Ibid.*, p. 60, fig. 26; pp. 156–7, nos. 288–291.

that of the clay. The whole lamp, both inside and outside, is covered with a thin wash, which cannot properly be called glaze or paint. In many cases it has all but disappeared. In addition to this surface treatment, many of the lamps of Type XVI have traces of a whitewash, applied after the lamp had been made, probably while it was in use in the Palaimonion. The same kind of whitewash is found on the Palaimonion lamps. For a possible explanation see below, p. 37.

There is really no appreciable difference in shape between the "glazed," Type XVI A, and the "unglazed" lamps, Type XVI B. In both groups there are some slight variations in profile, as shown in the sections on Plate 5; and in general the glazed lamps have slightly straighter sides without the pronounced flaring at the top that many of the unglazed lamps have. It is likely that Type XVI A as a group is slightly earlier than the more numerous variety of Type XVI B, but the two doubtless overlapped in date.

In the Palaimonion, lamps of Type XVI came to light at various levels, from just below the surface down to the floor of the Earlier Stadium. They were certainly in frequent use long before the fifth and last period of the Palaimonion, to which the Temple of Palaimon belongs. The earliest go back to the early years of the Christian era, when Sacrificial Pits A and B constituted the whole architectural apparatus of the cult of Palaimon. At that time the space at the northwest end of the Stadium, i.e. the area which later became the Peribolos proper of Palaimon, seems to have been an open court in which cult rites of the hero took place. This would account for the fact that lamps of Type XVI, together with the earlier forms of Palaimonion lamps, came from the lowest stratum only a little above the Stadium floor. Many of these lamps, together with some pottery and imported relief lamps, were found in nests at various points of the area. In the course of the years, at least three quarters of a century but probably more, the ground level in this area rose to a height of 0.50 m. to 0.75 m. above the Stadium floor. One fairly large area, east of the later temple, showed a well-marked strosis, and lamps of Type XVI were found both above and below this level[29] (*ca.* 0.75 m. above the Stadium floor).

It is a significant fact that lamps of Type XVI, with little or no change either in shape or in fabric and surfacing, came from such varied levels in the area of the Peribolos. This is to be explained partly by the fact that lamps of this type continued in use over a period of a century or more, and during that time there was no appreciable change in shape and fabric. But there is another explanation for this phenomenon. When the temple foundation was laid, a large square trench had to be dug through the layers of accumulated fill. The earth from this excavation would have been thrown out of the trench and later leveled out when the area round about was being landscaped. Whatever lamps and pottery this earth contained were scattered about above the level at which they had originally been deposited and became mixed with fill of later times. Thus the strosis mentioned above probably dates from before the construction of the Temple; and the fact that there were lamps and other objects with no distinction in date, both above and below the strosis, can be accounted for in this way.

It is obvious that Type XVI was mass-produced and sold in great numbers at a very small price to visitors at Isthmia and in particular to those who came there to participate in the cult rites of Palaimon.

In view of the uniformity of shape within the type, it seems aimless to describe in detail all the lamps and fragments of Type XVI. There are considerable differences in the clay and, in the case of the coated lamps, in the color and application of the wash. The following selection of 52 lamps, 28 of Type XVI A, and 24 of XVI B, illustrates all the variations of size, shape, wash, and fabric. The other lamps of the type are lumped together in the catalogue.

## TYPE XVI A. 339–477.

**339.** IP 2607. From northeast of the Temple of Poseidon.

Nozzle with part of side and top attached. Light gray clay; brown wash. The nozzle is rounded at the end and slightly spreading. The side is nearly straight, but diverging toward the top. This fragment is probably a forerunner of the fully developed Type XVI.

So far as can be judged from the small fragment, it belongs to the second group of Corinth Type XVI. *Corinth* IV, ii, p. 56.

**340.** IP 1902. Pl. 20. From Palaimonion Area, east of Temple, *ca.* 0.75 m. above Stadium floor.
L. 0.085; D. 0.058; H. 0.029.

Handle missing. Greenish buff clay; patches of dark brown and light brown wash.

**341.** IP 1640. Pl. 20. From Palaimonion Area, east of Temple.
D. 0.059; H. 0.0225.

Nozzle broken away. Pale buff clay; traces of light brown wash.

**342.** IP 924. Pl. 20. From Palaimonion, *ca.* 0.60 m. above Stadium floor.
D. 0.0585; H. 0.0315.

Handle and most of nozzle missing. Reddish buff clay, rather friable; slight traces of brown wash.

---

[29] See *Isthmia* II, p. 109.

343. IP 1597. Pls. 5, 20. From Palaimonion Area, South Stoa Wall Trench.
L. 0.087; D. 0.062; H. 0.031.
Handle missing. Pale buff clay; mottled light and dark brown wash, poor quality.

344. IP 782. Pls. 5, 20. From Palaimonion, middle section.
L. 0.081; D. 0.0565; H. 0.0305.
Handle restored. Grayish buff clay; mottled dark gray and brown wash.

345. IP 1893. Pl. 20. From Palaimonion Area, east of Temple, 0.25 m. above Stadium floor.
L. 0.085; D. 0.060; H. 0.027.
Handle missing. Greenish buff clay; poor, thin brown wash. Nozzle attached askew.

346. IP 1863. Pls. 5, 19, 20. From Palaimonion Area, east of Temple, 0.50 m. above Stadium floor.
L. 0.080; D. 0.060; H. 0.0285.
Mended but complete. Reddish buff clay; mottled light and dark brown wash.

347. IP 911. Pls. 5, 20. From Palaimonion Area, 0.60 m. above Stadium floor.
L. 0.089; D. 0.064; H. 0.035.
Handle restored. Red mealy clay; red wash. Handle and nozzle very unsymmetrical. Nozzle much darkened.

348. IP 923. Pl. 20. From Palaimonion, high level.
L. 0.092; D. 0.063; H. 0.025.
Much mended and handle restored. Pale yellow clay; faint traces of thin, light brown wash. Nozzle askew, i.e. top of nozzle is at a considerable angle to top of lamp.

349. IP 1629. Pl. 20. From Palaimonion, east of Temple, 0.30 m. above Stadium floor.
L. 0.080; D. 0.056; H. 0.029.
Handle missing. Reddish buff clay; bright red and light brown wash.

350. IP 951. Pl. 20. From Palaimonion, 0.20 m. above Stadium floor (pit).
D. 0.0645; H. 0.030.
Handle and end of nozzle broken away. Light buff clay; mottled dark and light brown wash.

351. IP 916. Pl. 20. From Palaimonion, ca. 0.095 m. above Stadium floor.
L. 0.090; D. 0.066; H. 0.032.
Handle restored. Buff clay; purplish brown wash, which tends to come off.

352. IP 919. Pls. 5, 19, 20. From Palaimonion, 0.55 m. above Stadium floor.
L. (0.0925); D. 0.062; H. 0.036.
Handle and part of nozzle restored. Light buff clay; mottled brown and purplish wash, very thin and poor.

353. IP 948. Pls. 5, 20. From Palaimonion, imbedded in Temple foundation.[30]
L. 0.092; D. 0.0635; H. 0.033.
Small part of handle restored. Reddish buff clay; mottled red and brown wash.

354. IP 1607. Pls. 5, 20. From Palaimonion Area, east of Temple, 0.35 m. above Stadium floor.
L. 0.0925; D. 0.064; H. 0.031.
Unbroken except for corners of nozzle. Brick-red clay; bright red wash.

355. IP 1666. Pl. 20. From Palaimonion, northeast of Temple.
L. (0.089); D. 0.0655; H. 0.034.
End of nozzle and parts of top broken away. Light red clay; mottled light and dark brown wash.

356. IP 1658. Pl. 20. From Palaimonion, east of Temple, 0.35 m. above Stadium floor.
L. 0.086; D. 0.061; H. 0.0315.
Handle and parts of side and top missing. Light red clay; mottled light and dark brown wash.

357. IP 890. Pl. 20. From Palaimonion, 0.60–0.50 m. above Stadium floor.
D. 0.0635; H. 0.031.
Handle and nozzle missing. Grayish buff clay; dark brown wash.

358. IP 1903. Pl. 20. From Palaimonion Area, east of Temple, ca. 0.70 m. above Stadium floor.
D. 0.064; H. 0.034.
Nozzle and part of side missing. Light red, mealy clay; mottled brown and red wash.

---

[30] The lamp, which is practically complete, cannot be used to indicate the exact date of construction of the Temple. The accumulated fill of the area round about the Temple contained many hundreds of lamps of this kind, and it is quite likely that one of them, 353, accidentally found its way into the mixture of stones and mortar that formed the foundation. Thus the lamp is earlier than the laying of the Temple foundation, but it must remain uncertain by how much. This matter has been discussed above in the introductory comments to the chapter on Lamps of Roman Imperial Times, p. 28. Footnote 29 gives reference to the literature in which this situation is explained in terms of the architectural development of the Temple and its temenos. See also below, footnote 31.

**359.** IP 976. Pls. 5, 20. Lamp found imbedded in South Stoa foundation at balbides sill.[31]
L. 0.093; D. 0.066; H. 0.0325.
Mended but almost complete. Buff clay; light brown wash.

**360.** IP 1871. Pl. 20. From Palaimonion Area, east of Temple, 0.50 m. above Stadium floor.
D. 0.062; H. 0.033.
Nozzle and part of top missing. Reddish buff clay; mottled dark and light brown wash.

**361.** IP 1884. Pl. 20. From Palaimonion, east of Temple, in nest 1.00 m. above Stadium floor.
L. (0.0935); D. 0.065; H. 0.033.
Handle and part of side missing. Light red clay; red wash.

**362.** IP 656. From Palaimonion, northeast of Temple, 1.00–0.75 m. above Stadium floor.
L. 0.091; D. 0.0625; H. 0.032.
Mended but complete. Light buff clay; light red wash.

**363.** IP 1890. From Palaimonion, east of Temple, 0.50 m. above Stadium floor.
D. 0.059; H. 0.030.
Handle and nozzle missing. Greenish buff clay; light brown wash.

**364.** IP 1870. From Palaimonion, east of Temple, 0.50 m. above Stadium floor.
L. (0.090); D. 0.061; H. 0.033.
Handle, most of top and part of side missing. Light buff, mealy clay; traces of light brown wash.

**365.** IP 6101. From Palaimonion, east of Temple.
D. 0.0605; H. 0.0305.
Handle and nozzle missing. Reddish buff clay; mottled light and dark brown wash.

**366.** IP 5954. From Palaimonion, east of Temple.
D. 0.060; H. 0.0315.
Handle and front part of body missing. Greenish buff clay; dark gray wash.

**367–477.** In addition to these 28 lamps, individually described, there are 111 other lamps and fragments of the "glazed" group.

| | | | |
|---|---|---|---|
| **367.** IP 1642. | **395.** IP 4026. | **423.** IP 5017. | **451.** IP 4445 a–d. |
| **368.** IP 2206. | **396.** IP 5530. | **424.** IP 5265. | **452.** IP 4676 a, b. |
| **369.** IP 315. | **397.** IP 5575. | **425.** IP 6308. | **453.** IP 4450 a, b. |
| **370.** IP 5087. | **398.** IP 5274. | **426.** IP 5596. | **454.** IP 5916 a, b. |
| **371.** IP 5088. | **399.** IP 5941. | **427.** IP 4790. | **455.** IP 4453 a–c. |
| **372.** IP 4788. | **400.** IP 5952. | **428.** IP 4769. | **456.** IP 4988 a, b. |
| **373.** IP 5740. | **401.** IP 5911. | **429.** IP 4652. | **457.** IP 4746 a, b. |
| **374.** IP 4540. | **402.** IP 4084. | **430.** IP 5475. | **458.** IP 5959 a, b. |
| **375.** IP 4364. | **403.** IP 6204. | **431.** IP 5123. | **459.** IP 4456 a, b. |
| **376.** IP 6303. | **404.** IP 5455. | **432.** IP 6071. | **460.** IP 5247 a–c. |
| **377.** IP 4863. | **405.** IP 5855. | **433.** IP 6067. | **461.** IP 4457 a, b. |
| **378.** IP 5376. | **406.** IP 4680. | **434.** IP 5038. | **462.** IP 4744 a, b. |
| **379.** IP 5238. | **407.** IP 5451. | **435.** IP 5533. | **463.** IP 6336 a, b. |
| **380.** IP 4656. | **408.** IP 4781. | **436.** IP 4373. | **464.** IP 5374 a, b. |
| **381.** IP 4890. | **409.** IP 5814. | **437.** IP 5524. | **465.** IP 5906 a, b. |
| **382.** IP 6285. | **410.** IP 5747. | **438.** IP 5230. | **466.** IP 4949 a, b. |
| **383.** IP 6226. | **411.** IP 4826. | **439.** IP 6230. | **467.** IP 4477 a–c. |
| **384.** IP 4995. | **412.** IP 4726. | **440.** IP 5385. | **468.** IP 5833 a, b. |
| **385.** IP 5654. | **413.** IP 5714. | **441.** IP 5590. | **469.** IP 4787 a, b. |
| **386.** IP 6032. | **414.** IP 5517. | **442.** IP 4435. | **470.** IP 4827. |
| **387.** IP 5514. | **415.** IP 4861. | **443.** IP 5910. | **471.** IP 4736. |
| **388.** IP 5145. | **416.** IP 5504. | **444.** IP 4649. | **472.** IP 4725. |
| **389.** IP 5824. | **417.** IP 5188. | **445.** IP 4800. | **473.** IP 5476. |
| **390.** IP 5586. | **418.** IP 4819. | **446.** IP 5908. | **474.** IP 5752. |
| **391.** IP 4446. | **419.** IP 5102. | **447.** IP 4143. | **475.** IP 4857 a. |
| **392.** IP 6311. | **420.** IP 5665. | **448.** IP 5825. | **476.** IP 4990. |
| **393.** IP 5821. | **421.** IP 6293. | **449.** IP 4055. | **477.** IP 4218. |
| **394.** IP 5098. | **422.** IP 5120. | **450.** IP 4451 a, b. | |

[31] What has been said in footnote 30 about the relationship of lamp **353** to the Temple foundation applies to **359** and its bearing on the date of the South Stoa. Both lamps, **353** and **359**, are probably considerably earlier than the foundations in which they were imbedded. The South Stoa and the fifth period of the Palaimonion appear to be part of the same construction program, in the first half of the 2nd century after Christ. See further *Isthmia* II, p. 83.

## TYPE XVI B. **478–1108.**

**478.** IP 891. Pls. 5, 21. From Palaimonion, 0.50 m. above Stadium floor.
L. 0.089; D. 0.066; H. 0.030.
Handle restored. Dull red clay.

**479.** IP 1662. Pls. 5, 21. From Palaimonion, east of Temple, 0.60 m. above Stadium floor.
L. 0.089; D. 0.0615; H. 0.035.
Complete. Buff clay with greenish tinge on the surface.

**480.** IP 1856. Pls. 5, 19, 21. From Palaimonion, east of Temple, 0.60 m. above Stadium floor.
L. 0.089; D. 0.064; H. 0.031.
Complete. Brick-red clay; nozzle much blackened.

**481.** IP 853. Pl. 21. From Palaimonion, *ca.* 1.00 m. above Stadium floor.
L. 0.089; D. 0.061; H. 0.031.
Complete. Pale red clay. The whole nozzle is blackened.

**482.** IP 783. Pls. 5, 21. From Palaimonion, middle section.
L. 0.092; D. 0.061; H. 0.0345.
Complete. Mottled dark and light gray clay with reddish tinge on bottom.

**483.** IP 1605. Pl. 21. From Palaimonion, east of Temple.
L. 0.086; D. 0.0625; H. 0.033.
Complete. Dull reddish clay; traces of whitewash or accidental lime deposit.

**484.** IP 654. Pl. 21. From Palaimonion, northeast of Temple, 1.00–0.75 m. above Stadium floor.
L. 0.0905; D. 0.062; H. 0.034.
Mended and top partly restored. Brick-red clay.

**485.** IP 1850. Pl. 21. From Palaimonion, east of Pit A, *ca.* 0.20 m. above Stoa floor.
L. 0.087; D. 0.063; H. 0.034.
Complete. Brick-red clay, darkened in spots to a dark brown.

**486.** IP 1602. Pl. 21. From Palaimonion, *ca.* 0.50 m. above Stadium floor.
L. 0.091; D. 0.063; H. 0.0325.
Complete. Brick-red clay; unglazed; traces of white-wash. Handle and nozzle unsymmetrically attached.

**487.** IP 1106. Pl. 21. From North Temenos Dump.
L. 0.0935; D. 0.064; H. 0.033.
Unbroken. Brick-red clay, darkened in places.

**488.** IP 206. Pls. 5, 21. From North Temenos Dump, at depth of *ca.* 1.70 m.
L. 0.091; D. 0.068; H. 0.0325.
Top mended and partly restored. Brick-red clay; fired to a darker color on the underside.

**489.** IP 1911. Pl. 21. From Palaimonion, northeast of Temple.
L. 0.092; D. 0.063; H. 0.031.
Complete. Dark gray clay slightly brownish in spots. Nozzle not blackened.

**490.** IP 1857. Pl. 21. From Palaimonion, east of Temple, 0.60 m. above Stadium floor.
L. 0.090; D. 0.060; H. 0.030.
Mended but complete. Reddish brown clay, darker on the front part.

**491.** IP 1644. Pl. 21. From Palaimonion, east of Temple, 0.35 m. above Stadium floor.
L. 0.088; D. 0.060; H. 0.0295.
Complete but handle mended. Dull red clay. Handle and nozzle unsymmetrical.

**492.** IP 1854. Pls. 5, 21. From Palaimonion, northeast of Temple.
L. 0.078; D. 0.056; H. 0.031.
Mended but complete. Brick-red clay with darker spots. Filling-hole very small.

**493.** IP 889. Pls. 5, 21. From Palaimonion, 0.20 m. above Stadium floor.
L. 0.085; D. 0.064; H. 0.034.
Partly restored. Dark gray, almost black clay.

**494.** IP 943. Pl. 21. From Palaimonion, 0.90 m. above Stadium floor.
L. 0.091; D. 0.0595; H. 0.035.
Handle and part of edge restored. Dark gray clay with brownish tinge in spots.

**495.** IP 859. Pl. 21. From Palaimonion.
L. 0.084; D. 0.059; H. 0.030.
Complete. Brick-red clay with dark areas probably discolored by fire.

**496.** IP 1861. Pl. 21. From Palaimonion, east of Temple, 0.50 m. above Stadium floor.
L. 0.086; D. 0.055; H. 0.028.
Complete. Dark gray clay almost black on top, possibly from use.

**497.** IP 784. Pls. 5, 19, 21. From Palaimonion, middle section.
L. 0.088; D. 0.062; H. 0.030.

Handle partly restored. Dark gray clay with reddish tinge. The lamp was squashed out of shape in firing, and yet the nozzle shows signs of use.

**498.** IP 1853. Pls. 19, 21. From Palaimonion, northeast of Temple.
L. 0.077; D. 0.055; H. 0.028.
Complete. Reddish brown clay.

**499.** IP 1858. From Palaimonion, east of Temple, 0.60 m. above Stadium floor.
L. 0.092; D. 0.061; H. 0.0345.
Handle missing. Light red clay. In the bottom is a blob of clay resulting from the piercing of the nozzle. Nozzle very much askew.

**500.** IP 1912. Pl. 21. From Palaimonion, southeast of Temple, close to Stadium floor.
L. 0.099; D. 0.063; H. 0.0345.
Unbroken, except for a slight chip on the nozzle. Nozzle unsymmetrically placed and much blackened at the end.

**501.** IP 1595. From Palaimonion, 1.00 m. above Stadium floor.
L. 0.099; D. 0.063; H. 0.0345.
Handle missing. Light red clay; traces of thick whitewash. Nozzle much blackened.

**502–1108.** In addition to the 24 specimens of Type XVI B described above, there are 607 whole lamps and fragments.

| | | | |
|---|---|---|---|
| **502.** IP 1608. | **542.** IP 1869. | **582.** IP 1634. | **622.** IP 1594. |
| **503.** IP 1648. | **543.** IP 1895. | **583.** IP 657. | **623.** IP 1866. |
| **504.** IP 975. | **544.** IP 1623. | **584.** IP 2324. | **624.** IP 1897. |
| **505.** IP 1649. | **545.** IP 1615. | **585.** IP 1880. | **625.** IP 855. |
| **506.** IP 1609. | **546.** IP 1635. | **586.** IP 1905. | **626.** IP 933. |
| **507.** IP 655. | **547.** IP 1878. | **587.** IP 1872. | **627.** IP 1891. |
| **508.** IP 1855. | **548.** IP 1596. | **588.** IP 920. | **628.** IP 1630. |
| **509.** IP 1852. | **549.** IP 2213. | **589.** IP 1654. | **629.** IP 949. |
| **510.** IP 1881. | **550.** IP 1646. | **590.** IP 1651. | **630.** IP 1659. |
| **511.** IP 1616. | **551.** IP 1851. | **591.** IP 1867. | **631.** IP 1598. |
| **512.** IP 1625. | **552.** IP 1886. | **592.** IP 1862. | **632.** IP 1641. |
| **513.** IP 91. | **553.** IP 2583. | **593.** IP 1612. | **633.** IP 849. |
| **514.** IP 1907. | **554.** IP 75. | **594.** IP 918. | **634.** IP 1874. |
| **515.** IP 798. | **555.** IP 1628. | **595.** IP 1909. | **635.** IP 1663. |
| **516.** IP 925. | **556.** IP 1639. | **596.** IP 1621. | **636.** IP 1679. |
| **517.** IP 1876. | **557.** IP 1873. | **597.** IP 848. | **637.** IP 1888. |
| **518.** IP 2580. | **558.** IP 1618. | **598.** IP 1614. | **638.** IP 1859. |
| **519.** IP 1647. | **559.** IP 2334. | **599.** IP 1883. | **639.** IP 1896. |
| **520.** IP 1894. | **560.** IP 1603. | **600.** IP 922. | **640.** IP 1632. |
| **521.** IP 1868. | **561.** IP 1627. | **601.** IP 2733. | **641.** IP 1665. |
| **522.** IP 1626. | **562.** IP 1638. | **602.** IP 1652. | **642.** IP 1901. |
| **523.** IP 1914. | **563.** IP 1668. | **603.** IP 1610. | **643.** IP 875. |
| **524.** IP 1906. | **564.** IP 1637. | **604.** IP 1904. | **644.** IP 1617. |
| **525.** IP 1613. | **565.** IP 1599. | **605.** IP 1910. | **645.** IP 1865. |
| **526.** IP 1887. | **566.** IP 1669. | **606.** IP 1900. | **646.** IP 1624. |
| **527.** IP 1913. | **567.** IP 1892. | **607.** IP 1899. | **647.** IP 1882. |
| **528.** IP 1600. | **568.** IP 1889. | **608.** IP 915. | **648.** IP 1951. |
| **529.** IP 1650. | **569.** IP 2613. | **609.** IP 1864. | **649.** IP 862. |
| **530.** IP 1678. | **570.** IP 1898. | **610.** IP 1606. | **650.** IP 3926. |
| **531.** IP 1645. | **571.** IP 658. | **611.** IP 1604. | **651.** IP 2738. |
| **532.** IP 1860. | **572.** IP 781. | **612.** IP 1656. | **652.** IP 1633. |
| **533.** IP 1657. | **573.** IP 1620. | **613.** IP 1879. | **653.** IP 2716. |
| **534.** IP 1655. | **574.** IP 1877. | **614.** IP 2533. | **654.** IP 216. |
| **535.** IP 1000. | **575.** IP 1875. | **615.** IP 1611. | **655.** IP 316. |
| **536.** IP 1908. | **576.** IP 921. | **616.** IP 1619. | **656.** IP 311. |
| **537.** IP 932. | **577.** IP 1601. | **617.** IP 888. | **657.** IP 1643. |
| **538.** IP 917. | **578.** IP 1631. | **618.** IP 1622. | **658.** IP 1661. |
| **539.** IP 1885. | **579.** IP 934. | **619.** IP 1667. | **659.** IP 1660. |
| **540.** IP 913. | **580.** IP 1664. | **620.** IP 205. | **660.** IP 3991. |
| **541.** IP 2211. | **581.** IP 1636. | **621.** IP 1653. | **661.** IP 1670. |

| | | | |
|---|---|---|---|
| **662.** IP 2616. | **718.** IP 4465 a–c. | **775.** IP 4775. | **832.** IP 4057. |
| **663.** IP 113. | **719.** IP 4860 a, b. | **776.** IP 4397. | **833.** IP 4969. |
| **664.** IP 2668 a, b, b'. | **720.** IP 4460 a, b. | **777.** IP 4375. | **834.** IP 4655. |
| **665.** IP 2545. | **721.** IP 4675. | **778.** IP 4427. | **835.** IP 4855. |
| **666.** IP 2710. | **722.** IP 4444 a, b. | **779.** IP 4889. | **836.** IP 4948. |
| **667.** IP 3970. | **723.** IP 4674. | **780.** IP 4821. | **837.** IP 4768. |
| **668.** IP 3971. | **724.** IP 4757. | **781.** IP 4247. | **838.** IP 4463 a, c. |
| **669.** IP 3962. | **725.** IP 4740. | **782.** IP 4250. | **839.** IP 4935. |
| **670.** IP 3988. | **726.** IP 4472 a–d. | **783.** IP 4820. | **840.** IP 4900. |
| **671.** IP 2671. | **727.** IP 4479 a–c. | **784.** IP 4864. | **841.** IP 4745 b. |
| **672.** IP 4812. | **728.** IP 4667 a, b. | **785.** IP 4707. | **842.** IP 4752 b. |
| **673.** IP 4829. | **729.** IP 4467 a–c. | **786.** IP 4780. | **843.** IP 4945 a–c. |
| **674.** IP 4678. | **730.** IP 4033. | **787.** IP 4607. | **844.** IP 4783. |
| **675.** IP 4934. | **731.** IP 4468 a, b. | **788.** IP 4910. | **845.** IP 5907. |
| **676.** IP 4942. | **732.** IP 4478 a, b. | **789.** IP 4665. | **846.** IP 5448. |
| **677.** IP 4724. | **733.** IP 4464 a, b. | **790.** IP 4083. | **847.** IP 5951. |
| **678.** IP 4459. | **734.** IP 4480 a, b. | **791.** IP 4971. | **848.** IP 5447. |
| **679.** IP 4470 a, b. | **735.** IP 4779. | **792.** IP 4606. | **849.** IP 5142. |
| **680.** IP 4959. | **736.** IP 4614. | **793.** IP 4997. | **850.** IP 5739. |
| **681.** IP 4532. | **737.** IP 4677 a, b. | **794.** IP 4176. | **851.** IP 5576. |
| **682.** IP 4474 a, b. | **738.** IP 4754. | **795.** IP 4150. | **852.** IP 5816. |
| **683.** IP 4116. | **739.** IP 4869. | **796.** IP 4854. | **853.** IP 5143. |
| **684.** IP 4722. | **740.** IP 4891. | **797.** IP 4668. | **854.** IP 5686. |
| **685.** IP 4922. | **741.** IP 4778. | **798.** IP 4831. | **855.** IP 5568. |
| **686.** IP 4813. | **742.** IP 4511. | **799.** IP 4730. | **856.** IP 5089. |
| **687.** IP 4735. | **743.** IP 4970. | **800.** IP 4246. | **857.** IP 5510. |
| **688.** IP 4784. | **744.** IP 4888. | **801.** IP 4786. | **858.** IP 5848. |
| **689.** IP 4471 a, b. | **745.** IP 4530. | **802.** IP 4830. | **859.** IP 5519. |
| **690.** IP 4447 a–c. | **746.** IP 4475. | **803.** IP 4653. | **860.** IP 5502. |
| **691.** IP 4859. | **747.** IP 4731. | **804.** IP 4765. | **861.** IP 5793. |
| **692.** IP 4866. | **748.** IP 4300. | **805.** IP 4312. | **862.** IP 5953. |
| **693.** IP 4073. | **749.** IP 4777. | **806.** IP 4666. | **863.** IP 5822. |
| **694.** IP 4466. | **750.** IP 4454. | **807.** IP 4054. | **864.** IP 5506. |
| **695.** IP 4461 a, b. | **751.** IP 4764. | **808.** IP 4304. | **865.** IP 5445. |
| **696.** IP 4755 a, b. | **752.** IP 4870. | **809.** IP 4785. | **866.** IP 5131. |
| **697.** IP 4782. | **753.** IP 4401. | **810.** IP 4798. | **867.** IP 5521. |
| **698.** IP 4925. | **754.** IP 4521. | **811.** IP 4301. | **868.** IP 5294. |
| **699.** IP 4448. | **755.** IP 4452. | **812.** IP 4668 A. | **869.** IP 5141. |
| **700.** IP 4303. | **756.** IP 4529. | **813.** IP 4056. | **870.** IP 5547. |
| **701.** IP 4473 a, b. | **757.** IP 4958. | **814.** IP 4163. | **871.** IP 5877. |
| **702.** IP 4458 a, b. | **758.** IP 4750. | **815.** IP 4795. | **872.** IP 5508. |
| **703.** IP 4865 a–c. | **759.** IP 4280. | **816.** IP 4550. | **873.** IP 5144. |
| **704.** IP 4756 a, b. | **760.** IP 4531. | **817.** IP 4650. | **874.** IP 5386. |
| **705.** IP 4449 a, b. | **761.** IP 4611. | **818.** IP 4018. | **875.** IP 5550. |
| **706.** IP 4462 a–d. | **762.** IP 4469. | **819.** IP 4818 a, b. | **876.** IP 5446. |
| **707.** IP 4117. | **763.** IP 4938. | **820.** IP 4648 a, b. | **877.** IP 5252. |
| **707A.** IP 4947. | **764.** IP 4654. | **821.** IP 4541 a, b. | **878.** IP 5461. |
| **708.** IP 4590. | **765.** IP 4111. | **822.** IP 4745 a. | **879.** IP 5818. |
| **709.** IP 4302. | **766.** IP 4862. | **823.** IP 4728. | **880.** IP 5094. |
| **710.** IP 4679. | **767.** IP 4727. | **824.** IP 4749 a, b. | **881.** IP 5820. |
| **711.** IP 4476 a, b. | **768.** IP 4858. | **825.** IP 4899. | **881 A.** IP 4960. |
| **712.** IP 4751 a, b. | **769.** IP 4651. | **826.** IP 4989 a, b. | **882.** IP 5086. |
| **713.** IP 4455 a, b. | **770.** IP 4770. | **827.** IP 4961. | **883.** IP 5509. |
| **714.** IP 4955. | **771.** IP 4124. | **828.** IP 4767. | **884.** IP 5784. |
| **715.** IP 4403. | **772.** IP 4776. | **829.** IP 4799. | **885.** IP 5095. |
| **716.** IP 4867 a, b. | **773.** IP 4828. | **830.** IP 4522. | **886.** IP 5956. |
| **717.** IP 4436. | **774.** IP 4766. | **831.** IP 4434. | **887.** IP 5710. |

| | | | |
|---|---|---|---|
| **888.** IP 5223. | **944.** IP 5272. | **1000.** IP 5507. | **1056.** IP 6078. |
| **889.** IP 5574. | **945.** IP 5729. | **1001.** IP 5012. | **1057.** IP 6288. |
| **890.** IP 5753. | **946.** IP 5121. | **1002.** IP 5264. | **1058.** IP 6289. |
| **891.** IP 5092. | **947.** IP 5955. | **1003.** IP 5742. | **1059.** IP 6033. |
| **892.** IP 5097. | **948.** IP 5370. | **1004.** IP 5515. | **1060.** IP 6034. |
| **893.** IP 5549. | **949.** IP 5728. | **1005.** IP 5727. | **1061.** IP 6069. |
| **894.** IP 5817. | **950.** IP 5581. | **1006.** IP 5831. | **1062.** IP 6321. |
| **895.** IP 5091. | **951.** IP 5512. | **1007.** IP 5746. | **1063.** IP 6012. |
| **896.** IP 5122. | **952.** IP 5018. | **1008.** IP 5516. | **1064.** IP 6066. |
| **897.** IP 5096. | **953.** IP 5371. | **1009.** IP 5591. | **1065.** IP 6205. |
| **898.** IP 5853. | **954.** IP 5744. | **1010.** IP 5893. | **1066.** IP 6095. |
| **899.** IP 5560. | **955.** IP 5147. | **1011.** IP 5231. | **1067.** IP 6294. |
| **900.** IP 5548. | **956.** IP 5093. | **1012.** IP 5601. | **1068.** IP 6291. |
| **901.** IP 5529. | **957.** IP 5477. | **1013.** IP 5544. | **1069.** IP 6286. |
| **902.** IP 5099. | **958.** IP 5557. | **1014.** IP 5798. | **1070.** IP 6029. |
| **903.** IP 5511. | **959.** IP 5505. | **1015.** IP 5513. | **1071.** IP 6322. |
| **904.** IP 5792. | **960.** IP 5592. | **1016.** IP 5273. | **1072.** IP 6013. |
| **905.** IP 5106. | **961.** IP 5149. | **1017.** IP 5193. | **1073.** IP 6307. |
| **906.** IP 5909. | **962.** IP 5498. | **1018.** IP 4729. | **1074.** IP 6334. |
| **907.** IP 5890. | **963.** IP 5931. | **1019.** IP 5687 a, b. | **1075.** IP 6332. |
| **908.** IP 5292. | **964.** IP 5387. | **1020.** IP 5373 a, b. | **1076.** IP 6315. |
| **909.** IP 5499. | **965.** IP 5222. | **1021.** IP 5375 a, b. | **1077.** IP 6313. |
| **910.** IP 5234. | **966.** IP 5525. | **1022.** IP 5340 a, b. | **1078.** IP 6320. |
| **911.** IP 5399. | **967.** IP 5950. | **1023.** IP 5751 a, b. | **1079.** IP 6295. |
| **912.** IP 5845. | **968.** IP 5166. | **1024.** IP 5717 a, b. | **1080.** IP 6290. |
| **913.** IP 5858. | **969.** IP 5562. | **1025.** IP 5851 a–c. | **1081.** IP 6222. |
| **914.** IP 5532. | **970.** IP 5369. | **1026.** IP 5819 a, b. | **1082.** IP 6125. |
| **915.** IP 5372. | **971.** IP 5799. | **1027.** IP 5826 a, b. | **1083.** IP 6030. |
| **916.** IP 5804. | **972.** IP 5531. | **1028.** IP 5892 a–c. | **1084.** IP 6292. |
| **917.** IP 5828. | **973.** IP 5783. | **1029.** IP 5945 a, b. | **1085.** IP 6228. |
| **918.** IP 5503. | **974.** IP 5782. | **1030.** IP 5944 a, b. | **1086.** IP 6112. |
| **919.** IP 5296. | **975.** IP 5165. | **1031.** IP 5958 a, b. | **1087.** IP 6316. |
| **920.** IP 5949. | **976.** IP 5232. | **1032.** IP 5235 a–c. | **1088.** IP 6141. |
| **921.** IP 5146. | **977.** IP 5764. | **1033.** IP 5236 a, b. | **1089.** IP 6091. |
| **922.** IP 5501. | **978.** IP 5119. | **1034.** IP 5940 a, b. | **1090.** IP 6076. |
| **923.** IP 5520. | **979.** IP 5526. | **1035.** IP 5085 a, b. | **1091.** IP 6306. |
| **924.** IP 5879. | **980.** IP 5518. | **1036.** IP 5016 a, b. | **1092.** IP 4748. |
| **925.** IP 5167. | **981.** IP 5434. | **1037.** IP 5957 a–c. | **1093.** IP 6065. |
| **926.** IP 5827. | **982.** IP 5293. | **1038.** IP 5960 a, b. | **1094.** IP 6070. |
| **927.** IP 5832. | **983.** IP 5726. | **1039.** IP 5716 a, b. | **1095.** IP 6072. |
| **928.** IP 5565. | **984.** IP 5450. | **1040.** IP 5745 a. | **1096.** IP 5612. |
| **929.** IP 5595. | **985.** IP 5932. | **1041.** IP 5295 a, b. | **1097.** IP 4923. |
| **930.** IP 5741. | **986.** IP 5640. | **1042.** IP 6296 a, b. | **1098.** IP 4752 a. |
| **931.** IP 5261. | **987.** IP 5368. | **1043.** IP 6133 a, b. | **1099.** IP 4921. |
| **932.** IP 5090. | **988.** IP 5811. | **1044.** IP 6333 a, b. | **1100.** IP 5449. |
| **933.** IP 5148. | **989.** IP 5297. | **1045.** IP 5635. | **1101.** IP 5835. |
| **934.** IP 5101. | **990.** IP 5398. | **1046.** IP 5021. | **1102.** IP 5237. |
| **935.** IP 5523. | **991.** IP 5578. | **1047.** IP 6028. | **1103.** IP 5566. |
| **936.** IP 5904. | **992.** IP 5905. | **1048.** IP 6225. | **1104.** IP 6035. |
| **937.** IP 5253. | **993.** IP 5948. | **1049.** IP 6031. | **1105.** IP 6038. |
| **938.** IP 5823. | **994.** IP 5594. | **1050.** IP 6224. | **1106.** IP 6054. |
| **939.** IP 5339. | **995.** IP 5943. | **1051.** IP 6304. | **1107.** IP 6305. |
| **940.** IP 5942. | **996.** IP 5500. | **1052.** IP 6287. | **1108.** IP 6068. |
| **941.** IP 5579. | **997.** IP 5341. | **1053.** IP 6301. | |
| **942.** IP 5367. | **998.** IP 5233. | **1054.** IP 6299. | |
| **943.** IP 5743. | **999.** IP 5353. | **1055.** IP 6086. | |

## TYPE XVII. **1109–1110.**

There is only one complete example (**1109**) of Corinth Type XVII from Isthmia, and one related lamp of earlier date. By shape this type would go with Type X, but because of the quality of the clay and absence of glaze it seems to range itself after Type XVI B. In no other type is that kind of clay used.

Date, *ca.* middle of 2nd century B.C. See below under **1109**. Chronologically this type should come before Type XVI, since the shape is very similar to Type X. For reasons stated in the introductory comments (p. 2), the typology of *Corinth* IV, ii has been retained.

**1109.** IP 1687. Pls. 4, 19. From manhole to Southwest Reservoir, west end of South Side.
L. 0.084; D. 0.058; H. 0.027.

Unbroken. Brick-red clay; unglazed. Curving sides merging into the rim. Short nozzle with triangular tip, much blackened. Slightly raised base not clearly set off from the sides. The date, based on its provenance, is probably about the middle of the 2nd century B.C. The shape is not very different from *Agora* IV, Type 39, no. 516, which is dated in "last quarter of 2nd century B.C." See also *Argos*, pl. 4, no. 187, which is very similar to our **1109**; *Délos* XXVI, pl. 5, planche D, no. 267: "Dernier quart du IIe—debut du Ier."

At Corinth a lamp of this type came from a manhole (8) in the Anaploga Cistern area. At the depth from which the lamp came the fill was dated to the middle of the 2nd century B.C. See Robinson, *Hesperia* 38, 1969, p. 19, no. 35, pl. 3. From these indications we may date Type XVII to the years just prior to the destruction of Corinth by Mummius.

**1110.** IP 750. Pls. 4, 19. From Rachi, South Cistern.
L. 0.0935; D. 0.063; H. 0.037.

Unbroken. Brick-red clay; no trace of glaze. The nozzle shows paring and smoothing and is heavily blackened from use. Rounded sides curving into top and bottom. No handle. Nozzle with its wide base merging gradually into the curving sides. No raised base, but in the center of the bottom is a deep circular groove, 0.016 m. in diameter, and inside the groove the bottom rises by steps to a point in the center (see section, Pl. 4). This lamp is unique both in shape and material and has here been grouped with Type XVII because it comes closer to that type than any other. By clay and absence of glaze it resembles Types XVI B and XVII, but its provenance shows that it belongs with the lamps of the 3rd century B.C. and rather before than after the middle of the century.

# PALAIMONION LAMPS

The Palaimonion lamp is a type peculiar to the Sanctuary of Palaimon at Isthmia. It is not, so far as I am aware, represented at Corinth itself and is all but unknown from other sites in Greece. At Isthmia it has been found in greater numbers than any other type, and most of them came from the Palaimonion. Thus, it is in a true sense of the word a cult vessel, designed exclusively for the Sanctuary of Palaimon. The lamps are all wheelmade, consisting of a large bowl that contained the oil and in the center a tubular wick-holder with one or more openings to permit the oil to reach the wick. Nearly all the lamps show blackening at the top of their sockets. The wick would have been large and was probably rolled into a tube, as on large modern kerosene lamps. A solid wick large enough to fill the socket would have used up oil too fast and would probably have produced an undue amount of smoke. The base is slightly raised and in most cases it is rough underneath, showing the marks of the string used for removing the lamp from the wheel. On several of the lamps, however, the base has been trimmed after removal from the wheel. The Palaimonion lamps have no handle; consequently they were intended to be set on the ground or on some lamp stand.

Lamps of comparable, but not similar, shape have been found in small numbers at several sites in the western provinces of the Roman Empire. They are as a rule smaller, the walls are more nearly vertical, and most of them had handles. This shows that they were intended to be carried about like oil lamps of ordinary shapes. The following have been published and there are probably other, both published and unpublished, examples:

1) Lerat: Pl. XXIII, 170. Lamp with central socket. D. 0.062 m.; H. 0.022 m. Handle broken away. Found presumably in Besançon.

2) Iványi: Pl. LVI, 1 and 3. No. 4120, D. 0.070 m.; H. 0.037 m.; no. 4121, D. 0.056 m., H. 0.026 m. Both have central sockets; no handles indicated and no oil-holes shown. Presumably such openings existed, because the author refers to a lamp illustrated and described by Walters, as shown below.

3) Walters: P. 215, no. 1414, fig. 339. "Saucer-shaped, with central socket, pierced with two triangular holes; flat handle. Diam. 2-7/8 in. (0.072 m.). From Rheims." One other lamp illustrated by Walters (p. 216, no. 1430, fig. 343) and called by him "lamp stand," seems to be a socket from a Palaimonion type. "Found in the Old Fish Street Hill, London." A third example (no. 1431), not illustrated, is similar.

4) Vegas gives a very exact description of a lamp from Novaesium, her no. 300, pls. 5 and 10. Listed under "Tüllenlampen": "Sie hat die Form eines Schälchens mit konkaver Wandung und wenig sorgfältig geglätteter Standfläche. In der Mitte eine Tülle, die sich nach oben verjüngt und etwas niedriger als der Schälchenrand ist. Sie ist von zwei Öffnungen durchbrochen. Der Henkel ist abgebrochen, sein oberer Ansatz greift auf den Rand des Näpfchens und der untere auf die Unterseite der Bodenfläche über. Dm. 8 cm.; H. 3,8 cm. Scherben [i.e. clay]: rotbraun. Oberfläche: ohne Überzug, rauhwandig. Zeit: 2. Hälfte 1 Jahrh. n. Chr." The lamp differs from our Palaimonion lamps in three particulars: it has nearly vertical sides flaring out at the top; it had a handle (broken off); and it is smaller than the smallest of our lamps (D. 0.08 m. as compared with 0.0965 m. of **2119**). In other respects the lamp from Novaesium is like ours, and even the chronology agrees with the earlier of the Palaimonion lamps from Isthmia. Vegas goes on to correct the misconception that lamps of this kind were used as candlesticks: "Wir hätten also einen Lampentypus mit ausgesprochenem Zentralbrenner vor uns."

5) Loeschcke has a similar explanation for some of his lamps from Vindonissa. In the catalogue he lists six examples, nos. 1044–1049, four of which he illustrates in pls. I and XX. Three fragmentary examples, nos. 1044–1046, have sockets cut by two slits that extend from the top almost to the bottom. This variety corresponds most closely to our Palaimonion Type A-6. Two others, nos. 1047, 1048, have sockets with two irregularly shaped oil-holes near the bottom of the very short sockets. These are more nearly similar to our Palaimonion Type A-4. On a third variety from Vindonissa, no. 1049, there is a low socket with a single opening, wider at the bottom than at the top, but extending all the way to the top, much as on our Palaimonion Types A-1 and A-2. All the lamps of this kind, Loeschcke's Typus XIV, are smaller (D. at the base 0.044–0.060 m.) than the lamps from Isthmia. Loeschcke dates them all in the second half of the 1st century after Christ. They are thus approximately of the same date as the Palaimonion lamps from Isthmia. In view of the marked differences in size and shape and the great distance from Vindonissa to Corinth, it would be hazardous to conclude that there is any direct connection between the few examples from the western provinces and the more numerous lamps from Isthmia. Loeschcke also illustrates some socket lamps from Avenches and Trier (p. 315, fig. 16), others from Strassburg and Nymwegen (p. 317, fig. 17), and one from Rome (p. 318, fig. 18). All of these are provided with central socket, into which the oil had access through holes or slits, but in other respects they differ radically from the Vindonissa socket lamps. The author suggests that these may have been used both as oil lamps and as candlesticks.[32] The lamps with sockets from Isthmia would hardly have been intended for such a double purpose.

6) Oleiro: Among the lamps in Coimbra, Oleiro (pl. VIII, 14) has one socket lamp without handle and bowl with incurving rim. D. 0.068 m., H. 0.040 m. He describes it thus: "Curiosa lucerna de barro escuro, circular, sem pegas e sem bico. De fogo central." The socket has two oil-holes. This is very similar to our Palaimonion lamps of Group B.

7) Cardaillac: Among the lamps from North African sites (Carthage, Tebessa, Algiers), published by Cardaillac, there are four examples (figs. 180–183) of bowl-shaped lamps without handles or nozzles and with a dome-shaped inner part narrowing at the top to form a socket. Near the bottom of the dome is a large oil-hole. The author gives no dimensions ("ces lampes étaient de dimensions variées"). He

---

[32] Candles were a Roman invention, which came to Greece only through contact with Roman practices, and became common after the introduction of Christianity. See Martin P. Nilsson, *Opus. Arch.* 6, 1950, p. 108.

calls them Vandalic and dates them in the 5th century after Christ. Though superficially resembling our Palaimonion lamps, they really belong to a different category, a late formation, more closely related to some proto-Byzantine lamps of Type XXXV from Corinth; *Corinth* IV, ii, nos. 1519–1530, pl. XXIV.

The Palaimonion lamps fall into two large groups, differing from each other chiefly in size and in the color of the clay. Within each group are several varieties distinguished mainly by the kind of central socket. Group A is certainly earlier than B, and some of the subtypes of A, especially A-4 and A-5, which are transitional, show features of both groups.

ADDENDUM *see* page 83.

## GROUP A. **1111—2078.**

In the first group the socket, except in the transitional A-4 and A-5, was made separately and added after the bowl had been cast on the wheel. After attaching the tubular piece of clay, the lampmaker often added some soft clay round the base of the tube to make it anneal properly to the bottom of the bowl. He would then trim the inside with his finger. This is shown by the fact that the bottom of the tube is in many cases lower than the bottom of the bowl (see under **1210**). In cases where the socket had not been carefully attached, perhaps because the clay was too dry when the tube was added, the socket has broken away from the bowl, leaving a collar of added clay. After the socket had been fixed to the bowl, the lampmaker made two or more vertical cuts in the side of the tube and then removed the narrow strip of clay between the cuts. The knife with which he made these cuts sometimes left marks on the edge of the bowl (see **1206**). In at least one case, **1246**, there are clear marks at the bottom of the tube, made unintentionally with the curved gouge used to cut loose the strip of clay.

Group A, which occurs in larger numbers than Group B, is the earlier of the two divisions. It goes back to the first period of the Sanctuary of Palaimon, which is to be dated in the reign of Augustus, either a little before or a little after the turn of the century. Although this group seems to have been in use over a period of some three quarters of a century and shows several variations, it is difficult to detect any clear chronological development within the group. The clay varies in color from a brick red to a pale yellow. In most cases it has a rather mealy surface, and in no case is there a glaze or wash. Many of the lamps, however, have traces of a white chalky surfacing applied both on the inside and the outside, and even on the base and inside the socket. This crumbly substance, which seems to be pure lime, can hardly have been made for decoration. I would venture a guess that it is mere whitewash applied at times for purification of the whole area.[33] This would seem to follow from the fact that in some cases, e.g. **1139**, it has been splashed over fragmentary and probably discarded lamps.

### PALAIMONION TYPE A-1. **1111–1205.**

This is the largest variety of Group A. Even within this subclass there are considerable differences in the color of the clay, the height and diameter of the central socket, and in other peculiarities which are pointed out in the catalogue. What distinguishes this type from the other lamps of Group A is the comparatively large socket, slightly flaring toward the top, with a single, rather wide cut (*ca.* 0.01 m. and less) extending from the top to the base of the socket. This single opening is wide enough for the oil to flow freely from the bowl to the wick. All the lamps of A-1 have a comparatively narrow rim, *ca.* 0.008–0.014 m., usually flat on top and projecting somewhat toward the outside. The socket, which in all cases is lower than the top of the rim, varies in inside diameter between 0.019 and 0.035 m. Its depth, measured on the inside, varies from 0.040 to 0.062 m. The measurements can be only approximate since the bowl is rarely quite circular and the height is not the same all around the rim.

---

[33] It is customary in Greece, especially before the Easter holidays, to whitewash garden walls, curbstones, etc. This is done by means of lime dissolved in water, which is liberally applied with a brush or broom. In particular the cemeteries with their funeral chapels and tombstones are so treated. The custom may go back to Jewish practices, as we learn from *Matthew* 23, 27, where Jesus speaks to the Pharisees: Παρομοιάξετε τάφοις κεκονιαμένοις, i.e. whitewashed sepulchers. It is possible that similar practices obtained in the case of some pagan cults. The lime pit found in the Palaimonion could have been used for such purposes; it is rather small to be used for slaking lime for construction, as suggested in my publication of the pit, *Isthmia* II, pp. 104–105.

**1111.** IP 647. Pls. 6, 22. From Palaimonion.

D. 0.167; H. 0.061; inner depth of socket, 0.045; inner D. of socket 0.026.

Much restored; brick-red clay. Heavy, slightly flaring socket with rounded edge at top. Single opening.

**1112.** IP 645. From Palaimonion.

D. 0.176; H. 0.068.

Much mended and restored. Brick-red clay. Narrow rim projecting toward the outside. Socket with thick walls flaring slightly and coming to a broad edge.

**1113.** IP 2155. From Palaimonion, east of Temple, 0.60–0.20 m. above Stadium floor.

D. 0.170; H. 0.066; inner depth of socket 0.040; inner D. of socket 0.025.

Mended and partly restored. Somewhat mealy, brick-red clay. Rather short socket, blackened on top.

**1114.** IP 648. From Palaimonion, Sacrificial Pits A and B.

D. 0.170; H. 0.065.

Much mended and partly restored. Red clay. Narrow rim; socket coming to a blunt edge at the top.

**1115.** IP 1587. Pls. 6, 22. From Palaimonion, north of Sacrificial Pit A.

D. 0.163; H. 0.084; rim 0.0115 wide; inner depth of socket 0.060; inside D. of socket 0.029.

Mended. Reddish buff clay. Socket with flaring top much lower than level of the rim; top of socket much blackened by fire.

**1116.** IP 953. From Palaimonion, 0.20 m. above Stadium floor.

D. 0.168; H. 0.067; rim 0.013 m. wide; H. of socket 0.039; inside D. of socket 0.035.

Mended and part of rim restored. Pinkish buff clay. Socket blackened at the top.

**1117.** IP 1586. Pls. 6, 22. From Palaimonion, 0.55 m. above Stadium floor.

D. 0.192; H. 0.071; inner depth of socket 0.037; D. of socket 0.035.

Mended but complete, except for a small patch on one side. Pale red clay, somewhat mealy on the surface. Rather narrow rim and thin walls. Small socket, blackened at the top.

**1118.** IP 900. From Palaimonion, 0.90 m. above Stadium floor.

D. 0.170; H. 0.076; inner depth of socket 0.058; D. of socket 0.045.

Mended and partly restored. Pale red clay. Rim of medium width, fairly thick walls. Socket much blackened at the top.

**1119.** IP 1673. Pls. 6, 22. From Palaimonion, east of Temple.

D. 0.180; H. 0.0635; W. of rim 0.011; depth of socket 0.043.

Reddish buff clay; patches of whitewash both inside and outside. Socket flaring toward the top.

**1120.** IP 964. From Palaimonion, 0.60–0.30 m. above Stadium floor.

D. 0.177; H. 0.080.

Mended and partly restored. Greenish yellow clay, heavy fabric. Large socket, tapering and forming a collar at the top; wide slit.

**1121.** IP 977. From Roman Altar Area, below macadam floor.

D. 0.168; H. 0.068.

Mended but complete. Buff clay with reddish tinge. Large socket with slight flare and blunt edge at the top.

**1122.** IP 945. From Palaimonion, 0.75 m. above Stadium floor.

D. 0.185; H. 0.071.

Much mended and partly restored. Light red clay. Small socket with slight flare.

**1123.** IP 876. Pls. 6, 22. From Palaimonion, 0.070 m. above Stadium floor.

D. 0.180; H. 0.088.

Mended. Mottled pale buff and pinkish clay. Narrow rim; low socket with almost straight sides coming to a blunt edge; single wide slit.

**1124.** IP 877. From Palaimonion, 0.70 m. above Stadium floor.

D. 0.173; H. 0.075.

Mended but complete. Light buff clay with greenish tinge on the inside. Narrow rim; very wide, low socket, flaring toward the top.

**1125.** IP 2208. From Palaimonion, South Building.

D. 0.181; H. 0.0825; depth of socket 0.060.

Mended and partly restored. Reddish buff clay. Rather narrow rim, only 0.008 m. wide. Large socket with blunt edge. Surface heavily covered with whitewash on the outside and inside. At the bottom of the bowl the white is particularly thick, but does not seem to have extended to the inside of the socket.

**1126.** IP 2207. From Palaimonion, South Building.

D. 0.192; H. 0.0705.

Mended and partly restored. Pale buff clay. The surface on the inside heavily pitted. Rather narrow rim and thin walls. Relatively tall socket with thin walls, flaring toward the top.

**1127.** IP 959. From Palaimonion, 1.25 m. above Stadium floor.

D. 0.187; H. 0.0735.

Mended and partly restored. Light red clay. Rather narrow rim. Low socket, its walls coming to a blunt edge at the top; big slit cut on a slant.

**1128.** IP 1674. From Palaimonion, east of Temple, *ca.* 0.70 m. above Stadium floor.

Complete, except for small mend at the top of the bowl. Reddish buff clay. Narrow rim. Large socket with thick walls coming to a blunt edge at the top and with broad slit cut on a slant.

**1129.** IP 902. From Palaimonion, *ca.* 1.00 m. above Stadium floor.

D. 0.173; H. 0.072.

Somewhat less than half of the bowl missing. Light red clay. Rim of medium width, projecting toward the outside. Broad socket with thick walls coming to a blunt edge at the top. Wide gash forming a single slit.

**1130.** IP 1011. From Palaimonion, 1.10–0.70 m. above Stadium floor.

Fragmentary. Greenish buff clay, rather friable. Narrow rim; socket with slight flare and blunt edge at the top.

**1131.** IP 1672. From Palaimonion, east of Temple.

Fragment. Brick-red clay; whitewash inside and outside. Rather narrow socket, blackened at top.

**1132.** IP 984. From Palaimonion, near surface.

H. 0.067.

Fragment. Pinkish buff clay. Thin fabric. Very narrow rim; socket narrow in the middle and flaring widely at the top.

**1133.** IP 2189 a. From Palaimonion, Sacrificial Pit B.

Fragment. Reddish buff clay. Prominent ridges on the sides. Walls of central socket rather heavy, flaring toward top. White coating inside and outside and within the socket.

**1134.** IP 954. From Palaimonion, 0.20 m. above Stadium floor.

H. 0.072.

Fragment. Brick-red clay, mealy. Small socket flaring slightly at the top.

**1135.** IP 884. From Palaimonion, 0.80 m. above Stadium floor.

Half of the bowl and part of the socket missing. Pinkish buff clay and rather heavy fabric. No trace of whitewash preserved.

**1136.** IP 893 a. From Palaimonion, 1.25 m. above Stadium floor.

H. *ca.* 0.080.

Fragment. Buff clay with pinkish tinge in spots. Rather narrow rim. Prominent groove in bottom around base of socket.

**1137.** IP 912. From Palaimonion, *ca.* 0.85 m. above Stadium floor.

H. 0.067.

Fragment. Pinkish buff clay, rather heavy fabric. Narrow rim, low socket flaring and coming to a blunt edge.

**1138.** IP 1676. From Palaimonion, east of Temple, *ca.* 0.70 m. above Stadium floor.

Fragment. Buff clay, tending to flake. Rather small socket flaring toward the top and coming to a comparatively thin edge.

**1139.** IP 926. From Palaimonion.

Fragment. Dark gray clay with reddish surface; heavy fabric. Narrow socket flaring toward the top. Wide slit set at an angle. Traces of whitewash which covers bottom of socket and the broken edge. This seems to indicate that the whitewash was applied indiscriminately from time to time on lamps and vases in the Palaimonion.

**1140.** IP 5155. From Palaimonion, northeast of Temple.

D. 0.175; H. 0.065.

Slightly restored. Pale yellow clay; traces of white coating more on the outside than inside.

**1141.** IP 4537. From Palaimonion, southeast of Temple.

D. 0.195; H. 0.073.

Parts of sides broken away. Pale yellow clay; prominent ridges on the outside of the bowl.

**1142–1205.** In addition to the 31 items described above there are 64 other fragmentary Palaimonion lamps of Type A-1.

| | | | |
|---|---|---|---|
| **1142.** IP 5333. | **1148.** IP 4806. | **1154.** IP 5082. | **1160.** IP 5335. |
| **1143.** IP 5255. | **1149.** IP 4534. | **1155.** IP 4966. | **1161.** IP 4943. |
| **1144.** IP 5332. | **1150.** IP 4497. | **1156.** IP 4851. | **1162.** IP 4874. |
| **1145.** IP 4157. | **1151.** IP 5337. | **1157.** IP 6309. | **1163.** IP 5291 a, b. |
| **1146.** IP 4737. | **1152.** IP 6343. | **1158.** IP 4848. | **1164.** IP 6312. |
| **1147.** IP 5152. | **1153.** IP 4895. | **1159.** IP 4887 a. | **1165.** IP 4853. |

| | | | |
|---|---|---|---|
| **1166.** IP 4367. | **1176.** IP 4575 a. | **1186.** IP 4718. | **1196.** IP 5788 a. |
| **1167.** IP 5585. | **1177.** IP 5177. | **1187.** IP 5839. | **1197.** IP 4314. |
| **1168.** IP 5176 a, b. | **1178.** IP 4709. | **1188.** IP 4416. | **1198.** IP 4539. |
| **1169.** IP 5380. | **1179.** IP 5761. | **1189.** IP 5537. | **1199.** IP 4179. |
| **1170.** IP 4797. | **1180.** IP 4824. | **1190.** IP 5215. | **1200.** IP 5546. |
| **1171.** IP 5358. | **1181.** IP 5695. | **1191.** IP 4368. | **1201.** IP 6043. |
| **1172.** IP 4807. | **1182.** IP 5662. | **1192.** IP 5698. | **1202.** IP 4645. |
| **1173.** IP 4589 a–c. | **1183.** IP 5194. | **1193.** IP 5674. | **1203.** IP 4811. |
| **1174.** IP 5187 a. | **1184.** IP 5214. | **1194.** IP 5196. | **1204.** IP 4810 a. |
| **1175.** IP 4362 a–d. | **1185.** IP 6318. | **1195.** IP 5785. | **1205.** IP 5217. |

PALAIMONION TYPE A-2. **1206–1249.**

The chief difference between this and the preceding variety consists in the shape of the socket. The walls of the socket in Type A-2 come to a thin, or sometimes blunt, edge at the top and lack the flare characteristic of A-1. In most cases the socket is somewhat taller, and in one lamp, **1208**, it rises slightly above the level of the rim. As in A-1, there is a single opening or slit extending from the top to the base of the socket. On several examples of Type A-2 the rim is broader than in A-1, but some have a very narrow rim, e.g. **1206** and **1212**. In clay and fabric the two groups are very much alike, and on both are found traces of the chalky white covering of the surface. There is no apparent chronological difference between Types A-1 and A-2.

**1206.** IP 944. Pls. 6, 22. From Palaimonion, 0.90 m. above Stadium floor.
D. 0.175; H. 0.070.
Complete, but somewhat mended. Pinkish buff clay. Rather prominent ridges on the outside. Narrow rim; tall socket with blunt edge at the top. The socket extends almost to the level of the rim. There are two marks of the knife on the rim made when the slit was cut out.

**1207.** IP 1671. Pls. 6, 22. From Palaimonion, west of Sacrificial Pit C, in small hollow below Stadium floor.
D. 0.183; H. 0.079.
Intact, but for a slight crack in the side. Brick-red clay. Broad rim, 0.019 m. wide. Sharply tapering socket with thin edge at the top; single narrow slit. Rather prominent ridges on the outside of the bowl.

**1208.** IP 2187. Pls. 6, 22. From Palaimonion, Sacrificial Pit B.
D. 0.186; H. 0.074; depth of socket 0.073.
Mended and partly restored. Pale red clay with heavy white coating inside and outside. Narrow rim, 0.009 m. wide. Socket extends slightly above level of rim. Single wide slit.

**1209.** IP 1978. From Palaimonion, south of Temple.
D. 0.196; H. 0.087; W. of rim 0.019.
Mended and restored. Brick-red clay. Broad rim, projecting far toward the outside. Rather thick walls showing prominent horizontal ridges. The walls of the socket make a blunt edge at the top, which shows marks of burning.

**1210.** IP 1014. Pls. 6, 22. From Palaimonion, northwest of Temple.
D. 0.178; H. 0.076; W. of rim 0.020.
Small part on one side of the bowl and top of socket restored. Bright red, mealy clay; heavy fabric. Broad rim with wide projection toward the outside. Bottom of socket extends below the bottom of the bowl.

**1211.** IP 1972. From Palaimonion, northeast of Temple.
D. 0.195; H. 0.0785.
Half of the bowl and part of the socket missing. Light red clay; traces of whitewash, mostly on the outside. Top of socket comes to thin edge. Prominent ridges on the outside of the bowl.

**1212.** IP 942. Pls. 6, 22. From Palaimonion.
D. 0.200; H. 0.0675.
Much mended and partly restored. Pale, greenish buff clay; thin fabric. Very narrow rim with slight projection toward the outside. Small socket.

**1213.** IP 662. From Palaimonion.
Fragment from bottom of bowl with socket completely preserved. Bright red clay; traces of whitewash. Large socket, 0.067 m. deep on the inside. Slit at a considerable angle and rough at the bottom. The top of the socket shows no clear sign of burning, but the blackening may have disappeared in the washing.

**1214–1249.** Besides the eight lamps described above, there are 36 other items in varying states of preservation that can be identified as belonging to Type A-2.

| | | | |
|---|---|---|---|
| **1214.** IP 5069. | **1223.** IP 5790. | **1232.** IP 6202. | **1241.** IP 4578 b. |
| **1215.** IP 6212. | **1224.** IP 5694. | **1233.** IP 4967. | **1242.** IP 4579. |
| **1216.** IP 4411 b. | **1225.** IP 5938. | **1234.** IP 5195. | **1243.** IP 4742. |
| **1217.** IP 4415. | **1226.** IP 4504 b. | **1235.** IP 4939. | **1244.** IP 5171. |
| **1218.** IP 5080. | **1227.** IP 6190 a–c. | **1236.** IP 6196. | **1245.** IP 4621. |
| **1219.** IP 5963. | **1228.** IP 6189. | **1237.** IP 6339. | **1246.** IP 4634. |
| **1220.** IP 5212. | **1229.** IP 5842. | **1238.** IP 5269. | **1247.** IP 4641 a–c. |
| **1221.** IP 5077. | **1230.** IP 5190. | **1239.** IP 5796. | **1248.** IP 4588 a. |
| **1222.** IP 5071. | **1231.** IP 4538. | **1240.** IP 4717. | **1249.** IP 4586 c. |

PALAIMONION TYPE A-3. **1250–1255.**

Type A-3 differs from A-1 only in the shape of the opening through the side of the socket; in other respects the two types are similar. The socket flares at the top and has a single opening that begins below the top and extends almost to the bottom. It is usually wider in the middle than at the top and bottom, but in one case, **1284**, the two sides of the opening are nearly parallel. Only one lamp, **1250**, preserves part of the rim, which is very narrow and does not project toward the outside.

**1250.** IP 1970. Pl. 6. From Palaimonion, northeast corner, in nest of lamps.

D. (0.178); H. 0.067.

Fragment preserving half the bowl and most of the socket. Mealy, brick-red clay. Very narrow rim with no projection toward the outside. Socket with slight flare toward the top. Single slit extending from *ca.* 0.020 m. below the top to the bottom of the socket.

**1251.** IP 653. Pl. 6. From Palaimonion, southeast corner.

Socket and bottom of bowl preserved. Pale red clay; slight traces of whitewash. Rather low, slightly flaring socket, coming to a broad edge at the top. Single oval slit which begins well below the top.

**1252.** IP 6218. Pl. 26. From Palaimonion, east of Temple.

Socket and base preserved. Buff clay; thin fabric. Rather tall socket, flaring out at the top. Slit with nearly parallel sides.

**1253.** IP 5664. Pl. 26. From Palaimonion, northeast of Temple.

Socket and base preserved. Reddish buff clay, friable.

**1254.** IP 4980. Pl. 26. From Palaimonion, southeast of Temple, 1.15–0.40 m. above Stadium floor.

Socket and part of base preserved. Red clay. Nearly rectangular slit.

**1255.** IP 5708. From Palaimonion, northeast of Temple.

Top of socket preserved. Mealy, brick-red clay.

PALAIMONION TYPES A-1–A-3. **1256–1480.** These 225 fragmentary lamps preserve some lower part of the socket, showing that they had single slits; they therefore belong to subtypes A-1, A-2, or A-3.

| | | | |
|---|---|---|---|
| **1256.** IP 2204. | **1274.** IP 4994 a, b. | **1292.** IP 4067. | **1310.** IP 5381. |
| **1257.** IP 967. | **1275.** IP 4360. | **1293.** IP 5009. | **1311.** IP 5357. |
| **1258.** IP 1675. | **1276.** IP 5266. | **1294.** IP 4104. | **1312.** IP 5170. |
| **1259.** IP 1971. | **1277.** IP 4424. | **1295.** IP 5055. | **1313.** IP 5359. |
| **1260.** IP 886. | **1278.** IP 4122. | **1296.** IP 4371. | **1314.** IP 5180. |
| **1261.** IP 2630. | **1279.** IP 5061. | **1297.** IP 5218. | **1315.** IP 5179. |
| **1262.** IP 1977. | **1280.** IP 4068. | **1298.** IP 4273. | **1316.** IP 5393. |
| **1263.** IP 2203. | **1281.** IP 5134 a. | **1299.** IP 5207. | **1317.** IP 5352. |
| **1264.** IP 2154. | **1282.** IP 2606 a–c. | **1300.** IP 5067. | **1318.** IP 5126 a, b. |
| **1265.** IP 1328. | **1283.** IP 4361 a. | **1301.** IP 5211 a. | **1319.** IP 5363 a, b. |
| **1266.** IP 2188. | **1284.** IP 5219. | **1302.** IP 5361. | **1320.** IP 5162. |
| **1267.** IP 2603. | **1285.** IP 4293. | **1303.** IP 5344. | **1321.** IP 4443. |
| **1268.** IP 2619. | **1286.** IP 5064. | **1304.** IP 5334. | **1322.** IP 5153. |
| **1269.** IP 2614 a. | **1287.** IP 4370 a. | **1305.** IP 5191. | **1323.** IP 5198. |
| **1270.** IP 893 b. | **1288.** IP 5345. | **1306.** IP 5185. | **1324.** IP 5182. |
| **1271.** IP 2648. | **1289.** IP 5159. | **1307.** IP 5316. | **1325.** IP 5305. |
| **1272.** IP 2209. | **1290.** IP 6075. | **1308.** IP 5172. | **1326.** IP 5136. |
| **1273.** IP 5271. | **1291.** IP 4628. | **1309.** IP 5382. | **1327.** IP 5151. |

| | | | |
|---|---|---|---|
| **1328.** IP 5115. | **1367.** IP 4984. | **1406.** IP 4605. | **1445.** IP 5922. |
| **1329.** IP 5154. | **1368.** IP 6220. | **1407.** IP 4583 a, b. | **1446.** IP 5733. |
| **1330.** IP 5181. | **1369.** IP 6206. | **1408.** IP 4839. | **1447.** IP 5919. |
| **1331.** IP 6044 a. | **1370.** IP 4808. | **1409.** IP 4803. | **1448.** IP 5900. |
| **1332.** IP 5111. | **1371.** IP 5997. | **1410.** IP 4585. | **1449.** IP 4383 b. |
| **1333.** IP 4599. | **1372.** IP 6310. | **1411.** IP 4568 a, b. | **1450.** IP 4386 b. |
| **1334.** IP 5314. | **1373.** IP 4716. | **1412.** IP 4594. | **1451.** IP 5456. |
| **1335.** IP 4627. | **1374.** IP 6283. | **1413.** IP 4705. | **1452.** IP 5702. |
| **1336.** IP 5135. | **1375.** IP 4902. | **1414.** IP 5270. | **1453.** IP 5473. |
| **1337.** IP 5005. | **1376.** IP 4559. | **1415.** IP 4844. | **1454.** IP 5699. |
| **1338.** IP 5133. | **1377.** IP 5227. | **1416.** IP 5841 a. | **1455.** IP 5669. |
| **1339.** IP 4847, IP 4881. | **1378.** IP 5838. | **1417.** IP 4572 a–c. | **1456.** IP 4566. |
| **1340.** IP 5178. | **1379.** IP 4720. | **1418.** IP 4631 a. | **1457.** IP 5661. |
| **1341.** IP 5161. | **1380.** IP 4714. | **1419.** IP 4738 a. | **1458.** IP 4518. |
| **1342.** IP 5113. | **1381.** IP 5996. | **1420.** IP 6327 a. | **1459.** IP 5791. |
| **1343.** IP 5140 a, b. | **1382.** IP 6284. | **1421.** IP 6136 a. | **1460.** IP 4525. |
| **1344.** IP 5139. | **1383.** IP 4836. | **1422.** IP 5786. | **1461.** IP 4494. |
| **1345.** IP 4845. | **1384.** IP 4983. | **1423.** IP 5668. | **1462.** IP 5797. |
| **1346.** IP 4849. | **1385.** IP 6099. | **1424.** IP 5701. | **1463.** IP 6328. |
| **1347.** IP 6214. | **1386.** IP 4551. | **1425.** IP 5676. | **1464.** IP 5780. |
| **1348.** IP 4846. | **1387.** IP 4719. | **1426.** IP 5538. | **1465.** IP 4526. |
| **1349.** IP 4905. | **1388.** IP 4721. | **1427.** IP 5610. | **1466.** IP 4349 a, b. |
| **1350.** IP 6346. | **1389.** IP 4554. | **1428.** IP 5675. | **1467.** IP 4499. |
| **1351.** IP 5283. | **1390.** IP 6215. | **1429.** IP 5608. | **1468.** IP 5467. |
| **1352.** IP 5840. | **1391.** IP 5970. | **1430.** IP 5553. | **1469.** IP 5410. |
| **1353.** IP 4928. | **1392.** IP 4686. | **1431.** IP 5683. | **1470.** IP 4527. |
| **1354.** IP 6281. | **1393.** IP 4536. | **1432.** IP 5611. | **1471.** IP 5763. |
| **1355.** IP 6317. | **1394.** IP 4596. | **1433.** IP 5545. | **1472.** IP 5787 a. |
| **1356.** IP 5802. | **1395.** IP 5989. | **1434.** IP 5425. | **1473.** IP 5660. |
| **1357.** IP 5282. | **1396.** IP 4986. | **1435.** IP 5901. | **1474.** IP 5721. |
| **1358.** IP 5288. | **1397.** IP 4636. | **1436.** IP 5418. | **1475.** IP 5552. |
| **1359.** IP 4924. | **1398.** IP 4692. | **1437.** IP 5926. | **1476.** IP 5888. |
| **1360.** IP 5800. | **1399.** IP 4637. | **1438.** IP 5541. | **1477.** IP 5731. |
| **1361.** IP 5299. | **1400.** IP 4884. | **1439.** IP 5422. | **1478.** IP 5738. |
| **1362.** IP 4500. | **1401.** IP 4571. | **1440.** IP 4382. | **1479.** IP 5697. |
| **1363.** IP 5981. | **1402.** IP 4689. | **1441.** IP 5433. | **1480.** IP 5730. |
| **1364.** IP 4886. | **1403.** IP 4992. | **1442.** IP 5540. | |
| **1365.** IP 4883. | **1404.** IP 6331. | **1443.** IP 5417. | |
| **1366.** IP 6098. | **1405.** IP 4600. | **1444.** IP 5929. | |

PALAIMONION TYPE A-4. **1481–1511.**

Type A-4 lamps have two, usually rather broad, elongated openings near the bottom of the socket. In other respects they conform to the shape of A-1 through A-3, but there are considerable differences within the subclass. In some instances the socket flares at the top, as in A-1 and A-3; in others it comes up to a sharp edge, as in A-2, and in a few cases it tapers toward the top. Two of the better-preserved lamps, **1488** and **1489**, have very broad rims with wide projection toward the outside and prominent ridges on the body. In both these lamps the socket flares at the top. Others, e.g. **1486**, have comparatively narrow rims with no projection toward the outside, but with a slight inward projection. A few lamps in this subclass are made of the usual pale yellow or light red clay; all the others are made of hard, brick-red clay. In ten cases, e.g. **1481, 1482**, the base has been trimmed after removal from the wheel. In the case of **1481**, the base is now quite flat and smooth; in **1482** the trimming of the base has resulted in a series of circular grooves and ridges.

Another important difference between Types A-4 and A-1-3 is the attachment of the socket to the bottom of the bowl. In Types A-1-3 the socket was added separately after the bowl had been finished; in most of the lamps of Type A-4 it was made in a single process, while the lamp was turned on the wheel. This peculiarity together with the type of clay, the shape of the oil-hole, and the trimming of the base in a large number of cases, seem to indicate that the lamps of Type A-4 were made in a different shop and probably at a slightly later time than the more numerous lamps of A-1-3, which are likely to have been produced at approximately the same time.

**1481.** IP 1313. Pls. 6, 23. From Large Circular Pit, depth 0.36 m.

Fragment with complete socket. Brick-red clay; very thin fabric. Steeply rising sides and narrow rim. Broad socket with two very short holes at the bottom. Low flat base, trimmed after lamp had been removed from the wheel.

**1482.** IP 956 a–d. Pls. 6, 23. From Palaimonion, 0.20 m. above Stadium floor.

Fragmentary. Brick-red clay; very friable. Narrow rim with no projection toward the outside, but a slight overhang on the inside. The base has been trimmed in a series of three circular ridges. Tall socket widening toward the top with two short irregular slits at the bottom.

**1483.** IP 873. Pl. 6. From Palaimonion, east end.

Fragment, preserving part of bowl and complete socket. Coarse, brick-red clay. Short socket with walls coming to a comparatively thin edge at the top. Two carelessly gouged slits at the bottom, set at a decided angle to the vertical.

**1484.** IP 1310. From Large Circular Pit, depth 0.25 m.

Fragment. Bright red clay; rather thin fabric. Short socket with walls coming to a thin edge. Two small slits at the bottom.

**1485.** IP 928. From Palaimonion.

Only socket preserved. Dark red clay, tapering socket with thin upper edge heavily blackened. Two slits at base.

**1486.** IP 1571. Pls. 6, 23. From Large Circular Pit, depth 0.20 m.

D. 0.170; H. 0.0655.

Part of bowl missing and socket slightly restored. Light red clay. Narrow rim with no projection on the outside, but projecting slightly toward the inside. Short, wide socket with walls coming to a thin edge at the top. Two roughly gouged slits at the bottom of the socket.

**1487.** IP 842. From Palaimonion, 0.60 m. above balbides sill.

Base and complete socket. Reddish buff clay. Short socket flaring slightly with two small slits at base.

**1488.** IP 1973. Pl. 6. From Palaimonion, northeast corner, in nest of lamps.

D. 0.176; H. 0.058; W. of rim 0.020.

Mended and partly restored. Light red clay; rather coarse fabric with prominent ridges on the outside. Broad rim with downward slant and wide overhang toward the outside. Large, flaring socket. Traces of white coating inside and outside.

**1489.** IP 1976. Pls. 6, 23. From Palaimonion, northeast corner, in nest of lamps.

D. 0.178; H. 0.065.

Much mended and somewhat restored. Light red clay with traces of whitewash both inside and outside. Broad rim, 0.018 m. wide, with prominent slant towards the outside, as on **1488**. Broad ridges on the body. Large socket flaring toward the top and coming to a blunt edge. Two broad slits at bottom of socket.

**1490.** IP 5132. From Temenos, east end of South Side.

Orange-pink clay. Base trimmed to form a series of concentric rings, as in **1482**.

**1491.** IP 5864 a, b. From Palaimonion, east section, ca. 0.70 m. above Stadium floor.

Brick-red clay with darker surface, coarse fabric. Traces of whitewash. Low socket with two short slits at bottom.

**1492.** IP 4929. From Palaimonion, middle section, 0.70–0.00 m. above Stadium floor.

Brick-red clay; socket much blackened from use.

**1493.** IP 5257. From Temenos, East Side.

Coarse, brick-red clay with darker surface. Very short socket with two oil-holes of irregular shape at the bottom.

**1494.** IP 5280. From Palaimonion, northwest of Temple.

H. 0.062.

Parts of rim and of socket preserved. Reddish buff clay.

**1495.** IP 5539. Pl. 26. From Palaimonion, east of Temple, 1.15–1.00 m. above Stadium floor.

Part of socket and base preserved. Orange clay, very crumbly. Trimmed underneath. This is an unusually high socket for this type, flaring slightly at the top; and the oil-holes are close to the bottom.

**1496.** IP 6025. Pl. 26. From Palaimonion, northwest of Temple.

Only socket and part of base preserved. Reddish brown clay. Base trimmed.

**1497.** IP 6344. Pl. 26. From Palaimonion, east section.

Socket and base preserved. Red clay; coarse fabric. Very low socket.

**1498–1511.** To Palaimonion Type A-4 belong also 14 smaller fragments, which preserve all or most of the socket with two openings at the base.

**1498.** IP 4601 (Pl. 26).    **1502.** IP 4914.    **1506.** IP 5197.    **1510.** IP 4918.
**1499.** IP 5307.                  **1503.** IP 5980.    **1507.** IP 5174.    **1511.** IP 4931 (Pl. 26).
**1500.** IP 5813.                  **1504.** IP 5302.    **1508.** IP 4396.
**1501.** IP 5114.                  **1505.** IP 5405.    **1509.** IP 4919.

PALAIMONION TYPE A-5. **1512–1529.**

Of A-5 there are several fragmentary examples. All seem to have been made like those of Type A-4, with the socket shaped on the wheel in one piece with the bowl. Consequently, when it breaks off, a piece from the bottom of the bowl goes with it. The type falls into two varieties.

*Type A-5a.* **1512–1517.**

The lamps of the less numerous variety, Type A-5a, are made of red clay and thin fabric of good quality. In three instances the base has been trimmed after the lamp was removed from the wheel. The lamps of this subtype have a very low socket, the walls of which rise vertically and usually have three approximately equidistant circular holes at the base. One fragment, **1517**, preserving the complete socket, differs from all the other Palaimonion lamps by the total absence of holes of any kind. Since the edge of the socket has been blackened, the lamp must have been in use. It is difficult to see how the oil reached the wick, unless it was poured directly into the socket. The omission of the holes may have been an oversight on the part of the lampmaker.

**1512.** IP 1102. Pls. 7, 23. From Palaimonion, 0.60–0.30 m. above Stadium floor.

Fragment of bottom of lamp, preserving the complete socket. Brick-red clay, thin fabric. Small socket, 0.028 m. deep on the inside, with three oil-holes near the bottom. The base is flat and has been neatly trimmed (see Pl. 23).

**1513.** IP 4987. From Palaimonion, southeast of Temple, 1.15–0.95 m. above Stadium floor.

Light gray clay; thin fabric. Base trimmed flat underneath. Socket low and thin walled with three holes at the base.

**1514.** IP 5670. Pl. 26. From Temenos, east end of South Side.

Red, crumbly clay. Very low socket, 0.022 m. on the outside, with three circular holes at bottom. Flat, raised base that seems to have been trimmed, but the surface is now corroded.

**1515.** IP 4963. From Palaimonion, southeast of Temple.

Small fragment of socket. Light red clay. Only one circular hole preserved at the lower edge, but there could have been others.

**1516.** IP 5723. From Palaimonion, northeast of Temple.

Small fragment from lower part of socket. Red clay. A single hole is preserved near the base of the socket, but there are traces of a second, and there were probably three.

**1517.** IP 4372. Pl. 26. From Palaimonion, east of Temple, depth 0.00–0.45 m.

Socket and base preserved. Light red clay. Comparatively low socket with no oil-holes, but blackened at the top.

*Type A-5b.* **1518–1529.**

The lamps of the second variety, A-5b, are of coarse fabric, also of red color. They have two small circular oil-holes at the base, and these come fairly close together, never opposite each other. The socket, which tapers markedly toward the top, was made on the wheel together with the bowl in one process. The only lamp well enough preserved to show the whole profile, **1518**, has rather heavy walls coming to a blunt edge, which does not widen into a proper rim as on most of the lamps of Group A. The socket is high, its top projecting above the height of the rim. On none of the lamps of this subtype has the base been trimmed underneath.

**1518.** IP 1418. Pl. 7. From Palaimonion, Sacrificial Pit C, lower deposit.
D. (0.180); H. 0.070.

Much mended, but socket original and complete. Light red clay, heavy fabric. The sides come to a blunt edge at the top and with no proper rim. Tall tapering socket, slightly uneven at the top, with two holes near the bottom.

**1519.** IP 4274. Pl. 26. From Temenos, west end of South Side, depth 0.90 m.

Very heavy fabric; light reddish color. The two oil-holes are rather close together.

**1520.** IP 5421. Pl. 26. From Temenos, South Side.

Very heavy fabric of light red color. The two oil-holes are rather close together.

**1521–1529.** There are nine more fragments that belong to the subtype A-5b.

**1521.** IP 6005.

**1522.** IP 6347.

**1523.** IP 4906 a.

**1524.** IP 5692.

**1525.** IP 4553.

**1526.** IP 5281.

**1527.** IP 4515.

**1528.** IP 4004.

**1529.** IP 5164.

PALAIMONION TYPE A-6. **1530–1649.**

Type A-6 is made up of rather large lamps with rims of medium width and with two slits through the socket, extending from the top all the way down to the bottom. In one case at least, **1538**, a comparatively broad strip was removed from the socket on either side, then the two halves were pushed together so as to make the openings narrower at the top than at the bottom. By this process the socket took on a decided taper toward the top. In some instances, e.g. **1532, 1537**, the openings consist of single slits through the wall of the socket with no strip of clay removed. An unusually large number of lamps and fragments of Type A-6 have bases neatly trimmed with a wide groove surrounding the flat circular base at the center; but in some cases the trimming has produced a base ring with a flat circular disc in the center. The rim varies somewhat in width, and in all cases it projects toward the outside. There is great contrast in the color of the clay within the type. In a large percentage of the lamps the clay is red, some dark red or brick red, others a lighter red. Not a few of the lamps, however, are made of a pale buff or greenish clay, but there is no other detectable difference among the lamps of these contrasting colors.

**1530.** IP 994. Pls. 7, 23. From Palaimonion.

D. 0.170; H. 0.061.

Mended but practically complete. Pinkish buff clay with patches of thick whitewash chiefly on the inside. Low socket, only 0.032 m. deep on the inside and coming to a thin edge. Two slits, both at an angle to the vertical. The socket seems to have been partly damaged in antiquity, as shown by discoloration on a broken edge.

**1531.** IP 2205. Pls. 7, 23. From Palaimonion, east of Temple, from hollow below the Stadium floor.

D. 0.194; H. 0.076.

Mended and slightly restored. Brick-red clay with traces of whitewash on outside and inside. Rather broad rim, 0.015 m. wide, with wide projection slanting down toward the outside. Socket rising to a blunt edge, with two wide slits.

**1532.** IP 1975. Pls. 7, 23. From Palaimonion, northeast of Temple, in nest of lamps.

D. 0.172; H. 0.073.

Mended but complete. Reddish buff clay; prominent ridges on the outside. Relatively broad rim projecting toward the outside. Wide socket with walls coming to a thin edge at the top. Two narrow slits, made as single gashes without removal of the strip of clay.

**1533.** IP 872. Pls. 7, 23. From Palaimonion, east of Temple.

D. 0.183; H. 0.081.

Part of side missing, and half of socket restored. Reddish buff clay. Rim of medium width. Rather short socket, only half preserved, tapering toward the top and coming to a blunt edge. Two slits, apparently made like those of **1532** with a single slash on either side.

**1534.** IP 2608 a. Pl. 23. From northeast of Temple of Poseidon.

Fragment from bottom. Buff clay, slightly pinkish on the inside. The base has been trimmed to produce a base ring on the outside and smooth disc in the center. Socket missing but bottom of the two slits preserved.

**1535.** IP 2608 b. Pl. 23. From Palaimonion.

Small fragment. Buff clay, slightly pinkish on the inside. The base has been trimmed to form a base ring on the outside and smooth disc in the center. Socket mostly missing but bottom of two slits preserved.

**1536.** IP 2614 b. Pl. 23. From Palaimonion.

Fragment from bottom of bowl. Pinkish buff clay. Socket missing but traces of a gash on either side show that there were two slits that seem to have been made without removal of strips of clay. The base has not been trimmed as shown by marks on bottom.

**1537.** IP 1561. From Large Circular Pit, depth 0.40 m.

D. 0.183; H. 0.0675.

Mended and restored. Pale buff clay. Rather wide rim with projection toward the outside. The socket has two slits, preserved only at the bottom. They were made as single gashes with no clay strip removed.

**1538.** IP 1974. Pls. 7, 23. From Palaimonion, northeast of Temple, in nest of lamps.

D. 0.197; H. 0.086.

Much mended and partly restored. Pale buff clay. Rim of medium width projecting somewhat toward the outside. Tall socket, tapering perceptibly toward top, with two slits wider at the bottom than at the top. Apparently the top was squeezed together after the strips of clay in the two slits had been cut out.

**1539–1649.** There are 111 smaller fragments that can be recognized as belonging to Type A-6.

| | | | |
|---|---|---|---|
| **1539.** IP 6221 a, b. | **1567.** IP 5536. | **1595.** IP 4880. | **1623.** IP 4894 a, b. |
| **1540.** IP 5995. | **1568.** IP 5734. | **1596.** IP 5206. | **1624.** IP 4842. |
| **1541.** IP 5409. | **1569.** IP 5789. | **1597.** IP 5303. | **1625.** IP 4712. |
| **1542.** IP 6219. | **1570.** IP 5720. | **1598.** IP 4025. | **1626.** IP 4879. |
| **1543.** IP 4563 a. | **1571.** IP 4552. | **1599.** IP 5390. | **1627.** IP 4968. |
| **1544.** IP 5068. | **1572.** IP 5663. | **1600.** IP 6083. | **1628.** IP 5735. |
| **1545.** IP 5408. | **1573.** IP 4498. | **1601.** IP 5396 a. | **1629.** IP 4598. |
| **1546.** IP 4519. | **1574.** IP 5677. | **1602.** IP 4419. | **1630.** IP 4591 a. |
| **1547.** IP 5413. | **1575.** IP 4421. | **1603.** IP 5312. | **1631.** IP 5313. |
| **1548.** IP 6000. | **1576.** IP 4985. | **1604.** IP 4420. | **1632.** IP 4573. |
| **1549.** IP 5856. | **1577.** IP 5754. | **1605.** IP 5928. | **1633.** IP 4662. |
| **1550.** IP 4330. | **1578.** IP 5815. | **1606.** IP 4121. | **1634.** IP 4592 a. |
| **1551.** IP 4558. | **1579.** IP 6094. | **1607.** IP 5110. | **1635.** IP 4715. |
| **1552.** IP 5920. | **1580.** IP 5679. | **1608.** IP 5074. | **1636.** IP 4690. |
| **1553.** IP 5315. | **1581.** IP 5079. | **1609.** IP 5066. | **1637.** IP 4893. |
| **1554.** IP 5974. | **1582.** IP 4560. | **1610.** IP 5301. | **1638.** IP 5983 b, c. |
| **1555.** IP 4323 a, b. | **1583.** IP 5737. | **1611.** IP 5100 a, b. | **1639.** IP 4763. |
| **1556.** IP 4659. | **1584.** IP 4843. | **1612.** IP 5065. | **1640.** IP 4907. |
| **1557.** IP 4395. | **1585.** IP 6199. | **1613.** IP 5062. | **1641.** IP 4593 a, c. |
| **1558.** IP 4412. | **1586.** IP 4335. | **1614.** IP 5072. | **1642.** IP 4603 b. |
| **1559.** IP 5850. | **1587.** IP 4520 c. | **1615.** IP 5073. | **1643.** IP 4602 b. |
| **1560.** IP 4423. | **1588.** IP 4561. | **1616.** IP 5070. | **1644.** IP 4625. |
| **1561.** IP 4414. | **1589.** IP 6279. | **1617.** IP 5052. | **1645.** IP 4761. |
| **1562.** IP 5862. | **1590.** IP 4693. | **1618.** IP 5063. | **1646.** IP 5336. |
| **1563.** IP 4326. | **1591.** IP 5158. | **1619.** IP 5169. | **1647.** IP 4619 a, b. |
| **1564.** IP 4937. | **1592.** IP 5156. | **1620.** IP 4417. | **1648.** IP 4698. |
| **1565.** IP 5867. | **1593.** IP 5320 a. | **1621.** IP 5983 a. | **1649.** IP 6348. |
| **1566.** IP 5657. | **1594.** IP 5992 a. | **1622.** IP 4574. | |

**1650–2078.**

These 429 items also belong to Group A. In the kinds of clay and frequent presence of whitewash they do not differ from the described lamps of Types A-1 to A-6. Although none of the particular features that determine the subtype are present, they can with fair certainty be distinguished from fragments of Group B. They are important as indicative of the distribution of the types comprising Group A in a particular area.

| | | | |
|---|---|---|---|
| **1650.** IP 5722 a. | **1672.** IP 1566. | **1694.** IP 4957. | **1716.** IP 4810 b. |
| **1651.** IP 5615. | **1673.** IP 5300. | **1695.** IP 6026. | **1717.** IP 4633 a. |
| **1652.** IP 5964. | **1674.** IP 4597. | **1696.** IP 4941 a–c. | **1718.** IP 4642 a, c. |
| **1653.** IP 5758. | **1675.** IP 4595. | **1697.** IP 5982. | **1719.** IP 4631 b. |
| **1654.** IP 5869. | **1676.** IP 4837. | **1698.** IP 4981. | **1720.** IP 4758 a, b. |
| **1655.** IP 4555. | **1677.** IP 5412. | **1699.** IP 4940. | **1721.** IP 4796 a–c. |
| **1656.** IP 4021. | **1678.** IP 5649. | **1700.** IP 4882. | **1722.** IP 4739 a, b. |
| **1657.** IP 5861. | **1679.** IP 5673. | **1701.** IP 4759. | **1723.** IP 5992 b. |
| **1658.** IP 5868. | **1680.** IP 4713. | **1702.** IP 4885. | **1724.** IP 4741 a, b. |
| **1659.** IP 5865. | **1681.** IP 4711. | **1703.** IP 4809. | **1725.** IP 4840 a–c. |
| **1660.** IP 5691. | **1682.** IP 5078. | **1704.** IP 6350 b. | **1726.** IP 4738 b. |
| **1661.** IP 4241. | **1683.** IP 5360. | **1705.** IP 4908. | **1727.** IP 4996. |
| **1662.** IP 4061. | **1684.** IP 6340. | **1706.** IP 4936. | **1728.** IP 4852 a, b. |
| **1663.** IP 6338. | **1685.** IP 5607. | **1707.** IP 4760. | **1729.** IP 5947. |
| **1664.** IP 5075. | **1686.** IP 4493 a. | **1708.** IP 4582. | **1730.** IP 4977 b. |
| **1665.** IP 6341. | **1687.** IP 4993. | **1709.** IP 4823. | **1731.** IP 4762 a, b. |
| **1666.** IP 5647. | **1688.** IP 4916. | **1710.** IP 4897. | **1732.** IP 4906 b. |
| **1667.** IP 5076. | **1689.** IP 4850. | **1711.** IP 4825. | **1733.** IP 4710. |
| **1668.** IP 5857. | **1690.** IP 4390. | **1712.** IP 4896. | **1734.** IP 4700 a, b. |
| **1669.** IP 5495. | **1691.** IP 5863. | **1713.** IP 4841. | **1735.** IP 4643. |
| **1670.** IP 5810. | **1692.** IP 6345. | **1714.** IP 4646. | **1736.** IP 5684. |
| **1671.** IP 4567. | **1693.** IP 4933. | **1715.** IP 4635 a–c. | **1737.** IP 4685. |

1738. IP 5672.
1739. IP 4603 a.
1740. IP 4696.
1741. IP 4683.
1742. IP 5645.
1743. IP 5781.
1744. IP 5921.
1745. IP 4592 b.
1746. IP 4591 b, c.
1747. IP 4586 a, b.
1748. IP 5732 a–d.
1749. IP 5622.
1750. IP 4632 a, b.
1751. IP 5966.
1752. IP 5787 b.
1753. IP 5722 b.
1754. IP 5924.
1755. IP 5937.
1756. IP 5652.
1757. IP 5923.
1758. IP 5651.
1759. IP 4052.
1760. IP 5760.
1761. IP 4023.
1762. IP 5646.
1763. IP 4629.
1764. IP 5736.
1765. IP 4022.
1766. IP 4681.
1767. IP 4638 a.
1768. IP 4703.
1769. IP 4699.
1770. IP 3945.
1771. IP 4644.
1772. IP 4695.
1773. IP 5930.
1774. IP 4612 b.
1775. IP 4633 b.
1776. IP 4604 b.
1777. IP 5605.
1778. IP 5712.
1779. IP 5700.
1780. IP 5556.
1781. IP 5604.
1782. IP 5671.
1783. IP 5494.
1784. IP 5682.
1785. IP 5681.
1786. IP 5606.
1787. IP 5693.
1788. IP 5788 b.
1789. IP 5711.
1790. IP 5613 a, b.
1791. IP 5571.
1792. IP 5678.
1793. IP 5554.
1794. IP 5680.

1795. IP 4570 a.
1796. IP 5757.
1797. IP 4702.
1798. IP 4688 a, b.
1799. IP 4575 b, c.
1800. IP 4624.
1801. IP 4691.
1802. IP 4687.
1803. IP 5659.
1804. IP 5779.
1805. IP 4630.
1806. IP 5914 a, b.
1807. IP 5703.
1808. IP 4374.
1809. IP 5453.
1810. IP 5134 b.
1811. IP 4570 b.
1812. IP 4602 a.
1813. IP 4580.
1814. IP 4622.
1815. IP 4660.
1816. IP 5650.
1817. IP 4429.
1818. IP 4363.
1819. IP 4697.
1820. IP 4587.
1821. IP 4669.
1822. IP 5555.
1823. IP 4576 b, c.
1824. IP 4638 b.
1825. IP 4604 a, c.
1826. IP 4626.
1827. IP 4704.
1828. IP 4615.
1829. IP 5618.
1830. IP 4661.
1831. IP 4578 a.
1832. IP 4613.
1833. IP 4584 a, b.
1834. IP 4581 a, b.
1835. IP 5602.
1836. IP 4593 b.
1837. IP 5603.
1838. IP 4670.
1839. IP 4588 b.
1840. IP 5927.
1841. IP 4642 b.
1842. IP 5965.
1843. IP 5355.
1844. IP 4366.
1845. IP 5715.
1846. IP 4901.
1847. IP 5124.
1848. IP 5202.
1849. IP 4370 b–d.
1850. IP 5356.
1851. IP 5138.

1852. IP 5319.
1853. IP 5320 b.
1854. IP 4440.
1855. IP 5318.
1856. IP 5348.
1857. IP 5125.
1858. IP 4438.
1859. IP 4439.
1860. IP 4430 a, b.
1861. IP 4442.
1862. IP 4433.
1863. IP 4432.
1864. IP 5383 a, b.
1865. IP 6044 b, c.
1866. IP 4975.
1867. IP 5653.
1868. IP 5704.
1869. IP 5658.
1870. IP 4612 a.
1871. IP 5396 b.
1872. IP 4999.
1873. IP 5311 a–c.
1874. IP 5112.
1875. IP 5419.
1876. IP 5338.
1877. IP 5454.
1878. IP 4898.
1879. IP 5362.
1880. IP 5187 b, c.
1881. IP 5184 a–c'.
1882. IP 5459.
1882 A. IP 5192.
1883. IP 5535 a, b.
1884. IP 4425.
1885. IP 5457.
1886. IP 4380.
1887. IP 5199.
1888. IP 4381.
1889. IP 4977 a.
1890. IP 5474.
1891. IP 6335.
1892. IP 6209.
1893. IP 6198.
1894. IP 5173.
1895. IP 4318.
1896. IP 5411.
1897. IP 6207.
1898. IP 4426.
1899. IP 4324.
1900. IP 5458.
1901. IP 5321.
1902. IP 4377.
1903. IP 5186.
1904. IP 5346.
1905. IP 5384.
1906. IP 4418 a, b.
1907. IP 4350.

1908. IP 6327 b, c.
1909. IP 6282.
1910. IP 5889.
1911. IP 4386 a.
1912. IP 6053.
1913. IP 6170.
1914. IP 6325.
1915. IP 4932.
1916. IP 6298.
1917. IP 5226.
1918. IP 5882.
1919. IP 5849.
1920. IP 6171 a, b.
1921. IP 6197.
1922. IP 6330.
1923. IP 5878.
1924. IP 5263.
1925. IP 5262.
1926. IP 4410 a, b.
1927. IP 6136 b.
1928. IP 4402.
1929. IP 5854.
1930. IP 4322.
1931. IP 4354.
1932. IP 6327 d.
1933. IP 6326 a, b.
1934. IP 5843.
1935. IP 4441.
1936. IP 4917.
1937. IP 4915.
1938. IP 5936.
1939. IP 4930.
1940. IP 4495 a.
1941. IP 4071.
1942. IP 4516.
1943. IP 5003 b.
1944. IP 6349.
1945. IP 4557.
1946. IP 5762.
1947. IP 5935.
1948. IP 5175.
1949. IP 5801.
1950. IP 4546 b.
1951. IP 6103.
1952. IP 5841 b.
1953. IP 4422.
1954. IP 4508.
1955. IP 5860.
1956. IP 4391 a, b.
1957. IP 5268.
1958. IP 4505 a, b.
1959. IP 5157 A.
1960. IP 4404.
1961. IP 4406.
1962. IP 5994.
1963. IP 4528.
1964. IP 4507.

| | | | |
|---|---|---|---|
| **1965.** IP 4509. | **1994.** IP 5030. | **2023.** IP 4400. | **2052.** IP 4562. |
| **1966.** IP 6324. | **1995.** IP 5054. | **2024.** IP 5250 a, b. | **2053.** IP 4123. |
| **1967.** IP 4405. | **1996.** IP 4266. | **2025.** IP 5278. | **2054.** IP 5200. |
| **1968.** IP 4512. | **1997.** IP 5137. | **2026.** IP 5993. | **2055.** IP 4128. |
| **1969.** IP 6319. | **1998.** IP 4013. | **2027.** IP 4556. | **2056.** IP 5211 b. |
| **1970.** IP 4398. | **1999.** IP 4569 c, d. | **2028.** IP 6006. | **2057.** IP 5000 a, b. |
| **1971.** IP 4409 b. | **2000.** IP 5228. | **2029.** IP 3996. | **2058.** IP 5026. |
| **1972.** IP 5213 a, b. | **2001.** IP 5967. | **2030.** IP 4504 a. | **2059.** IP 4310. |
| **1973.** IP 4506 b. | **2002.** IP 5006. | **2031.** IP 4572 d. | **2060.** IP 4313. |
| **1974.** IP 4545 a, b. | **2003.** IP 5015. | **2032.** IP 4394. | **2061.** IP 4275. |
| **1975.** IP 4383 a. | **2004.** IP 3982. | **2033.** IP 3994 b, c. | **2062.** IP 4127 a. |
| **1976.** IP 4524. | **2005.** IP 5002. | **2034.** IP 4298. | **2063.** IP 4307. |
| **1977.** IP 4503 a. | **2006.** IP 5004. | **2035.** IP 4255. | **2064.** IP 5201. |
| **1978.** IP 4393. | **2007.** IP 4062. | **2036.** IP 4295. | **2065.** IP 5001. |
| **1979.** IP 4520 b. | **2008.** IP 4978. | **2037.** IP 4378. | **2066.** IP 5047. |
| **1980.** IP 4563 b. | **2009.** IP 4501. | **2038.** IP 4546 a. | **2067.** IP 4072. |
| **1981.** IP 4569 a, b. | **2010.** IP 4506 a. | **2039.** IP 4502. | **2068.** IP 4001. |
| **1982.** IP 4496 a, b. | **2011.** IP 4119. | **2040.** IP 5003 a. | **2069.** IP 5279. |
| **1983.** IP 6297. | **2012.** IP 5014 a. | **2041.** IP 4305. | **2070.** IP 4409 a. |
| **1984.** IP 6329. | **2013.** IP 5267. | **2042.** IP 3946. | **2071.** IP 4503 b. |
| **1985.** IP 4334. | **2014.** IP 4520 a. | **2043.** IP 4309. | **2072.** IP 5014 b. |
| **1986.** IP 5157. | **2015.** IP 4238. | **2044.** IP 4299. | **2073.** IP 4495 b. |
| **1987.** IP 4110. | **2016.** IP 4064. | **2045.** IP 4170. | **2074.** IP 4496 c. |
| **1988.** IP 4120. | **2017.** IP 4308. | **2046.** IP 5010. | **2075.** IP 4887 b. |
| **1989.** IP 4127 b. | **2018.** IP 6116. | **2047.** IP 4376. | **2076.** IP 4078. |
| **1990.** IP 6027 a–g. | **2019.** IP 4384. | **2048.** IP 4014. | **2077.** IP 5846. |
| **1991.** IP 5969. | **2020.** IP 5317. | **2049.** IP 4493 b. | **2078.** IP 5925. |
| **1992.** IP 5986. | **2021.** IP 5249. | **2050.** IP 5059. | |
| **1993.** IP 5988. | **2022.** IP 4392. | **2051.** IP 4184. | |

## GROUP B. 2079–2332.

The second group of Palaimonion lamps comprises several subtypes, B-1–B-4, differing from the lamps of Group A in size, in the color of the clay, in the mode of manufacture, and particularly in the profile of the rim. Most of them are smaller than the lamps of Group A, and the clay is mostly dark brown, of rather hard, coarse, gritty consistency. There are some of brick-red color, but the difference may be due to firing rather than the mixture of the clay. In one variety of this group, Type B-2, the lamps are pale yellow in color, and most of these are covered with a dull, light brown or gray wash, much like that on the lamps of Type XVI A. In the lamps of Group B, as in Types A-4 and A-5, the central socket, in most cases at least, was made on the wheel in one piece with the bowl, not added separately, as in the other types of Group A. Because of this the socket rarely breaks away from the bowl at the base, as so often happens in Palaimonion Types A-1–A-3 and A-6. When it does break off, it usually takes with it a piece from the bottom of the bowl.

Another distinguishing feature of Group B is the greater height of the socket, which in most cases, except on B-1, extends above the level of the top of the bowl. This will be pointed out in the catalogue of the whole lamps of Group B. Lamps of Group B, with very few exceptions, have three narrow slits near the base of the socket, cut with a knife or some thin instrument without removing any part of the wall of the socket. The three slits are rarely vertical, and in some cases they are fairly close together on one side leaving the other side without oil-hole. With the exception of one transitional specimen, **2085**, the lamps of Group B have no proper rim, such as we have observed in nearly all the lamps of Group A. The walls of the bowls come up rather steeply and terminate in a blunt edge, sometimes with an inward curve at the top. Although there are relatively slight differences among the lamps of Group B, they are here arranged into four subtypes, distinguished mainly by size. This, however, is not true of B-1, of which there are only two complete examples, both larger than the others and differing from them in several particulars. Some of the fragments, preserving only the socket and classed as Group A of uncertain subtype, may indeed belong to B-1.

That Group B is later than Group A is obvious from the deterioration of the type, as shown by a gradual decrease in size, the disappearance of the rim, and the poorer quality of the fabric. This conclusion is corroborated by the provenance of the two groups. The lamps of Types A-1–A-4 and A-6 were found in large numbers in the lowest strata of the Palaimonion area, especially in the area east of the Temple of Palaimon. They came from the same context as lamps of Type XVI, both "glazed" and unglazed, and with them were many imported lamps of Types XXII–XXV. The Palaimonion lamps of Group A were produced throughout most of the 1st century after Christ. The transition from Group A to Group B took place in the second half of the 1st century of our era. The earlier lamps of Group B are to be dated in the late 1st or early 2nd century after Christ, and the group continued well into the 2nd century, at least as late as the middle of the century and probably into the second half.

PALAIMONION TYPE B-1. **2079–2081.**

The bowl of this type is of comparatively thin fabric, the walls of which rise more steeply than in the later lamps, but, like those, terminate in a blunt edge, forming no rim proper. The socket is very short, only about half as high as the depth of the bowl. The clay in the two nearly complete examples of this variety is of rather fine consistency, brick red in color, shifting to dark brown or gray in spots. This type, which in size compares with some of the smaller lamps of Group A, is transitional. Except for the fact that they have three gashes, rather than circular holes, they resemble the lamps of A-5a, which represent an earlier stage in the transition between Groups A and B.

**2079.** IP 1560. Pls. 7, 24. From Large Circular Pit, depth 1.60–2.20 m.
D. 0.150; H. 0.0635.
Much mended and restored. Dark brown and brick-red fabric, probably darkened by fire after it had left the potter's shop. Thin walls with no proper rim, but with a small lip set off from the walls by a shallow groove on the outside. Short, narrow socket with three small slits at the base.

**2080.** IP 1410. Pls. 7, 24. From Palaimonion, northeast corner of Sacrificial Pit C, lower deposit.
D. 0.145; H. 0.078.

Bowl mended and restored. Mottled red and brown clay, partly discolored by fire. Rather thin walls coming to a blunt edge with a lip, as in **2079**, and without a proper rim. Sides smooth on the outside and with prominent horizontal ridges on the inside. Short socket with walls growing thinner toward the top.
Date: A.D. 75–125; see *Isthmia* II, p. 102, note 8.

**2081.** IP 5324. From Temenos, west end of South Side.
Fragmentary. Very short socket, entirely preserved. Bright red clay, hard fabric with deep grooves on the inside of the bowl.

PALAIMONION TYPE B-2. **2082–2093.**

Palaimonion Type B-2 comprises a few lamps, all made with clay of a light color, pale yellow or grayish buff. At least three, and perhaps a fourth, had a dull gray wash, reminiscent of the surfacing of Type XVI A. These are the only examples of Palaimonion lamps with this kind of wash on the surface. In shape they differ little from B-3 and B-4, except that in several cases, **2083**, **2084**, and **2085**, the bottom has been trimmed after removal from the wheel. One example, **2085**, has a flat rim, projecting toward the outside; on all the others the sides come up to a blunt edge. In size they go with Type B-3 rather than with the smaller lamps of B-4.

**2082.** IP 1297. Pl. 24. From Palaimonion, upper deposit of Sacrificial Pit C.
D. 0.135; H. 0.0485.
Mended and partly restored. Pinkish buff clay. Curving sides coming to a blunt edge. Narrow, tapering socket, partly restored; three narrow slits at the bottom.
Date: ca. A.D. 125–150; see *Isthmia* II, p. 102, note 8.

**2083.** IP 1415. Pls. 7, 24. From Sacrificial Pit C, upper layer.
D. 0.125; H. 0.038.
Mended and partly restored. Buff clay with mottled, light brown surface consisting of a thin wash, like that on Type XVI A. Very shallow bowl, walls with blunt edge, and no rim proper. The base has been trimmed

with a deep groove, creating a kind of base ring (Pl. 24), which is not set off from the walls. Tapering, tall socket with three slits at the base.

**2084.** IP 996. Pl. 23. From Roman Altar Area.
Fragment, but socket complete. Reddish buff clay; thin orange-pink wash. The bottom has been trimmed with a deep groove and shaped into a base ring. Tapering, rather short socket, with three slits at base.

**2085.** IP 992. Pls. 7, 23. From Palaimonion, east of Temple, 2.00–1.00 m. above Stadium floor.
H. 0.0565.
Fragmentary. Pinkish gray, rather coarse clay. Curving walls, flattened at top to form narrow rim projecting toward the outside. Socket, largely missing,

had three oil-holes at the base. The base has been trimmed and is slightly concave underneath. This lamp is not a typical example of B-2. It has so much in common with Type A-5 that it could be classed as such; it marks the transition from A-5 to B-2.

**2086.** IP 4976. From Palaimonion, northeast of Temple, surface.

Socket and base preserved. Light red clay.

**2087.** IP 3944. Pls. 7, 26. From Temenos, South Side.

Socket and most of base preserved. Buff clay, orange-brown wash. Base trimmed to form ring.

**2088–2093.** Small fragments of Palaimonion Lamps B-2.

| | | |
|---|---|---|
| **2088.** IP 4974. | **2090.** IP 5325. | **2092.** IP 6210. |
| **2089.** IP 4239. | **2091.** IP 6165. | **2093.** IP 4237. |

PALAIMONION TYPE B-3. **2094–2110.**

Type B-3 is made up of lamps of rather heavy, coarse fabric of dark brown, less commonly red, color. Since several of these and also many lamps of B-4 came from Sacrificial Pit C, it is quite possible that the dark color is partly due to contact with fire in the pit rather than to the original firing in the potter's oven. The bowls are of medium size, considerably smaller than those of Group A, but somewhat larger than in the lamps of B-4. The central socket was made in the same process as the rest of the lamp and is comparatively high. In one case, **2094,** it extends 0.030 m. above the top of the bowl. In the others, however, the socket is lower, but in all the complete lamps of this type, it reaches somewhat higher than the top of the bowl. All have three narrow slits at the base of the socket. One lamp of this variety, **2096,** is of rather crumbly fabric that may have been damaged through the fire in the pit; its base is comparatively smooth and may have been trimmed.

Date: *ca.* A.D. 75–150.

**2094.** IP 1296. Pls. 7, 25. From Sacrificial Pit C, upper deposit.

D. 0.133; H. 0.051.

Bowl partly restored but socket complete. Dark gray clay of coarse fabric. Height of socket from bottom of bowl, 0.066 m. Walls with a slight inward curve and forming a blunt edge with no proper rim. Tall tapering socket with three narrow slits at bottom.

**2095.** IP 1032. Pls. 7, 25. From Palaimonion, Sacrificial Pit C.

D. 0.130; H. 0.040.

Mended but nearly complete. Coarse fabric, dark brown almost black color. Socket projecting well above the rim; three narrow slits.

**2096.** IP 1034. Pls. 7, 25. From Palaimonion, Sacrificial Pit C.

D. 0.135; H. 0.043.

Much mended but almost complete. Very coarse, dark gray clay, probably darkened in fire after being thrown into the pit. Curving walls with blunt edge. Tall socket with three narrow slits at the bottom.

**2097.** IP 1033. Pls. 7, 25. From Palaimonion, Sacrificial Pit C.

D. 0.128; H. 0.0405.

Mended but complete. Coarse dark gray clay probably darkened after firing; surface orange gray. Sides coming to a blunt edge. Socket projecting above level of rim; three narrow slits at base.

**2098.** IP 1010. From Palaimonion, Sacrificial Pit C.

Mended and part of bowl missing. Coarse fabric, dark brown clay with slightly lighter surface. Slightly incurving rim. Top of socket almost level with top of rim. Three narrow slits at the base.

**2099–2110.** There are 12 more fragmentary lamps of Type B-3.

| | | | |
|---|---|---|---|
| **2099.** IP 6176. | **2103.** IP 4333. | **2106.** IP 5284. | **2109.** IP 3943 |
| **2100.** IP 4926 (Pl. 26). | **2104.** IP 4640. | **2107.** IP 5423. | (Pls. 7, 26). |
| **2101.** IP 4297 (Pl. 26). | **2105.** IP 4514. | **2108.** IP 4510. | **2110.** IP 6097. |
| **2102.** IP 6350 a. | | | |

PALAIMONION TYPE B-4. **2111–2159.**

The lamps of B-4 are the smallest of the Palaimonion lamps and also the latest. One, **2119,** is only 0.0965 m. in diameter, as compared with the lamps of A-1–A-3, the largest of which is nearly twice as large, measuring 0.185 m. in diameter. Most of the well-preserved examples of B-4 came from the upper layer of Sacrificial Pit C; and several fragmentary lamps of this type came from the upper strata of the Large Circular Pit. The lamps of

B-4 differ from those of B-3 not in fabric and shape but only in size. In some cases, e.g. **2121**, the crumbly material and very dark color may well be due to the action of fire in the pit. The fabric of some is lighter in color, a reddish brown or gray, and a few fragmentary specimens are brick red. The central socket in all the well-preserved cases rises above the top of the bowl, but not as pronouncedly as in the lamps of B-3. In no case has the base been trimmed after removal from the wheel. A few fragmentary lamps of B-4 have only two slits in the socket, and two partly preserved sockets seem to have had no opening for the flow of oil. All the rest have three thin slits, like those of B-3.

**2111.** IP 1123. Pls. 7, 25. From Palaimonion, Sacrificial Pit C, upper layer.
D. 0.120; H. 0.042.
Mended and partly restored. Coarse, gritty fabric of dark gray and pinkish brown color. Shallow bowl with blunt edge and no proper rim. Tapering socket with three rather wide, irregular slits at the base.

**2112.** IP 1007. Pls. 7, 25. From Palaimonion, Sacrificial Pit C.
D. 0.116; H. 0.043.
Unbroken. Very heavy fabric, almost black in color. Sides with slight inward curve, terminating in a broad lip with no proper rim. Narrow socket projecting above level of the rim. Three thin narrow slits at the base.

**2113.** IP 1004. From Palaimonion, Sacrificial Pit C.
D. 0.121; H. 0.035.
Complete. Coarse, dark brown and gray clay with light brown, almost whitish surface in spots, possibly accidental discoloration. Shallow bowl coming to blunt edge. Tapering socket extending high above the rim, and three narrow slits at base.

**2114.** IP 1311. From Large Circular Pit, depth 0.10 m.
D. (0.117); H. 0.040.
One half of bowl and top of socket restored. Coarse fabric; dark gray color. Three slits at base of socket.

**2115.** IP 1031. From Palaimonion, Sacrificial Pit C.
D. 0.1185; H. 0.0395.
Mended but nearly complete. Very coarse, gritty fabric; dark gray and brown, almost black color, probably blackened after it had been thrown into the pit. Socket projects above level of rim; three narrow slits at the base.

**2116.** IP 1122. Pls. 7, 25. From Palaimonion, Sacrificial Pit C.
D. 0.123; H. 0.0385.
Mended and slightly restored. Coarse, gray and reddish brown clay. Shallow bowl with socket projecting considerably above the edge. Three slits at the base of the socket.

**2117.** IP 1005. From Palaimonion, Sacrificial Pit C.
D. 0.114; H. 0.043.
Bowl slightly mended. Coarse, dark brown and gray clay. Walls slightly incurving, forming a blunt lip at the top. Tapering socket extending above level of rim.

**2118.** IP 1299. From Palaimonion, Sacrificial Pit C, upper deposit.
D. 0.115; H. 0.035.
Slightly restored. Reddish brown and dark gray clay, probably discolored by fire in the pit. Tall socket with three narrow slits at the base.

**2119.** IP 854. Pls. 7, 25. From Palaimonion, 1.20 m. above Stadium floor.
D. 0.0965; H. 0.040.
Slightly restored. Reddish brown and dark gray clay; coarse fabric. Socket projects slightly above level of rim; three narrow slits at the bottom.

**2120–2159.** In addition to the nine lamps of Group B-4 described above, there are numerous other fragmentary examples that have been classified as B-4, although the distinction between B-4 and B-3, in the case of smaller pieces, cannot be sharply drawn. At least 40 examples, **2120–2159**, seem to go with B-4.

| | | | |
|---|---|---|---|
| **2120.** IP 1006. | **2130.** IP 6211. | **2140.** IP 5326. | **2150.** IP 4513. |
| **2121.** IP 1030. | **2131.** IP 5330. | **2141.** IP 5242. | **2151.** IP 6314. |
| **2122.** IP 1564. | **2132.** IP 5309. | **2142.** IP 4272. | **2152.** IP 6223. |
| **2123.** IP 1309. | **2133.** IP 5614. | **2143.** IP 5210. | **2153.** IP 5705. |
| **2124.** IP 1677. | **2134.** IP 4332. | **2144.** IP 5873. | **2154.** IP 5081. |
| **2125.** IP 1013. | **2135.** IP 5872. | **2145.** IP 4271. | **2155.** IP 4351. |
| **2126.** IP 1563. | **2136.** IP 3998. | **2146.** IP 5696. | **2156.** IP 5884. |
| **2127.** IP 1312. | **2137.** IP 6058. | **2147.** IP 4413 a, b. | **2157.** IP 6302. |
| **2128.** IP 1565. | **2138.** IP 5331. | **2148.** IP 5208. | **2158.** IP 5874. |
| **2129.** IP 1562. | **2139.** IP 5975. | **2149.** IP 5328. | **2159.** IP 5246. |

**2160–2332.**

These are numerous minor pieces, too small to show the subtype. Most of them belong to Types B-3 and B-4. Of these, 72 came from the Palaimonion. A large number lay scattered in the surface soil in the southwest sector of the Temenos, along the east end of the South Stoa, in the areas of the Roman Altar, the Southeast Propylon, and the Southeast House.[34] Others came from as far away as the Theater and the Early Christian Fortress. A very large number of fragments of Types B-3 and B-4 were picked up off the ground and thus have no meaningful provenance. They represent a late stage in the cult history of the Palaimonion. Lamps of these types must have been brought to the Sanctuary in very large numbers to have become mixed so liberally in the topsoil of the area.

| | | | |
|---|---|---|---|
| 2160. IP 6052. | 2204. IP 5481. | 2248. IP 5648. | 2292. IP 5163. |
| 2161. IP 5837. | 2205. IP 5402. | 2249. IP 3995. | 2293. IP 4878. |
| 2162. IP 5871. | 2206. IP 5407. | 2250. IP 5689. | 2294. IP 4663. |
| 2163. IP 6216. | 2207. IP 5656. | 2251. IP 4270. | 2295. IP 4877. |
| 2164. IP 5876. | 2208. IP 5707. | 2252. IP 4251. | 2296. IP 4904. |
| 2165. IP 5885. | 2209. IP 5483. | 2253. IP 3994 a. | 2297. IP 5306. |
| 2166. IP 5899. | 2210. IP 5482. | 2254. IP 5496. | 2298. IP 6004. |
| 2167. IP 4565. | 2211. IP 5414. | 2255. IP 4149. | 2299. IP 4701. |
| 2168. IP 5898. | 2212. IP 5183. | 2256. IP 4066. | 2300. IP 5322. |
| 2169. IP 6096. | 2213. IP 5364. | 2257. IP 4059. | 2301. IP 4639. |
| 2170. IP 5847. | 2214. IP 5349. | 2258. IP 4053. | 2302. IP 4682. |
| 2171. IP 5859. | 2215. IP 5323. | 2259. IP 3949. | 2303. IP 4913. |
| 2172. IP 6323. | 2216. IP 4320. | 2260. IP 5655. | 2304. IP 6003. |
| 2173. IP 4564. | 2217. IP 4240. | 2261. IP 5756 a, b. | 2305. IP 4876. |
| 2174. IP 4327. | 2218. IP 4203. | 2262. IP 4005. | 2306. IP 4875. |
| 2175. IP 6047. | 2219. IP 5327. | 2263. IP 4162. | 2307. IP 5394. |
| 2176. IP 6164. | 2220. IP 5365. | 2264. IP 5939. | 2308. IP 5984. |
| 2177. IP 6087. | 2221. IP 4235. | 2265. IP 4028. | 2309. IP 6342. |
| 2178. IP 6337. | 2222. IP 4254. | 2266. IP 3947. | 2310. IP 5985. |
| 2179. IP 5866. | 2223. IP 4317. | 2267. IP 5755. | 2311. IP 5259. |
| 2180. IP 5844. | 2224. IP 4196. | 2268. IP 4079. | 2312. IP 5286. |
| 2181. IP 4408. | 2225. IP 5209. | 2269. IP 5778. | 2313. IP 5285. |
| 2182. IP 6045. | 2226. IP 5609. | 2270. IP 4060. | 2314. IP 5229. |
| 2183. IP 6300. | 2227. IP 4024. | 2271. IP 4081. | 2315. IP 5244. |
| 2184. IP 4399. | 2228. IP 4233. | 2272. IP 4000. | 2316. IP 4838. |
| 2185. IP 4321. | 2229. IP 5366. | 2273. IP 4003. | 2317. IP 5245. |
| 2186. IP 6240. | 2230. IP 4165. | 2274. IP 4236. | 2318. IP 6007. |
| 2187. IP 4319. | 2231. IP 4287. | 2275. IP 5304. | 2319. IP 4684. |
| 2188. IP 4979. | 2232. IP 5203. | 2276. IP 5308. | 2320. IP 5979. |
| 2189. IP 6208. | 2233. IP 4289. | 2277. IP 5395. | 2321. IP 5998. |
| 2190. IP 4348. | 2234. IP 5351. | 2278. IP 4623. | 2322. IP 5287. |
| 2191. IP 4331. | 2235. IP 3999. | 2279. IP 5350. | 2323. IP 4903. |
| 2192. IP 5401. | 2236. IP 3950. | 2280. IP 5388. | 2324. IP 4927. |
| 2193. IP 5406. | 2237. IP 5041. | 2281. IP 5329. | 2325. IP 5999. |
| 2194. IP 5465. | 2238. IP 3997. | 2282. IP 5391. | 2326. IP 4911. |
| 2195. IP 4336. | 2239. IP 5690. | 2283. IP 5389. | 2327. IP 5260. |
| 2196. IP 5424. | 2240. IP 4017. | 2284. IP 4706. | 2328. IP 5243. |
| 2197. IP 5484. | 2241. IP 4234. | 2285. IP 5403. | 2329. IP 6022. |
| 2198. IP 5468. | 2242. IP 4171. | 2286. IP 4616. | 2330. IP 5083. |
| 2199. IP 5400 a, b. | 2243. IP 3948. | 2287. IP 4664. | 2331. IP 4982. |
| 2200. IP 5464. | 2244. IP 4065. | 2288. IP 5392. | 2332. IP 6001. |
| 2201. IP 5404. | 2245. IP 5561. | 2289. IP 4694. | |
| 2202. IP 5466. | 2246. IP 4063. | 2290. IP 4647. | |
| 2203. IP 5706. | 2247. IP 5685. | 2291. IP 4912. | |

[34] For the location of these buildings see *Isthmia* II, pp. 69, 73–78; and see below, Provenance and Distribution of Types, pp. 84–91.

# LAMPS OF ROMAN IMPERIAL TIMES, TYPES XX – XXVII

## TYPE XX. **2333–2335.**

The first type of molded lamp is of non-Corinthian origin. The fully developed lamps have a loop handle, made separately, and attached after the two halves of the body had been stuck together. The lower end of the handle was attached at the suture, and the upper end to the edge of the discus. There is usually a broad groove through the middle of the handle. The discus is small, plain, and deeply concave, and usually surrounded by two raised lines. The nozzle is small with rounded end and set off with double volutes on the top and with a single raised line underneath. A similar line encircles the base on which there is a large raised *alpha* with broken crossbar. The whole lamp, above and below the suture, except the nozzle and handle, is covered with rows of tiny globules, made from the mold. At the seam the globules were rubbed off when the two halves were joined.

Type XX is an Athenian product which was exported to Corinth in early Imperial times. Fragments of three molds for such lamps came from the Athenian Agora Excavations,[35] and in Athens the type is very common. No less than 210 are listed in *Agora* VII and the author states, with perhaps some exaggeration: "A conservative estimate would place the total number of moulds in the thousands, the lamps in the hundreds of thousands."[36] In her otherwise thorough discussion of these lamps, she does not refer to the fact that some lamps of Type XX lack both globules and the *alpha* (see below under **2333**).

Our collection of lamps from Isthmia contains only one certain fragment, **2334**, and two doubtful pieces of this type. The paucity may be explained by the fact that the type was in use chiefly during the period when the Isthmian Sanctuary was not functioning as a religious and agonistic center. In Corinth itself the type occurs somewhat more frequently. The founding of the Roman colony by Julius Caesar, probably in 44 B.C., led to a rapid rebuilding of the city during Augustus' reign; but the Isthmian Sanctuary seems to have been in neglect until the first decade of the Christian era, when the Isthmian Games were again held at Isthmia under Corinthian management.[37] Such evidence as we have points to a large-scale rebuilding of Isthmia later, perhaps in the time of Claudius.[38]

None of the fragments of Type XX from Isthmia came from a datable context. The distinguishing feature apart from the globules is the presence of the large A in relief on the reverse. This signature in much the same form is found on other molded lamps from the end of the 1st century B.C. and throughout the 1st century of the Christian era. Cf. *Agora* IV, Types 54 D, 58 B, etc. The evidence—admittedly meager—from Corinth and from Isthmia, would rather tend to show that Type XX was in use there in the early part of the 1st century after Christ.

**2333.** IP 4048 c. Pls. 9, 27. From Temenos, West End. W. (0.065); H. 0.034.

Handle, nozzle and part of body missing. Buff clay; reddish brown glaze. Plain rim separated from the deeply concave, plain discus by two raised lines. On the body are faint traces of dots that suggest globules. Slightly concave base, partly missing. This is either an early form of what eventually evolved into the A-Globule Type XX, or—more likely—a late copy made in a mold produced from a lamp with globules.

See *Corinth* IV, ii, p. 167, no. 382, fig. 93, which likewise has no globules and no *alpha*, and is clearly a late example of the type. This is probably true also of **2333**, although the clay and glaze are of good quality. The volutes and the raised lines that on other examples of Type XX set off the neck from the body may have been purposely rubbed off in the wet mold made from a normal A-globule lamp. This would then explain some uncertain traces of surface decorations.

**2334.** IP 3580. Pl. 27. From northwest of Temple of Poseidon.

Two adjoining fragments with part of the top and attachment of the handle preserved. Light red clay, light and dark brown glaze. On the rim are rows of small globules. A series of three raised lines surrounds the discus.

Cf. *Agora* VII, pp. 15–17, and nos. 418–627; *Corinth* IV, ii, nos. 372–382. Since my publication of the Corinth lamps in 1930, which includes eleven lamps of Type XX, only one lamp of this type (L 4161) has been inventoried at Corinth.

**2335.** IP 4294. From Temenos, west end of South Side.

Small fragment from lower part of lamp. Buff clay, light and dark brown glaze. On the body are rows of dots which seem to have resulted, as in **2333**, from rubbed-off globules, but the type is not certain.

---

[35] *Agora* VII, pp. 107–108, nos. 439–441.
[36] *Agora* VII, p. 15.
[37] *Isthmia* II, p. 67, note 2.
[38] *Isthmia* I, pp. 100–102; *Isthmia* II, pp. 21, 67; Gebhard, *The Theater at Isthmia*, p. 63.

## TYPE XXI. **2336–2347.**

The lamps of Type XXI are mostly large, decorative lamps, the characteristic feature of which is an attachment above the handle. This may have originated as a reflector in use on lamps made of metal, but on the terracotta lamps it is purely ornamental. There are two varieties that differ in shape and more particularly in fabric.

### TYPE XXI A. **2336–2340.**

Several of the lamps of this type from Corinth and Athens are made of ash-gray or grayish brown clay, covered with a black metallic glaze. It is likely that they were produced in imitation of metal lamps. Compare *Corinth* IV, ii, no. 383, and *Agora* VII, no. 16. Only a few fragmentary examples came from Isthmia.

**2336.** IP 2975. Pls. 8, 27. From Southeast House.
H. 0.070.

Several fragments of a large decorative lamp, preserving parts of top, nozzle and base, and one complete side knob. Gray clay; dark gray, almost black, glaze. Inside unglazed. The lamp resembles the better-preserved *Corinth* IV, ii, no. 383, pl. VIII, but has only one nozzle with volutes. On the neck is an indistinct design. Plain, flat rim with two grooves encircling the discus, which is decorated with a rosette. The one preserved side knob, a purely decorative feature, is a nearly rectangular piece but somewhat wider at the end than at the attachment, and in the top are seven grooves. The handle attachment has been conjecturally restored from the Corinth lamp. Unlike the latter, the Isthmia lamp has no vent hole at the base of the nozzle. Raised base ring.

Cf. *Corinth* IV, ii, no. 383; *Agora* VII, pl. 2, no. 16; *Argos*, pl. 5, no. 209. A fragmentary lamp of the same kind was found in the Athenian Agora, in a cistern filled up "not long after the middle of the 1st century after Christ"; *Agora* V, pp. 22, 37, pl. 47, G 149. It is likely that the lamp is a great deal earlier, inasmuch as a highly decorative—and consequently costly—vessel of this kind would have been in use over several decades before being discarded.

**2337.** IP 3649. Pl. 27. From northwest of Temple of Poseidon.

Fragments of the underside from front part of large decorative lamp. Ash-gray clay; dark gray, metallic glaze. Long narrow neck; high base ring.

**2338.** IP 2640. Pl. 27. From northwest of Temple of Poseidon.

Part of nozzle of large decorative lamp. Ash-gray clay; black, metallic glaze, which tends to peel off. The top of the neck has a deep groove at either edge extending to the wick-hole.

**2339.** IP 2666. Pls. 11, 27. From Temenos, North Side, 0.25–0.00 m. above Stadium floor.

Fragment of large lamp preserving parts of base and side, together with one side knob and part of one volute. Brownish gray clay with black, metallic glaze. Within the base ring is preserved part of a signature engraved in the wet clay. Perhaps: Δα[μ] ίπ[π] ο[υ] ?

**2340.** IP 3556. Pl. 27. From Northeast Cave.

Handle attachment with part of the handle preserved. Dark gray clay, apparently unglazed, but perhaps covered with a thin wash. The attachment is in the form of a poorly executed palmette with rudimentary spirals at the base.

### TYPE XXI B. **2341–2347.**

Lamps of the second variety are made of light red or buff clay and are usually glazed. There are fragments of at least six examples of this kind from Isthmia. One, **2341 A**, was a very large lamp, but the fragments are small.

**2341.** IP 109 + IP 308. Pl. 27. From Temple of Poseidon and North Temenos Dump.

Two fragments of handle attachment of a very large lamp. Reddish brown clay; dark brown glaze. The handle is pierced with a hole, 0.011 m. in diameter. The smaller fragment (IP 308), which does not join the larger piece (IP 109), has been attached to it with plaster. The design consists of two spreading leaves held together with a double slip knot. In the space between the two leaves, just below the break, there was some object that looks like the nose of an animal with prominent nostrils, but was probably part of the floral design.

**2341 A.** IM 2205. Pl. 27. Found at west end of South Stoa.
L. of head 0.045.

Horse's head, almost certainly from the same lamp as **2341**.

Reddish brown clay, good brown glaze, slightly darker than the color of the clay. The head is completely preserved, attached to a piece from the left side of the lamp. On the top side the features of the head are very carefully rendered. The mane consists of flame-like locks. The ear, the eye, and the headgear are reproduced in relief; and to the left of the ear are three small globules, presumably indicating some decorative feature of the bridle. The details on the other side of the head, i.e. the underside of the lamp, are roughly indicated by impressed lines.

**2342.** IP 105. Pl. 27. From North Temenos Dump.

Small fragment from nozzle of large decorative lamp. Reddish brown clay; dark brown glaze on the outside, reddish brown on inside. Preserved is only part of the flat rim round the wick-hole and the volute on the right side, with a triangular neck design between the two volutes. This too may be part of the lamp **2341**; the clay is of a slightly darker color, yet the glaze is very similar. It seems unlikely that there was a second decorative lamp of jumbo size, and that two of its fragments should be found in the same place.

The lamp must have resembled a better-preserved lamp from Corinth published in *Corinth* IV, ii, pl. IX, no. 409, but the Isthmia lamp was somewhat smaller. The Corinth lamp has now been more completely restored and is shown here in Plate 39. The handle attachment on the lamp from Isthmia was different, and it may be that the discus had a different design. The details of the head from Isthmia are more meticulously rendered. The clay and glaze of the two lamps are very much alike, and it seems a safe conclusion that both were produced in the same shop, probably in Italy.

A lamp from Herculaneum of the same type but with different discus is illustrated in Loeschcke, p. 223, fig. 3.

**2343.** IP 321. Pl. 27. From Temenos, west end of North Side.

Handle attachment. Reddish buff clay; no glaze preserved. On the face is an indistinct leaf in very low relief.

**2344.** IP 1967. Pl. 27. From Palaimonion, east of Temple, 0.45 m. above Stadium floor.

Small part of rim and discus from near the nozzle. Reddish brown clay; dark brown glaze. Very narrow rim with a row of globules. The discus seems to have been decorated with a shell pattern.

For the rim and shoulder volute, compare *Corinth* IV, ii, no. 453, fig. 103, which has plain discus, however.

**2345.** IP 3519. Pl. 27. From Temple of Poseidon, east side.

Nozzle of large lamp. Buff, crumbly clay; no glaze preserved. On top two grooves extend to diamond-shaped nozzle.

**2346.** IP 4040. Pls. 11, 27. From Northwest Dump.

Small fragment from bottom of lamp. Buff clay; reddish brown glaze. Within the base ring was a signature of which only one short, slanting stroke remains.

**2347.** IP 4038. Pl. 27. From Northwest Dump.

Small fragment from top of lamp. Preserved is one spiral of a shoulder volute and a small part of the rim. Buff clay with thin reddish brown glaze.

## TYPE XXII. **2348–2371.**

There is only one complete lamp, **2348**, of Type XXII from Isthmia, but several fragmentary examples can be recognized as belonging to the type. They are circular lamps, usually without handle and with a nozzle set off from the rim with shoulder volutes. The nozzle has a triangular termination. The rim is narrow and has one or more grooves, enframing the discus, which usually carries a relief. On the earlier specimens the band at the outer edge of the rim is comparatively narrow and those have a base ring. On the later lamps of the type the base is flat and set off from the sides by a groove. The clay comes in a variety of colors and the surface on the outside is always glazed, usually in some shade of brown.

Type XXII was produced throughout the 1st century after Christ. The lamps of this type are probably all imported, most of them from Italy. At Isthmia this type of lamp came from the earliest strata in the Palaimonion area, chiefly in the space east and northeast of the Temple of Palaimon, where the fill goes back to the early years of the 1st century of our era. From the same context came Palaimonion lamps of Group A and many Type XVI lamps. Relative dates within the type are indicated chiefly by the rim profile. See Loeschcke, p. 213 and fig. 2; and cf. *Corinth* IV, ii, pp. 76–78. In *Agora* VII lamps of this type, nos. 36, 48, 67, have been dated in the early 1st century after Christ.

**2348.** IP 827. Pls. 9, 27. From Southeast Propylon Area.

L. 0.096; D. 0.0695; H. 0.027.

Complete, except for a small break on the base. Reddish buff clay; light brown glaze, shifting to red. Circular body with narrow rim and grooves around the discus. Broad triangular nozzle with shoulder volutes. On the discus is a horseman to left mounted on the nearer of two horses; rather indistinct design.

The scene seems to be the same as in *Corinth* IV, ii, pl. XXV, no. 442.

**2349.** IP 6187. Pls. 9, 27. From Palaimonion.

L. 0.094; W. 0.0695; H. 0.026.

Fragmentary. Light buff clay; thin light brown glaze. No handle. Narrow rim with double groove surrounding the discus. On discus, relief of lion running to right.

For the design, cf. Loeschcke, pl. XII, no. 202.

**2350–2366.** Small fragments of Type XXII.

| | | | |
|---|---|---|---|
| **2350.** IP 5643. | **2355.** IP 5129. | **2359.** IP 6155. | **2363.** IP 4835. |
| **2351.** IP 5558. | **2356.** IP 4019. | **2360.** IP 5632. | **2364.** IP 6234. |
| **2352.** IP 6040. | **2357.** IP 4463 b. | **2361.** IP 4281 b. | **2365.** IP 4793. |
| **2353.** IP 4956. | **2358.** IP 5128. | **2362.** IP 5551 b. | **2366.** IP 4973. |
| **2354.** IP 6151. | | | |

**2367.** IP 929. Pl. 27. From Palaimonion, 0.25 m. above
Stadium floor.
D. 0.075.

Several fragments of a lamp, probably Type XXII.
Preserved are most of the discus, parts of rim and side,
and most of the base. Reddish buff clay; light brown
glaze on top, shifting to red on the bottom. Flat,
slightly raised base. Double groove on the rim. On the
discus, an indistinct figure, probably Dionysos (possibly
a maenad) holding a thyrsos or scepter in his left hand,
his right arm crossing his chest. There seems to be a
wreath of flowers or leaves round the head. He was
probably represented as seated on a throne, the top
of which appears faintly on the left side of the head.

**2368.** IP 1096. Pl. 27. From Palaimonion Area.

Fragment probably of Type XXII, preserving most
of the discus, parts of the rim and one shoulder volute.
Reddish buff clay; dark brown glaze. On the discus
with triple groove is the picture of a barking dog to
the left.

For the design, cf. Loeschcke, pl. XIII, no. 274.
First half of 1st century after Christ.

**2369.** IP 81. Pl. 27. From North Temenos Dump.

Part of discus and rim of large lamp, probably of
Type XXII. Greenish buff clay; brown glaze. Rim with
double groove surrounding the discus. There is a
picture of Pegasos to right, standing in front of what
appears to be a smoking censor, but by analogy with
similar pictures is meant to be a tree growing out of
a kantharos. Above his head is a circular shield, and
there was another object, probably a rectangular shield,
at the edge of the break, just above the rump. On the
chest of the horse is a cross.[39]

**2370.** IP 4488. From Palaimonion, east of Temple,
0.60–0.30 m. above Stadium floor.

Fragment preserving about half of rim, side, and
part of bottom. Reddish buff clay; brown glaze,
largely rubbed off. On the bottom is a depression which
could be part of a signature, but is probably accidental.

**2371.** IP 5225. From Palaimonion, Temple Area, *ca.*
1.00–0.60 m. above Stadium floor.
W. 0.075.

Two joined fragments. Preserved is most of the rim
and part of a shoulder volute. Buff clay, darkened in
fire; thin brown glaze.

## TYPE XXIII. 2372–2441.

Type XXIII is characterized by double volutes and nozzle with rounded end; rim usually somewhat wider
than in Type XXII; discus rarely plain, commonly decorated with relief; flat or slightly concave base. Most
of the lamps are without handle; but one fragment, **2374**, has a handle. Like all other relief lamps, Type XXIII
consists of two halves, each made in a separate mold and the two put together while the clay was soft. When
there is a handle, it too has been made in the molds, and has grooves. The seam between the two halves can be
seen on the inside; on the outside it was smoothed over before the lamp was glazed and fired. There are only
a few fragments from Isthmia that have the complete nozzle with double volutes indicative of the type. Others,
which preserve only the shoulder volutes and could thus be either Type XXII or XXIII, have been grouped
with the latter.

The lamps of Type XXIII were imported to Corinth, mostly from Italian centers. They are made of red or
brown clay and covered with glaze of good quality. A few examples with indistinct reliefs, e.g. **2386, 2387**, are
made of buff clay and have poor brown glaze that has largely rubbed off. These may be local copies out of molds
made from imported lamps.

The date of Type XXIII is about the same as that of Type XXII, and the lamps of the two types came from
the same contexts. The shape of the rim indicates that most of them are to be dated in the first half of the 1st
century after Christ.

---

[39] A figure of Pegasos in the Corinth collection (*Corinth* IV, ii, no. 428, fig. 100) has a similar cross on the chest; and
the same symbol appears on a lamp from Vindonissa (Loeschcke, pl. XVI, no. 199). Presumably these marks have the
same significance as the rosettes that are found on horses on Classical vases, there usually on the haunches. For a discussion
with references to some examples see *Hesperia* 6, 1937, p. 472, note 2.

**2372.** IP 2618. Pl. 28. From Temenos, North Side.

Fragment preserving complete nozzle and two double volutes. Red clay, bright red glaze. Three grooves surround the discus, which probably had a relief.

**2373.** IP 3960. Pl. 28. From Northwest Reservoir.

Nozzle and part of discus and rim preserved. Grayish brown clay; mottled light and dark brown glaze. Very narrow rim and three grooves surrounding the discus, slight traces of a relief of uncertain nature.

**2374.** IP 121. Pls. 9, 28. From North Temenos Dump.
 D. 0.069; H. 0.022.

| | |
|---|---|
| **2375.** IP 5597. | **2378.** IP 430. |
| **2376.** IP 5379. | **2379.** IP 4543. |
| **2377.** IP 5589. | **2380.** IP 5725. |

**2386.** IP 649. Pls. 9, 28. From Palaimonion.
 L. (0.109); W. (0.075); H. 0.0235.

Poorly preserved lamp put together out of many fragments and partly restored. Crumbly buff clay; dark brown glaze, largely peeled off. On the rim a narrow plain band on the outer edge and double groove surrounding discus. The relief consists of an erotic *symplegma*, very indistinct. The scene seems to be the same as in Loeschcke, pl. VIII, nos. 95 and 412.

**2387.** IP 785. Pls. 9 (discus only), 28. From Palaimonion, middle section.
 L. (0.101); D. (0.072); H. 0.022.

Part of right side and most of nozzle restored. Enough is preserved to show that the nozzle had a rounded end and thus that the lamp does not belong to Type XXII. Buff clay; brown and red glaze, poorly

End of nozzle and most of the base missing, part of the top restored. Red clay; hard, mottled red and brown glaze of good quality. Both shoulder volutes preserved; on the neck is an air-hole. Rim consists of a rather broad, flat band and two grooves round the discus. Handle with double groove above the suture, single below. On the discus is the figure of a rabbit to right, munching on a leafy plant.

Loeschcke, p. 403, pls. III, no. 512, and XIII, no. 663, says that the rabbit is eating grapes.

**2375–2385.** Small fragments of Type XXIII.

| | |
|---|---|
| **2381.** IP 4753 b. | **2384.** IP 6255. |
| **2382.** IP 5522. | **2385.** IP 5452. |
| **2383.** IP 5588. | |

preserved. The rim consists of a plain band and a double groove surrounding the discus. Shoulder volutes, mostly restored. Slightly concave reverse. On the discus is a chariot with driver and two galloping horses to left, very indistinct. No handle.

For the relief, cf. *Agora* VII, pl. 3, no. 65.

**2388.** IP 4140. From Temenos, west end of North Side.
 W. 0.080; H. 0.030.

Fragmentary, but probably Type XXIII; one shoulder volute and attachment of handle preserved. Reddish brown clay; dark brown glaze. Plain rim and triple groove around deeply concave, plain discus. Concave base with circular blob near the center.

**2389–2441.** Small fragments of Type XXIII.

| | | | |
|---|---|---|---|
| **2389.** IP 4734. | **2403.** IP 4481 b. | **2416.** IP 4547 d, e. | **2429.** IP 5105. |
| **2390.** IP 2578. | **2404.** IP 4481 c. | **2417.** IP 4834. | **2430.** IP 4789. |
| **2391.** IP 4487 (Pl. 28). | **2405.** IP 4964. | **2418.** IP 5795. | **2431.** IP 4871. |
| **2392.** IP 6252. | **2406.** IP 4365. | **2419.** IP 6148. | **2432.** IP 4954. |
| **2393.** IP 6036. | **2407.** IP 4952. | **2420.** IP 5633. | **2433.** IP 6261. |
| **2394.** IP 6039. | **2408.** IP 6203. | **2421.** IP 4873. | **2434.** IP 5343 a. |
| **2395.** IP 4620. | **2409.** IP 6156. | **2422.** IP 5634. | **2435.** IP 6235. |
| **2396.** IP 6088. | **2410.** IP 6128. | **2423.** IP 5103. | **2436.** IP 6147. |
| **2397.** IP 4773. | **2411.** IP 5961 b. | **2424.** IP 6042. | **2437.** IP 1917. |
| **2398.** IP 4747 a. | **2412.** IP 6245. | **2425.** IP 6149. | **2438.** IP 5275. |
| **2399.** IP 5084. | **2413.** IP 4816. | **2426.** IP 6250. | **2439.** IP 5241 a. |
| **2400.** IP 4484. | **2414.** IP 6248. | **2427.** IP 4209 a. | **2440.** IP 4491 d. |
| **2401.** IP 4037. | **2415.** IP 6351. | **2428.** IP 4132 b. | **2441.** IP 6237 c. |
| **2402.** IP 5205. | | | |

## TYPE XXIV. 2442–2457.

Type XXIV differs from XXIII chiefly in the nozzle which is without shoulder volutes; the rim continues on the neck and (except on Type XXIV C) terminates in single volutes at the nozzle. The rim is wider and the discus correspondingly smaller than in Types XXII and XXIII. In some cases, where the discus carries elaborate reliefs, as in **2442**, the rim is narrower, and yet wider than in Types XXII and XXIII. Nearly all the lamps of Type XXIV have moldmade handles. The date is later than that of the preceding two types, but Type XXIV still comes within the 1st century after Christ, chiefly in the second and third quarters.

Type XXIV came to Corinth from Italy, but some lamps like **2444** and **2445** are probably of local make. There are four varieties of Type XXIV.

TYPE XXIV A. **2442–2444.**

This is the most common variety, but at Isthmia there are so few lamps of Type XXIV that the relative frequency of the four varieties does not represent the true proportions. Type XXIV A is best represented by **2442** and **2444**. For the shape see Plates 9 and 28 and descriptions of individual lamps.

**2442.** IP 3484. Pl. 9, 28. From Temenos, East End.
L. (0.102); W. 0.074; H. (0.0335).

Put together out of many fragments and partly restored, with parts of the relief and of the reverse missing. Red clay; red and brown glaze. Handle with double groove above suture, plain below; volutes at the nozzle partly preserved. Comparatively narrow, plain rim and three grooves surrounding the discus. Imported. The relief, not very clear, shows a procession to left with soldiers carrying standards; in the middle the figure of a horse to left, partly broken away, but there was no horseman. There is a similar lamp from Pozzuoli in the British Museum, completely preserved and with sharp features. Walters (pl. XXIII, no. 788) correctly interprets the relief as follows: "Within a border of stamped egg-pattern, a horse victorious in a race. The horse walks to left, preceded by two beardless men in short chiton, one of whom carries a standard on which are indications of an inscription; the other leads the horse which has a wreath round his neck. Behind it walk three similar men, the first with uplifted hands, the other two carrying palm branches. In the background is incised ROMA. Underneath a stamp, COPPI." The lamp from Isthmia preserves no parts of the inscriptions mentioned by Walters.

**2443.** IP 2212. Pl. 28. From Palaimonion, South Building.
D. 0.067; H. 0.031.

Fragment; front part missing; the type is probably XXIV A. Light red clay with red and brown glaze, which has largely disappeared. Broad, slanting rim with single groove surrounding discus. Handle with double groove both above and below the suture. On the discus is preserved the upper part of what appears to be a floral design.

**2443 A.** IP 5903. Pl. 28. From Palaimonion, east of Temple, 0.60–0.30 m. above Stadium floor.

Fragment preserving parts of rim, discus, and side. Light red clay; reddish brown glaze. Three grooves surround discus, which carried some representation, probably a floral design.

**2444.** IP 5060. Pls. 9, 28. From North Temenos Dump.
L. (0.105); W. 0.072; H. 0.0385.

Mended; handle and parts of body restored. Light red clay; brown glaze, which has largely peeled off. Plain, wide rim, separated from the small undecorated discus by a single groove. This is probably a local copy of the imported lamps of Type XXIV.

Cf. *Corinth* IV, ii, pl. X, no. 467.

TYPE XXIV B. **2445–2449.**

The second variety of Type XXIV has crescent-shaped side lugs; in other respects it is similar to XXIV A. It rarely has reliefs on the discus.

**2445.** IP 958. Pl. 9. From North Temenos Dump.
L. (0.100); D. (0.075); H. 0.030.

Most of nozzle and part of left side restored. Buff clay; light brown and red glaze. Handle with large hole and double groove above suture, plain below. Broad, slanting rim with triple groove around plain discus. Air-hole and one nozzle volute preserved. On the sides are crescent-shaped lugs with grooves. From the type of clay one might conclude that this is a locally made lamp, but more probably it is imported.

For the shape, cf. *Agora* VII, pl. 4, no. 80.

**2446.** IP 4481 d. Pl. 28. From Palaimonion, east of Temple, 1.35–1.00 m. above Stadium floor.

Small fragment preserving side lug and part of rim. Buff clay; brown glaze.

This and **2447** probably belong to Type XXIV, but side lugs are not limited to Type XXIV B. See, for example, *Délos* XXVI, pl. 31, no. 4650.

**2447.** IP 6251. Pl. 28. From Palaimonion, east of Temple, 1.35–1.00 m. above Stadium floor.

Small fragment preserving side lug and part of rim. Reddish buff clay; red glaze over a coat of white. The side lug is pierced.

This is an example of the rather rare red-on-white lamps.[40]

---

[40] For discussion see below under Type XXV, footnote 42.

**2448.** IP 6260. From Palaimonion, east of Temple, 1.00–0.60 m. above Stadium floor.

Side lug and parts of base and body preserved. Buff clay; traces of brown glaze. This may be of local make.

**2449.** IP 4950. From Roman Altar Area.

Parts of rim and of both side lugs preserved. Buff clay; brown glaze.

TYPE XXIV C. **2450, 2451.**

On the third variety of Type XXIV the discus is elongated, and the rim is usually decorated with oblique leaf design. There are no volutes, properly speaking, but the rim turns out at the nozzle which has a triangular termination.

**2450.** IP 320. Pl. 9. From Temple of Poseidon, east end of cella.

L. *ca.* (0.102); W. 0.0715; H. 0.033.

Many adjoining fragments preserving most of the top, the handle and part of the nozzle, and a small part of the base. Light red clay; orange-brown glaze. Handle with large hole, and double groove above, plain below. Elongated top with small plain discus. On the rim a series of leaves, separately impressed in the wet clay, and circles stamped on either side of the neck. Air-hole in channel leading to the wick-hole.

Flat, elongated base, set off by single groove. Probably imported.

Cf. *Corinth* IV, ii, pl. X, no. 474. Lamps of the same general shape, without glaze, were made in Corinth in the 2nd century.

**2451.** IP 6253. From Palaimonion, east of Temple, 0.60–0.30 m. above Stadium floor.

Fragment of lamp, probably like **2450** with impressed leaf design. Light red clay; reddish brown glaze.

TYPE XXIV D. **2452, 2453.**

A fourth variety of Type XXIV, of which there are only two fragments from Isthmia, has a broad rim with a raised tongue pattern terminating toward the nozzle with a spiral, also in relief. The discus is very small and plain, set off from the rim by a series of grooves. This type of lamp, very rare in Greece, is explained by Loeschcke, pp. 229–230, as going back to Hellenistic forms of decoration. It has, in fact, much in common with Corinth Types XVIII and XIX. See, for example, *Corinth* IV, ii, pl. VI, no. 367, and pp. 21 and 67, fig. 29, no. 50. A more remote example is *Agora* IV, pl. 49, no. 654, which came from a context of about 100 B.C.

**2452.** IP 4242. Pl. 28. From Temenos, North Side.

Top of lamp, right half. Light red clay; orange-red glaze. Broad rim with elongated tongue pattern and spirals at shoulder, all in relief. Small plain discus within triple groove.

Cf. *Corinth* IV, ii, pl. XXV, no. 458.

**2453.** IP 6256. Pl. 28. From Palaimonion, east of Temple, 0.60–0.30 m. above Stadium floor.

Small fragment of lamp like the preceding, with part of the tongue pattern and spiral on left side preserved. Buff mealy clay; the glaze has disappeared.

**2454–2457.** Fragments of Type XXIV of uncertain subtype.

**2454.** IP 2732.          **2455.** IP 4609.          **2456.** IP 5534.          **2457.** IP 2615.

## TYPE XXV. **2458–2516.**

Of Type XXV there are several certain examples and a large number of fragments that are probably to be ascribed to this type but cannot be clearly distinguished from Type XXIV. Some have handles; others do not. A single example, **2458**, has a base ring; the others have a flat base, sometimes slightly raised. Most of the lamps of Type XXV resemble the other imported lamps, Types XXII–XXIV, in fabric. There is one exception, a nearly complete lamp, **2461**, which is made of mealy, almost white clay. This can hardly be from the same production centers as the others. The fabric is unique among the lamps from Isthmia, and the lamp has other peculiar features. The pale yellow clay of Corinth, characteristic of the locally made lamps, is different.[41] A favorite discus decoration on most lamps of Type XXV is the rosette; but some have more elaborate reliefs, and many have a plain discus. The distinguishing feature of the type is the rather small, rounded nozzle without volutes.

---

[41] There are, however, a few late Roman or Christian lamps from Corinth, the clay of which resembles that of **2461** in color, but not in quality. The author of *Agora* VII, pp. 17–18, discussing Athenian lamps of the 3rd and 4th centuries after Christ, emphasizes the fact that Athenian lampmakers at first imitated the Corinthian models, not only in shape and decoration but in fabric. She speaks of Attic lamps "of a creamier white than ever appears in Corinthian lamps of the Roman period."

Sometimes it is roughly heart-shaped; in other cases it has a broad flat top that extends across the rim to the edge of the discus, like the nozzle of Type XXVII A–C. Other variations of nozzle occur on lamps in other collections. The rim is often plain but usually wider than on Types XXII–XXIV; others have ovules or an oblique leaf pattern. The latter were always impressed after the top part came out of the mold, whereas the ovules came from the molds themselves.

Many of the lamps and fragments of Type XXV from Isthmia are doubtless imports from the foreign centers that produced Types XXII–XXIV, but some are of local make. It is this type in particular that forms the transition from the imported relief lamps with glazed surface of the 1st century after Christ to the superb Corinthian lamps with no glaze, Type XXVII, that dominated the Greek market in the 2nd century. During the era of imitation the foreign lamps were in many cases so successfully copied that it is difficult to tell the locally made products from the imports. In general, the clay of imported lamps is red, and the glaze a red or reddish brown of good quality that adhered well to the surface. A few pieces belong to the red-on-white group of imported relief lamps.[42] The clay of the locally made lamps is of a lighter red or buff color and the glaze is thinner and tends to rub off. But there are many border cases in which the two classes of lamps are difficult to distinguish. And, of course, the imported lamps did not all come from the same region or even from the same part of the ancient world; and differences in the color of the clay and glaze are to be expected even among the products from the same lampmaking center.

**2458.** IP 1915. Pls. 10, 28. From Palaimonion, east of Temple, 0.25 m. above Stadium floor.

L. 0.088; D. 0.075; H. 0.027.

Complete, except for slight break at edge of wick-hole. Brick-red clay; bright red glaze. Vertical handle made separately and attached to edge of rim. Ovules on rim; rosette with fourteen petals on the discus within a single groove. Small, almost circular nozzle. Raised base ring. Imported.

Probable date, second half of 1st century after Christ.

**2459.** IP 860. Pls. 10, 28. From Palaimonion, 0.60 m. above Stadium floor.

L. 0.0905; D. 0.065; H. 0.0265.

Complete. Brick-red clay; bright red glaze. Grooved handle made in the mold. Plain rim set off from discus by double groove. On the discus, rosette with eight pointed petals. Large heart-shaped nozzle; circular base with two indistinct depressions, probably a misshapen *planta pedis*.

Cf. *Agora* VII, pl. 5, no. 130, which, however, has no handle; and see *Délos* XXVI, pl. 30, no. 4624, which is signed by the prolific lamp firm of Romanesis.

**2460.** IP 892. From Palaimonion, 0.70 m. above Stadium floor.

L. 0.092; D. 0.077; H. 0.026.

Most of the top and much of the base missing. Red clay; light red and brownish glaze. Rim consists of plain outer band and two grooves surrounding discus, which may have been decorated with relief of which

nothing remains. Small, semicircular nozzle. Slightly raised base; no handle.

For the shape compare *Agora* VII, pl. 5, no. 126, which has a handle, however; dated in the second half of the 1st century after Christ.

**2461.** IP 955. Pls. 10, 11, 28. From Palaimonion, 0.20 m. above Stadium floor.

L. 0.087; D. 0.075; H. 0.023.

Much mended and partly restored, but almost complete lamp. White mealy clay which seems to be unglazed. The rim has an egg-and-dart pattern, an elaborate variation of the common ovules. Plain discus within series of grooves and raised rings. Very small, almost circular nozzle, at the base of which are two raised circles with a dot in the center. Slightly raised, flat base with stamped *planta pedis*. No handle.

**2462.** IP 2632. Pl. 28. From north of Temple of Poseidon.

H. 0.028.

Fragment of imported relief lamp. Red clay; bright red glaze. Handle with double groove above, plain below. Plain rim with triple groove surrounding discus. The discus carried a relief, of which only slight traces remain. Slightly raised base.

**2463.** IP 5883. Pl. 28. From East Temenos Wall.

Fragment preserving the handle and parts of rim and discus. Light red clay; red glaze. Imported.

**2464–2467.** Five fragments of Type XXV, too small to merit description.

[42] Lamps with red-on-white glaze appear in limited numbers at Corinth (*Corinth* IV, ii, p. 86, nos. 508, 511, 518, 519) and more frequently in Athens (*Agora* VII, nos. 155–204); they are very sparingly represented among the lamps from Isthmia. Three fragments, one, **2447**, of Type XXIV, and two, **2468, 2469**, probably of Type XXV, clearly belong to that category. Judith Perlzweig (*Agora* VII, pp. 5–6), who made an extensive study of these lamps, came to the conclusion that the factories for the red-on-white lamps probably were located in Ephesos or in a nearby town. That is probably correct; if so, we must assume that other relief lamps besides the red-on-white were imported to Corinth from Asia Minor factories in the 1st century after Christ. Much remains to be done in tracing the provenance of these Asia Minor lamps and the extent of their exportation to Greece.

**2464.** IP 4044.     **2465 A.** IP 4791.     **2466.** IP 2288.     **2467.** IP 5584.
**2465.** IP 1137.

**2468.** IP 6021. Pl. 28. From Palaimonion.
Fragment of rim and handle of red-on-white ware. Imported. For this and **2469** see footnote 42.

**2469.** IP 4010. From Temenos, North Side.
Fragment of base of red-on-white lamp. Imported.

**2470–2516.** Other small fragments of Type XXV.

| | | | |
|---|---|---|---|
| **2470.** IP 4481 a. | **2482.** IP 5626 (Pl. 28). | **2494.** IP 4190 b. | **2506.** IP 4610. |
| **2471.** IP 4547 b. | **2483.** IP 2660. | **2495.** IP 5023 a. | **2507.** IP 5765. |
| **2472.** IP 214. | **2484.** IP 4009. | **2496.** IP 4190 a. | **2508.** IP 5043. |
| **2473.** IP 2617 b. | **2485.** IP 1918. | **2497.** IP 5109. | **2509.** IP 313. |
| **2474.** IP 4211. | **2486.** IP 5577. | **2498.** IP 6154. | **2510.** IP 4108. |
| **2475.** IP 5377. | **2487.** IP 4743. | **2499.** IP 4657. | **2511.** IP 6257. |
| **2476.** IP 4249. | **2488.** IP 4872. | **2500.** IP 5569. | **2512.** IP 6055. |
| **2477.** IP 6239 b. | **2489.** IP 4732. | **2501.** IP 5978 (Pl. 28). | **2513.** IP 6077. |
| **2478.** IP 1916. | **2490.** IP 1919. | **2502.** IP 1151. | **2514.** IP 5056. |
| **2479.** IP 5048. | **2491.** IP 4106. | **2503.** IP 5019. | **2515.** IP 5600 (Pl. 28). |
| **2480.** IP 2617 a. | **2492.** IP 4965. | **2504.** IP 5528 (Pl. 28). | **2516.** IP 4998. |
| **2481.** IP 4733. | **2493.** IP 5239. | **2505.** IP 5042. | |

### TYPE XXVI. Factory Lamps and Related Forms. 2517–2520.

Type XXVI, the so-called factory lamp, is poorly represented in Greece, and is all but absent among the lamps from Isthmia. The transitional fragment, **2517**, is almost certainly imported. Two other fragments, **2518** and **2519**, seem to be from lamps of Type XXVI. The nozzle, **2518**, is an imported piece. One other small piece, **2520**, from the top of a lamp, may to belong to the Argive type with triangular handle. One such lamp was published in *Corinth* IV, ii, pl. XI, no. 532. There are no examples of this type among the published lamps from the Athenian Agora, but the comparatively small collection from Argos contains no less than 19 such lamps. Anne Bovon, *Argos*, p. 40 and nos. 232–250, was certainly right in attributing the type to Argos. She dated the type chiefly in the 1st century after Christ, but thought that it may have extended into the 2nd century. The Corinth lamp has rather high lugs on the rim, and that feature shows the relation of the Argos type to the factory lamps. The lamps from Argos, however, and two unpublished lamps from Corinth (L 4241 and L 4229, Pl. 40, k) lack the lugs; they may represent a later development than the published Corinth example. These lugs led to the formation of the rim panels that characterize Type XXVII C and D.

**2517.** IP 309. Pl. 28. From gully northwest of Temple of Poseidon.
Handle and part of rim preserved. Light red clay; bright red and brown glaze. Moldmade handle with large hole. Ovules and side knobs on the rim. The discus was sunken and surrounded with an almost vertical high edge, as on the regular factory lamps. There appears to have been a raised base ring most of which is missing.

This appears to be an imported lamp of unusual form, a combination of Types XXV and XXVI. The ovules on the rim it has in common with Type XXV; they do not occur on the fully developed factory lamps of Type XXVI. The knob on the rim and the sunken discus are characteristic of Type XXVI.

**2518.** IP 2766. Pl. 28. From Northeast Area.
Nozzle of lamp, probably of Type XXVI. Light red clay; reddish brown glaze. Imported. There are no volutes, but a raised ridge extending from the discus surrounds the flat top of the nozzle. This kind of nozzle occurs on factory lamps; see Loeschcke, p. 446, fig. 36, nos. 996, 998, and pl. I, nos. 997, 999.

**2519.** IP 4210 a. Pl. 28. From Temenos, West End.
Fragment from top of lamp. Light red clay; reddish brown glaze. Broad rim with part of panel preserved, and depressed plain discus. The type is not absolutely certain, but most likely XXVI. A completely preserved factory lamp from Corinth (L 4217) is shown on Plate 40 (j).

**2520.** IP 4094. From Later Stadium, surface fill.
Small fragment from top of lamp. Buff clay; reddish brown glaze. The lamp had a broad, plain rim and a deeply concave discus. This fragment is too small to show for certain to which type it belongs, but it looks like the Argos type with triangular handle.

For a discussion of the Argos type, see introductory remarks above.

## FRAGMENTS (FROM THE DISCUS) OF TYPES XXII–XXVI. 2521–2780 A.

**2521.** IP 2064. Pl. 28. From west of Temple of Poseidon.

Part of discus. Buff clay; light brown glaze. Discus with bearded male head in profile to left. The discus design is the same as Loeschcke, pl. VII, no. 395. This is a Herakles head, or perhaps an emperor represented as Herakles.

**2522.** IP 1048. Pl. 28. From Palaimonion Area, 0.90–0.70 m. above Stadium floor.

Part of discus. Buff clay; dark brown glaze. On discus, bust of Selene, front face.

Cf. Loeschcke, pl. XVII, no. 638.

**2523.** IP 5713. Pl. 29. From Palaimonion, east of Temple, 0.70–0.10 m. above Stadium floor.

Fragment of discus with relief of some object that I cannot interpret.

**2524.** IP 4031. Pl. 29. From North Temenos Dump.

Part of the top of a lamp. What remains of the relief seems to be a wing, perhaps of Eros or Nike.

**2525.** IP 5107. Pl. 29. From Palaimonion, northeast of Temple.

Fragment of discus with figure of Eros riding on lion (?).

**2526.** IP 3007. Pl. 28. From Temenos, West End.

Part of discus. Reddish buff clay; dark brown glaze. Discus design consists of small draped figure seated on elephant to right.

Cf. *Corinth* IV, ii, p. 181, fig. 108, no. 502; and *Agora* VII, pl. 7, no. 228, where other references are given.

**2527.** IP 1057. Pls. 9, 28. From Palaimonion Area.

Most of discus preserved. Mealy red clay; light red glaze. On the discus, indistinct figure of centaur to right with kantharos on his shoulder.

**2528.** IP 4129. Pl. 29. From Temenos, west end of North Side.

Fragment of discus. Grayish buff clay; slight traces of brown glaze. Preserved is rear part of sphinx to left.

**2529.** IP 1938. Pl. 29. From Palaimonion, Semicircular Gate Foundation.

Fragment of discus. Light gray clay; dark brown glaze. On the discus, nude figure advancing to right, perhaps part of gladiatorial scene. His stance is much like that of the figure in **2530**, and of the gladiator on the right in Loeschcke, pl. IX, no. 122, but a trace of the filling-hole on our fragment shows that he was in the left half of the discus.

**2530.** IP 1059. Pl. 29. From Roman Altar Area.

Part of discus. Mealy reddish clay; red and brown glaze, poorly preserved. On the discus, male figure striding toward right, probably gladiator. The pose is the same as that of **2529**, but in this case he is on the right side of the filling-hole. There can hardly have been a second gladiator.

**2531.** IP 4262. Pl. 29. From Temenos, North Side.

Fragment of discus. Light brown clay; brown glaze. Preserved is figure striding to right with drapery over his left arm. The pose is almost the same as on **2529** and **2530**, but he cannot represent a gladiator. Possibly Herakles, but too indistinct to make identification certain.

**2532.** IP 6123. Pl. 29. From Palaimonion, Temple Area.

Fragment of discus. Reddish buff clay; thin brown glaze. Figure of gladiator wearing greaves and holding rectangular shield in left hand. There was a second figure on the right side of the filling-hole, but only a slight trace of him is preserved. For the pose of single gladiator, cf. Loeschcke, pl. X, no. 435.

**2533.** IP 5666. Pl. 29. From Palaimonion, northeast of Temple.

Fragment of discus. Light red clay; brown glaze. Preserved on right side of filling-hole is a figure to left, probably gladiator.

**2534.** IP 2663. Pl. 29. From north of Temple of Poseidon.

Fragment of discus. Reddish gray clay; dark brown glaze. The design consists of an erotic *symplegma*; male reclining on couch and woman seated above.

The scene is the same as in Loeschcke, pl. VIII, no. 423.

**2535.** IP 6233. Pl. 29. From Palaimonion, northeast of Temple.

Fragment of discus. Pale buff, mealy clay; no glaze preserved. All that remains of the picture is the tail of a dolphin.

**2536.** IP 1080. Pl. 29. From Palaimonion Area.

Fragment of discus. Reddish buff clay; brown glaze. Design, rather indistinct, consists of an animal galloping to right.

**2536 A.** IP 1060. Pl. 29. From Roman Altar Area.

Fragment of discus. Reddish buff clay; traces of brown glaze. On the discus, figure of cock to right.

Cf. *Agora* VII, pl. 6, no. 171, which is slightly different. Loeschcke, pl. XIII, no. 523, seems to have the same figure as ours.

**2537.** IP 905. Pl. 29. From Palaimonion, middle section, 1.25 m. above Stadium floor.

Small fragment of discus. Pale reddish clay; light reddish brown glaze. On the discus forepart of animal, probably lion, galloping to right.

**2538.** IP 1049. Pl. 29. From Palaimonion Area.

Fragment of discus. Red clay; bright red glaze. Kantharos with floral stalks hanging down on either side and rising from the center. This is a rather common design, but details differ. Cf. *Délos* XXVI, pl. 29, no. 4596, and pl. 30, no. 4625.

**2539–2780 A.** Smaller fragments of lamps of Types XXII–XXVI.

| | | | |
|---|---|---|---|
| **2539.** IP 6140. | **2583.** IP 4946 a, b, d. | **2627.** IP 4192. | **2671.** IP 4006. |
| **2540.** IP 4892. | **2584.** IP 5432 a, b. | **2628.** IP 4212. | **2672.** IP 4115. |
| **2541.** IP 3009. | **2585.** IP 6239 c–e. | **2629.** IP 4200. | **2673.** IP 4953. |
| **2542.** IP 2552. | **2586.** IP 4281 a. | **2630.** IP 5829. | **2674.** IP 6244. |
| **2543.** IP 1933 (Pl. 11). | **2587.** IP 5962 a, b. | **2631.** IP 6118. | **2675.** IP 4185. |
| **2544.** IP 2816. | **2588.** IP 4141 c. | **2632.** IP 4771. | **2676.** IP 6254. |
| **2545.** IP 5248. | **2589.** IP 6237 a, b. | **2633.** IP 6263. | **2677.** IP 4822. |
| **2546.** IP 6145. | **2590.** IP 6265 a, b. | **2634.** IP 5053. | **2678.** IP 4805. |
| **2547.** IP 4951. | **2591.** IP 5241 b. | **2635.** IP 4191. | **2679.** IP 4187. |
| **2548.** IP 4041. | **2592.** IP 5343 b. | **2636.** IP 4523. | **2680.** IP 4671. |
| **2549.** IP 4723. | **2593.** IP 6238 a, b. | **2637.** IP 4105. | **2681.** IP 4544. |
| **2550.** IP 6129. | **2594.** IP 5946 a. | **2638.** IP 5629. | **2682.** IP 5619. |
| **2551.** IP 5251. | **2595.** IP 5542 b, c. | **2639.** IP 5020. | **2683.** IP 5852. |
| **2552.** IP 5587. | **2596.** IP 6188 a, b. | **2640.** IP 5667. | **2684.** IP 4548. |
| **2553.** IP 4216. | **2597.** IP 4482 a–c. | **2641.** IP 5204. | **2685.** IP 4135. |
| **2554.** IP 5130. | **2598.** IP 4944 a–c. | **2642.** IP 4388. | **2686.** IP 4285. |
| **2555.** IP 4036. | **2599.** IP 4483 b. | **2643.** IP 5220. | **2687.** IP 6231. |
| **2556.** IP 4284. | **2600.** IP 4857 b. | **2644.** IP 5750. | **2688.** IP 5104. |
| **2557.** IP 4107. | **2601.** IP 4491 a–c. | **2645.** IP 4972. | **2689.** IP 4492. |
| **2558.** IP 4542. | **2602.** IP 5961 a. | **2646.** IP 4096. | **2690.** IP 5216. |
| **2559.** IP 5342. | **2603.** IP 5551 a. | **2647.** IP 4991. | **2691.** IP 4485. |
| **2560.** IP 6152. | **2604.** IP 4132 a, c. | **2648.** IP 4801. | **2692.** IP 5830. |
| **2561.** IP 6236. | **2605.** IP 4213 c. | **2649.** IP 4148. | **2693.** IP 6085. |
| **2562.** IP 6117. | **2606.** IP 5023 b. | **2650.** IP 4151. | **2694.** IP 5913. |
| **2563.** IP 5572. | **2607.** IP 4210 b. | **2651.** IP 6090. | **2695.** IP 5912. |
| **2564.** IP 5224. | **2608.** IP 6262. | **2652.** IP 6232. | **2696.** IP 4672. |
| **2565.** IP 5058. | **2609.** IP 5641. | **2653.** IP 4962. | **2697.** IP 4087. |
| **2566.** IP 4772. | **2610.** IP 5463. | **2654.** IP 6048. | **2698.** IP 4804. |
| **2567.** IP 4133. | **2611.** IP 4486. | **2655.** IP 6247. | **2699.** IP 5902. |
| **2568.** IP 4490. | **2612.** IP 4043. | **2656.** IP 5718. | **2700.** IP 5298. |
| **2569.** IP 4243. | **2613.** IP 4186. | **2657.** IP 6146. | **2701.** IP 4792. |
| **2570.** IP 5583. | **2614.** IP 5719. | **2658.** IP 5748. | **2702.** IP 6073. |
| **2571.** IP 6227. | **2615.** IP 5582. | **2659.** IP 5050. | **2703.** IP 6153. |
| **2572.** IP 6074. | **2616.** IP 5625. | **2660.** IP 6249. | **2704.** IP 5630. |
| **2573.** IP 5933. | **2617.** IP 6169. | **2661.** IP 4113. | **2705.** IP 5543 a, b. |
| **2574.** IP 6217. | **2618.** IP 4144. | **2662.** IP 4035. | **2706.** IP 4547 a, c. |
| **2575.** IP 5968. | **2619.** IP 4269. | **2663.** IP 4032. | **2707.** IP 4102. |
| **2576.** IP 6037. | **2620.** IP 5493. | **2664.** IP 5420. | **2708.** IP 4134. |
| **2577.** IP 6002. | **2621.** IP 4201. | **2665.** IP 6124. | **2709.** IP 5542 a. |
| **2578.** IP 4802. | **2622.** IP 6150. | **2666.** IP 4856. | **2710.** IP 5946 b. |
| **2579.** IP 4658. | **2623.** IP 4042. | **2667.** IP 6008. | **2711.** IP 5127. |
| **2580.** IP 4178. | **2624.** IP 4774. | **2668.** IP 4039. | **2712.** IP 6100. |
| **2581.** IP 5881. | **2625.** IP 4175. | **2669.** IP 6229. | **2713.** IP 4209 b. |
| **2582.** IP 5567. | **2626.** IP 5573. | **2670.** IP 6041. | **2714.** IP 4306. |

| | | | |
|---|---|---|---|
| **2715.** IP 4673. | **2732.** IP 6142. | **2749.** IP 5378. | **2766.** IP 5354. |
| **2716.** IP 5492. | **2733.** IP 5599. | **2750.** IP 5593. | **2767.** IP 4172. |
| **2717.** IP 2723. | **2734.** IP 6264. | **2751.** IP 5598. | **2768.** IP 4070. |
| **2718.** IP 5444. | **2735.** IP 5870. | **2752.** IP 4489. | **2769.** IP 5934. |
| **2719.** IP 6213. | **2736.** IP 4141 a. | **2753.** IP 5724. | **2770.** IP 6201. |
| **2720.** IP 4817. | **2737.** IP 4385. | **2754.** IP 4145. | **2771.** IP 3975. |
| **2721.** IP 3985. | **2738.** IP 6259. | **2755.** IP 6143. | **2772.** IP 5108. |
| **2722.** IP 4137. | **2739.** IP 6246. | **2756.** IP 5628. | **2773.** IP 4261. |
| **2723.** IP 5031. | **2740.** IP 4244. | **2757.** IP 5527. | **2774.** IP 4549. |
| **2724.** IP 5057. | **2741.** IP 3956. | **2758.** IP 5991. | **2775.** IP 4034. |
| **2725.** IP 5749. | **2742.** IP 4142. | **2759.** IP 5977. | **2776.** IP 4131. |
| **2726.** IP 6011. | **2743.** IP 5631. | **2760.** IP 4747 b. | **2777.** IP 4139. |
| **2727.** IP 4753 a. | **2744.** IP 4220. | **2761.** IP 3981. | **2778.** IP 4832. |
| **2728.** IP 4257. | **2745.** IP 4008. | **2762.** IP 4245. | **2779.** IP 5221. |
| **2729.** IP 5580. | **2746.** IP 4112. | **2763.** IP 5486. | **2780.** IP 5189. |
| **2730.** IP 3992. | **2747.** IP 6144. | **2764.** IP 5469. | **2780 A.** IP 4379. |
| **2731.** IP 6243. | **2748.** IP 4608. | **2765.** IP 4533. | |

## TYPE XXVII. **2781–2963.**

Type XXVII is a local Corinthian product which was exported extensively to other parts of Greece and even to very distant places. The lamps are made of the pale yellow, sometimes pink, Corinthian clay; and nearly all are unglazed. Like most relief lamps, they were made in double molds, one half for the top and the other for the bottom. Both the nozzle and the handle were made in the molds. The two halves were then stuck together while the clay was soft. On the inside the suture can be clearly seen, but on the outside the edges were trimmed before the lamp was fired.[43] The hole through the handle, as well as the wick-hole, was made after the lamp had been taken out of the molds. Many of the lamps have signatures, which were incised on the reverse before firing. The published lamps of Type XXVII from Corinth are divided into four groups, three of which are represented at Isthmia by a few whole lamps, but mostly by fragments; the fourth is almost entirely lacking. To these groups I shall add a fifth, of which there are one nearly complete example and small fragments of others in the Isthmia collection.

The development of the type took place about the turn of the 1st to the 2nd centuries of our era, and the type continued to be made throughout the 2nd century and well into the 3rd. By the beginning of the 3rd century Type XXVII had deteriorated, and soon thereafter the center of the lamp industry was shifted to Athens.

The origin of Type XXVII presents some problems. It appears at Corinth as a fully developed product of superior craftsmanship in the early years of the 2nd century. The author of *Agora* VII, p. 7, explains this phenomenon by suggesting that the Corinthian lampmakers "began imitating Italian glazed lamps as early as the third quarter of the 1st century, and that they produced a good many lamps of Broneer types XXIII, XXIV, XXV and XXX." This is partly correct. That such imitation took place has been pointed out above under Type XXV. But this leaves some questions still unanswered. Of the imported lamps, only Type XXV is closely related in shape to the Corinthian Type XXVII, and that only to one of its varieties, XXVII A. The lamps of Type XXVII B, C, D, and E have no close analogies among the imported relief lamps of the 1st century. The side panels on the rim of Type XXVII C were doubtless borrowed from the factory lamps, Type XXVI (see above, p. 61), which, so far as we know, were not produced in Corinth and only sparingly imported there. It is a significant fact that the lamps of the Argos type with triangular handle that were found at Argos (*Argos*, nos. 232–250, pl. 6) have no rim panels, but a single lamp of the same type from Corinth (*Corinth* IV, ii, pl. XI, no. 532) has rudimentary panels. Two other specimens from Corinth, L 4229 (Pl. 40, k) and L 4241, of the same type and of non-Corinthian fabric, lack the rim panels. We may conclude from this that the lamp in *Corinth* IV, ii, no. 532, is a local imitation of the Argive lamps, made perhaps shortly before the evolution of Type XXVII C.

A likely link between Type XXVII and the imported relief lamps is presented by a series of lamps from North Africa. Among the lamps published by Johanna Brants there are three specimens (pl. VII, nos. 1036, 1038, 1040) like our Type XXV, but with knobs on the rim. The author says that they are of Greek origin, though

---

[43] For a sketch showing how lamps were made in the molds and stacked in the oven, see Lepikowna, p. 56, fig. 31. The illustration seems to have been lifted out of Fremersdorf, pp. 67–75, figs. 66, 69, 71. In the lamp pictured there, however, the making of the handle is rather like that on Type XVI. In most molded lamps the handle was shaped solid and pierced after the molds had been removed.

found at North African sites. In the recent publication of the lamps from Carthage by Jean Deneauve, there are many lamps of that kind (pls. LXXX–LXXXI, nos. 878–898). Most of these have two knobs—not panels—on the rim, mostly on the cross axis, but sometimes (nos. 878, 898) closer to the nozzle than to the handle, as is the case on many of the factory lamps. These are grouped under his Type VII C, which the author characterizes as "Lampes à protuberances sur le marli." Many have Latin signatures. The nozzle is very much as on our Type XXV. A single fragmentary lamp from Isthmia, **2517**, probably also of Type XXV, but included in the small heterogeneous collection with Type XXVI, had ovules and raised panels, or rather knobs, on the rim. It is probably an imported lamp and may be regarded, like the lamps from North Africa and Xanten, as transitional between Type XXV and the factory lamps, on the one hand, and Type XXVII on the other.

Whatever were the successive steps that led to the creation of Type XXVII, especially XXVII C, we have to recognize in the creation of these lowly utilitarian objects of markedly artistic quality one evidence for the renaissance of arts and crafts that Greece experienced in the 2nd century of the Christian era, and more specifically during the reign of Hadrian. At such junctures in the history of human progress creativity rises to a pitch that defies logical explanation. The impossible becomes commonplace. This is a very different phenomenon from the flourishing of Athenian lampmaking in the 3rd century of our era, which began as a closely imitative process. At that period Corinthian lamps of Type XXVII were first imported into Athens in quantities, and these were so neatly copied by the Athenian lampmakers that, except for the type of clay, the earliest Athenian lamps would be almost indistinguishable from the Corinthian products.[44]

The development of Type XXVII has been fully discussed in *Corinth* IV, ii, pp. 83–88, and 90–102; and in *Agora* VII, pp. 6–9.[45] The lamps from Isthmia of Types XXV and XXVII are too few and too unrepresentative to form the basis for a fruitful review of the observations made in these studies. The details of development of the five varieties of Type XXVII and their relative and absolute chronology should be studied at Corinth itself, which was the home of Greek lampmaking from the end of the 1st century into the 3rd century of our era. The excavations there have brought to light a large number of lamps of Type XXVII since my publication of *Corinth* IV, ii. There are about 80 inventoried pieces in the Corinth collection and probably many more fragments kept among the pottery. These have come from carefully controlled excavations with all the stratigraphic information recorded. Many lamps of this type, both published and unpublished, have been discovered at other recent excavations in Greece. The type has found its way to many sites in Greece proper: Delos,[46] Delphi,[47] Nikopolis,[48] Patras,[49] Sparta,[50] and many others; and to such remote places as Alexandria in Egypt,[51] Salona and Spalato in Dalmatia,[52] Cyprus,[53] and to several sites in Italy and Asia Minor.[54] A complete

---

[44] See for example *Agora* VII, pl. 15, nos. 634, 649, 671; pl. 17, nos. 748, 751; pl. 19, nos. 838, 844.

[45] Two articles dealing with these lamps have been published by members of the French School in Athens: Gérard Siebert, "Lampes corinthiennes et imitations au Musée National d'Athènes," *B.C.H.* 90, 1966, pp. 472–513; and Philippe Bruneau, "Lampes corinthiennes," *B.C.H.* 95, 1971, pp. 437–501.

[46] W. Deonna, *B.C.H.* 32, 1908, pp. 133–136; Bruneau, pl. 31, nos. 4655–4662.

[47] P. Perdrizet, *Fouilles de Delphes* V, pp. 188–192; Bruneau, *B.C.H.* 95, 1971, pp. 460–479.

[48] Nikopolis has produced the most representative collection of Type XXVII outside Corinthian sites and Athens. In a cursory glance at the collection we counted well over 40 examples—and there are numerous other fragments—many of them with signatures of well-known makers. Some that were discovered in the 1920's were published by A. Philadelpheus, and these are referred to in *Corinth* IV, ii, pp. 91, no. 1; 93, no. 6. They were originally stored away in Preveza before the small Museum was constructed at Nikopolis. Many others came from more recent excavations at Nikopolis.

[49] Some Type XXVII lamps in the Patras collection are included in Bruneau's article, *op. cit.* (above, footnote 47), pp. 479–492.

[50] For the remarkable collection of lamps in the Sparta Museum, see below, footnote 54.

[51] In the Lucas Benachi collection from Egypt, now in the National Museum in Athens, there are several lamps of our Type XXVII. At least three appear to be genuine products of Corinthian manufacture. Two belong to XXVII A: one (no. 745) has the signature Ἀντωνίου, the other (no. 750) has Κρησκέντος on the reverse. A third (no. 747), without signature, is a fine specimen of Type XXVII C, with a discus figure of a sphinx, very similar to—but not identical with—that of *Corinth* IV, ii, pl. XXVII, no. 628. A fourth example, also XXVII C, with an erotic scene on the discus and no signature, is more likely a non-Corinthian product. There are other examples of Type XXVII in the collection, some with signatures of non-Greek names but in Greek letters. Those are obvious Egyptian imitations of the imported Corinthian lamps. I am deeply indebted to my long-time friend, Lucas Benachi, and to the Ephor, Barbara Philippaki, for the privilege of seeing and making cursory study of this superb collection of lamps, which still awaits publication.

[52] See *Corinth* IV, ii, p. 93, notes 2 and 3.

[53] D. M. Bailey, *Opus. Athen.* VI, 1965, pl. VIII, nos. 161–163.

[54] There are lamps of Type XXVII in most European collections, but only rarely are there reliable records of their provenance. Mercando, pl. VI, 1, 2, shows two Corinthian lamps, signed Loukiou and Preimou, but does not state where they came from. Lerat, pl. IX, 80, 81, shows two lamps of our Type XXVII, presumably found at Besançon itself. Szent.

record of all this material, together with available data, is an urgent desideratum;[55] it must precede a full study of the origin and development, the distribution, and chronology of these lamps, which mark the perfection of lampmaking in Greece during Roman Imperial times.

TYPE XXVII A. **2781–2795.**

The rim of Type XXVII A is sometimes plain; more commonly it is decorated with stamped ovules, but lacks the panels found on subtypes C and D. In most cases the ovules were stamped in the mold, but occasionally, if the mold was worn, such details appear to have been retouched after the molds had been removed. The discus is nearly always decorated with rays but occasionally it is plain. Besides the filling-hole, there is always a small air-hole at the edge of the discus, close to the nozzle.[56] One slight feature which distinguishes the earlier from the later lamps of the type is the double groove on the handle. On the earlier lamps, particularly on subtype A, these grooves are limited to the top half of the handle; below the suture the grooves are lacking. This would seem to indicate that the grooves were made in the top half of the mold, but not in the lower half. Some specimens have one or more impressed circles or an X at the bottom of the handle.

Type XXVII A is the first variety of the type to have come into existence. This is shown by its close resemblance to Type XXV and by the peculiarities of the handle shown above. The other subtypes, B–E, made their appearance not much later, and after they had been perfected all the varieties seem to have been produced simultaneously. The production of one of the subtypes was not limited to a single shop; this is shown by the presence of several signatures on any given variety. The relief lamps of Types XXII–XXV, whether imported or locally made, disappeared from the market as soon as Type XXVII became available. This is shown by the absence of this type in the nests of lamps found at floor level in the Palaimonion. These contained lamps of the locally produced Palaimonion Type and of Type XVI, and many imported relief lamps of Types XXII–XXV. Sacrificial Pit C, which continued in use well into the 2nd century, contained the large cult lamp **2843** of Type XXVII E.

---

records a lamp in the Debrecen Deri Museum (Hungary), no. 171, which the author says is our Type XXVIII, but color of clay (creamy yellow, unpainted) and signature (Ὀλυμπίου) show that it is Type XXVII. Cardaillac, p. 70, fig. 77, shows a lamp of our Type XXVII in his collection of lamps from North Africa. Iconomu, p. 22, fig. 42, has a late example of Type XXVII B, and many Attic lamps of Type XXVIII, in Dobrogea, Rumania. Menzel has a Type XXVII C lamp, no. 537, which he says is from Miletos; another was (fig. 47:7) signed by the Corinthian maker Φλάβιος. The author (p. 82) thinks that such Latin names on Greek lamps were copied from the factory lamps, but very few factory lamps have been found in Corinth.

Wherever Type XXVII was imported from Corinth it was imitated and modified by local manufacturers. That process is best illustrated in Athens, where, to quote from *Agora* VII, p. 51, "Attic lamp makers—in the early 3rd century—blindly imitated Corinthian models." Copying and retouching seem to have been practiced on a large scale in Cyprus; see Bailey, *op. cit.* (above, footnote 53), pp. 15–17. In one case, his pl. VIII, no. 162, he says that "the Cypriote maker apparently copied the shape from an imported Corinthian or Athenian lamp and the scene [gladiators] from an imported Italian lamp, the dates of which could, but need not, be more than a century apart." The most remarkable instance of such copying is illustrated by a unique, as yet unpublished, collection of some 200 lamps, found at Sparta, briefly mentioned in Δελτίον 19, 1964 (Athens, 1966), Χρονικά, p. 145, pls. 145, 146. All, or nearly all, are blackened by a fire that destroyed the building in which they were found. This cannot be anything but a lamp factory specializing in copies of lamps of widely differing periods. There are 21 whole, and probably fragments of many more, lamps of Type XXIV, with a gladiatorial scene, underneath which is the signature Γαίου. (The name occurs also as signature on lamps of Type XXVII; *Corinth* IV, ii, nos. 706, 717; *Agora* VII, p. 7, note 17; and on a lamp from Cyprus, now in the British Museum, Walters, no. 1105.) The originals from which these were copied are not later than about the middle of the 1st century after Christ. Many came from the same mold. Most numerous are the copies of Type XXVII B, of which there are at least 87, plus numerous fragments. Many carry the signatures of Sekoundos, Loukios, Posphoros; but since the lamps have not been washed only a few signatures can be read. There are many imprints from molds of Type XXVII C with various discus decorations. There are also lamps with plain rim and discus and without signatures. The latest are lamps of Type XXVIII A of Athenian manufacture, many with some form of erotic *symplegma* and the signature of Pireithos. The originals of which these are copies are to be dated in the first half of the 3rd century of our era. From a cursory look at the collection, one gets the impression that they were all produced about the same time in molds taken from imported lamps, most of them Corinthian and Athenian but some of Italian origin. They must have been stacked on shelves when the fire broke out. Thus the originals from which the molds were made differ in date by as much as two centuries.

[55] Specialized studies like those of Siebert, *B.C.H.* 90, 1966, pp. 472–513, and Bruneau, *B.C.H.* 95, 1971, pp. 437–501, and the more general publications such as the *Athenian Agora* VII and *Corinth* IV, ii, cover the ground in part, but much more is needed to include all the sites where lamps of Type XXVII have been discovered. It would constitute an important chapter on the economics, commerce, and artistic activities of Corinth during the 2nd and 3rd centuries after Christ.

[56] For the significance of this feature, see *Corinth* IV, ii, pp. 9–16.

**2781.** IP 2325. Pl. 30. From Northwest Reservoir, Manhole 4.

W. 0.079.

Front part and base missing. Light red clay with pinkish buff surface; no glaze. Molded handle with grooves in upper half only. Ovules on rim; rays on discus; air-hole.

**2782.** IP 1965. Pl. 30. Early Christian Fortress.

Fragment with handle, parts of rim, and discus preserved. Light gray clay. The handle has double grooves both above and below the suture; it terminates in a sharp point, and on its end and on either side are stamped circles. Ovules with double outline on the rim; rays on the discus, all very sharp.

**2783.** IP 2667. From Northeast Area, depth *ca.* 1.10 m.

Fragment preserving parts of rim and discus of lamp similar to **2782**. Ash-gray clay shifting to pinkish color in center of discus.

**2784–2795.** Small fragments of Type XXVII A.

| | | | |
|---|---|---|---|
| **2784.** IP 2840. | **2787.** IP 2292 (Pl. 30). | **2790.** IP 5258. | **2793.** IP 4174. |
| **2785.** IP 2669. | **2788.** IP 2623. | **2791.** IP 4080 a. | **2794.** IP 4206. |
| **2786.** IP 6352. | **2789.** IP 4177. | **2792.** IP 5427. | **2795.** IP 5429 a, b. |

TYPE XXVII B. **2796–2821.**

The lamps of XXVII B have a vine pattern with leaves and clusters of grapes on the rim and rays on the discus. There seems to be no variation in these features. The handle is like that on XXVII A, except that in all extant examples the grooves extend both above and below the suture. Several of these lamps have signatures that were incised with a pointed instrument while the clay was still wet. The deterioration of the lamps of this variety is clearly shown by comparison of the two lamps with the signature of Euporos, **2796** and **2797**, in which all the features are sharp, with the later specimens of the same subtype, **2801**, signed Posphorou, and **2800**, signed Eugodou. The latter two are to be dated in the 3rd century.

**2796.** IP 1960. Pls. 10, 11, 30. From area south of Fortress.

L. 0.094; W. 0.078; H. 0.032.

Complete. Pale buff clay with pinkish tinge on top. Handle with double groove extending all the way to the bottom. Vine pattern on rim; rays on discus; air-hole at the edge of discus. On the bottom, the signature: Εὐπόρου.

Cf. *Hesperia* 28, 1959, p. 336, nos. 11, 12, pl. 71, c. For the signature see *Corinth* IV, ii, pl. XXXI, nos. 731–734.

**2797.** IP 1959. Pl. 30. From area south of Fortress.

L. (0.094); W. 0.0775; H. 0.0315.

Tip of nozzle missing. Pale buff clay with pinkish tinge on left side of top. Shape and decoration exactly like that of **2796** and the same signature on the reverse. The two lamps were made in the same mold. Another lamp of the same type, not from the same mold but with Euporos' signature, came from a deposit in the area east of the sanctuary (Δελτίον 26, 1971, Χρονικά, p. 107, pl. 87, a–b).

See *Hesperia* 28, 1959, p. 336, nos. 11, 12, pl. 71, c.

**2798.** IP 988. Pl. 30. From area of Southeast Propylon.

Fragment with handle and part of top preserved. Buff clay; no glaze. Vine pattern on rim; rays on discus; air-hole at the edge. Moldmade handle with double groove, extending all the way down.

**2799.** IP 2518. Pl. 30. From Sacred Glen Well, depth 4.30–5.80 m.

L. *ca.* 0.099; D. 0.084.

Fragment with handle, top and part of nozzle preserved. Reddish buff clay. Vine pattern with large leaves on rim. On discus, rays and air-hole at edge. Handle with double grooves extending all the way to the bottom.

**2800.** IP 2848. Pls. 11, 30. From Theater Cave.

L. 0.102; D. 0.088; H. 0.035.

Mended and partly restored. Light red clay, darkened by fire. Pierced handle with double groove above and below. Vine pattern on rim; rays on the discus. The details are distinct but coarsely rendered. On the reverse is the signature: Εὐγόδου.

**2801.** IP 6353. Pls. 11, 30. Provenance not recorded.

L. 0.090; W. 0.075; H. 0.030.

Mended and some small pieces missing. Pale red clay. Handle with double groove above and below suture. Vine pattern on rim; rays on discus. Nozzle and discus much blackened. Signature: Πωσφόρου.

**2802–2821.** Fragments of Type XXVII B, too insignificant to warrant individual description.

| | | | |
|---|---|---|---|
| **2802.** IP 2558. | **2807.** IP 2708. | **2812.** IP 6024. | **2817.** IP 3976. |
| **2803.** IP 2784. | **2808.** IP 2569 a, b. | **2813.** IP 6023. | **2818.** IP 4164. |
| **2804.** IP 2773. | **2809.** IP 4159. | **2814.** IP 4199 a. | **2819.** IP 4224. |
| **2805.** IP 2277 a, b, | **2810.** IP 5027. | **2815.** IP 4095. | **2820.** IP 5240. |
|     IP 2289 a, b. | **2811.** IP 4228. | **2816.** IP 5460. | **2821.** IP 4080 b. |
| **2806.** IP 2625. | | | |

TYPE XXVII C. **2822–2841.**

The third variety of Type XXVII is poorly represented at Isthmia. There are many fragments but no whole lamp. All have pictorial representations on the discus. The rim is usually either plain or decorated with ovules, and always has a plain panel on either side at the cross axis. One fragmentary example, **2833**, is unusual in having buds and tendrils together with plain panels. The panels owe their origin to the factory lamps, which in the early period of their development had two rather high knobs usually so placed as to be equidistant from each other and from the handle. Some factory lamps without handles have three equidistant knobs on the rim.[57] These were originally intended to be perforated so that triple strings or chains could be attached to the holes and held together with a ring for suspension. On Type XXVII the panels serve no such practical purpose, but seem to have been added as decoration to emphasize the cross axis. Their original purpose was forgotten, and in time they degenerated into two parallel lines, usually with a herringbone pattern or some other device in the middle. This late development can be followed in Type XXVIII, *q.v.* pp. 74–75.

**2822.** IP 3629. Pl. 30. From Northeast Cave, West Chamber.

Fragment preserving handle and parts of rim and discus. Pinkish yellow clay; no glaze. Moldmade handle with double groove above and below suture. Ovules and panels on the rim. On the discus is preserved the upper part of a female figure and some indistinct object just below the handle.

**2823.** IP 1964. Pl. 30. From area south of Fortress. H. 0.0335.

Several adjoining fragments from left side of lamp. Pale red clay much discolored in fire; no glaze. Handle with double groove above and below. Plain rim; on discus is preserved only a small unrecognizable part of some object, perhaps right hand of Athena casting a ballot for Orestes. On the reverse was a signature of which only the final *upsilon* is extant.

Cf. *Corinth* IV, ii, no. 581.

**2824.** IP 2781. Pl. 31. From Northeast Reservoir.

Fragment of discus. Greenish buff clay; unglazed. On discus figure of Dionysos standing, holding thyrsos in left hand and kantharos in right; leopard skin over left shoulder. On his right side is the figure of a leopard.

Cf. *Corinth* IV, ii, pl. XII, no. 598, on which the animal is not shown. See also lamp in Delphi, signed by Sposianos; Bruneau, *B.C.H.* 95, 1971, p. 466, figs. 24 and 25.

**2825.** IP 2256. Pl. 31. From Northeast Cave.

Fragment from top of lamp. Reddish buff clay; unglazed. Plain rim with panels and stamped circles on either side. On the discus, within double groove, is

a figure of Herakles strangling the lion. Head of lion and upper part of Herakles missing. All the features are very sharp.

A marble statuette from a fountain showing Herakles with the Nemean lion was found in a field at Isthmia, *Hesperia* 31, 1962, pp. 18–19, pl. 9, a; and on lamps of Type XXXVIII the scene occurs very frequently. See *Corinth* IV, ii, nos. 1169–1171; *Agora* VII, no. 773. A bowl from Alexandria with a similar scene is reproduced by Margarete Bieber, *Sculpture of the Hellenistic Age*, fig. 399.

**2826.** IP 1969. Pl. 31. From Palaimonion, northeast of Temple, 0.70–0.40 m. above Stadium floor.

Fragment of discus. Mealy yellow clay. On discus, indistinct semi-nude figure to right, crouching before some object at the right edge (nurse recognizing Odysseus?).

**2827.** IP 2337. Pl. 31. From east edge of Sanctuary.

Small fragment of discus. Light buff clay. Part of erotic *symplegma*.

**2828.** IP 2785. Pl. 31. From area of Northeast Reservoir.

Parts of discus and rim preserved. Red clay, very crumbly. Plain rim with panels. On discus, heavily draped figure to left, holding some objects in either hand. In front of her an indistinct stand, perhaps an altar. The prominent headgear and formal drapery indicate that this is probably a sacrificial scene.

**2829.** IP 2544. Pl. 31. From Theater Cave, well in East Chamber, depth 2.97 m.

---

[57] The matter is fully discussed by Loeschcke, pp. 256–258; see also his fig. 10, no. 1, and pl. XIX; and *Corinth* IV, ii, pp. 87–88, 93.

Part of rim and discus preserved. Light red clay. Plain rim with panels on which herringbone pattern is scratched. On discus, indistinct figure holding object in right hand. At the left edge, large vessel. Perhaps Eros in front of altar or thymiaterion.

**2830.** IP 3533. Pl. 31. From Later Stadium.

Small fragment of discus. Reddish clay; unglazed. Preserved, front part of centaur holding lyre in left hand.

Cf. *Agora* VII, pl. 15, no. 671.

**2831.** IP 2775. Pl. 31. From Northeast Reservoir.

Fragment of rim and discus. Buff clay; unglazed. On the rim a double row of elongated globules arranged like herringbone. On the discus, nude figure to right with raised left hand, an erotic *symplegma*.

The same scene is on a lamp from Delphi, see Bruneau, *B.C.H.* 95, 1971, p. 469, fig. 28.

**2832.** IP 2553. From Theater Cave, East Entrance Court.

Tiny fragment of rim and discus preserving plain panel and some of the ovules. Pale red clay; unglazed.

**2833.** IP 1963. Pls. 10, 11, 30. From area south of Fortress.

D. 0.077; H. 0.027.

Top of handle and front part missing. Mottled red and gray fabric. Handle with grooves above and below suture. On the rim, pattern of buds and tendrils interrupted by panels. On discus, square rosette and four pecten shells. On the reverse within triple groove, the signature: Ἐπιτυνχάνου.

Cf. *Hesperia* 28, 1959, p. 336, no. 13, pl. 71, c; *Agora* VII, pl. 9, no. 283. A lamp in *Corinth* IV, ii, p. 204, no. 691, fig. 137, also made by Epitynchanos, has two intertwined, four-pointed figures, producing an effect somewhat similar to that of the lamp from Isthmia. The lamp from Athens referred to above is listed among the lamps from Corinth and dated in the first half of the 3rd century. A fragment from the base of a lamp by Epitynchanos, *Agora* VII, no. 296, Perlzweig dates in the first half of the 2nd century. A lamp found in 1965 in a grave at Stobi, and published by Ivan Mikulčić (*Studies in the Antiquities of Stobi* I, 1973, pp. 75–76, fig. 49), has a "seven-angled figure," giving a comparable effect. That too is presumably

Corinthian, although of red clay. No signature is recorded.

**2834.** IP 2642. Pl. 30. From Entrance Court of Northeast Cave.

Fragment of rim and discus. Gray clay with reddish tinge on top; no glaze. Ovules and panels on the rim. Of the relief on the discus, only a tiny part remains close to the break.

**2835.** IP 2709. Pl. 31. From Theater.

Most of discus preserved. Red clay. Figure of bearded Herakles to right, nude, with lion skin hanging down from his shoulders. In the right hand he holds the club.

For the picture cf. *Corinth* IV, ii, p. 196, no. 622, fig. 118.

**2836.** IP 2721. Pl. 31. From Theater.

Small fragment of discus. Greenish buff clay. On discus an indistinct figure to right raising right hand, probably part of an erotic *symplegma*.

**2837.** IP 3933. Pl. 31. From Theater Cave.

Fragment of discus. Greenish buff clay; relief very unclear. Draped figure to left holding staff in left hand and patera (?) in right.

**2838.** IP 3932. Pl. 31. From Theater Cave.

Fragment of discus. Pale buff mealy clay. Unsharp relief of Eros to left playing the flute.

Cf. *Corinth* IV, ii, pl. XXVII, no. 616.

**2839.** IP 5805 a. Pl. 31. From Temenos, North Side.

Fragment from top of lamp; one plain side panel and part of relief preserved. Pale buff mealy clay. Ovules on rim; on discus, indistinct relief, probably part of gladiatorial scene.

**2840.** IP 4277. Pl. 31. From Early Christian Fortress.

Grayish buff clay. Plain rim; fragment of relief on discus too small to show what it represents.

**2841.** IP 4276. Pl. 30. From Early Christian Fortress.

Fragment. Greenish buff clay. Ovules on rim; traces of relief on discus. Handle with double groove above and below.

TYPE XXVII D. **2842.**

The characteristic feature of Type XXVII D is the rim, which consists of an outer plain band and a sunken channel, separated from the discus by a narrow raised fillet. A plain panel on either side divides each half of the rim into two parts. The nozzle is very small, and from it a raised spool-shaped design runs across the rim. The discus carries reliefs. Of this fourth group, there is only one uncertain fragment, **2842**, preserving the handle and a very small part of the rim.

**2842.** IP 2326. Pl. 30. From Roman Cistern, southwest of Northwest Cistern.

Handle and part of right side preserved. Greenish
gray clay; no glaze. Rim consists of outer plain band
with depression on the inside indicating that the fragment probably belongs with XXVII D. Double groove
on handle, above and below, and an X impressed at
the lower end.

TYPE XXVII E. **2843–2849.**

The lamps of Type XXVII E are about twice as large as the more common lamps of Type XXVII. A single,
nearly complete specimen of this subtype was found in Sacrificial Pit C of the Palaimonion. Although most
of the bottom has been restored in plaster, enough is preserved of the name to indicate that the lamp was signed
by Sekoundos.

There are other lamps of the same general type and large size, but they differ from each other in several important details. One is in the local museum at Patras,[58] and another, said to be from Sparta, is now in the
Staatliche Museum in Berlin.[59] The lamps in Patras and Berlin have vine patterns on the rim interrupted by
plain panels. Both are of Corinthian make, and they have on the discus a figure of Attis reclining under a pine
tree with his paraphernalia about him. In his detailed description of the lamps from Sparta and Patras, Bruneau
(*B.C.H.* 95, 1971, pp. 483–491) discusses the close relationship between them. He believes that they were made
in separate molds which derived from the same patrix. The relation of the two lamps is rather more complicated.
It is quite clear that the lamp in Patras came out of molds made from the lamp now in Berlin or from some
other lamp made from the same original mold. The differences that appear in the Patras lamp are due to
retouching. All the objects in the two lamps are of the same scale and stand in the same relationship to each
other. The retouching is clear in the vine leaves on the rim, the branches and root of the tree, in the two hands
and the drapery of Attis, and in the flutes and tympanon. The unretouched features on the Patras lamp, as
is inevitably the case in a copy, are much less sharp than on the lamp in Berlin. This is particularly clear in the
rendering of the musculature on the nude parts of Attis' body.

Regarding the interpretation of the scene, Bruneau cites M. J. Vermaseren, "The Legend of Attis in Greek
and Roman Art" (*Études préliminaires aux religions orientales dans l'empire romain* IX, 1966, pp. 35, no. 2).
Attis, according to this view, is here shown at the time of his self-mutilation and death. But the pose does not
seem to be that of a dying man; he is shown seated on the ground with legs crossed and leaning on his left
elbow; that is, the relaxed pose of a shepherd. The circular object below his left hand is a tympanon, as Furtwängler explained it. On the lamp at Patras the lower edge of this object shows a ragged line, which Bruneau
took to be water from an overturned jar used in preparation for Attis' castration. On the lamp in Berlin, which
has not been retouched, the circle is complete. It is the picture of a tympanon, and the destruction of the edge
on the Patras lamp probably resulted from carelessness at the time of retouching. On the two lamps under
discussion there is a small crescent-shaped object hanging by a double string from the tree, a little to the left
of Attis' head. This, according to Bruneau, is a pair of cymbals (castanets?). It seems more likely that this is
the shepherd's scrip, which on the lamp from Isthmia Attis holds in his right hand. The lamps in Patras and
Berlin do not show the figure of Kybele; but there is enough similarity between the three lamps to indicate that
the representation of Attis on all three goes back to a common origin. This was probably some well-known
painting or perhaps a mosaic or marble relief. The Isthmia lamp shows the whole scene, whereas the other
two omit the major deity.

These large decorative specimens constitute a separate subtype, inasmuch as they combine features of Types
XXVII B (vine pattern on rim) and XXVII C (panels on the rim and reliefs on the discus). They did not come
from the same atelier in Corinth. The lamp in Patras has the signature of Posphoros; that in Berlin is signed
by Preimos, and the lamp from Isthmia, almost certainly, was made in the shop of Sekoundos.

Type XXVII E occurs much less frequently than the other subtypes of XXVII, but it may have been more
common than appears from the extant examples. They were probably all intended for use in the cults of some
deities. The picture of Kybele and Attis, with its allusions to the mystery cult of the Asiatic goddess, would have
been an appropriate dedication in the shrine of Palaimon in which nocturnal rites of a mystic nature played a
prominent role. Among the unpublished lamps from Corinth there are some fragments of large lamps of Type
XXVII and the publication of the lamps from the Athenian Agora contains one large Corinthian lamp of Type
XXVII D (*Agora* VII, pl. 9, no. 283), with rosette and four pecten shells on the discus. The Athenian lampmakers
of the 3rd and 4th centuries, who owed much to their Corinthian forerunners, occasionally created lamps of
large size with interesting scenes of religious content. For a superb example of such a lamp see *Agora* VII,
no. 781, frontispiece.

---

[58] Published by Bruneau, in *B.C.H.* 95, 1971, pp. 483–484, fig. 46.
[59] Published by Furtwängler, pl. LXXV, no. 4; and Bruneau, *loc. cit.*, pp. 483, 485, fig. 47.

**2843.** IP 1055. Pls. 8, 30. From Sacrificial Pit C.
L. (0.210); D. 0.179; H. 0.067.

Large lamp put together from many fragments. Nozzle, most of the handle, parts of the discus and of rim and base restored. Mottled buff and gray clay, much discolored in fire; no glaze. Handle probably with two holes and three grooves terminating in an X above a leaf design. On the rim are tendrils, vine leaves, and clusters of grapes. The discus is decorated with a cult scene showing Kybele and Attis. To the left of the filling-hole Kybele is seated to right, in three-quarter view, holding staff in left hand and resting her right hand on a large tympanon at the edge of the throne. She is fully draped; her loose garment, the himation, covers her hair, and above it she wears a crown or kalathos. Her feet rest on a footstool. On her right side is the standing figure of a lion; the head of a second lion is faintly indicated on her left side. Attis reclines beneath a pine tree. From its branches hangs a Panpipe, just above the head of the second lion. Attis' two flutes, one straight, the other showing stops and curved end, lie on the ground below the figure of Attis. He is holding a shepherd's scrip in the right hand and rests his head on the left elbow. He wears a pointed cap, a garment with long sleeves and trousers. On the reverse of the lamp is preserved the beginning of a signature. The first letter is a lunate *sigma*, the second is a curving letter, probably *epsilon*, from Σε[κούνδου] the well-known Corinthian lampmaker.[60]

**2844.** IP 5256 a–d. Pl. 30. From East Propylon.

Four fragments of a large lamp, including the handle, a fragment from the rim, and two small pieces of the base; only the largest piece shown on Plate 30. Light red clay. Ovules on rim; the handle had a cross at the lower end. The lamp was somewhat smaller than **2843**, about twice the size of the more common lamps of Type XXVII.

**2845–2849.** Lamps of unusual shape related to Type XXVII.

**2845.** IP 4248. Pl. 30. From North Temenos Dump.

Fragment of large lamp. Reddish buff clay, unglazed. Volutes at the nozzle as on Type XXIV, but by clay and absence of glaze it resembles the lamps of Type XXVII.

Cf. *Corinth* IV, ii, pl. XXI, no. 1434, which, however, had two nozzles without volutes. For the shape see Corinth lamp L 4168 (Pl. 40, i) and cf. *Agora* VII, pl. 9, nos. 286 and 287, which also are of Corinthian manufacture.

**2846.** IP 4125 a and b. Pl. 30. From Temenos, North Side.

Small fragments of large lamp. Reddish buff clay. Rudimentary volute at shoulder.

**2848.** IP 2799. From area of Northeast Reservoir.

Handle from top of suspension lamp, with handle rising from center of discus. Reddish buff clay; unglazed. The clay is rather similar to that of **2849**, and it is possible that the two fragments are from the same lamp.

**2847.** IP 3958. Pl. 30. From Northwest Reservoir.

Top of lamp preserved. Light red clay. This lamp had ovules on the rim, and a handle in the center of the discus, but only one nozzle.

**2849.** IP 2763. Pl. 11. From Northeast Reservoir.

Part of bottom preserved. Pinkish buff clay. Oval base; within double groove the signature:[Π]ωσφό[ρ]ου

**2850–2858.** Inscribed fragments of Type XXVII, uncertain subtype.

**2850.** IP 3528. Pl. 12. From area of Northeast Reservoir.

Small fragment of inscribed base. Grayish buff clay. Signature: Μιχ [ικιανοῦ].

**2853.** IP 1929. Pl. 12. From South Stoa, middle sector.

Fragment of inscribed base. Pale red clay. Signature: Πριε [– – –].

**2851.** IP 2999. Pl. 11. From Sacred Glen Well, depth 4.30 m.

Fragment of inscribed base. Light red clay. Signature: 'Ολυμ[πι] ανοῦ.

**2854.** IP 6200. Pl. 11. From Palaimonion, northeast of Temple.

Fragment of base. Red clay. What remains seems to be ισ, perhaps from [Καλλ-] ίσ [του]?

**2852.** IP 2777. Pl. 11. From area of Northeast Reservoir.

Fragment of inscribed base. Pale red clay. Signature: [Κρ] ησκέ γτος.

**2855.** IP 3977. Pl. 11. No context.

Fragment of base and side. Red clay. Signature: Π [ιρεἰϑ] ου?

---

[60] *Corinth* IV ii, pp. 97, 311, and pl. XXXII, record 21 examples, all fragments of bases, on which this signature appears.

**2856.** IP 4099 a and b. Pl. 11. From Rachi, Cistern.
Fragment from base and side. Grayish buff clay.
Signature: [Σεκούν] δου.

**2857.** IP 2776. Pl. 12. From area of Northeast Reservoir.
Fragment of inscribed base. Light gray clay. Inscription undeciphered.

**2858.** IP 2801. Pl. 11. From area of Northeast Reservoir.
Small fragment of inscribed base. Light gray clay.
Part of signature, perhaps [Πρεί] μου?
Cf. *Corinth* IV, ii, pl. XXX, no. 692.

**2859–2963.** Other fragments of lamps of Type XXVII, uncertain subtype.

| | | | |
|---|---|---|---|
| **2859.** IP 4088. | **2886.** IP 4225 b. | **2912.** IP 4369. | **2938.** IP 3969. |
| **2860.** IP 2252. | **2887.** IP 5805 b. | **2913.** IP 4225 a. | **2939.** IP 4077. |
| **2861.** IP 2557. | **2888.** IP 4229 b. | **2914.** IP 5426. | **2940.** IP 6121. |
| **2862.** IP 2782. | **2889.** IP 4231. | **2915.** IP 5637. | **2941.** IP 3980. |
| **2863.** IP 2634. | **2890.** IP 4217. | **2916.** IP 5485. | **2942.** IP 4263. |
| **2864.** IP 2720. | **2891.** IP 5254. | **2917.** IP 4222. | **2943.** IP 5636. |
| **2865.** IP 2622. | **2892.** IP 4130. | **2918.** IP 5168. | **2944.** IP 4230. |
| **2866.** IP 2547. | **2893.** IP 3986. | **2919.** IP 6010. | **2945.** IP 4226. |
| **2867.** IP 2644. | **2894.** IP 5807. | **2920.** IP 3967. | **2946.** IP 4092. |
| **2868.** IP 2567. | **2895.** IP 4075. | **2921.** IP 4221. | **2947.** IP 4161. |
| **2869.** IP 2566. | **2896.** IP 4208. | **2922.** IP 5809. | **2948.** IP 4085. |
| **2870.** IP 2712. | **2897.** IP 4213 b. | **2923.** IP 6119. | **2949.** IP 4279. |
| **2871.** IP 2722. | **2898.** IP 4283. | **2924.** IP 5040. | **2950.** IP 5428. |
| **2872.** IP 1593. | **2899.** IP 4207 b. | **2925.** IP 3973. | **2951.** IP 4356. |
| **2873.** IP 2291. | **2900.** IP 4708. | **2926.** IP 3990. | **2952.** IP 4219 b. |
| **2874.** IP 5971. | **2901.** IP 4197. | **2927.** IP 5035. | **2953.** IP 3979. |
| **2875.** IP 6056. | **2902.** IP 3961. | **2928.** IP 4074. | **2954.** IP 4229 a, c. |
| **2876.** IP 5032. | **2903.** IP 5497. | **2929.** IP 3968. | **2955.** IP 4098. |
| **2877.** IP 4278. | **2904.** IP 3993. | **2930.** IP 5621. | **2956.** IP 5037. |
| **2878.** IP 4219 a. | **2905.** IP 5564. | **2931.** IP 5470. | **2957.** IP 4214. |
| **2879.** IP 5028. | **2906.** IP 4160. | **2932.** IP 3984. | **2958.** IP 4202 b. |
| **2880.** IP 3931. | **2907.** IP 4199 b. | **2933.** IP 4002. | **2959.** IP 4082. |
| **2881.** IP 5033. | **2908.** IP 4195. | **2934.** IP 4086. | **2960.** IP 5034. |
| **2882.** IP 5973. | **2909.** IP 4194. | **2935.** IP 5039. | **2961.** IP 5806. |
| **2883.** IP 3930. | **2910.** IP 4076. | **2936.** IP 4207 a. | **2962.** IP 6358. |
| **2884.** IP 4202 a. | **2911.** IP 4097. | **2937.** IP 3972. | **2963.** IP 4016. |
| **2885.** IP 4337. | | | |

# LATE ROMAN AND EARLY CHRISTIAN LAMPS,
# TYPES XXVIII—XXXIII

### TYPE XXVIII. 2964–3141.

Throughout the 2nd century after Christ and in the early decades of the 3rd century, Corinth was the chief center of the lamp industry in Greece. That was the period when lamps of Type XXVII were produced and exported in vast quantities. The later lamps of that type show a decline in workmanship. In many cases, especially in lamps of Type XXVII B, the details are blunted, and it is obvious that such lamps were not made from original molds but were produced with the use of molds made from earlier specimens. Each time such copying was done the resulting lamp lost much of its sharpness. In the 3rd century the lamp industry shifted to Athens, where the lampmakers at first imitated the Corinthian models.[61] Some of the Corinthian makers may have migrated to Athens and established themselves in the Kerameikos.[62] Several lamps from Isthmia which belong to the transition between Types XXVII and XXVIII are made of a pale yellow, sometimes slightly reddish clay which has a tendency to flake. It is less well levigated than the clay in the best lamps of Type XXVII; on the other hand the color looks more like the color of these Corinthian lamps. Although many of these lamps may have been made in Corinth, one of them, **2964**, which seems to have come from the same mold as a lamp from the Athenian Agora, is almost certainly of Athenian manufacture. The signature Πιρείθου, which occurs on both lamps, is in raised letters, and was thus engraved in negative form in the mold. The lamp in Athens has been dated in the second half of the 3rd century (*Agora* VII, p. 122, no. 814). In view of the fact that the later, more fully developed lamps of Type XXVIII in Athens are generally made of a brick-red or reddish brown clay typical of the Athenian pottery, it is not unlikely that Corinthian lampmakers who migrated to Athens brought clay from Corinth in the early stages of their activities in the new center. One characteristic of the transitional lamps is the handle, which is smaller than on the earlier lamps, and the hole through the handle gradually became smaller and was eventually eliminated altogether.

The development of Type XXVIII, its relation to Type XXVII, and its gradual deterioration, are discussed in *Corinth* IV, ii, pp. 102–114. The small collection of lamps of Type XXVIII from Isthmia is not in good enough condition to illustrate these changes. Since the publication of *Corinth* IV, ii, large numbers of whole lamps of Type XXVIII have been found at Corinth, especially in the excavations carried on in 1965–1971 by James Wiseman in the Gymnasion area, "Fountain of the Lamps." This remarkable collection of about 4000 lamps, most of them complete, has now been studied by Karen Garnett. It has enabled her now for the first time to establish a satisfactory classification and chronology of the Late Roman and Early Christian lamps found at Corinth.[63]

TYPE XXVIII A. **2964–2968.**

This is an early group of Type XXVIII forming the transition from Type XXVII. All but the small fragment **2968** are made of a clay with pale buff or light red color, more like that of Corinth than the Athenian clay; and yet one of them, **2964**, is certainly Attic, as is shown by the signature (see above). The other three, **2965–2967**, are likely to be Attic too. It may be only accidental but is worth noting that these four, which distinguish themselves so clearly from the more common varieties of Type XXVIII, all came from the same restricted area, the Theater Cave.[64] The small piece, **2968**, is of the common red fabric.

[61] Perlzweig, *Agora* VII, pp. 17 and 112, no. 649, emphasizes the close imitation of Corinthian lamps and postulates the use of Corinthian molds by the Athenian lampmakers. But is her no. 649 certainly Attic? The same question may be raised about *Agora* VII, no. 1784. Both are made of light buff clay and have all the earmarks of the Corinth lamps.

[62] See *Corinth* IV, ii, pp. 111–112. In *Agora* VII, p. 8, the author argues for the extension of Type XXVII through the 3rd century, her chief reason being to fill a near vacuum of a whole century during which few Athenian lamps reached Corinth. This seems to be correct. Some of the lamps signed by Sposianos especially show great decline in the art of lampmaking. But if the Corinthian lampmakers made use of material that is virtually indistinct from that of Athens there is no criterion by which the two can be distinguished. The color of the clay is often misleading.

[63] When I wrote the text and catalogue for this section of the book, Mrs. Garnett was still at work on the lamps from the Fountain; consequently I was unable to incorporate her conclusions into my study of the Late Roman and Early Christian lamps from Isthmia. Before I sent my manuscript to the publishers, I had received a copy of Mrs. Garnett's manuscript, but her article (*Hesperia* 44, 1975, pp. 173–206) had not appeared in print. Instead of making a new study and rewriting the whole section, thereby delaying the publication of the Isthmia lamps, it seemed preferable to let my old classification stand as it was. This decision is further justifiable on the ground of the paucity of whole or nearly whole lamps of this kind from Isthmia. The numerous fragments of Type XXVIII that came chiefly from the Theater are too minute to permit detailed classification of the kind that Mrs. Garnett has achieved. The most startling result of her study is that of the *ca.* 4000 lamps from the Fountain only about 10% are Attic imports; nearly all the rest are of Corinthian manufacture. The Corinthian lamp industry, which had become justly famous throughout the ancient world in the 2nd century after Christ, deteriorated in the 3rd century and lost the market to the Athenian lampmakers. After their products also had deteriorated lampmaking again flourished in Corinth for more than a century (early 5th century to middle of the 6th). But the quality of the new products—like the contemporary lamps from other centers—is not to be compared with that of the lamps produced some three centuries earlier. "Unoriginal, uninspired, mechanical," with "greater concern for quantity than for quality or individuality" are the terms Mrs. Garnett employs to describe the Corinthian lampmakers' craft in the Early Christian Era. Anyone who, like the present author, has had to handle and describe countless specimens of these unbeautiful creations can readily agree with her appraisal.

I am greatly indebted to the Editor, Marian McAllister, for sending me a copy of Mrs. Garnett's manuscript, and to James R. Wiseman and Mrs. Garnett for the privilege of being able to read it prior to its publication. Professor Wiseman's preliminary articles on the excavations should be consulted for a description of the Fountain and the discovery of the lamps; *Hesperia* 38, 1969, pp. 75–78 and pl. 24, a; 41, 1972, pp. 9–33, and pl. 10, a, b.

[64] See Gebhard, *The Theater at Isthmia*, and *Isthmia* II, pp. 37–40.

**2964.** IP 2546. Pls. 10, 12, 33. From Theater Cave, West Chamber.
W. 0.079; H. 0.031.

Nozzle missing. Reddish buff clay with darker patches; very crumbly with pitted surface; no glaze. On the rim are panels and tendrils with clusters of berries. Large air-hole on discus. Small perforated handle, grooved only in upper part and terminating in heart-shaped design (shown on Pl. 12). On discus, erotic couple on couch; rather similar to, but not identical with, that on **2534**. Some furniture is showing in background on left side. Within base ring in raised letters, signature: Πιρείθου. Attic.

From same molds as *Agora* VII, pl. 18, no. 814. The author notes, p. 17, the significant fact that "fifty lamps signed by Pireithos have been found in Athens, none in Corinth," i.e. up to the time of her writing (1959).

**2965.** IP 2550. Pl. 33. From Theater Cave, West Chamber.

Fragment preserving handle and rear part of body. Pale yellow clay, very crumbly and tending to flake off. Plain rim; handle with traces of grooves on top only, pierced with small hole. There seems to be a signature in raised letters too faint to decipher.

**2966.** IP 2245. Pl. 33. From Theater Cave.
H. 0.035.

TYPE XXVIII B. **2969–2976.**

Put together out of many fragments from the top, handle and side of the lamp; base and left side missing. Pale red clay, very crumbly; no glaze. Plain rim with panels. Handle with triple groove on upper part only. On the discus, bust of Hermes, front view but with head turned slightly toward his right. In his left hand he holds the Kerykeion.

The figure of Hermes is the same as in *Agora* VII, pl. 17, no. 778, but the two lamps cannot have been made in the same molds since the rims are different. The Athens lamp is dated in the "late 3rd century."

**2967.** IP 2554 + IP 2559. Pl. 33. From Theater Cave, manhole in East Chamber.
W. 0.070; H. 0.028.

Handle and rear half missing. Light red clay; no glaze. Single row of globules on the rim terminating on either side of the nozzle in raised circles. The discus has a series of raised bands. Rather large, U-shaped nozzle, with the top at a lower level than the top of the rim. On the base a series of concentric raised circles.
*Agora* VII, pl. 12, no. 1152 is very similar but lacks the globules on the rim.

**2968.** IP 3505. Pl. 32. From Later Stadium.
Small fragment of discus. Bright red clay; unglazed. Part of an erotic *symplegma*.
Cf. **2964.**

The distinguishing feature of Type XXVIII B is four pairs of double spirals on the rim, interrupted in the middle by two lines or circles, all that survives of the original panels.[65] The nozzle is much like that of Type XXVII. The handle, whenever preserved, is solid and has two or three grooves above and usually two grooves on the lower half. The discus usually has a relief, often the picture of an animal. The clay is either dark red or mottled gray and dark brown. Most of the extant examples from Isthmia are unglazed. Out of eight items of this subtype, six came from the Theater Area.

**2969.** IP 2246 + IP 2249. Pls. 13, 33. From Theater Cave.
W. 0.077; H. 0.037.

Put together out of fragments from the top, bottom and sides; handle and nozzle missing. Dark gray clay. On the rim eight double spirals and rudimentary panels. On the discus, figure of dog, to left. No air-hole. On the base, raised heart-shaped leaf design.

The top is quite like that of *Agora* VII, pl. 20, no. 924, but less distinct. It might have come from a mold made from a lamp of that kind. But the Athens lamp has the signature ΛΕ. The "leaf" signature is common in Athens (94 from the Agora), rare in Corinth.

**2970.** IP 2917. Pl. 33. From the Later Stadium.
Handle and part of rim preserved. Pale red clay;

unglazed. Solid handle with triple groove above and double below. On rim, double spirals. There was probably a relief on the discus, but only small traces are preserved.

**2971.** IP 2562. From Theater Cave, manhole in East Chamber.
Handle and part of rim preserved. Pale red clay; unglazed. Solid handle with triple groove above, double below. On rim, double spirals.

**2972.** IP 2565. From Theater Cave, East Chamber.
Fragments preserving part of handle and rim. Dark gray clay; unglazed. Fabric like that of **2969.** Solid handle with double groove above. On the rim, double spiral pattern.

---

[65] In *Agora* VII, there are many lamps with this kind of rim design, there referred to as "8-S pattern," but the lamps are arranged by discus decoration; consequently lamps of our Type XXVIII B are scattered throughout the catalogue.

**2973.** IP 2711. Pl. 33. From Theater.

Fragment from top with handle, parts of rim and discus preserved. Brick-red clay; unglazed. Handle with triple groove above and double below suture. Hole begun on either side but not pierced through. On the rim double spiral design interrupted by plain panels. A triple groove separates discus from rim. On the discus is preserved a head to left wearing a pointed headdress. Only the top of the head is preserved. The complete picture shows the bust of a person to left holding a double ax.

In *Corinth* IV, ii, p. 255, I suggested that it may represent Men-Mithras, who is often shown with a double ax. Karl Kübler (p. 118) also thinks the figure represents Mithras; Bernhard (p. 326) suggests Men. Haken (p. 100), refers to his Phrygian cap; and he believes that the bust with the double ax is a *pars pro toto* representation of Attis, borrowed from scenes such as appear on the large lamps of Type XXVII E. These, however, are of Corinthian manufacture, whereas the series of lamps with a figure holding the double ax more likely originated in Athens; from there they were exported to Corinth, Argos, and other sites in Greece. Whatever person or deity it represents, whether male or female, we may take for granted that the head was readily recognizable at least in Athens and perhaps in Corinth as well. In *Agora* VII, p. 117, the figure is said to be "that of a woman, and the small round object above her forehead, which was formerly taken to be the curving peak of a Phrygian cap," is there said to be "the end of a long braid starting at the nape of her neck." That is possible but not as certain as the author's statement makes it seem.[66] The author of *Agora* VII cites many instances of female figures holding a double ax, but admits that "the identity of the figure is not known." And as long as the identity remains unknown, it seems wise not to be dogmatic about the sex that the head is intended to portray. The folds on the sharply rendered figure on our Isthmia lamp do not look like braids but more like a turban. The only reliefs that look like a woman's "bushy coiffure" are on the late examples of the type (*Corinth* IV, ii, nos. 1188 and 1189), where the hairdo and the whole face have been retouched and distorted.

A plausible explanation has been suggested to me by Kathleen Slane Wright. The figure on the early lamps is a male wearing a Phrygian cap or a turban and holding a double ax. In the process of retouching the mold, lampmakers unfamiliar with the headdress mistook it and retouched it as hair. Therefore the later lamps seem to show a woman with a 4th century hairstyle and a double ax. A comparable change is illustrated by a Type XXVII lamp, *Corinth* IV, ii, p. 100, fig. 46, nos. 584 and 592; see also **2979**.

For the relief, cf. *Corinth* IV, ii, pl. XVI, nos. 1185, 1189, 1190. *Argos*, no. 592, pl. 12, also p. 72, where several other references are given.

**2974** (now joined to **3140**). IP 2702 b. Pl. 33. From Theater Trench.

Parts of rim, base and body preserved. Reddish brown clay; brown glaze. On the rim, double spirals separated by globules and interrupted in the middle on either side by a panel with stamped circles, four of which are preserved.

**2975.** IP 2905. Pl. 33. From Theater Orchestra, depth *ca.* 0.10 m.

Fragment from rim. Brown clay; dark brown glaze. Double spirals, separated by globules.

**2976.** IP 5972. From Southeast House.

Fragment from rim with double spirals and plain panels. Light red clay; unglazed.

## TYPE XXVIII C. 2977–3034.

Type XXVIII C comprises a large number of lamps, some of which appear to be of local manufacture. The rim is sometimes plain with rudimentary panels on the sides; in one case, **2995**, the panels are missing. The handle is usually solid, but in several cases perforation has been started on either side, but rarely goes through the full thickness. The nozzle is shorter than on the earlier types and the wick-hole is comparatively large. There is a filling-hole in the center of the discus and an air-hole at the base of the nozzle. The discus has some kind of decoration, frequently an animal or human figure, sometimes a rosette, and occasionally nothing at all. On the reverse are circular grooves, sometimes a single one, more often two or three.

---

[66] The author of *Agora* VII, p. 117, refers to "terracotta figurines of goddesses with the same coiffure" in *Agora* VI, but does not specify which figures she has in mind. In fig. 1, p. 15 of that volume are depicted twelve female heads in profile, two of which show some resemblance to the head on the lamps. Photos of these two heads appear on plate 5. One, no. 145, is a small "head of matrona" from late 3rd to early 4th century, and thus somewhat later than the best of the lamps. The other, no. 189, is dated in the 4th century. This is characterized by "elaborate exaggerated hairstyle, like tower crown of Kybele." On neither of these two heads do the braids of the hair end in a knot above the forehead. On plate 7 of the same volume are shown photos of nine heads labeled as boys in Phrygian caps. All are said to be closely related types, and there are several copies from the same mold. They may be intended to represent the same figure: "Harpokratos (?), Telesphoros, Dioskouroi (?), Attis." Only the heads are preserved with no other marks of identification than the Phrygian cap. They all show similarity to the head on the lamps, especially so no. 331, which has some impressed herringbone designs that resemble braids. The heads may not all represent the same person or deity.

**2977.** IP 2916. Pl. 32. From Later Stadium.

Small fragment of discus. Reddish brown clay; apparently unglazed. Bear to left and man turning somersault above.

**2978.** IP 4015. Pl. 33. From Later Stadium.

W. (0.080); H. 0.032.

Nozzle and lower left half missing. Brick-red clay with bright red surface. Solid handle with double groove above and below. Herringbone pattern and plain panels on the rim. On the discus, scene from the arena, like that on **2977**; bear to left, below, and man turning somersault above. On the reverse, base ring and branch.

Cf. *Corinth* IV, ii, p. 262, fig. 185, no. 1243; *Agora* VII, pl. 19, nos. 861, 863. For the type of performance see *Corinth* X, pp. 54–55.

**2979.** IP 4045. Pls. 10, 33. From Later Stadium.

L. 0.092; W. 0.079; H. 0.033.

Most of handle and part of rim missing. Reddish brown clay, with dark brown surface. Handle with double groove underneath. Plain rim with panels indicated by herringbone pattern. On the discus, within double groove, Pan walking to right but looking back and playing the syrinx. The relief was originally used to represent Eros (cf. *Corinth* IV, ii, pl. XV, no. 1134), but was later converted into a figure of Pan. Similar figures of Eros are common on lamps from Athens (*Agora* VII, pl. 16, nos. 689–702, and p. 114), where more than 250 such lamps have been found. Cf. *Argos*, pl. 7, no. 262, and see next item. On Plate 40 are shown two lamps from the Corinth collection: one, 40, 1 (L-69-116), showing Eros with wings and wearing mantle, the other, 40, m (L-69-215), showing Pan without wings but wearing similar mantle.

**2980.** IP 2778. Pl. 33. From Northeast Reservoir.

Handle and part of top preserved. Reddish brown clay with darker surface, probably darkened by fire. Triple groove on handle, hole started on either side but not pierced through. Plain rim. On the discus, figure of Eros playing Panpipe, very indistinct. The pose is the same as that of Pan in **2979**.

**2981.** IP 2915. Pl. 32. From Theater Orchestra.

Small fragment of discus. Dark brown clay; unglazed. Figure of Eros to right as in *Corinth* IV, ii, pl. XV, nos. 1115–1121; cf. *Agora* VII, pl. 16, nos. 725–733.

**2982.** IP 4091. Pls. 13, 33. From Theater Cave.

L. 0.093; W. 0.072; H. 0.033.

Fragmentary. Reddish brown clay; slightly darker brown glaze. Solid handle with triple groove above and below suture. Plain rim with single circle indicating place of panels and similar circles on either side of nozzle and handle. Double groove sets off nozzle from rim and surrounds the discus. The base is heart-shaped, outlined with double grooves. If there was a signature it has been broken away. On the discus, of which only the upper part has been preserved, is a figure of a winged Eros, head turned left, playing the flute; very indistinct. The figure is the same as on **2980**.

For references see under **2979**.

**2983.** IP 2724. Pl. 32. From Theater.

Part of top with most of discus preserved. Dark brown clay with reddish brown surface. Plain rim; on the discus, figure of centaur to right, holding lyre.

Cf. *Agora* VII, nos. 671–673 and pl. 15.

**2984.** IP 2254. Pl. 32. From Theater.

Small fragment of discus. Brick-red clay and glaze of the same color. On the discus, part of hairy animal to left, probably stag.

Cf. *Corinth* IV, ii, pl. XXIX, no. 1253.

**2985.** IP 2253. Pl. 32. From Theater.

Fragment of rim and discus. Dark gray clay with dark brown glaze. On discus, part of furry animal, probably bear, to right.

**2986.** IP 2693. Pl. 32. From Theater.

Most of discus preserved. Brick-red clay with thin glaze or wash of slightly darker hue. On the discus, bear walking to left.

Cf. *Corinth* IV, ii, pl. XXIX, no. 1246; *Agora* VII, pl. 20, no. 901.

**2987.** IP 3546. Pl. 32. From Theater, east parodos.

Fragment of discus. Red clay with wash of the same color. Figure of lion to right.

Cf. *Corinth* IV, ii, pl. XVIII; *Agora* VII, pl. 21, nos. 970, 974.

**2988.** IP 2814. Pl. 32. From Later Stadium.

Fragment from rim and discus. Red clay with bright red wash. On the rim a row of small globules. On the discus, lion to right; only head preserved. Same figure as in **2987**.

**2989.** IP 2542 a. Pl. 32. From Sacred Glen Well.

Fragment of discus. Reddish brown clay, darkened by fire. Plain rim; on discus, bear to right, more likely standing upright on hind legs, from scene with revolving "turnstile", with man on the other side missing.

See *Corinth* X, pp. 54–55; *Agora* VII, pl. 19, nos. 853 and 855.

**2990.** IP 2282. Pl. 32. From Theater.

Small fragment from discus. Brick-red clay with no apparent indication of glaze. On discus, boukranion.

Cf. *Corinth* IV, ii, nos. 1301–1307, and p. 268, figs. 190–192; *Agora* VII, pl. 22, nos. 1036–1060.

**2991.** IP 1926. Pl. 32. From Theater.
Fragment from top of lamp. Brick-red clay, bright red glaze. Plain rim with panels. On discus, figure of boukranion, rather indistinct.

**2992.** IP 2742. Pl. 32. From Theater.
Fragment of discus. Dark brown clay, with surface of the same color. The rim seems to have been plain. On the discus, part of sail with hatchings.
For complete picture of the boat, see *Agora* VII, pl. 21, no. 1029.

**2993.** IP 2729. Pl. 32. From Theater.
Fragment of discus. Brick-red clay. On the discus, figure of Eros looking left. The figure seems to be the same as in **2981**, but very indistinct.

**2994.** IP 6355. Pl. 33. No provenance available.
L. (0.099); W. 0.075; H. 0.0335.
Handle and part of base restored. Dark red clay; dark brown and reddish brown glaze. Plain rim with panels marked by herringbone pattern. Round the discus, two deep grooves and air-hole at nozzle. Discus decorated with a crescent. On the base, three deep grooves and a signature, mostly broken away.
Cf. *Corinth* IV, ii, pl. XIX, no. 1308.

**2995.** IP 1922. Pl. 33. From West Stoa.
H. 0.030.
Left half missing. Reddish buff clay; red glaze. Solid handle with triple groove above and double below. Plain rim; rosette with air-hole on the discus. On the base, double groove.

**2996.** IP 2904. Pls. 10, 33. From Later Stadium, Cistern.

| | | |
|---|---|---|
| **3001.** IP 2717. | **3004.** IP 2698. | |
| **3002.** IP 2735. | **3005.** IP 2725. | |
| **3003.** IP 2737. | **3006.** IP 2688. | |

**3011.** IP 2561. Pl. 33. From Theater Cave.
L. 0.0905; W. 0.0715; H. 0.0335.
Repaired; parts of nozzle and side missing. Bright red clay; no glaze. Handle with triple groove above, double below suture; hole started on either side but not cut through. Plain rim, double raised lines around discus. The discus design consists of a garland in relief. On the bottom a base ring and several grooves.

L. (0.092); W. 0.078; H. 0.035.
Complete, except for a slight chip at the tip of the nozzle. Red clay; purplish brown, metallic glaze. Handle with triple groove above and double below, perforated on either side, but not cut through. Plain rim with herringbone pattern on panels. Rosette on the discus. Two concentric circular grooves on reverse.

**2997.** IP 2919. Pl. 12. From Later Stadium.
L. 0.087; W. 0.076; H. 0.037.
Part of left side and half of nozzle missing. Dark brown clay with glaze of slightly lighter color. Handle with double groove above and below; hole started on either side but not cut through. Rim with herringbone pattern, very indistinct, and plain panels. Rosette on discus. On the reverse, two grooves with small impressed circles. Trace of signature.

**2998.** IP 2278. Pl. 33. From Theater.
Fragment of top. Brick-red clay; unglazed. Wave pattern on rim; plain discus.

**2999.** IP 2568. Pl. 33. From Theater Cave.
H. 0.031.
Most of nozzle and right side missing. Light brown clay; purplish brown glaze. Solid handle. On the rim, herringbone pattern; on the discus a rosette.

**3000.** IP 2718. Pl. 32. From Theater.
Fragment preserving parts of handle, rim and discus. Brick-red clay; dark brown glaze. Solid handle with triple groove above. Plain rim, very narrow, three concentric lines surrounding discus, decorated with mask. Very indistinct.

**3001–3010.** Fragments of Type XXVIII C, not deserving description.

| | | |
|---|---|---|
| **3007.** IP 2727. | **3009.** IP 2743. | |
| **3008.** IP 2734. | **3010.** IP 2694. | |

**3012.** IP 5834. Pl. 33. From Later Stadium.
Fragment from top of lamp. Light red clay, brighter red glaze. Solid handle with triple groove above suture. On the rim, wave pattern without panels. Rosette on discus. Nozzle set off by raised notched bar at right angles to the main axis.

**3013–3034.** Fragments of Type XXVIII C, not deserving description.

| | | | |
|---|---|---|---|
| **3013.** IP 5642. | **3019.** IP 4093. | **3025.** IP 5803. | **3031.** IP 2283. |
| **3014.** IP 3952. | **3020.** IP 4909. | **3026.** IP 5617. | **3032.** IP 2068 (Pl. 13). |
| **3015.** IP 4315. | **3021.** IP 4258. | **3027.** IP 3953. | **3033.** IP 2692. |
| **3016.** IP 5276. | **3022.** IP 4814. | **3028.** IP 2687, IP 2704. | **3034.** IP 2740. |
| **3017.** IP 4168. | **3023.** IP 5794. | **3029.** IP 2719. | |
| **3018.** IP 5808. | **3024.** IP 6356. | **3030.** IP 4193. | |

Type XXVIII D. **3035–3053.**

This subtype comprises a number of poorly made lamps, of red or dark brown clay. Mostly they have solid handles with grooves above and below. In two cases, **3035** and **3037**, the handle has been perforated, and in some others a hole is started on either side but not bored through. The rim has a herringbone pattern, and the top of the lamp is elongated, with the nozzle less sharply set off from the rim than in the earlier lamps. They are all of late date and several have the Christian monogram (cross with *rho*), and more than one filling-hole on the discus.

**3035.** IP 2767. Pl. 34. From Northeast Reservoir.

Handle and part of rim preserved. Reddish brown, very hard fabric, dark brown glaze. Small hole through handle; triple groove above, double below. Herringbone pattern on rim. This is a comparatively early specimen, probably first half of 4th century.

**3036.** IP 1921. Pl. 34. From Temenos, east end of South Side.
H. 0.034.

Most of nozzle and part of left side missing. Brick-red clay; unglazed. Solid handle with triple groove above and below. Herringbone pattern on rim. Rosette on discus. Double circular groove on base.
Cf. *Agora* VII, pl. 31, no. 1871, "second half of 4th century."

**3037.** IP 2824. Pls. 10, 12, 34. From Theater.
L. 0.0935; W. 0.074; H. 0.0325.

Complete. Reddish brown clay; no glaze. Perforated handle with double groove above and below. Herringbone pattern on the rim; on the discus, six-bar monogram with closed *rho* turned right, five filling-holes and air-hole. On the leaf-shaped base, signature: Χιόνης.
Cf. *Corinth* IV, ii, pl. XIX, no. 1337, where the *rho* is turned left; *Agora* VII, pl. 24, nos. 1139–1141. They have been dated to the late 4th and early 5th century.

**3038.** IP 1925. Pls. 10, 13, 34. From Theater.
L. 0.087; W. 0.0695; H. 0.0365.

Part of discus missing. Brick-red clay; no glaze.

Handle with double groove above and single below; hole started on either side but not pierced through. Herringbone pattern on rim. On the discus, damaged, four-bar monogram with the *rho* turned left. On the reverse, large **A** within double groove.

**3039.** IP 2826. Pls. 10, 13, 34. From Later Stadium.
L. 0.076; W. 0.059; H. 0.0295.

Top part of handle missing. Brick-red clay; unglazed. Handle with single groove underneath. Herringbone pattern on the rim. On the discus, studded four-bar monogram with closed *rho* to right. On the reverse, leaf and four circles as on Plate 13, **3032.**

**3040.** IP 1923. Pl. 34. From Temenos, west end of South Side.
L. 0.100; W. 0.072; H. 0.036.

Most of base and part of side broken away. Brick-red clay; unglazed. Handle with faint triple groove on upper side only; hole begun on either side but not cut through. Raised herringbone pattern on the rim. Plain leaf-shaped discus.
Cf. *Corinth* IV, ii, pl. XIII, no. 862; *Agora* VII, pl. 27, no. 1413.

**3041.** IP 2731. Pl. 34. From Theater.
L. 0.063; W. (0.049).

Miniature lamp; bottom broken away. Brick-red clay; unglazed. Solid handle with double groove above and below. Herringbone pattern on rim; plain discus.

**3042–3048.** Insignificant fragments of Type XXVIII D.

| | |
|---|---|
| **3042.** IP 2739. | **3044.** IP 2695. |
| **3043.** IP 2685. | **3045.** IP 2726. |

| | |
|---|---|
| **3046.** IP 2701. | **3048.** IP 5160. |
| **3047.** IP 3965 a, b. | |

**3049.** IP 2570. Pl. 34. Theater Cave.
W. (0.106).

Fragment of large lamp. Bright red clay with lighter red outer surface; no glaze. On the rim, herringbone pattern. Nozzle with double grooves on either

side, and with single groove in middle. On the discus, rosette with large filling-hole in the center and four smaller holes among the leaves.

**3050–3053.** Insignificant fragments of Type XXVIII D.

| | |
|---|---|
| **3050.** IP 2906. | **3051.** IP 4358. |

| | |
|---|---|
| **3052.** IP 2672. | **3053.** IP 5623. |

Type XXVIII E. **3054–3085.**

The distinguishing feature of this type is the rim which is decorated with one, two, or three rows of globules. Only fragments of this type are preserved at Isthmia.

**3054.** IP 5559. Pl. 34. From Palaimonion, middle section, 0.70–0.40 m. above Stadium floor.

Handle and part of right side preserved. Reddish brown clay with slightly darker brown glaze. Solid handle with triple groove above, double below. On the rim are two rows of globules, and nearer the handle, three rows of the same.

**3055.** IP 2548. Pl. 34. From Theater Cave, East Chamber.

H. 0.0325; W. (0.088).

Fragment of large lamp preserving handle and rear

| | |
|---|---|
| **3056.** IP 2700. | **3059.** IP 3978. |
| **3057.** IP 2551. | **3060.** IP 4109. |
| **3058.** IP 4007. | **3061.** IP 5570. |

**3066.** IP 2250. Pl. 13. From Theater.

Fragment of base and lower part. Brick-red clay; purplish red glaze. On the bottom within small circle, large A.

**3067.** IP 2745. Pl. 12. From Theater.

Fragment from bottom of lamp. Brick-red clay; glaze of slightly darker color. On the base within double groove, signature, ending in Y.

**3068.** IP 2746. Pl. 12. From Theater.

Fragment of base. Red clay; apparently unglazed. Within double circular groove, the signature: Pοῦ[φος]. The lamps bearing this signature, according to *Agora* VII, p. 50, were made chiefly in the first half of the 4th century. There are no Rouphos lamps from Corinth among those published in *Corinth* IV, ii.

**3069.** IP 3578. Pl. 12. From Temenos, North Side.

Fragment from base. Red clay; unglazed. This is presumably from the Karpeme shop (*Agora* VII, p. 40). Kα[ρπή]? The third letter, of which a slight trace remains, does not look like a *rho*; it may be because of the blur at the top.

**3070.** IP 2819. Pl. 13. From West Foundation.

Small fragment from base. Pale reddish, mealy clay; unglazed. Leaf design on reverse.

**3071.** IP 2914. Pl. 13. From Theater Court.

Fragment from base. Dark brown clay and glaze. Double circular groove and branch pattern on base.

**3072.** IP 2706. Pl. 34. From Theater.

Fragment from base. Bright red clay; unglazed. On the reverse a series of concentric circles.

Cf. *Agora* VII, pl. 34, no. 2078.

part. Brick-red clay; unglazed. Handle with triple groove above, double below, terminating in a raised heart design. Hole started on either side, but not cut through. Rim divided by raised band into two halves, the outer decorated with a row of small globules and plain panel; the inner part has small circles and elongated dots, indistinct. Two raised bands surround the discus, which seems to have been plain. On the bottom, four circular grooves.

Cf. *Agora* VII, pl. 25, no. 1307.

**3056–3065.** Minor fragments of Type XXVIII E.

| | |
|---|---|
| **3062.** IP 5013. | **3064.** IP 2697. |
| **3063.** IP 6258. | **3065.** IP 5987. |

**3073.** IP 1924. Pl. 34. From Temenos, west end of South Side.

Handle and parts of base and rim preserved. Brick-red clay; unglazed. Solid handle with double groove above, single below. Rectangular discus. Double groove on base with two circles at lower end of handle.

**3074.** IP 319. Pl. 12. From Temple of Poseidon, northeast sector.

Fragment of base and lower part of handle. Mealy red clay; no glaze. Double groove on handle below suture; elongated base set off by double groove. Signature: Χιό[νης].

**3075.** IP 4180. Pl. 12. From Theater Cave.

Fragment of lower part. Red clay, thin glaze or wash of darker red. On base: Δ.

**3076.** IP 4265. Pls. 13, 34. From Temple of Poseidon.

Fragment of grayish brown clay; unglazed. Elongated base with leaf design.

**3077.** IP 312. Pl. 34. From Early Christian Fortress.

Fragment from lower part of large lamp. Brick-red clay; unglazed. Triple groove on lower part of handle. On base, series of grooves and ridges.

**3078.** IP 2908. Pl. 12. From Theater.

Reddish brown clay with darker surface. On base: KY.

For this signature see *Corinth* IV, ii, pls. XXXII and XXXIII; *Agora* VII, p. 41.

**3079.** IP 5117. Pl. 13. From Southeast House.

Red clay; no glaze. On the base: T.

Cf. *Corinth* IV, ii, pl. XXXIII, no. 1398; *Agora* VII, p. 54.

**3080.** IP 2555. Pls. 12, 34. From Theater Cave.

Fragment preserving handle and part of base. Dark gray clay; unglazed. Triple groove on upper part of handle, and on lower part, double groove with middle strip hatched. Hole cut on either side, but not pierced through. On the reverse within double groove, what seems to be part of a signature.

**3081.** IP 4169. From Theater Cave.

Fragment from bottom of lamp. Light red clay; reddish brown glaze. On the reverse what was probably a signature, now illegible.

**3082.** IP 2744. Pl. 34. From Theater.

Lower half of lamp. Reddish brown clay; unglazed. On the reverse within double circular groove are some marks, probably impressed circles.

**3083.** IP 3951. Pl. 34. No provenance.

Fragment preserving handle and parts of side and base. Reddish brown clay, dark brown glaze. On

handle, double groove above and below, and hatchings on middle strip above suture. On reverse within double circular groove, part of one letter, probably *upsilon* or *chi*.

See *Agora* VII, p. 55.

**3084.** IP 4090. Pl. 34. From Theater Cave.

Lamp of uncertain type originally attached to stand. Fragment preserves lower part of handle, part of the side and the attachment to the stand. Bright red clay; slightly darker red glaze. Very crumbly, coarse fabric.

**3085.** IP 5290. Pl. 34. From Temenos, west end of South Side.

Fragment from the lower part of lamp. Reddish buff clay with thin light brown wash. This was the same type of lamp as **3084**. The attachment is quite clear, the rest of the lamp is missing. Before it was attached to the stand the reverse was carefully finished with base ring and small raised circle in the center.

**3086–3141.** Fragments, mostly of Type XXVIII, but uncertain subtype.

| | | | |
|---|---|---|---|
| **3086.** IP 2284. | **3101.** IP 5277. | **3116.** IP 5116. | **3131.** IP 5036. |
| **3087.** IP 1682. | **3102.** IP 4328. | **3117.** IP 4353. | **3132.** IP 3983. |
| **3088.** IP 314. | **3103.** IP 4089. | **3118.** IP 5976. | **3133.** IP 2907. |
| **3089.** IP 2696. | **3104.** IP 4204. | **3119.** IP 4198. | **3134.** IP 3987. |
| **3090.** IP 2293. | **3105.** IP 6051. | **3120.** IP 5051. | **3135.** IP 5462. |
| **3091.** IP 2686. | **3106.** IP 4311. | **3121.** IP 5471. | **3136.** IP 4288. |
| **3092.** IP 2728. | **3107.** IP 4167. | **3122.** IP 4282. | **3137.** IP 4152. |
| **3093.** IP 2713. | **3108.** IP 4389. | **3123.** IP 4136. | **3138.** IP 5917. |
| **3094.** IP 2699. | **3109.** IP 4920. | **3124.** IP 4126. | **3139.** IP 4483 a. |
| **3095.** IP 2736. | **3110.** IP 3974. | **3125.** IP 5472. | **3140.** IP 2702 a |
| **3096.** IP 2703. | **3111.** IP 5118. | **3126.** IP 4058. | (now joined to |
| **3097.** IP 2715. | **3112.** IP 4227. | **3127.** IP 4617. | **2974**). |
| **3098.** IP 2287. | **3113.** IP 6049. | **3128.** IP 4577. | **3141.** IP 4048 a, b. |
| **3099.** IP 2705. | **3114.** IP 6184. | **3129.** IP 4118. | |
| **3100.** IP 2707 a–c. | **3115.** IP 5049. | **3130.** IP 5616. | |

## TYPE XXIX. 3142, 3143.

There are only two fragments from Isthmia of this very puzzling type of lamp. One is from the top, the other from the bottom, with part of the enigmatic signature preserved. Two photographs of a lamp of this kind from Corinth are shown on Plate 40 (n). The handle is an unperforated elongated knob. There is a raised edge round the wick-hole and elongated loops or rays extend from it toward the edge of the top. There is no rim in the proper sense, but a projecting edge marks the suture between the two halves. Circular nozzle with rather large wick-hole. On the lower half, the handle with triple groove extends down to the base ring, and two double raised lines set off the nozzle. The letters, which are raised and thus were made in the mold, run in a circle, but it is not clear in which direction they are to be read. All attempts to decipher the inscription have been unsuccessful (see *Corinth* IV, ii, p. 280, no. 1413: Θαυμασις?; *Agora* VII, p. 102, nos. 362–366: Λαδοσω[δ], and pl. 52; *Argos*, p. 86, nos. 603–607, and planche F; Walters, no. 1491; and cf. *Délos* XXVI, nos. 4726–4728, without signature.

**3142.** IP 4260. Pl. 35. From Temenos, North Side.

Handle and small part of rim preserved. Red clay; unglazed.

**3143.** IP 5759. Pls. 13, 35. From Temenos, South Side.

Part of side and base preserved. Pale buff clay; unglazed. Part of inscription in raised letters. For attempted interpretations see above.

## TYPE XXX. **3144.**

This is not a type in the proper sense, but rather a catchall of heterogeneous pieces that do not fit into the classification of regular types. A single fragment from Isthmia belongs to that category.

**3144.** IP 1700. Pl. 35. Not found by excavators.

Handle attachment in the form of a cross. Brick-red clay; unglazed. No decoration on the cross.

There is an almost identical cross in the Corinth collection, L 4170. Bronze lamps with similar handle attachments are common; see *Agora* VII, pl. 48, nos. 2948, 2949.

## TYPE XXXI. **3145–3169.**

Of Type XXXI there are two whole examples and many fragments from Isthmia. This is the Christian type, in a restricted sense, the prototypes of which came to Greece from North African sites. The lamps are boat shaped with solid knob handle; a broad flat rim, usually impressed with a variety of patterns; comparatively small discus, often with Biblical motives, taken from the Old and New Testaments, and usually with two or three holes. The nozzle, as in the later varieties of Type XXVIII, is not organically set off from the top of the lamp, and the wick-hole is often rather large. One feature found on all the best examples of the type, e.g. **3150**, is a raised ridge extending from the base of the handle to the raised base ring. Of the original imported lamps of the type there is only one certain fragment, **3146**, but three other fragments, **3147, 3148, 3149**, may also be imported.

**3145.** IP 215. Pl. 35. From Temple of Poseidon, southwest part.

Fragment from right side, preserving part of the rim and edge of discus. Red clay; bright red glaze, well preserved. On the depressed rim, some geometrical designs consisting of small raised circles in clusters, which are separated by a large circle with several concentric rings. On the discus is preserved one studded arm of a cross.

**3146.** IP 1927. Pl. 35. From Early Christian Fortress.

Nozzle and front part of lamp preserved. Reddish brown clay; light brown glaze. On the rim, leaf design. On the discus, series of raised dots, perhaps part of a cross.

Cf. *Agora* VII, no. 2591; *Argos*, no. 642.

**3147.** IP 2066. Pl. 35. From southwest corner of Temenos.

Front part of rim and discus. Brick-red clay; light red glaze. On the rim, some design made with small raised circles. In the channel between discus and wick-hole, a raised leaf, and on the discus, lower part of studded Christian monogram.

**3148.** IP 217. Pl. 35. From Temple of Poseidon.

Left half of top preserved. Reddish buff clay; light brown glaze. On the rim, a series of triangular designs made up of small circles; on the discus, similar circles probably from a cross.

**3149.** IP 1928. Pls. 10, 35. From Early Christian Fortress.

L. 0.115; W. 0.080; H. 0.031.

Complete and undamaged except for top of handle. Brick-red clay; unglazed. Solid knob handle; depressed rim decorated with a series of *tau*s, *lambda*s, and circles. On the discus small figure of bird to right, very indistinct. Tiny raised base ring, so uneven that the lamp is very unstable when set down on a flat surface. Ridge extends from the handle to the base ring.

Cf. *Corinth* IV, ii, no. 1483; *Argos*, no. 625; *Agora* VII, no. 2401.

**3150.** IP 1680. Pls. 10, 36. From Temenos, west end of South Side.

L. 0.087; W. 0.055; H. 0.0265.

Complete. Brick-red clay; unglazed. Solid knob handle. On depressed rim, a pattern of small raised lines; indistinct design on the discus, perhaps a bird. Base ring connected by ridge to handle.

Cf. *Argos*, no. 651.

**3151.** IP 317. Pl. 36. From Temple of Poseidon, east end.

Handle and half of top preserved. Brick-red clay; unglazed. Solid handle; on the rim, branches. On discus, indistinct figure of cross.

**3152.** IP 1698. Pl. 36. From Temenos, west end of South Side.

Small part of rim and nozzle close to the wick-hole. On the rim, design in the form of a chalice. On the discus, part of a relief resembling a fish.

**3153.** IP 2063. Pl. 36. From southwest of Temple of Poseidon.

Small part of rim and top. Dark brown clay, darkened by fire from wick; no glaze. On the rim, depressed, a leaf design; on the discus, probably a cross.

**3154–3169.** Smaller fragments of Type XXXI.

| | | | |
|---|---|---|---|
| **3154.** IP 4352. | **3158.** IP 6009. | **3162.** IP 6019 (Pl. 36). | **3166.** IP 4256. |
| **3155.** IP 5347 (Pl. 36). | **3159.** IP 4286 (Pl. 36). | **3163.** IP 5289 (Pl. 36). | **3167.** IP 6014. |
| **3156.** IP 4329 (Pl. 36). | **3160.** IP 5895. | **3164.** IP 5624. | **3168.** IP 2831. |
| **3157.** IP 4252 (Pl. 36). | **3161.** IP 4296 (Pl. 36). | **3165.** IP 5479. | **3169.** IP 6050. |

## TYPE XXXII. 3170–3176.

Type XXXII is an imported product, probably originating in Sicily but exported in considerable numbers to Greek sites. Very few came from the Agora excavations, but both at Corinth (*Corinth* IV, ii, nos. 1501–1510, and at least 22 unpublished examples) and at Argos (*Argos*, nos. 661–666) the type is well represented. The best examples of the type are made of a fine levigated clay, light red in color, and with very sharp designs both on the rim and on the discus. These are the imported specimens. The local imitations are as a rule smaller, the designs are less distinct, and the clay is usually of a mud-gray color. They are flat, circular lamps with a pointed knob handle. The rim is broad and decorated with a variety of raised designs, and on the discus are raised radiating lines separating rows of circles and dots and more complicated patterns. There are seven small fragments of this type from Isthmia, all from the top, two of them preserving the handle. A complete example from Corinth (L-69-143) is shown on Plate 40 (o).

**3170.** IP 5880. Pl. 37. From North Temenos Dump.
Fragment from rim and edge of discus. Light red clay; no glaze. On the broad rim, raised leaf-shaped designs, with double spirals inside and separated by small raised circles. There seem to have been similar designs on the discus. Probably imported.

**3171.** IP 5480. Pl. 37. From Palaimonion, east section.
Fragment of rim and discus. Light red clay; no glaze. On broad rim and on discus, row of raised heart-shaped designs, separated by intertwined triangles with spirals. A row of raised dots separates rim from discus.

**3172.** IP 1095. Pl. 37. From Palaimonion, middle section.
Fragment. Pale yellow clay; traces of thin reddish glaze or a wash. On the rim, series of triangular designs separated by raised lines and rows of globules.

**3173.** IP 5563. Pl. 37. From Palaimonion, middle section.
Fragment of rim with raised floral designs. Pale yellow clay; no glaze.

**3174.** IP 1980. Pl. 37. From Temenos, South Side, middle section.
Fragment preserving handle and parts of rim and discus. Light red clay; unglazed. Pointed knob handle. On the rim, a series of S-shaped floral elements, and small raised circles. On the discus, raised lines and rows of circles, decreasing in size toward filling-hole in center. Probably imported.

**3175.** IP 310. Pl. 37. From Theater.
Handle and parts of rim and discus preserved. Red clay; unglazed. Pointed knob handle. On rim, row of meanders on the outside, and on the inside, row of floral spirals like those on **3174**. On the discus, rays and rows of globules.

**3176.** IP 6015. Pl. 37. From Palaimonion.
Small fragment from the rim with raised intricate design. Red clay; no glaze.

## TYPE XXXIII. 3177–3183.

In *Corinth* IV, ii a few fragments are described as Type XXXIII because of certain characteristics that they have in common, the most prominent of which is a depressed channel on the rim with raised dots or other decorative elements. The lower part of the rim usually has elongated dots or raised lines. A poorly preserved discus decoration was—probably incorrectly—thought to be part of the Menora (*Corinth* IV, ii, no. 1511). There are a few late fragments from Isthmia that show certain affinities to the lamps of Type XXXIII from Corinth. They are here grouped together as Type XXXIII, but they can hardly be said to constitute a type in any proper sense of that term. With these few heterogeneous pieces we have reached the end of the catalogue. The excavations at Isthmia produced no examples of Byzantine lamps with vitreous glaze, like those listed in *Corinth* IV, ii, under Type XXXV.

**3177.** IP 4517. Pl. 37. From Temenos, South Side.
Fragment. Light red clay; no glaze. Flat knob handle. Broad rim with outer band plain; at the inner edge, raised elongated dots.

**3178.** IP 2549. Pl. 36. From Theater Cave.
Fragment from rear of top. Reddish buff clay; no glaze. Flat knob handle; on rim in sunken channel, row of large globules with serrated edge. Most of

discus device is lost, but below handle are what seem to be branches of a tree.

A somewhat similar but not identical figure occurs on a lamp in Hungary, Szent., no. 237.

**3179.** IP 1681. Pl. 36. From Temenos, South Side.

Fragment from top. Ash-gray clay with reddish buff surface. Flat knob handle. On the rim, row of globules at outer edge and raised herringbone pattern at inner edge. On discus, rosette with raised leaves.

**3180.** IP 4253. Pl. 37. From Temple of Poseidon.

Fragment of rim. Grayish brown clay with red surface. On the rim row of globules separated by X's.

**3181.** IP 4387. Pl. 35. From Palaimonion, east of Temple.

Fragment from front part of top. Red clay; orange red glaze. On the rim, row of raised concentric circles.

In the groove separating rim from the discus, row of globules on the right side and elongated dots on the left. On the discus are preserved some elongated dots and raised concentric circles.

**3182.** IP 6354. Pl. 37. Provenance unknown.

Fragment of rim and side. Reddish brown clay; no glaze. On the rim within sunken channel, double row of elongated dots on the outside running lengthwise and single row of elongated dots on the inside at right angles to the above.

**3183.** IP 6357. Pl. 37. Provenance unknown.

Fragment from rim and discus. Grayish brown clay; no glaze. On the rim within sunken channel, double row of elongated dots on the outside running lengthwise and single row of elongated dots on the inside running crosswise. On the discus what seems to be a Christian cross outlined in rows of raised circles.

*Addendum*: It came to my attention too late to be added to the text and notes that lamps similar to our Palaimonion lamps were discovered in excavations at Samaria in Palestine, where they appear to have been used in cults of Kore. The excavators dated them in the 1st to 3rd centuries after Christ. (Crowfoot, J. W., Crowfoot, G. M., Kenyon, K. M., *Samaria-Sebaste* III: *The Objects from Samaria*, (Palestine Exploration Fund, London, 1957), pp. 373–374, fig. 88, 11.).

# PROVENANCE AND DISTRIBUTION OF TYPES

The main body of this volume, containing discussion of types with description and measurements of the individual pieces, inevitably lays emphasis on the lychnological aspect of the subject. From this viewpoint the Isthmia collection leaves much to be desired. With the exception of the Palaimonion lamps, it offers few novelties, and leaves many gaps in the study of Greek lamps. The purpose of the present chapter is to deal with these plain, ubiquitous objects of terracotta in their relation to the areas and buildings in which they were found. Some of the areas are well defined, as is the case with the Palaimonion, the Large Circular Pit, the Rachi; others have no fixed limits and no functional significance in themselves. Only their proximity to specific monuments lends importance to the lamps found in them. Two of the areas, the Rachi and the Fortress, are not in any obvious way concerned with the Isthmian Games or the cults of the gods; the others are by proximity or function parts of the Isthmian Sanctuary.

A large percentage of the very small fragments that are not described in the catalogue are here included and figure in the total number of lamps from a given area.

The Types are designated by Roman numerals. Whenever a dash appears between such numerals the types so indicated comprise fragments too small to show the type clearly. Thus I–VI means that the number of lamps shown after these numerals belong to one of the first six types of the series. There is a slight discrepancy between the number of lamps listed in the Catalogue (3183) and the total number from all the areas added together (3191). The difference of eight lamps is explained as follows. Two of these lamps, with the catalogue numbers **1339** and **2431**, were made up of fragments found in different places, and thus each lamp appears twice in the record of Provenance and Distribution. Six lamps are listed in the catalogue with the designation A, thus: **707 A, 2431 A, 2443 A, 2465 A, 2536 A, 2780 A**. The reason for this irregularity is obvious: faulty human calculating machine. In the course of our study, after the lamps had received their catalogue numbers, some rearrangement became necessary, and those six pieces that had earlier escaped our notice had to be added. To avoid renumbering the whole lot they were placed in their proper sequence bearing such numbers.

Twenty areas are here described; they have been designated as A–T, and their locations can be found on the plan, Plate A.

## A. AREA OF THE TEMPLE OF POSEIDON

The Archaic Temple, built in the early 7th century B.C., was destroyed by fire about the time of the Persian Wars. The Classical Temple was constructed in the 460's B.C. and extensively repaired subsequent to the fire of 390 B.C. After the reconditioning of the Sanctuary in the 1st century after Christ, the Temple appears to have been several times repaired, but remained standing until the final closing of the pagan cults (*Isthmia* I, p. 103).

The lamps from the Temple area do little to reflect the dramatic changes that took place in the pre-Roman era. The 1st and 2nd centuries after Christ are well represented, however, and somewhat less so the period of decay in Late Roman times.

| Type | | No. of Lamps | |
|---|---|---|---|
| I | | 1 | |
| IV | | 1 | |
| I–VI | | 1 | |
| | CLASSICAL GREEK | | 3 |
| VII | | 2 | |
| VII–XIII | | 1 | |
| | HELLENISTIC | | 3 |
| XVI | | 6 | |
| Palaimonion A | | 10 | |
| Palaimonion B | | 17 | |
| XXI | | 2 | |
| XXIV | | 1 | |
| XXII–XXVI | | 1 | |
| XXVII | | 2 | |
| | ROMAN IMPERIAL | | 39 |

| Type | No. of Lamps | |
|------|------------|---|
| XXVIII | 4 | |
| XXXI | 4 | |
| XXXIII | 1 | |
| LATE ROMAN & EARLY CHRISTIAN | 9 | |
| | TOTAL | 54 |

## B. LARGE CIRCULAR PIT

The lamps from the Large Circular Pit have to be separated into two groups, depending on the depth at which they were found. The fill below 5 meters gave the impression of having been thrown in at one time, probably soon after the middle of the 5th century B.C. It probably resulted from the landscaping of the area after the construction of the Classical Temple.

The topmost five meters of fill contained Roman pottery and lamps, in addition to large quantities of earlier pottery, mostly Classical vases of the 5th and 6th centuries before Christ. This can hardly have resulted from the filling in with Roman debris at the top after the usual settling had taken place. If such had been the case it would be difficult to account for so much early pottery of the same kind as that found at greater depths, with only a slight admixture of Roman. It seems more likely that the well had originally been filled to the top with debris of the 5th century and earlier; then in Roman times an attempt had been made to reopen the shaft by removing the fill of the first five meters at the top. Since no bottom was reached the hole was filled up both with the original earth that had been removed and with some contemporary Roman rubbish.

### LARGE CIRCULAR PIT (to 5 m.)

| Type | No. of Lamps | |
|------|------------|---|
| II | 1 | |
| III | 2 | |
| IV | 6 | |
| I–VI | 1 | |
| | CLASSICAL GREEK | 10 |
| Palaimonion A | 11 | |
| Palaimonion B | 8 | |
| XXVII | 1 | |
| | ROMAN IMPERIAL | 20 |
| | TOTAL | 30 |

### LARGE CIRCULAR PIT (below 5 m.)

| Type | No. of Lamps | |
|------|------------|---|
| I | 8 | |
| II | 11 | |
| III | 2 | |
| IV | 10 | |
| V | 9 | |
| I–VI | 7 | |
| | CLASSICAL GREEK | 47 |
| | TOTAL | 47 |

## C. TEMENOS, EAST END

This area extends in length from the northeast corner of the Palaimonion to the Northeast Area, and from the east façade of the Temple of Poseidon to the eastern limit of the Early Roman Temenos wall. The area underwent several changes of level and saw much building activity at widely different times. The eastward slope of the terrain, like that in the northwest corner of the Sanctuary, became a dumping ground, where debris from the Archaic Temple and from the fire of 390 B.C. was disposed of. The earliest building is the Earlier Stadium. Its two parallel retaining walls run diagonally through the area from northwest to southeast. Then, almost in the axis of the Temple of Poseidon, the East Gateway was built, probably in the 4th century B.C. (*Isthmia* II, p. 16). The first Roman Temenos Wall and the Roman Altar were constructed in the 1st century after Christ. Finally in the 2nd century the East Stoa and the Southeast Propylon came into existence. From this checkered history we would expect to find lamps of many types of different dates, and such in fact is the case. Only the Hellenistic and Late Roman-Early Christian periods are poorly represented. Nearness to the Palaimonion explains the discovery of rather large numbers of Palaimonion Types A and B, which make up nearly half of all the lamps from the area.

| Type | No. of Lamps | |
|------|------------|---|
| I | 1 | |
| II | 2 | |
| III | 1 | |
| IV | 4 | |
| I–VI | 1 | |
| VII A–D | 1 | |
| | CLASSICAL GREEK | 10 |
| VII | 2 | |
| X | 2 | |
| | HELLENISTIC | 4 |
| XVI | 5 | |
| Palaimonion A | 40 | |
| Palaimonion B | 21 | |
| XXI | 1 | |
| XXII | 2 | |
| XXIII | 2 | |
| XXIV | 2 | |
| XXV | 3 | |
| XXII–XXVI | 10 | |
| XXVII | 10 | |
| | ROMAN IMPERIAL | 96 |
| XXVIII | 9 | |
| XXXI | 1 | |
| LATE ROMAN & EARLY CHRISTIAN | 10 | |
| | TOTAL | 120 |

## D. NORTHEAST CAVE

The cave in the northeast corner of the Sanctuary, which apparently served the same purpose as the Theater Cave (see below), is probably the earlier of the two cult caves. It had already been abandoned when the Temple of Poseidon was rebuilt, after the fire of 390 B.C. (*Isthmia* II, pp. 33–37). Some of the debris from that fire was left on the floor of the chambers when the cave was reconditioned in Roman times, probably to serve as a storage room. Of the 52 lamps and lamp fragments found in the fill, all but two are Roman Imperial. The contents show clearly that most of the space had been filled with debris by the end of the 2nd century after Christ. That may have taken place in connection with the second abortive Roman reconstruction of the Theater in the Antonine period. See Gebhard, *The Theater at Isthmia*, pp. 89–135, 143.

| Type | No. of Lamps | |
|---|---|---|
| III | 1 | |
| CLASSICAL GREEK | | 1 |
| XVI | 3 | |
| Palaimonion A | 2 | |
| Palaimonion B | 1 | |
| XXI | 1 | |
| XXIII | 1 | |
| XXV | 1 | |
| XXII–XXVI | 4 | |
| XXVII | 37 | |
| ROMAN IMPERIAL | | 50 |
| XXVIII | 1 | |
| LATE ROMAN & EARLY CHRISTIAN | | 1 |
| TOTAL | | 52 |

## E. NORTHEAST RESERVOIR

The full story of the Northeast Reservoir cannot be written until the rest of the inside has been excavated. The lamps found in it, mostly Type XXVII, seem to indicate that the fill of the reservoir and the upper fill in the Northeast Cave were thrown in about the same time, perhaps as a result of the extensive rebuilding of the Theater, and the construction of the East Stoa.

| Type | No. of Lamps | |
|---|---|---|
| XXVII | 11 | |
| ROMAN IMPERIAL | | 11 |
| XXVIII | 2 | |
| LATE ROMAN & EARLY CHRISTIAN | | 2 |
| TOTAL | | 13 |

## F. NORTHEAST AREA

The northeast corner of the Sanctuary has a checkered history. In the pre-Roman era this area contained the Northeast Cave, and—at a higher level—the Northeast Altar Terrace. The lamps from the Cave and the Northeast Reservoir have been accounted for separately; they came from fill at a much lower level than those listed in this section of the Northeast Area. The latest architectural changes were brought about by the construction of the East Stoa and the Northeast Gate that served to facilitate communication between the Temenos of Poseidon and the Theater (*Isthmia* II, pp. 75–77). The Stoa was constructed in the 2nd century of our era, and the lamps show that this was the period in which the Northeast Area saw its greatest activity. Of the 88 lamps from this area 84% belong to Roman Imperial types.

| Type | No. of Lamps | |
|---|---|---|
| II | 1 | |
| VI | 1 | |
| CLASSICAL GREEK | | 2 |
| X | 1 | |
| XI | 1 | |
| VII–XIII | 4 | |
| HELLENISTIC | | 6 |
| XVI | 15 | |
| Palaimonion A | 21 | |
| Palaimonion B | 2 | |
| XXV | 3 | |
| XXVI | 1 | |
| XXII–XXVI | 9 | |
| XXVII | 23 | |
| ROMAN IMPERIAL | | 74 |
| XXVIII | 6 | |
| LATE ROMAN & EARLY CHRISTIAN | | 6 |
| TOTAL | | 88 |

## G. TEMENOS, NORTH SIDE

This area extends northward from the north flank of the Temple of Poseidon to the North Temenos wall. At the east and west ends the area merges without demarcation with the Northeast and Northwest Areas, *q.v.* From the east end of the North Temenos wall the area extends westward for the full length of the wall, beyond the west end of the Temple of Poseidon. Stratigraphically the Temenos, North Side has no unified character, and the fill in most places was very shallow, extending down only to the Late Roman pavement or to natural rock. But it contained pockets of earlier fill, especially in the western half. Here, because of late intrusions and the removal of foundations in Early Christian times, the fill was quite mixed.

Out of 100 items, including small pieces of uncertain subtypes, no less than 91 belong to the two and a half centuries (*ca.* A.D. 3–250) of Roman Imperial times, and of these 85 are to be dated in the 1st century of the Christian era and the first half of the 2nd century.

| Type | No. of Lamps | |
|------|------|------|
| VII | 2 | |
| VII–XIII | 1 | |
| XIV | 1 | |
| | HELLENISTIC | 4 |
| XVI | 7 | |
| Palaimonion A | 25 | |
| Palaimonion B | 7 | |
| XXI | 2 | |
| XXIII | 3 | |
| XXIV | 1 | |
| XXV | 11 | |
| XXII–XXVI | 29 | |
| XXVII | 6 | |
| | ROMAN IMPERIAL | 91 |
| XXVIII | 4 | |
| XXIX | 1 | |
| LATE ROMAN & EARLY CHRISTIAN | | 5 |
| | TOTAL | 100 |

## H. NORTHWEST AREA

This area is not easily definable either in extent or chronologically. It comprises the North Temenos Dump, which contained debris from the burned Archaic Temple of Poseidon but few lamps. The upper strata in this area contained lamps of Hellenistic and Roman types. Since the steep slope of the gully was used for a dump over a long period of time, and was later cut through for the West and North Stoa foundations in the 2nd century of our era, several periods are represented but not readily separated. The lamps show the hodgepodge nature of the fill, but here, as in most areas of the Sanctuary, the types of Roman Imperial times predominate.

| Type | No. of Lamps | |
|------|------|------|
| IV | 2 | |
| | CLASSICAL GREEK | 2 |
| VII E–F | 5 | |
| XI | 2 | |
| VII–XIII | 8 | |
| XII | 1 | |
| | HELLENISTIC | 16 |
| XVI | 10 | |
| Palaimonion A | 1 | |
| XX | 1 | |
| XXI | 6 | |
| XXII | 2 | |
| XXIII | 3 | |
| XXIV | 2 | |
| XXV | 3 | |
| XXVI | 1 | |
| XXII–XXVI | 18 | |
| XXVII | 4 | |
| | ROMAN IMPERIAL | 51 |

| Type | No. of Lamps | |
|------|------|------|
| XXVIII | 2 | |
| XXXII | 1 | |
| LATE ROMAN & EARLY CHRISTIAN | | 3 |
| | TOTAL | 72 |

## I. NORTHWEST RESERVOIR

The Northwest Reservoir, located *ca.* 100 m. northwest of the Temple of Poseidon, was made in pre-Roman times, probably in the 4th century B.C. (*Isthmia* II, p. 31). Since it is still in good condition, it probably suffered little damage during the 150 years (146 B.C. to *ca.* A.D. 3) when the Sanctuary and cult of Poseidon did not function. The stairway and three manholes appear to have remained accessible, and it is likely that the Reservoir was reconditioned after the reopening of the Sanctuary and continued to be used for at least a century. Since only three fragments of Type XXVII, two of them XXVII A, and no later lamps came from the fill, it is probable that the reservoir went out of use in the first half of the 2nd century after Christ. The five pre-Roman lamp fragments do not indicate the original period of use; more likely they were in the earth thrown down after the reservoir was abandoned.

| Type | No. of Lamps | |
|------|------|------|
| I–VI | 1 | |
| VII | 1 | |
| | CLASSICAL GREEK | 2 |
| Unclassified Hellenistic | 1 | |
| VII–XIII | 2 | |
| | HELLENISTIC | 3 |
| XVI | 3 | |
| Palaimonion A | 10 | |
| XXIII | 1 | |
| XXII–XXVI | 4 | |
| XXVII | 3 | |
| | ROMAN IMPERIAL | 21 |
| | TOTAL | 26 |

## J. TEMENOS, WEST END

The area extends in width from the west end of the Temple of Poseidon to the rear wall of the West Stoa. At the north end it begins at what we have called the Northwest Area, *q.v.*, and extends from there southward to the South Stoa. Thus the area is almost square. Three early channels cut across it below the temenos level of Roman times. One branch brought water to the Earlier Stadium; another ran along the north side of the temenos in the direction of the Theater. A third branch from the same source supplied the Southwest Reservoir and West Waterworks. These are the only pre-Roman remains in the area, and they were partly destroyed in the 2nd century after Christ, when the West Stoa was constructed. The top of the Reservoir with its manholes was cut down at that time, but this probably caused little serious contamination to the stratification. The majority of the lamps date from the 1st century after Christ, i.e. from the time prior to the construction of the Stoa. There is no way of telling what monuments may have existed here before the living rock was cut down to make room for the Stoa. Since most of the earlier Roman lamps are of Type XVI and the Palaimonion Types, they may well have found their way here with some removal of earth from the Palaimonion area. The Large Circular Pit is not far away, and from there too came quite a few Palaimonion lamps. There might have been some building in the southwest corner of the Sanctuary in which such lamps had been dedicated, but in view of the specific nature of the Palaimonion lamps, this is less likely.

| Type | No. of Lamps | |
|---|---|---|
| VII–XIII | 1 | |
| | HELLENISTIC | 1 |
| XVI | 6 | |
| Palaimonion A | 6 | |
| Palaimonion B | 5 | |
| XX | 1 | |
| XXI | 1 | |
| XXV | 1 | |
| XXVI | 1 | |
| XXII–XXVI | 3 | |
| XXVII | 2 | |
| | ROMAN IMPERIAL | 26 |
| XXVIII | 5 | |
| XXXI | 2 | |
| LATE ROMAN & EARLY CHRISTIAN | | 7 |
| | TOTAL | 34 |

## K. SOUTHWEST RESERVOIR

The Southwest Reservoir belongs to the same hydraulic system as the West Waterworks. The Reservoir (see *Isthmia* II, pp. 27–29), which has a length of 43.50 m., is of pre-Roman date, but it seems to have been reopened and used for a short time in the early Roman era. The top of the Reservoir was cut away in the 2nd century after Christ when the South Stoa was constructed. The lamps are here very revealing. They are predominantly Hellenistic, and the six specimens of later date belong to types that came into existence shortly before the Christian era and continued in use for over a century. It is significant that no lamps of distinctly later date came from the fill of the Reservoir.

| Type | No. of Lamps | |
|---|---|---|
| V | 1 | |
| VII A–D | 1 | |
| | CLASSICAL GREEK | 2 |
| X | 5 | |
| XI | 2 | |
| VII–XIII | 14 | |
| | HELLENISTIC | 21 |
| XVI | 5 | |
| XVII | 1 | |
| | ROMAN IMPERIAL | 6 |
| | TOTAL | 29 |

## L. TEMENOS, SOUTH SIDE

The area extends in width from the south flank of the Temple of Poseidon to the rear wall of the South Stoa, and from east to west it runs the full length of the Stoa. At the west end the original ground level was lowered when the South Stoa was constructed in the 2nd century of our era. This operation cut off the top part of the Southwest Reservoir with its manholes containing pottery and lamps of Hellenistic times. In this way we can account for the relatively large number of lamps of Hellenistic types (9 as compared with only 3 Classical Greek). In the eastern part the area covers the early Palaimonion, originally consisting only of Sacrificial Pits A and B with their enclosures (first and second periods, *Isthmia* II, pp. 100–101). It is no surprise therefore to find a large number (89) of Palaimonion Type A lamps. And over the whole area close to the cult place of Palaimon, lamps of Palaimonion B lay strewn in the upper levels of the accumulated fill. The two types, Palaimonion A and B, make up more than 66% of the total number of lamps from this area.

| Type | No. of Lamps | |
|---|---|---|
| IV | 2 | |
| I–VI | 1 | |
| | CLASSICAL GREEK | 3 |
| VII E–F | 8 | |
| VII–XIII | 1 | |
| | HELLENISTIC | 9 |
| XVI | 14 | |
| Palaimonion A | 89 | |
| Palaimonion B | 77 | |
| XX | 1 | |
| XXII | 1 | |
| XXIII | 2 | |
| XXV | 2 | |
| XXII–XXVI | 13 | |
| XXVII | 9 | |
| | ROMAN IMPERIAL | 208 |

| Type | No. of Lamps |
|------|-------------|
| XXVIII | 15 |
| XXIX | 1 |
| XXXI | 9 |
| XXXII | 1 |
| XXXIII | 2 |
| LATE ROMAN & EARLY CHRISTIAN | 28 |
| TOTAL | 248 |

## M. PALAIMONION

The second most important cult at Isthmia was that of Palaimon. Its location, to the left as one approached the Temple of Poseidon, i.e. to one arriving from the Later Stadium through the Southeast Propylon, is assured through Pausanias' description (II, ii, 1). It was a large complex of buildings that underwent five periods of construction within the 1st and 2nd centuries of our era. Only in the last period did it receive a temple, a very small circular building with columns but no cella walls.

More than 58% of all the lamps from Isthmia came from the Palaimonion area, and many more found in the adjoining areas had doubtless spilled over from there. That is particularly true of Type XVI and the Palaimonion Types A and B. The latter were certainly cult vessels in a restricted sense, and it is very probable that all the lamps of these types found at Isthmia had originally served in the cult of Palaimon. The presence of a few, only 8, Classical Greek and Hellenistic lamps from this area can be explained partly by the existence of the Earlier Stadium, which had covered nearly the whole area later occupied by the Palaimonion; others may have come from accidental intrusions in the earth fill. No trace of a pre-Roman Palaimonion has been found (*Isthmia* II, p. 99). It is significant that out of 1860 lamps, all but 34 belong to Roman Imperial types. The floruit of the Palaimonion was the first 150 years of our era. The history and importance of the Palaimon Cult during those years is amply reflected by the lamps.

| Type | No. of Lamps | |
|------|-------------|---|
| I | 1 | |
| III | 1 | |
| I–IV | 1 | |
| | CLASSICAL GREEK | 3 |
| VII | 1 | |
| VII–XIII | 3 | |
| XII | 1 | |
| | HELLENISTIC | 5 |
| XVI | 675 | |
| Palaimonion A | 753 | |
| Palaimonion B | 110 | |
| XXI | 1 | |
| XXII | 19 | |

| Type | No. of Lamps | |
|------|-------------|---|
| XXIII | 57 | |
| XXIV | 7 | |
| XXV | 31 | |
| XXII–XXVI | 156 | |
| XXVII | 17 | |
| | ROMAN IMPERIAL | 1826 |
| XXVIII | 17 | |
| XXXI | 4 | |
| XXXII | 4 | |
| XXXIII | 1 | |
| LATE ROMAN & EARLY CHRISTIAN | 26 | |
| | TOTAL | 1860 |

## N. THEATER CAVE

The Cave above the Theater was divided into two chambers, each with its own unroofed court in which meals were prepared. Couches carved out of the native hard clay (marl) show that the chambers were used as dining rooms. Each had its cult niche, a deep depression in the floor shaped to fit a large wine jar, and the entrance to a small side chamber. (For further description see *Isthmia* II, pp. 37–46.) From a deposit of pottery in the entrance court we know that the Theater Cave was abandoned about the middle of the 4th century B.C. But both chambers had been reopened in Roman times when they were probably used for storage. The large number of lamps of Roman Imperial types as well as Late Roman and Early Christian lamps testify to this later use of the cave. Only two lamp fragments are earlier, and these probably stem from the original use of the cave by some religious body connected with the Theater.

| Type | No. of Lamps | |
|------|-------------|---|
| I | 1 | |
| IV | 1 | |
| | CLASSICAL GREEK | 2 |
| XVI | 1 | |
| Palaimonion B | 1 | |
| XXII–XXVI | 2 | |
| XXVII | 14 | |
| | ROMAN IMPERIAL | 18 |
| XXVIII | 22 | |
| XXXIII | 1 | |
| LATE ROMAN & EARLY CHRISTIAN | 23 | |
| | TOTAL | 43 |

## O. THEATER

The Theater shows at least five periods of construction, three in Classical Greek times, two in the Roman era. Only three lamp fragments can go back to the early stages of the building. The very large number of Late Roman and Early Christian lamp fragments would tend to show that the building continued in use until late times, perhaps to the closing of the Games, probably in the early years of the 5th century. The last years of the Games, at the Isthmus as elsewhere, are shrouded in obscurity. It is unlikely that the Theater—or any athletic building at Isthmia—remained intact as late as the reign of the Emperor Justinian (A.D. 527–565).

| Type | No. of Lamps | |
|---|---|---|
| IV | 2 | |
| I–VI | 1 | |
| | CLASSICAL GREEK | 3 |
| XVI | 5 | |
| Palaimonion B | 1 | |
| XXV | 1 | |
| XXII–XXVI | 5 | |
| XXVII | 10 | |
| | ROMAN IMPERIAL | 22 |
| XXVIII | 69 | |
| XXXII | 1 | |
| | LATE ROMAN & EARLY CHRISTIAN | 70 |
| | TOTAL | 95 |

### P. LATER STADIUM

The Later Stadium is a creation of the Hellenistic age; its construction may have begun in the time of Alexander the Great (*Isthmia* II, p. 66). Like the other buildings at Isthmia, it probably suffered some depredation during the time after the destruction of Corinth in 146 B.C. It was reconditioned with some structural modifications in the 1st century after Christ and remained in use as long as the Isthmian Games continued to be held. Only a single lamp fragment, probably of Type VII, can be dated to the pre-Roman era. That is understandable in view of the fact that only small parts of the building have been revealed in trenches and tunnels, and nowhere did our digging extend below the Roman levels.

| Type | No. of Lamps | |
|---|---|---|
| VII | 1 | |
| | HELLENISTIC | 1 |
| Palaimonion A | 1 | |
| XXVI | 1 | |
| XXVII | 9 | |
| | ROMAN IMPERIAL | 11 |
| XXVIII | 13 | |
| | LATE ROMAN & EARLY CHRISTIAN | 13 |
| | TOTAL | 25 |

### Q. EARLY CHRISTIAN FORTRESS

A small-scale excavation, carried on some 250 m. east of the Palaimonion, outside the wall of the Fortress, produced six lamps of Type XXVII within a small structure that could not be identified. Other lamps of later date came from the area of the South Gate of the Fortress, and one complete, very late lamp (3149) came from the bottom of the fill within Tower 7, and should thus be contemporary with the construction of the tower (*Hesperia* 28, 1959, p. 336, no. 14).

The area, being well removed from the Temples of Poseidon and Palaimon, is of interest in itself and for the history of the Fortress, rather than in connection with the main sanctuary.

| Type | No. of Lamps | |
|---|---|---|
| Palaimonion B | 1 | |
| XXVII | 6 | |
| | ROMAN IMPERIAL | 7 |
| XXVIII | 1 | |
| XXXI | 3 | |
| | LATE ROMAN & EARLY CHRISTIAN | 4 |
| | TOTAL | 11 |

### R. SACRED GLEN

The Sacred Glen area has been only partly excavated and the trenches have since been filled up by the owners of the field. The objects found in the area show clearly that one of several cult places, that of Demeter, was in existence in the 4th century B.C., and remained in use in the Roman era. Though unconnected physically with the main cult area of Poseidon, it formed an important annex to the Isthmian sanctuary. The lamps, overwhelmingly Classical Greek and Hellenistic, though not exclusively so, agree in date with other finds of known date from the area (*Isthmia* II, pp. 113–116).

| Type | No. of Lamps | |
|---|---|---|
| IV | 8 | |
| VI | 1 | |
| I–VI | 2 | |
| VII A–D | 4 | |
| | CLASSICAL GREEK | 15 |
| VII | 11 | |
| Unclassified Hellenistic | 1 | |
| XI | 1 | |
| | HELLENISTIC | 13 |
| XVI | 2 | |
| XXII–XXVI | 2 | |
| XXVII | 2 | |
| | ROMAN IMPERIAL | 6 |
| XXVIII | 2 | |
| | LATE ROMAN & EARLY CHRISTIAN | 2 |
| | TOTAL | 36 |

## S. RACHI

This is the least complicated of the areas that produced impressive numbers of lamps. Pottery and other datable objects indicate that the ridge became the site of a fairly extensive textile industry about 360 B.C., and it seems to have come to a complete stop about 120 years later. (See Chrysoula Kardara, *A.J.A.* 65, 1961, p. 263.) There may have been a cult place of earlier date at the now highest point on the ridge. What remains is only a small part of the occupied area; the rest has disappeared as a result of quarrying. Possibly further digging in the area of the quarries would show that there had been earlier industrial establishments there.

The lamps agree well chronologically with the date of the industry established by Professor Kardara. The latest of the Hellenistic Types, IX, X, XI, came into vogue about the middle of the 3rd century and continued to be made later. The three lamps of Roman Imperial times could have been brought by visitors after the textile shops had ceased their production. It is also possible that the parts of the industrial establishment farther west, where the surface has been quarried away, continued in operation later.

| Type | No. of Lamps | | |
|---|---|---|---|
| IV | 2 | | |
| VI | 2 | | |
| I–VI | 2 | | |
| VII A–D | 16 | | |
| | | CLASSICAL GREEK | 22 |
| VII E–F | 36 | | |
| IX | 12 | | |
| Unclassified Hellenistic | 1 | | |
| X | 1 | | |
| XI | 44 | | |
| VII–XIII | 22 | | |
| | | HELLENISTIC | 116 |
| XVI | 1 | | |
| XVII | 1 | | |
| XXVII | 1 | | |
| | | ROMAN IMPERIAL | 3 |
| | | TOTAL | 141 |

## T. WEST FOUNDATION

This area—*ca.* 2 km. southwest of the Temple of Poseidon—is the farthest removed from the main sanctuary. The building, probably a grandstand of the Hippodrome built around a heroon (*Isthmia* II, pp. 117–122), is securely dated about the middle of the 4th century B.C. The few lamps culled from the fill stand in no significant relation to the date of construction or use of the building.

| Type | No. of Lamps | | |
|---|---|---|---|
| I–VI | 2 | | |
| | | CLASSICAL GREEK | 2 |
| XXVIII | 2 | | |
| XXXI | 1 | | |
| | LATE ROMAN & EARLY CHRISTIAN | | 3 |
| | | TOTAL | 5 |

## UNSPECIFIED AREAS

The 20 areas specified above account for all but 62 of the lamps and lamp fragments from our excavations. This residue makes up less than 2% of the total number. Some of these came from scattered trial trenches dug at some distance from the Sanctuary, as for example along the Hellenistic Trans-Isthmian Wall (James R. Wiseman, *Hesperia* 32, 1963, pp. 248–275). Others are chance finds picked up by workmen outside the excavations, sometimes in their own fields, or brought in by children of the neighborhood, for which they received some small compensation. In some instances faulty records or destruction of labels have caused the provenance to be omitted. These items are here grouped together under a single rubric to make the record complete.

| Type | No. of Lamps | | |
|---|---|---|---|
| III | 1 | | |
| IV | 1 | | |
| VII A–D | 1 | | |
| | | CLASSICAL GREEK | 3 |
| VII | 2 | | |
| VII–XIII | 2 | | |
| | | HELLENISTIC | 4 |
| XVI | 13 | | |
| Palaimonion A | 5 | | |
| Palaimonion B | 3 | | |
| XXIII | 1 | | |
| XXV | 4 | | |
| XXI–XXVI | 6 | | |
| XXVII | 14 | | |
| | | ROMAN IMPERIAL | 46 |
| XXVIII | 5 | | |
| XXX | 1 | | |
| XXXI | 1 | | |
| XXXIII | 2 | | |
| | LATE ROMAN & EARLY CHRISTIAN | | 9 |
| | | TOTAL | 62 |

# CONCLUSIONS

When we consider the areas described above in terms of the several types and the total number of lamps found in each, certain facts stand out as significant. Very striking is the small number of Classical Greek (132) and Hellenistic (206) lamps in comparison with the large quantities from Roman Imperial times (2632). The Late Roman and Early Christian types (220), though present in small quantities in all but four of the areas, are also poorly represented.

Lamps of Classical Greek types are found in significant quantities in only four areas: the Large Circular Pit (57), the Temenos, East End (10), Sacred Glen (15), and the Rachi (22). Those from the Large Circular Pit and the East End areas are to be explained as having served in connection with the precinct and Cult of Poseidon. Both these areas contained lamps of the early Types I, II, and III, which are too early to have been used in the Temple of the 5th century B.C., but of appropriate date for the Archaic Temple. The other two areas, the Sacred Glen and the Rachi, contained later Types, IV—VII A—D, which come down into the 4th century B.C. Both these areas are predominantly Hellenistic in date, and this is clearly shown by the lamps found in them.

The bulk of the lamps, more than $83^0/_0$ of them, belong to the Roman Imperial times. Of these by far the greater number are to be dated in the 1st century after Christ, the period when the cult of Palaimon flourished. It is the Palaimonion that produced most of the lamps of this period. The nightly mystery rites of Palaimon must have attracted large crowds of worshipers, and the lamps were needed for illumination of the whole area. The fact that many lamps, some quite intact, of Type XVI and the Palaimonion Types were found in the sacrifical pits (*Isthmia* II, pp. 100—102) tends to indicate that they were brought also as dedications. Whether they served other cult practices, such as lychnomanteia, is uncertain. The great number of lamps from the Palaimonion and the frequent architectural changes give the impression that the cult of Palaimon in the 1st century of our era eclipsed that of Poseidon in importance.

# CONCORDANCE

| Inv. No. | Cat. No. | Inv. No. | Cat. No. | Inv. No. | Cat. No. | Inv. No. | Cat. No. |
|---|---|---|---|---|---|---|---|
| IP 54 | 241 | IP 318 | 182 | IP 716 | 58 | IP 916 | 351 |
| 55 | 242 | 319 | 3074 | 718 | 219 | 917 | 538 |
| 56 | 133 | 320 | 2450 | 719 | 212 | 918 | 594 |
| 57 | 337 | 321 | 2343 | 720 | 141 | 919 | 352 |
| 75 | 554 | 368 | 181 | 743 | 183 | 920 | 588 |
| 81 | 2369 | 370 | 59 | 750 | 1110 | 921 | 576 |
| 91 | 513 | 371 | 109 | 754 | 129 | 922 | 600 |
| 105 | 2342 | 372 | 126 | 781 | 572 | 923 | 348 |
| 109 + 308 | 2341 | 373 | 85 | 782 | 344 | 924 | 342 |
| 113 | 663 | 430 | 2378 | 783 | 482 | 925 | 516 |
| 121 | 2374 | 431 | 83 | 784 | 497 | 926 | 1139 |
| 205 | 620 | 444 | 124 | 785 | 2387 | 928 | 1485 |
| 206 | 488 | 445 | 207 | 787 | 110 | 929 | 2367 |
| 207 | 237 | 446 | 114 | 798 | 515 | 932 | 537 |
| 208 | 227 | 447 | 137 | 802 | 116 | 933 | 626 |
| 209 | 228 | 452 | 113 | 827 | 2348 | 934 | 579 |
| 210 | 134 | 455 | 127 | 842 | 1487 | 942 | 1212 |
| 213 | 135 | 478 | 122 | 848 | 597 | 943 | 494 |
| 214 | 2472 | 483 | 205 | 849 | 633 | 944 | 1206 |
| 215 | 3145 | 486 | 138 | 853 | 481 | 945 | 1122 |
| 216 | 654 | 544 | 115 | 854 | 2119 | 948 | 353 |
| 217 | 3148 | 553 a | 136 | 855 | 625 | 949 | 629 |
| 245 | 245 | 553 b | 180 | 859 | 495 | 951 | 350 |
| 246 | 139 | 554 | 211 | 860 | 2459 | 953 | 1116 |
| 251 | 90 | 555 | 206 | 862 | 649 | 954 | 1134 |
| 254 | 234 | 556 | 233 | 872 | 1533 | 955 | 2461 |
| 265 | 239 | 590 | 236 | 873 | 1483 | 956 a–d | 1482 |
| 266 | 246 | 592 | 232 | 875 | 643 | 958 | 2445 |
| 267 | 240 | 593 | 214 | 876 | 1123 | 959 | 1127 |
| 268 | 244 | 594 | 201 | 877 | 1124 | 964 | 1120 |
| 269 | 231 | 596 | 229 | 884 | 1135 | 967 | 1257 |
| 270 | 208 | 599 | 243 | 886 | 1260 | 975 | 504 |
| 271 | 142 | 619 | 125 | 888 | 617 | 976 | 359 |
| 272 | 140 | 637 | 238 | 889 | 493 | 977 | 1121 |
| 273 | 203 | 645 | 1112 | 890 | 357 | 984 | 1132 |
| 274 | 204 | 647 | 1111 | 891 | 478 | 988 | 2798 |
| 284 | 215 | 648 | 1114 | 892 | 2460 | 992 | 2085 |
| 308 + 109 | 2341 | 649 | 2386 | 893 a | 1136 | 994 | 1530 |
| 309 | 2517 | 653 | 1251 | 893 b | 1270 | 996 | 2084 |
| 310 | 3175 | 654 | 484 | 900 | 1118 | 1000 | 535 |
| 311 | 656 | 655 | 507 | 902 | 1129 | 1004 | 2113 |
| 312 | 3077 | 656 | 362 | 905 | 2537 | 1005 | 2117 |
| 313 | 2509 | 657 | 583 | 911 | 347 | 1006 | 2120 |
| 314 | 3088 | 658 | 571 | 912 | 1137 | 1007 | 2112 |
| 315 | 369 | 662 | 1213 | 913 | 540 | 1009 | 218 |
| 316 | 655 | 697 | 213 | 914 | 336 | 1010 | 2098 |
| 317 | 3151 | 714 | 132 | 915 | 608 | 1011 | 1130 |

| Inv. No. | Cat. No. | Inv. No. | Cat. No. | Inv. No. | Cat. No. | Inv. No. | Cat. No. |
|---|---|---|---|---|---|---|---|
| IP 1013 | 2125 | IP 1587 | 1115 | IP 1648 | 503 | IP 1866 | 623 |
| 1014 | 1210 | 1593 | 2872 | 1649 | 505 | 1867 | 591 |
| 1017 | 3 | 1594 | 622 | 1650 | 529 | 1868 | 521 |
| 1030 | 2121 | 1595 | 501 | 1651 | 590 | 1869 | 542 |
| 1031 | 2115 | 1596 | 548 | 1652 | 602 | 1870 | 364 |
| 1032 | 2095 | 1597 | 343 | 1653 | 621 | 1871 | 360 |
| 1033 | 2097 | 1598 | 631 | 1654 | 589 | 1872 | 587 |
| 1034 | 2096 | 1599 | 565 | 1655 | 534 | 1873 | 557 |
| 1048 | 2522 | 1600 | 528 | 1656 | 612 | 1874 | 634 |
| 1049 | 2538 | 1601 | 577 | 1657 | 533 | 1875 | 575 |
| 1055 | 2843 | 1602 | 486 | 1658 | 356 | 1876 | 517 |
| 1057 | 2527 | 1603 | 560 | 1659 | 630 | 1877 | 574 |
| 1059 | 2530 | 1604 | 611 | 1660 | 659 | 1878 | 547 |
| 1060 | 2536 A | 1605 | 483 | 1661 | 658 | 1879 | 613 |
| 1080 | 2536 | 1606 | 610 | 1662 | 479 | 1880 | 585 |
| 1095 | 3172 | 1607 | 354 | 1663 | 635 | 1881 | 510 |
| 1096 | 2368 | 1608 | 502 | 1664 | 580 | 1882 | 647 |
| 1102 | 1512 | 1609 | 506 | 1665 | 641 | 1883 | 599 |
| 1106 | 487 | 1610 | 603 | 1666 | 355 | 1884 | 361 |
| 1122 | 2116 | 1611 | 615 | 1667 | 619 | 1885 | 539 |
| 1123 | 2111 | 1612 | 593 | 1668 | 563 | 1886 | 552 |
| 1137 | 2465 | 1613 | 525 | 1669 | 566 | 1887 | 526 |
| 1150 | 235 | 1614 | 598 | 1670 | 661 | 1888 | 637 |
| 1151 | 2502 | 1615 | 545 | 1671 | 1207 | 1889 | 568 |
| 1160 | 49 | 1616 | 511 | 1672 | 1131 | 1890 | 363 |
| 1296 | 2094 | 1617 | 644 | 1673 | 1119 | 1891 | 627 |
| 1297 | 2082 | 1618 | 558 | 1674 | 1128 | 1892 | 567 |
| 1299 | 2118 | 1619 | 616 | 1675 | 1258 | 1893 | 345 |
| 1308 | 31 | 1620 | 573 | 1676 | 1138 | 1894 | 520 |
| 1309 | 2123 | 1621 | 596 | 1677 | 2124 | 1895 | 543 |
| 1310 | 1484 | 1622 | 618 | 1678 | 530 | 1896 | 639 |
| 1311 | 2114 | 1623 | 544 | 1679 | 636 | 1897 | 624 |
| 1312 | 2127 | 1624 | 646 | 1680 | 3150 | 1898 | 570 |
| 1313 | 1481 | 1625 | 512 | 1681 | 3179 | 1899 | 607 |
| 1316 | 119 | 1626 | 522 | 1682 | 3087 | 1900 | 606 |
| 1318 | 50 | 1627 | 561 | 1687 | 1109 | 1901 | 642 |
| 1322 | 61 | 1628 | 555 | 1698 | 3152 | 1902 | 340 |
| 1323 | 51 | 1629 | 349 | 1700 | 3144 | 1903 | 358 |
| 1327 | 81 | 1630 | 628 | 1743 | 22 | 1904 | 604 |
| 1328 | 1265 | 1631 | 578 | 1798 | 30 | 1905 | 586 |
| 1329 | 98 | 1632 | 640 | 1850 | 485 | 1906 | 524 |
| 1410 | 2080 | 1633 | 652 | 1851 | 551 | 1907 | 514 |
| 1415 | 2083 | 1634 | 582 | 1852 | 509 | 1908 | 536 |
| 1418 | 1518 | 1635 | 546 | 1853 | 498 | 1909 | 595 |
| 1534 | 15 | 1636 | 581 | 1854 | 492 | 1910 | 605 |
| 1560 | 2079 | 1637 | 564 | 1855 | 508 | 1911 | 489 |
| 1561 | 1537 | 1638 | 562 | 1856 | 480 | 1912 | 500 |
| 1562 | 2129 | 1639 | 556 | 1857 | 490 | 1913 | 527 |
| 1563 | 2126 | 1640 | 341 | 1858 | 499 | 1914 | 523 |
| 1564 | 2122 | 1641 | 632 | 1859 | 638 | 1915 | 2458 |
| 1565 | 2128 | 1642 | 367 | 1860 | 532 | 1916 | 2478 |
| 1566 | 1672 | 1643 | 657 | 1861 | 496 | 1917 | 2437 |
| 1569 | 45 | 1644 | 491 | 1862 | 592 | 1918 | 2485 |
| 1571 | 1486 | 1645 | 531 | 1863 | 346 | 1919 | 2490 |
| 1578 | 14 | 1646 | 550 | 1864 | 609 | 1921 | 3036 |
| 1586 | 1117 | 1647 | 519 | 1865 | 645 | 1922 | 2995 |

| Inv. No. | Cat. No. | Inv. No. | Cat. No. | Inv. No. | Cat. No. | Inv. No. | Cat. No. |
|---|---|---|---|---|---|---|---|
| IP 1923 | 3040 | IP 2277 a, b | 2805 | IP 2551 | 3057 | IP 2685 | 3043 |
| 1924 | 3073 | 2278 | 2998 | 2552 | 2542 | 2686 | 3091 |
| 1925 | 3038 | 2282 | 2990 | 2553 | 2832 | 2687 + IP 2704 | 3028 |
| 1926 | 2991 | 2283 | 3031 | 2554 + 2559 | 2967 | 2688 | 3006 |
| 1927 | 3146 | 2284 | 3086 | 2555 | 3080 | 2692 | 3033 |
| 1928 | 3149 | 2287 | 3098 | 2557 | 2861 | 2693 | 2986 |
| 1929 | 2853 | 2288 | 2466 | 2558 | 2802 | 2694 | 3010 |
| 1933 | 2543 | 2289 a, b | 2805 | 2559 + 2554 | 2967 | 2695 | 3044 |
| 1938 | 2529 | 2291 | 2873 | 2561 | 3011 | 2696 | 3089 |
| 1951 | 648 | 2292 | 2787 | 2562 | 2971 | 2697 | 3064 |
| 1959 | 2797 | 2293 | 3090 | 2565 | 2972 | 2698 | 3004 |
| 1960 | 2796 | 2315 | 42 | 2566 | 2869 | 2699 | 3094 |
| 1963 | 2833 | 2317 | 43 | 2567 | 2868 | 2700 | 3056 |
| 1964 | 2823 | 2318 | 74 | 2568 | 2999 | 2701 | 3046 |
| 1965 | 2782 | 2322 | 6 | 2569 a, b | 2808 | 2702 a + 2702 b | 3140 + |
| 1967 | 2344 | 2323 | 91 | 2570 | 3049 | | 2974 |
| 1969 | 2826 | 2324 | 584 | 2572 | 48 | 2702 b + 2702 a | 2974 + |
| 1970 | 1250 | 2325 | 2781 | 2573 | 123 | | 3140 |
| 1971 | 1259 | 2326 | 2842 | 2578 | 2390 | 2703 | 3096 |
| 1972 | 1211 | 2334 | 559 | 2580 | 518 | 2704 + IP 2687 | 3028 |
| 1973 | 1488 | 2337 | 2827 | 2583 | 553 | 2705 | 3099 |
| 1974 | 1538 | 2373 | 38 | 2603 | 1267 | 2706 | 3072 |
| 1975 | 1532 | 2374 | 76 | 2604 | 220 | 2707 a–c | 3100 |
| 1976 | 1489 | 2375 | 44 | 2606 a–c | 1282 | 2708 | 2807 |
| 1977 | 1262 | 2376 | 19 | 2607 | 339 | 2709 | 2835 |
| 1978 | 1209 | 2442 | 7 | 2608 a | 1534 | 2710 | 666 |
| 1980 | 3174 | 2443 | 13 | 2608 b | 1535 | 2711 | 2973 |
| 2056 | 12 | 2444 | 41 | 2613 | 569 | 2712 | 2870 |
| 2063 | 3153 | 2445 | 5 | 2614 a | 1269 | 2713 | 3093 |
| 2064 | 2521 | 2446 | 16 | 2614 b | 1536 | 2715 | 3097 |
| 2066 | 3147 | 2447 | 47 | 2615 | 2457 | 2716 | 653 |
| 2068 | 3032 | 2448 | 75 | 2616 | 662 | 2717 | 3001 |
| 2154 | 1264 | 2449 | 80 | 2617 a | 2480 | 2718 | 3000 |
| 2155 | 1113 | 2450 | 39 | 2617 b | 2473 | 2719 | 3029 |
| 2187 | 1208 | 2451 | 10 | 2618 | 2372 | 2720 | 2864 |
| 2188 | 1266 | 2452 | 17 | 2619 | 1268 | 2721 | 2836 |
| 2189 a | 1133 | 2453 | 21 | 2622 | 2865 | 2722 | 2871 |
| 2203 | 1263 | 2454 | 37 | 2623 | 2788 | 2723 | 2717 |
| 2204 | 1256 | 2518 | 2799 | 2625 | 2806 | 2724 | 2983 |
| 2205 | 1531 | 2519 | 184 | 2630 | 1261 | 2725 | 3005 |
| 2206 | 368 | 2523 | 36 | 2632 | 2462 | 2726 | 3045 |
| 2207 | 1126 | 2524 + IP 5776 | 1 | 2634 | 2863 | 2727 | 3007 |
| 2208 | 1125 | 2525 | 18 | 2635 | 230 | 2728 | 3092 |
| 2209 | 1272 | 2526 | 2 | 2636 | 29 | 2729 | 2993 |
| 2211 | 541 | 2527 | 40 | 2640 | 2338 | 2731 | 3041 |
| 2212 | 2443 | 2528 | 100 | 2642 | 2834 | 2732 | 2454 |
| 2213 | 549 | 2529 | 89 | 2644 | 2867 | 2733 | 601 |
| 2245 | 2966 | 2533 | 614 | 2648 | 1271 | 2734 | 3008 |
| 2246 + 2249 | 2969 | 2542 a | 2989 | 2660 | 2483 | 2735 | 3002 |
| 2249 + 2246 | 2969 | 2544 | 2829 | 2663 | 2534 | 2736 | 3095 |
| 2250 | 3066 | 2545 | 665 | 2666 | 2339 | 2737 | 3003 |
| 2251 | 9 | 2546 | 2964 | 2667 | 2783 | 2738 | 651 |
| 2252 | 2860 | 2547 | 2866 | 2668 a, b, b′ | 664 | 2739 | 3042 |
| 2253 | 2985 | 2548 | 3055 | 2669 | 2785 | 2740 | 3034 |
| 2254 | 2984 | 2549 | 3178 | 2671 | 671 | 2742 | 2992 |
| 2256 | 2825 | 2550 | 2965 | 2672 | 3052 | 2743 | 3009 |

| Inv. No. | Cat. No. | Inv. No. | Cat. No. | Inv. No. | Cat. No. | Inv. No. | Cat. No. |
|---|---|---|---|---|---|---|---|
| IP 2744 | **3082** | IP 3649 | **2337** | IP 3991 | **660** | IP 4047 | **151** |
| 2745 | **3067** | 3926 | **650** | 3992 | **2730** | 4048 a, b | **3141** |
| 2746 | **3068** | 3927 | **338** | 3993 | **2904** | 4048 c | **2333** |
| 2751 | **86** | 3928 | **66** | 3994 a | **2253** | 4049 a–d | **276** |
| 2763 | **2849** | 3930 | **2883** | 3994 b, c | **2033** | 4050 | **226** |
| 2766 | **2518** | 3931 | **2880** | 3995 | **2249** | 4051 | **102** |
| 2767 | **3035** | 3932 | **2838** | 3996 | **2029** | 4052 | **1759** |
| 2773 | **2804** | 3933 | **2837** | 3997 | **2238** | 4053 | **2258** |
| 2775 | **2831** | 3938 | **28** | 3998 | **2136** | 4054 | **807** |
| 2776 | **2857** | 3943 | **2109** | 3999 | **2235** | 4055 | **449** |
| 2777 | **2852** | 3944 | **2087** | 4000 | **2272** | 4056 | **813** |
| 2778 | **2980** | 3945 | **1770** | 4001 | **2068** | 4057 | **832** |
| 2781 | **2824** | 3946 | **2042** | 4002 | **2933** | 4058 | **3126** |
| 2782 | **2862** | 3947 | **2266** | 4003 | **2273** | 4059 | **2257** |
| 2784 | **2803** | 3948 | **2243** | 4004 | **1528** | 4060 | **2270** |
| 2785 | **2828** | 3949 | **2259** | 4005 | **2262** | 4061 | **1662** |
| 2799 | **2848** | 3950 | **2236** | 4006 | **2671** | 4062 | **2007** |
| 2801 | **2858** | 3951 | **3083** | 4007 | **3058** | 4063 | **2246** |
| 2814 | **2988** | 3952 | **3014** | 4008 | **2745** | 4064 | **2016** |
| 2816 | **2544** | 3953 | **3027** | 4009 | **2484** | 4065 | **2244** |
| 2819 | **3070** | 3954 | **62** | 4010 | **2469** | 4066 | **2256** |
| 2824 | **3037** | 3955 | **153** | 4011 | **4** | 4067 | **1292** |
| 2826 | **3039** | 3956 | **2741** | 4012 | **70** | 4068 | **1280** |
| 2831 | **3168** | 3957 | **178** | 4013 | **1998** | 4069 | **332** |
| 2840 | **2784** | 3958 | **2847** | 4014 | **2048** | 4070 | **2768** |
| 2848 | **2800** | 3959 | **117** | 4015 | **2978** | 4071 | **1941** |
| 2904 | **2996** | 3960 | **2373** | 4016 | **2963** | 4072 | **2067** |
| 2905 | **2975** | 3961 | **2902** | 4017 | **2240** | 4073 | **693** |
| 2906 | **3050** | 3962 | **669** | 4018 | **818** | 4074 | **2928** |
| 2907 | **3133** | 3963 | **202** | 4019 | **2356** | 4075 | **2895** |
| 2908 | **3078** | 3964 | **216** | 4020 | **312** | 4076 | **2910** |
| 2914 | **3071** | 3965 a, b | **3047** | 4021 | **1656** | 4077 | **2939** |
| 2915 | **2981** | 3966 | **162** | 4022 | **1765** | 4078 | **2076** |
| 2916 | **2977** | 3967 | **2920** | 4023 | **1761** | 4079 | **2268** |
| 2917 | **2970** | 3968 | **2929** | 4024 | **2227** | 4080 a | **2791** |
| 2919 | **2997** | 3969 | **2938** | 4025 | **1598** | 4080 b | **2821** |
| 2975 | **2336** | 3970 | **667** | 4026 | **395** | 4081 | **2271** |
| 2999 | **2851** | 3971 | **668** | 4027 | **94** | 4082 | **2959** |
| 3007 | **2526** | 3972 | **2937** | 4028 | **2265** | 4083 | **790** |
| 3009 | **2541** | 3973 | **2925** | 4029 | **305** | 4084 | **402** |
| 3014 | **166** | 3974 | **3110** | 4031 | **2524** | 4085 | **2948** |
| 3015 | **121** | 3975 | **2771** | 4032 | **2663** | 4086 | **2934** |
| 3484 | **2442** | 3976 | **2817** | 4033 | **730** | 4087 | **2697** |
| 3489 a, b | **20** | 3977 | **2855** | 4034 | **2775** | 4088 | **2859** |
| 3505 | **2968** | 3978 | **3059** | 4035 | **2662** | 4089 | **3103** |
| 3507 | **179** | 3979 | **2953** | 4036 | **2555** | 4090 | **3084** |
| 3508 | **107** | 3980 | **2941** | 4037 | **2401** | 4091 | **2982** |
| 3519 | **2345** | 3981 | **2761** | 4038 | **2347** | 4092 | **2946** |
| 3524 | **128** | 3982 | **2004** | 4039 | **2668** | 4093 | **3019** |
| 3528 | **2850** | 3983 | **3132** | 4040 | **2346** | 4094 | **2520** |
| 3533 | **2830** | 3984 | **2932** | 4041 | **2548** | 4095 | **2815** |
| 3546 | **2987** | 3985 | **2721** | 4042 | **2623** | 4096 | **2646** |
| 3556 | **2340** | 3986 | **2893** | 4043 | **2612** | 4097 | **2911** |
| 3578 | **3069** | 3987 | **3134** | 4044 | **2464** | 4098 | **2955** |
| 3580 | **2334** | 3988 | **670** | 4045 | **2979** | 4099 a, b | **2856** |
| 3629 | **2822** | 3990 | **2926** | 4046 | **60** | 4100 | **165** |

| Inv. No. | Cat. No. | Inv. No. | Cat. No. | Inv. No. | Cat. No. | Inv. No. | Cat. No. |
|---|---|---|---|---|---|---|---|
| IP 4101 | 103 | IP 4157 | 1145 | IP 4209 a | 2427 | IP 4258 | 3021 |
| 4102 | 2707 | 4158 | 63 | 4209 b | 2713 | 4259 | 302 |
| 4103 | 156 | 4159 | 2809 | 4210 a | 2519 | 4260 | 3142 |
| 4104 | 1294 | 4160 | 2906 | 4210 b | 2607 | 4261 | 2773 |
| 4105 | 2637 | 4161 | 2947 | 4211 | 2474 | 4262 | 2531 |
| 4106 | 2491 | 4162 | 2263 | 4212 | 2628 | 4263 | 2942 |
| 4107 | 2557 | 4163 | 814 | 4213 b | 2897 | 4264 | 266 |
| 4108 | 2510 | 4164 | 2818 | 4213 c | 2605 | 4265 | 3076 |
| 4109 | 3060 | 4165 | 2230 | 4214 | 2957 | 4266 | 1996 |
| 4110 | 1987 | 4166 a, b | 330 | 4215 a | 326 | 4267 | 68 |
| 4111 | 765 | 4167 | 3107 | 4215 b, c | 108 | 4268 | 69 |
| 4112 | 2746 | 4168 | 3017 | 4216 | 2553 | 4269 | 2619 |
| 4113 | 2661 | 4169 | 3081 | 4217 | 2890 | 4270 | 2251 |
| 4114 | 282 | 4170 | 2045 | 4218 | 477 | 4271 | 2145 |
| 4115 | 2672 | 4171 | 2242 | 4219 a | 2878 | 4272 | 2142 |
| 4116 | 683 | 4172 | 2767 | 4219 b | 2952 | 4273 | 1298 |
| 4117 | 707 | 4173 | 163 | 4220 | 2744 | 4274 | 1519 |
| 4118 | 3129 | 4174 | 2793 | 4221 | 2921 | 4275 | 2061 |
| 4119 | 2011 | 4175 | 2625 | 4222 | 2917 | 4276 | 2841 |
| 4120 | 1988 | 4176 | 794 | 4223 | 55 | 4277 | 2840 |
| 4121 | 1606 | 4177 | 2789 | 4224 | 2819 | 4278 | 2877 |
| 4122 | 1278 | 4178 | 2580 | 4225 a | 2913 | 4279 | 2949 |
| 4123 | 2053 | 4179 | 1199 | 4225 b | 2886 | 4280 | 759 |
| 4124 | 771 | 4180 | 3075 | 4226 | 2945 | 4281 a | 2586 |
| 4125 a, b | 2846 | 4181 | 65 | 4227 | 3112 | 4281 b | 2361 |
| 4126 | 3124 | 4182 | 53 | 4228 | 2811 | 4282 | 3122 |
| 4127 a | 2062 | 4183 | 274 | 4229 a, c | 2954 | 4283 | 2898 |
| 4127 b | 1989 | 4184 | 2051 | 4229 b | 2888 | 4284 | 2556 |
| 4128 | 2055 | 4185 | 2675 | 4230 | 2944 | 4285 | 2686 |
| 4129 | 2528 | 4186 | 2613 | 4231 | 2889 | 4286 | 3159 |
| 4130 | 2892 | 4187 | 2679 | 4232 | 200 | 4287 | 2231 |
| 4131 | 2776 | 4188 | 189 | 4233 | 2228 | 4288 | 3136 |
| 4132 a, c | 2604 | 4189 | 157 | 4234 | 2241 | 4289 | 2233 |
| 4132 b | 2428 | 4190 a | 2496 | 4235 | 2221 | 4290 | 316 |
| 4133 | 2567 | 4190 b | 2494 | 4236 | 2274 | 4291 | 224 |
| 4134 | 2708 | 4191 | 2635 | 4237 | 2093 | 4292 | 290 |
| 4135 | 2685 | 4192 | 2627 | 4238 | 2015 | 4293 | 1285 |
| 4136 | 3123 | 4193 | 3030 | 4239 | 2089 | 4294 | 2335 |
| 4137 | 2722 | 4194 | 2909 | 4240 | 2217 | 4295 | 2036 |
| 4139 | 2777 | 4195 | 2908 | 4241 | 1661 | 4296 | 3161 |
| 4140 | 2388 | 4196 | 2224 | 4242 | 2452 | 4297 | 2101 |
| 4141 a | 2736 | 4197 | 2901 | 4243 | 2569 | 4298 | 2034 |
| 4141 c | 2588 | 4198 | 3119 | 4244 | 2740 | 4299 | 2044 |
| 4142 | 2742 | 4199 a | 2814 | 4245 | 2762 | 4300 | 748 |
| 4143 | 447 | 4199 b | 2907 | 4246 | 800 | 4301 | 811 |
| 4144 | 2618 | 4200 | 2629 | 4247 | 781 | 4302 | 709 |
| 4145 | 2754 | 4201 | 2621 | 4248 | 2845 | 4303 | 700 |
| 4146 | 176 | 4202 a | 2884 | 4249 | 2476 | 4304 | 808 |
| 4148 | 2649 | 4202 b | 2958 | 4250 | 782 | 4305 | 2041 |
| 4149 | 2255 | 4203 | 2218 | 4251 | 2252 | 4306 | 2714 |
| 4150 | 795 | 4204 | 3104 | 4252 | 3157 | 4307 | 2063 |
| 4151 | 2650 | 4205 | 170 | 4253 | 3180 | 4308 | 2017 |
| 4152 | 3137 | 4206 | 2794 | 4254 | 2222 | 4309 | 2043 |
| 4154 | 217 | 4207 a | 2936 | 4255 | 2035 | 4310 | 2059 |
| 4155 | 67 | 4207 b | 2899 | 4256 | 3166 | 4311 | 3106 |
| 4156 | 187 | 4208 | 2896 | 4257 | 2728 | 4312 | 805 |

| Inv. No. | Cat. No. | Inv. No. | Cat. No. | Inv. No. | Cat. No. | Inv. No. | Cat. No. |
|---|---|---|---|---|---|---|---|
| IP 4313 | 2060 | IP 4369 | 2912 | IP 4422 | 1953 | IP 4478 a, b | 732 |
| 4314 | 1197 | 4370 a | 1287 | 4423 | 1560 | 4479 a–c | 727 |
| 4315 | 3015 | 4370 b–d | 1849 | 4424 | 1277 | 4480 a, b | 734 |
| 4316 | 193 | 4371 | 1296 | 4425 | 1884 | 4481 a | 2470 |
| 4317 | 2223 | 4372 | 1517 | 4426 | 1898 | 4481 b | 2403 |
| 4318 | 1895 | 4373 | 436 | 4427 | 778 | 4481 c | 2404 |
| 4319 | 2187 | 4374 | 1808 | 4429 | 1817 | 4481 d | 2446 |
| 4320 | 2216 | 4375 | 777 | 4430 a, b | 1860 | 4482 a–c | 2597 |
| 4321 | 2185 | 4376 | 2047 | 4431 | 93 | 4483 a | 3139 |
| 4322 | 1930 | 4377 | 1902 | 4432 | 1863 | 4483 b | 2599 |
| 4323 a, b | 1555 | 4378 | 2037 | 4433 | 1862 | 4484 | 2400 |
| 4324 | 1899 | 4379 | 2780 A | 4434 | 831 | 4485 | 2691 |
| 4325 | 174 | 4380 | 1886 | 4435 | 442 | 4486 | 2611 |
| 4326 | 1563 | 4381 | 1888 | 4436 | 717 | 4487 | 2391 |
| 4327 | 2174 | 4382 | 1440 | 4437 | 105 | 4488 | 2370 |
| 4328 | 3102 | 4383 a | 1975 | 4438 | 1858 | 4489 | 2752 |
| 4329 | 3156 | 4383 b | 1449 | 4439 | 1859 | 4490 | 2568 |
| 4330 | 1550 | 4384 | 2019 | 4440 | 1854 | 4491 a–c | 2601 |
| 4331 | 2191 | 4385 | 2737 | 4441 | 1935 | 4491 d | 2440 |
| 4332 | 2134 | 4386 a | 1911 | 4442 | 1861 | 4492 | 2689 |
| 4333 | 2103 | 4386 b | 1450 | 4443 | 1321 | 4493 a | 1686 |
| 4334 | 1985 | 4387 | 3181 | 4444 a, b | 722 | 4493 b | 2049 |
| 4335 | 1586 | 4388 | 2642 | 4445 a–d | 451 | 4494 | 1461 |
| 4336 | 2195 | 4389 | 3108 | 4446 | 391 | 4495 a | 1940 |
| 4337 | 2885 | 4390 | 1690 | 4447 a–c | 690 | 4495 b | 2073 |
| 4338 | 287 | 4391 a, b | 1956 | 4448 | 699 | 4496 a, b | 1982 |
| 4339 | 335 | 4392 | 2022 | 4449 a, b | 705 | 4496 c | 2074 |
| 4340 | 258 | 4393 | 1978 | 4450 a, b | 453 | 4497 | 1150 |
| 4341 | 262 | 4394 | 2032 | 4451 a, b | 450 | 4498 | 1573 |
| 4342 | 313 | 4395 | 1557 | 4452 | 755 | 4499 | 1467 |
| 4343 | 308 | 4396 | 1508 | 4453 a–c | 455 | 4500 | 1362 |
| 4344 | 320 | 4397 | 776 | 4454 | 750 | 4501 | 2009 |
| 4345 | 198 | 4398 | 1970 | 4455 a, b | 713 | 4502 | 2039 |
| 4346 | 319 | 4399 | 2184 | 4456 a, b | 459 | 4503 a | 1977 |
| 4347 | 334 | 4400 | 2023 | 4457 a, b | 461 | 4503 b | 2071 |
| 4348 | 2190 | 4401 | 753 | 4458 a, b | 702 | 4504 a | 2030 |
| 4349 a, b | 1466 | 4402 | 1928 | 4459 | 678 | 4504 b | 1226 |
| 4350 | 1907 | 4403 | 715 | 4460 a, b | 720 | 4505 a, b | 1958 |
| 4351 | 2155 | 4404 | 1960 | 4461 a, b | 695 | 4506 a | 2010 |
| 4352 | 3154 | 4405 | 1967 | 4462 a–d | 706 | 4506 b | 1973 |
| 4353 | 3117 | 4406 | 1961 | 4463 a, c | 838 | 4507 | 1964 |
| 4354 | 1931 | 4408 | 2181 | 4463 b | 2357 | 4508 | 1954 |
| 4355 | 56 | 4409 a | 2070 | 4464 a, b | 733 | 4509 | 1965 |
| 4356 | 2951 | 4409 b | 1971 | 4465 a–c | 718 | 4510 | 2108 |
| 4357 | 195 | 4410 a, b | 1926 | 4466 | 694 | 4511 | 742 |
| 4358 | 3051 | 4411 b | 1216 | 4467 a–c | 729 | 4512 | 1968 |
| 4359 | 106 | 4412 | 1558 | 4468 a, b | 731 | 4513 | 2150 |
| 4360 | 1275 | 4413 a, b | 2147 | 4469 | 762 | 4514 | 2105 |
| 4361 a | 1283 | 4414 | 1561 | 4470 a, b | 679 | 4515 | 1527 |
| 4362 a–d | 1175 | 4415 | 1217 | 4471 a, b | 689 | 4516 | 1942 |
| 4363 | 1818 | 4416 | 1188 | 4472 a–d | 726 | 4517 | 3177 |
| 4364 | 375 | 4417 | 1620 | 4473 a, b | 701 | 4518 | 1458 |
| 4365 | 2406 | 4418 a, b | 1906 | 4474 a, b | 682 | 4519 | 1546 |
| 4366 | 1844 | 4419 | 1602 | 4475 | 746 | 4520 a | 2014 |
| 4367 | 1166 | 4420 | 1604 | 4476 a, b | 711 | 4520 b | 1979 |
| 4368 | 1191 | 4421 | 1575 | 4477 a–c | 467 | 4520 c | 1587 |

| Inv. No. | Cat. No. | Inv. No. | Cat. No. | Inv. No. | Cat. No. | Inv. No. | Cat. No. |
|---|---|---|---|---|---|---|---|
| IP 4521 | 754 | IP 4571 | 1401 | IP 4615 | 1828 | IP 4667 a, b | 728 |
| 4522 | 830 | 4572 a–c | 1417 | 4616 | 2286 | 4668 | 797 |
| 4523 | 2636 | 4572 d | 2031 | 4617 | 3127 | 4668 A | 812 |
| 4524 | 1976 | 4573 | 1632 | 4618 | 27 | 4669 | 1821 |
| 4525 | 1460 | 4574 | 1622 | 4619 a, b | 1647 | 4670 | 1838 |
| 4526 | 1465 | 4575 a | 1176 | 4620 | 2395 | 4671 | 2680 |
| 4527 | 1470 | 4575 b, c | 1799 | 4621 | 1245 | 4672 | 2696 |
| 4528 | 1963 | 4576 b, c | 1823 | 4622 | 1814 | 4673 | 2715 |
| 4529 | 756 | 4577 | 3128 | 4623 | 2278 | 4674 | 723 |
| 4530 | 745 | 4578 a | 1831 | 4624 | 1800 | 4675 | 721 |
| 4531 | 760 | 4578 b | 1241 | 4625 | 1644 | 4676 a, b | 452 |
| 4532 | 681 | 4579 | 1242 | 4626 | 1826 | 4677 a, b | 737 |
| 4533 | 2765 | 4580 | 1813 | 4627 | 1335 | 4678 | 674 |
| 4534 | 1149 | 4581 a, b | 1834 | 4628 | 1291 | 4679 | 710 |
| 4535 | 92 | 4582 | 1708 | 4629 | 1763 | 4680 | 406 |
| 4536 | 1393 | 4583 a, b | 1407 | 4630 | 1805 | 4681 | 1766 |
| 4537 | 1141 | 4584 a, b | 1833 | 4631 a | 1418 | 4682 | 2302 |
| 4538 | 1231 | 4585 | 1410 | 4631 b | 1719 | 4683 | 1741 |
| 4539 | 1198 | 4586 a, b | 1747 | 4632 a, b | 1750 | 4684 | 2319 |
| 4540 | 374 | 4586 c | 1249 | 4633 a | 1717 | 4685 | 1737 |
| 4541 a, b | 821 | 4587 | 1820 | 4633 b | 1775 | 4686 | 1392 |
| 4542 | 2558 | 4588 a | 1248 | 4634 | 1246 | 4687 | 1802 |
| 4543 | 2379 | 4588 b | 1839 | 4635 a–c | 1715 | 4688 a, b | 1798 |
| 4544 | 2681 | 4589 a–c | 1173 | 4636 | 1397 | 4689 | 1402 |
| 4545 a, b | 1974 | 4590 | 708 | 4637 | 1399 | 4690 | 1636 |
| 4546 a | 2038 | 4591 a | 1630 | 4638 a | 1767 | 4691 | 1801 |
| 4546 b | 1950 | 4591 b, c | 1746 | 4638 b | 1824 | 4692 | 1398 |
| 4547 a, c | 2706 | 4592 a | 1634 | 4639 | 2301 | 4693 | 1590 |
| 4547 b | 2471 | 4592 b | 1745 | 4640 | 2104 | 4694 | 2289 |
| 4547 d, e | 2416 | 4593 a, c | 1641 | 4641 a–c | 1247 | 4695 | 1772 |
| 4548 | 2684 | 4593 b | 1836 | 4642 a, c | 1718 | 4696 | 1740 |
| 4549 | 2774 | 4594 | 1412 | 4642 b | 1841 | 4697 | 1819 |
| 4550 | 816 | 4595 | 1675 | 4643 | 1735 | 4698 | 1648 |
| 4551 | 1386 | 4596 | 1394 | 4644 | 1771 | 4699 | 1769 |
| 4552 | 1571 | 4597 | 1674 | 4645 | 1202 | 4700 a, b | 1734 |
| 4553 | 1525 | 4598 | 1629 | 4646 | 1714 | 4701 | 2299 |
| 4554 | 1389 | 4599 | 1333 | 4647 | 2290 | 4702 | 1797 |
| 4555 | 1655 | 4600 | 1405 | 4648 a, b | 820 | 4703 | 1768 |
| 4556 | 2027 | 4601 | 1498 | 4649 | 444 | 4704 | 1827 |
| 4557 | 1945 | 4602 a | 1812 | 4650 | 817 | 4705 | 1413 |
| 4558 | 1551 | 4602 b | 1643 | 4651 | 769 | 4706 | 2284 |
| 4559 | 1376 | 4603 a | 1739 | 4652 | 429 | 4707 | 785 |
| 4560 | 1582 | 4603 b | 1642 | 4653 | 803 | 4708 | 2900 |
| 4561 | 1588 | 4604 a, c | 1825 | 4654 | 764 | 4709 | 1178 |
| 4562 | 2052 | 4604 b | 1776 | 4655 | 834 | 4710 | 1733 |
| 4563 a | 1543 | 4605 | 1406 | 4656 | 380 | 4711 | 1681 |
| 4563 b | 1980 | 4606 | 792 | 4657 | 2499 | 4712 | 1625 |
| 4564 | 2173 | 4607 | 787 | 4658 | 2579 | 4713 | 1680 |
| 4565 | 2167 | 4608 | 2748 | 4659 | 1556 | 4714 | 1380 |
| 4566 | 1456 | 4609 | 2455 | 4660 | 1815 | 4715 | 1635 |
| 4567 | 1671 | 4610 | 2506 | 4661 | 1830 | 4716 | 1373 |
| 4568 a, b | 1411 | 4611 | 761 | 4662 | 1633 | 4717 | 1240 |
| 4569 a, b | 1981 | 4612 a | 1870 | 4663 | 2294 | 4718 | 1186 |
| 4569 c, d | 1999 | 4612 b | 1774 | 4664 | 2287 | 4719 | 1387 |
| 4570 a | 1795 | 4613 | 1832 | 4665 | 789 | 4720 | 1379 |
| 4570 b | 1811 | 4614 | 736 | 4666 | 806 | 4721 | 1388 |

| Inv. No. | Cat. No. | Inv. No. | Cat. No. | Inv. No. | Cat. No. | Inv. No. | Cat. No. |
|---|---|---|---|---|---|---|---|
| IP 4722 | 684 | IP 4773 | 2397 | IP 4829 | 673 | IP 4885 | 1702 |
| 4723 | 2549 | 4774 | 2624 | 4830 | 802 | 4886 | 1364 |
| 4724 | 677 | 4775 | 775 | 4831 | 798 | 4887 a | 1159 |
| 4725 | 472 | 4776 | 772 | 4832 | 2778 | 4887 b | 2075 |
| 4726 | 412 | 4777 | 749 | 4833 | 307 | 4888 | 744 |
| 4727 | 767 | 4778 | 741 | 4834 | 2417 | 4889 | 779 |
| 4728 | 823 | 4779 | 735 | 4835 | 2363 | 4890 | 381 |
| 4729 | 1018 | 4780 | 786 | 4836 | 1383 | 4891 | 740 |
| 4730 | 799 | 4781 | 408 | 4837 | 1676 | 4892 | 2540 |
| 4731 | 747 | 4782 | 697 | 4838 | 2316 | 4893 | 1637 |
| 4732 | 2489 | 4783 | 844 | 4839 | 1408 | 4894 a, b | 1623 |
| 4733 | 2481 | 4784 | 688 | 4840 a–c | 1725 | 4895 | 1153 |
| 4734 | 2389 | 4785 | 809 | 4841 | 1713 | 4896 | 1712 |
| 4735 | 687 | 4786 | 801 | 4842 | 1624 | 4897 | 1710 |
| 4736 | 471 | 4787 a, b | 469 | 4843 | 1584 | 4898 | 1878 |
| 4737 | 1146 | 4788 | 372 | 4844 | 1415 | 4899 | 825 |
| 4738 a | 1419 | 4789 | 2430 | 4845 | 1345 | 4900 | 840 |
| 4738 b | 1726 | 4790 | 427 | 4846 | 1348 | 4901 | 1846 |
| 4739 a, b | 1722 | 4791 | 2465 A | 4847 + IP 4881 | 1339 | 4902 | 1375 |
| 4740 | 725 | 4792 | 2701 | 4848 | 1158 | 4903 | 2323 |
| 4741 a, b | 1724 | 4793 | 2365 | 4849 | 1346 | 4904 | 2296 |
| 4742 | 1243 | 4794 | 33 | 4850 | 1689 | 4905 | 1349 |
| 4743 | 2487 | 4795 | 815 | 4851 | 1156 | 4906 a | 1523 |
| 4744 a, b | 462 | 4796 a–c | 1721 | 4852 a, b | 1728 | 4906 b | 1732 |
| 4745 a | 822 | 4797 | 1170 | 4853 | 1165 | 4907 | 1640 |
| 4745 b | 841 | 4798 | 810 | 4854 | 796 | 4908 | 1705 |
| 4746 a, b | 457 | 4799 | 829 | 4855 | 835 | 4909 | 3020 |
| 4747 a | 2398 | 4800 | 445 | 4856 | 2666 | 4910 | 788 |
| 4747 b | 2760 | 4801 | 2648 | 4857 a | 475 | 4911 | 2326 |
| 4748 | 1092 | 4802 | 2578 | 4857 b | 2600 | 4912 | 2291 |
| 4749 a, b | 824 | 4803 | 1409 | 4858 | 768 | 4913 | 2303 |
| 4750 | 758 | 4804 | 2698 | 4859 | 691 | 4914 | 1502 |
| 4751 a, b | 712 | 4805 | 2678 | 4860 a, b | 719 | 4915 | 1937 |
| 4752 a | 1098 | 4806 | 1148 | 4861 | 415 | 4916 | 1688 |
| 4752 b | 842 | 4807 | 1172 | 4862 | 766 | 4917 | 1936 |
| 4753 a | 2727 | 4808 | 1370 | 4863 | 377 | 4918 | 1510 |
| 4753 b | 2381 | 4809 | 1703 | 4864 | 784 | 4919 | 1509 |
| 4754 | 738 | 4810 a | 1204 | 4865 a–c | 703 | 4920 | 3109 |
| 4755 a, b | 696 | 4810 b | 1716 | 4866 | 692 | 4921 | 1099 |
| 4756 a, b | 704 | 4811 | 1203 | 4867 a, b | 716 | 4922 | 685 |
| 4757 | 724 | 4812 | 672 | 4869 | 739 | 4923 | 1097 |
| 4758 a, b | 1720 | 4813 | 686 | 4870 | 752 | 4924 | 1359 |
| 4759 | 1701 | 4814 | 3022 | 4871 | 2431 | 4925 | 698 |
| 4760 | 1707 | 4816 | 2413 | 4872 | 2488 | 4926 | 2100 |
| 4761 | 1645 | 4817 | 2720 | 4873 | 2421 | 4927 | 2324 |
| 4762 a, b | 1731 | 4818 a, b | 819 | 4874 | 1162 | 4928 | 1353 |
| 4763 | 1639 | 4819 | 418 | 4875 | 2306 | 4929 | 1492 |
| 4764 | 751 | 4820 | 783 | 4876 | 2305 | 4930 | 1939 |
| 4765 | 804 | 4821 | 780 | 4877 | 2295 | 4931 | 1511 |
| 4766 | 774 | 4822 | 2677 | 4878 | 2293 | 4932 | 1915 |
| 4767 | 828 | 4823 | 1709 | 4879 | 1626 | 4933 | 1693 |
| 4768 | 837 | 4824 | 1180 | 4880 | 1595 | 4934 | 675 |
| 4769 | 428 | 4825 | 1711 | 4881 + IP 4847 | 1339 | 4935 | 839 |
| 4770 | 770 | 4826 | 411 | 4882 | 1700 | 4936 | 1706 |
| 4771 | 2632 | 4827 | 470 | 4883 | 1365 | 4937 | 1564 |
| 4772 | 2566 | 4828 | 773 | 4884 | 1400 | 4938 | 763 |

| Inv. No. | Cat. No. | Inv. No. | Cat. No. | Inv. No. | Cat. No. | Inv. No. | Cat. No. |
|---|---|---|---|---|---|---|---|
| IP 4939 | 1235 | IP 4994 a, b | 1274 | IP 5049 | 3115 | IP 5105 | 2429 |
| 4940 | 1699 | 4995 | 384 | 5050 | 2659 | 5106 | 905 |
| 4941 a–c | 1696 | 4996 | 1727 | 5051 | 3120 | 5107 | 2525 |
| 4942 | 676 | 4997 | 793 | 5052 | 1617 | 5108 | 2772 |
| 4943 | 1161 | 4998 | 2516 | 5053 | 2634 | 5109 | 2497 |
| 4944 a–c | 2598 | 4999 | 1872 | 5054 | 1995 | 5110 | 1607 |
| 4945 a–c | 843 | 5000 a, b | 2057 | 5055 | 1295 | 5111 | 1332 |
| 4946 a, b, d | 2583 | 5001 | 2065 | 5056 | 2514 | 5112 | 1874 |
| 4947 | 707 A | 5002 | 2005 | 5057 | 2724 | 5113 | 1342 |
| 4948 | 836 | 5003 a | 2040 | 5058 | 2565 | 5114 | 1501 |
| 4949 a, b | 466 | 5003 b | 1943 | 5059 | 2050 | 5115 | 1328 |
| 4950 | 2449 | 5004 | 2006 | 5060 | 2444 | 5116 | 3116 |
| 4951 | 2547 | 5005 | 1337 | 5061 | 1279 | 5117 | 3079 |
| 4952 | 2407 | 5006 | 2002 | 5062 | 1613 | 5118 | 3111 |
| 4953 | 2673 | 5007 | 185 | 5063 | 1618 | 5119 | 978 |
| 4954 | 2432 | 5008 | 24 | 5064 | 1286 | 5120 | 422 |
| 4955 | 714 | 5009 | 1293 | 5065 | 1612 | 5121 | 946 |
| 4956 | 2353 | 5010 | 2046 | 5066 | 1609 | 5122 | 896 |
| 4957 | 1694 | 5012 | 1001 | 5067 | 1300 | 5123 | 431 |
| 4958 | 757 | 5013 | 3062 | 5068 | 1544 | 5124 | 1847 |
| 4959 | 680 | 5014 a | 2012 | 5069 | 1214 | 5125 | 1857 |
| 4960 | 881 A | 5014 b | 2072 | 5070 | 1616 | 5126 a, b | 1318 |
| 4961 | 827 | 5015 | 2003 | 5071 | 1222 | 5127 | 2711 |
| 4962 | 2653 | 5016 a, b | 1036 | 5072 | 1614 | 5128 | 2358 |
| 4963 | 1515 | 5017 | 423 | 5073 | 1615 | 5129 | 2355 |
| 4964 | 2405 | 5018 | 952 | 5074 | 1608 | 5130 | 2554 |
| 4965 | 2492 | 5019 | 2503 | 5075 | 1664 | 5131 | 866 |
| 4966 | 1155 | 5020 | 2639 | 5076 | 1667 | 5132 | 1490 |
| 4967 | 1233 | 5021 | 1046 | 5077 | 1221 | 5133 | 1338 |
| 4968 | 1627 | 5022 | 11 | 5078 | 1682 | 5134 a | 1281 |
| 4969 | 833 | 5023 a | 2495 | 5079 | 1581 | 5134 b | 1810 |
| 4970 | 743 | 5023 b | 2606 | 5080 | 1218 | 5135 | 1336 |
| 4971 | 791 | 5024 | 292 | 5081 | 2154 | 5136 | 1326 |
| 4972 | 2645 | 5025 | 323 | 5082 | 1154 | 5137 | 1997 |
| 4973 | 2366 | 5026 | 2058 | 5083 | 2330 | 5138 | 1851 |
| 4974 | 2088 | 5027 | 2810 | 5084 | 2399 | 5139 | 1344 |
| 4975 | 1866 | 5028 | 2879 | 5085 a, b | 1035 | 5140 a, b | 1343 |
| 4976 | 2086 | 5030 | 1994 | 5086 | 882 | 5141 | 869 |
| 4977 a | 1889 | 5031 | 2723 | 5087 | 370 | 5142 | 849 |
| 4977 b | 1730 | 5032 | 2876 | 5088 | 371 | 5143 | 853 |
| 4978 | 2008 | 5033 | 2881 | 5089 | 856 | 5144 | 873 |
| 4979 | 2188 | 5034 | 2960 | 5090 | 932 | 5145 | 388 |
| 4980 | 1254 | 5035 | 2927 | 5091 | 895 | 5146 | 921 |
| 4981 | 1698 | 5036 | 3131 | 5092 | 891 | 5147 | 955 |
| 4982 | 2331 | 5037 | 2956 | 5093 | 956 | 5148 | 933 |
| 4983 | 1384 | 5038 | 434 | 5094 | 880 | 5149 | 961 |
| 4984 | 1367 | 5039 | 2935 | 5095 | 885 | 5151 | 1327 |
| 4985 | 1576 | 5040 | 2924 | 5096 | 897 | 5152 | 1147 |
| 4986 | 1396 | 5041 | 2237 | 5097 | 892 | 5153 | 1322 |
| 4987 | 1513 | 5042 | 2505 | 5098 | 394 | 5154 | 1329 |
| 4988 a, b | 456 | 5043 | 2508 | 5099 | 902 | 5155 | 1140 |
| 4989 a, b | 826 | 5044 | 120 | 5100 a, b | 1611 | 5156 | 1592 |
| 4990 | 476 | 5045 | 32 | 5101 | 934 | 5157 | 1986 |
| 4991 | 2647 | 5046 | 57 | 5102 | 419 | 5157 A | 1959 |
| 4992 | 1403 | 5047 | 2066 | 5103 | 2423 | 5158 | 1591 |
| 4993 | 1687 | 5048 | 2479 | 5104 | 2688 | 5159 | 1289 |

| Inv. No. | Cat. No. | Inv. No. | Cat. No. | Inv. No. | Cat. No. | Inv. No. | Cat. No. |
|---|---|---|---|---|---|---|---|
| IP 5160 | 3048 | IP 5214 | 1184 | IP 5269 | 1238 | IP 5325 | 2090 |
| 5161 | 1341 | 5215 | 1190 | 5270 | 1414 | 5326 | 2140 |
| 5162 | 1320 | 5216 | 2690 | 5271 | 1273 | 5327 | 2219 |
| 5163 | 2292 | 5217 | 1205 | 5272 | 944 | 5328 | 2149 |
| 5164 | 1529 | 5218 | 1297 | 5273 | 1016 | 5329 | 2281 |
| 5165 | 975 | 5219 | 1284 | 5274 | 398 | 5330 | 2131 |
| 5166 | 968 | 5220 | 2643 | 5275 | 2438 | 5331 | 2138 |
| 5167 | 925 | 5221 | 2779 | 5276 | 3016 | 5332 | 1144 |
| 5168 | 2918 | 5222 | 965 | 5277 | 3101 | 5333 | 1142 |
| 5169 | 1619 | 5223 | 888 | 5278 | 2025 | 5334 | 1304 |
| 5170 | 1312 | 5224 | 2564 | 5279 | 2069 | 5335 | 1160 |
| 5171 | 1244 | 5225 | 2371 | 5280 | 1494 | 5336 | 1646 |
| 5172 | 1308 | 5226 | 1917 | 5281 | 1526 | 5337 | 1151 |
| 5173 | 1894 | 5227 | 1377 | 5282 | 1357 | 5338 | 1876 |
| 5174 | 1507 | 5228 | 2000 | 5283 | 1351 | 5339 | 939 |
| 5175 | 1948 | 5229 | 2314 | 5284 | 2106 | 5340 a, b | 1022 |
| 5176 a, b | 1168 | 5230 | 438 | 5285 | 2313 | 5341 | 997 |
| 5177 | 1177 | 5231 | 1011 | 5286 | 2312 | 5342 | 2559 |
| 5178 | 1340 | 5232 | 976 | 5287 | 2322 | 5343 a | 2434 |
| 5179 | 1315 | 5233 | 998 | 5288 | 1358 | 5343 b | 2592 |
| 5180 | 1314 | 5234 | 910 | 5289 | 3163 | 5344 | 1303 |
| 5181 | 1330 | 5235 a–c | 1032 | 5290 | 3085 | 5345 | 1288 |
| 5182 | 1324 | 5236 a, b | 1033 | 5291 a, b | 1163 | 5346 | 1904 |
| 5183 | 2212 | 5237 | 1102 | 5292 | 908 | 5347 | 3155 |
| 5184 a–c′ | 1881 | 5238 | 379 | 5293 | 982 | 5348 | 1856 |
| 5185 | 1306 | 5239 | 2493 | 5294 | 868 | 5349 | 2214 |
| 5186 | 1903 | 5240 | 2820 | 5295 a, b | 1041 | 5350 | 2279 |
| 5187 a | 1174 | 5241 a | 2439 | 5296 | 919 | 5351 | 2234 |
| 5187 b, c | 1880 | 5241 b | 2591 | 5297 | 989 | 5352 | 1317 |
| 5188 | 417 | 5242 | 2141 | 5298 | 2700 | 5353 | 999 |
| 5189 | 2780 | 5243 | 2328 | 5299 | 1361 | 5354 | 2766 |
| 5190 | 1230 | 5244 | 2315 | 5300 | 1673 | 5355 | 1843 |
| 5191 | 1305 | 5245 | 2317 | 5301 | 1610 | 5356 | 1850 |
| 5192 | 1882 A | 5246 | 2159 | 5302 | 1504 | 5357 | 1311 |
| 5193 | 1017 | 5247 a–c | 460 | 5303 | 1597 | 5358 | 1171 |
| 5194 | 1183 | 5248 | 2545 | 5304 | 2275 | 5359 | 1313 |
| 5195 | 1234 | 5249 | 2021 | 5305 | 1325 | 5360 | 1683 |
| 5196 | 1194 | 5250 a, b | 2024 | 5306 | 2297 | 5361 | 1302 |
| 5197 | 1506 | 5251 | 2551 | 5307 | 1499 | 5362 | 1879 |
| 5198 | 1323 | 5252 | 877 | 5308 | 2276 | 5363 a, b | 1319 |
| 5199 | 1887 | 5253 | 937 | 5309 | 2132 | 5364 | 2213 |
| 5200 | 2054 | 5254 | 2891 | 5311 a–c | 1873 | 5365 | 2220 |
| 5201 | 2064 | 5255 | 1143 | 5312 | 1603 | 5366 | 2229 |
| 5202 | 1848 | 5256 a–d | 2844 | 5313 | 1631 | 5367 | 942 |
| 5203 | 2232 | 5257 | 1493 | 5314 | 1334 | 5368 | 987 |
| 5204 | 2641 | 5258 | 2790 | 5315 | 1553 | 5369 | 970 |
| 5205 | 2402 | 5259 | 2311 | 5316 | 1307 | 5370 | 948 |
| 5206 | 1596 | 5260 | 2327 | 5317 | 2020 | 5371 | 953 |
| 5207 | 1299 | 5261 | 931 | 5318 | 1855 | 5372 | 915 |
| 5208 | 2148 | 5262 | 1925 | 5319 | 1852 | 5373 a, b | 1020 |
| 5209 | 2225 | 5263 | 1924 | 5320 a | 1593 | 5374 a, b | 464 |
| 5210 | 2143 | 5264 | 1002 | 5320 b | 1853 | 5375 a, b | 1021 |
| 5211 a | 1301 | 5265 | 424 | 5321 | 1901 | 5376 | 378 |
| 5211 b | 2056 | 5266 | 1276 | 5322 | 2300 | 5377 | 2475 |
| 5212 | 1220 | 5267 | 2013 | 5323 | 2215 | 5378 | 2749 |
| 5213 a, b | 1972 | 5268 | 1957 | 5324 | 2081 | 5379 | 2376 |

| Inv. No. | Cat. No. | Inv. No. | Cat. No. | Inv. No. | Cat. No. | Inv. No. | Cat. No. |
|---|---|---|---|---|---|---|---|
| IP 5380 | 1169 | IP 5435 | 35 | IP 5491 | 301 | IP 5546 | 1200 |
| 5381 | 1310 | 5436 | 191 | 5492 | 2716 | 5547 | 870 |
| 5382 | 1309 | 5437 | 82 | 5493 | 2620 | 5548 | 900 |
| 5383 a, b | 1864 | 5438 | 46 | 5494 | 1783 | 5549 | 893 |
| 5384 | 1905 | 5439 | 333 | 5495 | 1669 | 5550 | 875 |
| 5385 | 440 | 5440 | 112 | 5496 | 2254 | 5551 a | 2603 |
| 5386 | 874 | 5441 | 171 | 5497 | 2903 | 5551 b | 2362 |
| 5387 | 964 | 5442 | 194 | 5498 | 962 | 5552 | 1475 |
| 5388 | 2280 | 5443 | 152 | 5499 | 909 | 5553 | 1430 |
| 5389 | 2283 | 5444 | 2718 | 5500 | 996 | 5554 | 1793 |
| 5390 | 1599 | 5445 | 865 | 5501 | 922 | 5555 | 1822 |
| 5391 | 2282 | 5446 | 876 | 5502 | 860 | 5556 | 1780 |
| 5392 | 2288 | 5447 | 848 | 5503 | 918 | 5557 | 958 |
| 5393 | 1316 | 5448 | 846 | 5504 | 416 | 5558 | 2351 |
| 5394 | 2307 | 5449 | 1100 | 5505 | 959 | 5559 | 3054 |
| 5395 | 2277 | 5450 | 984 | 5506 | 864 | 5560 | 899 |
| 5396 a | 1601 | 5451 | 407 | 5507 | 1000 | 5561 | 2245 |
| 5396 b | 1871 | 5452 | 2385 | 5508 | 872 | 5562 | 969 |
| 5397 | 188 | 5453 | 1809 | 5509 | 883 | 5563 | 3173 |
| 5398 | 990 | 5454 | 1877 | 5510 | 857 | 5564 | 2905 |
| 5399 | 911 | 5455 | 404 | 5511 | 903 | 5565 | 928 |
| 5400 a, b | 2199 | 5456 | 1451 | 5512 | 951 | 5566 | 1103 |
| 5401 | 2192 | 5457 | 1885 | 5513 | 1015 | 5567 | 2582 |
| 5402 | 2205 | 5458 | 1900 | 5514 | 387 | 5568 | 855 |
| 5403 | 2285 | 5459 | 1882 | 5515 | 1004 | 5569 | 2500 |
| 5404 | 2201 | 5460 | 2816 | 5516 | 1008 | 5570 | 3061 |
| 5405 | 1505 | 5461 | 878 | 5517 | 414 | 5571 | 1791 |
| 5406 | 2193 | 5462 | 3135 | 5518 | 980 | 5572 | 2563 |
| 5407 | 2206 | 5463 | 2610 | 5519 | 859 | 5573 | 2626 |
| 5408 | 1545 | 5464 | 2200 | 5520 | 923 | 5574 | 889 |
| 5409 | 1541 | 5465 | 2194 | 5521 | 867 | 5575 | 397 |
| 5410 | 1469 | 5466 | 2202 | 5522 | 2382 | 5576 | 851 |
| 5411 | 1896 | 5467 | 1468 | 5523 | 935 | 5577 | 2486 |
| 5412 | 1677 | 5468 | 2198 | 5524 | 437 | 5578 | 991 |
| 5413 | 1547 | 5469 | 2764 | 5525 | 966 | 5579 | 941 |
| 5414 | 2211 | 5470 | 2931 | 5526 | 979 | 5580 | 2729 |
| 5415 | 303 | 5471 | 3121 | 5527 | 2757 | 5581 | 950 |
| 5416 | 197 | 5472 | 3125 | 5528 | 2504 | 5582 | 2615 |
| 5417 | 1443 | 5473 | 1453 | 5529 | 901 | 5583 | 2570 |
| 5418 | 1436 | 5474 | 1890 | 5530 | 396 | 5584 | 2467 |
| 5419 | 1875 | 5475 | 430 | 5531 | 972 | 5585 | 1167 |
| 5420 | 2664 | 5476 | 473 | 5532 | 914 | 5586 | 390 |
| 5421 | 1520 | 5477 | 957 | 5533 | 435 | 5587 | 2552 |
| 5422 | 1439 | 5479 | 3165 | 5534 | 2456 | 5588 | 2383 |
| 5423 | 2107 | 5480 | 3171 | 5535 a, b | 1883 | 5589 | 2377 |
| 5424 | 2196 | 5481 | 2204 | 5536 | 1567 | 5590 | 441 |
| 5425 | 1434 | 5482 | 2210 | 5537 | 1189 | 5591 | 1009 |
| 5426 | 2914 | 5483 | 2209 | 5538 | 1426 | 5592 | 960 |
| 5427 | 2792 | 5484 | 2197 | 5539 | 1495 | 5593 | 2750 |
| 5428 | 2950 | 5485 | 2916 | 5540 | 1442 | 5594 | 994 |
| 5429 a, b | 2795 | 5486 | 2763 | 5541 | 1438 | 5595 | 929 |
| 5430 | 154 | 5487 a | 221 | 5542 a | 2709 | 5596 | 426 |
| 5431 | 325 | 5487 b | 286 | 5542 b, c | 2595 | 5597 | 2375 |
| 5432 a, b | 2584 | 5488 | 223 | 5543 a, b | 2705 | 5598 | 2751 |
| 5433 | 1441 | 5489 | 322 | 5544 | 1013 | 5599 | 2733 |
| 5434 | 981 | 5490 | 155 | 5545 | 1433 | 5600 | 2515 |

| Inv. No. | Cat. No. | Inv. No. | Cat. No. | Inv. No. | Cat. No. | Inv. No. | Cat. No. |
|---|---|---|---|---|---|---|---|
| IP 5601 | 1012 | IP 5657 | 1566 | IP 5715 | 1845 | IP 5770 | 78 |
| 5602 | 1835 | 5658 | 1869 | 5716 a, b | 1039 | 5771 | 79 |
| 5603 | 1837 | 5659 | 1803 | 5717 a, b | 1024 | 5772 | 84 |
| 5604 | 1781 | 5660 | 1473 | 5718 | 2656 | 5773 | 101 |
| 5605 | 1777 | 5661 | 1457 | 5719 | 2614 | 5774 | 8 |
| 5606 | 1786 | 5662 | 1182 | 5720 | 1570 | 5775 | 34 |
| 5607 | 1685 | 5663 | 1572 | 5721 | 1474 | 5776 + IP 2524 | 1 |
| 5608 | 1429 | 5664 | 1253 | 5722 a | 1650 | 5777 | 131 |
| 5609 | 2226 | 5665 | 420 | 5722 b | 1753 | 5778 | 2269 |
| 5610 | 1427 | 5666 | 2533 | 5723 | 1516 | 5779 | 1804 |
| 5611 | 1432 | 5667 | 2640 | 5724 | 2753 | 5780 | 1464 |
| 5612 | 1096 | 5668 | 1423 | 5725 | 2380 | 5781 | 1743 |
| 5613 a, b | 1790 | 5669 | 1455 | 5726 | 983 | 5782 | 974 |
| 5614 | 2133 | 5670 | 1514 | 5727 | 1005 | 5783 | 973 |
| 5615 | 1651 | 5671 | 1782 | 5728 | 949 | 5784 | 884 |
| 5616 | 3130 | 5672 | 1738 | 5729 | 945 | 5785 | 1195 |
| 5617 | 3026 | 5673 | 1679 | 5730 | 1480 | 5786 | 1422 |
| 5618 | 1829 | 5674 | 1193 | 5731 | 1477 | 5787 a | 1472 |
| 5619 | 2682 | 5675 | 1428 | 5732 a–d | 1748 | 5787 b | 1752 |
| 5620 | 95 | 5676 | 1425 | 5733 | 1446 | 5788 a | 1196 |
| 5621 | 2930 | 5677 | 1574 | 5734 | 1568 | 5788 b | 1788 |
| 5622 | 1749 | 5678 | 1792 | 5735 | 1628 | 5789 | 1569 |
| 5623 | 3053 | 5679 | 1580 | 5736 | 1764 | 5790 | 1223 |
| 5624 | 3164 | 5680 | 1794 | 5737 | 1583 | 5791 | 1459 |
| 5625 | 2616 | 5681 | 1785 | 5738 | 1478 | 5792 | 904 |
| 5626 | 2482 | 5682 | 1784 | 5739 | 850 | 5793 | 861 |
| 5627 | 97 | 5683 | 1431 | 5740 | 373 | 5794 | 3023 |
| 5628 | 2756 | 5684 | 1736 | 5741 | 930 | 5795 | 2418 |
| 5629 | 2638 | 5685 | 2247 | 5742 | 1003 | 5796 | 1239 |
| 5630 | 2704 | 5686 | 854 | 5743 | 943 | 5797 | 1462 |
| 5631 | 2743 | 5687 a, b | 1019 | 5744 | 954 | 5798 | 1014 |
| 5632 | 2360 | 5689 | 2250 | 5745 a | 1040 | 5799 | 971 |
| 5633 | 2420 | 5690 | 2239 | 5746 | 1007 | 5800 | 1360 |
| 5634 | 2422 | 5691 | 1660 | 5747 | 410 | 5801 | 1949 |
| 5635 | 1045 | 5692 | 1524 | 5748 | 2658 | 5802 | 1356 |
| 5636 | 2943 | 5693 | 1787 | 5749 | 2725 | 5803 | 3025 |
| 5637 | 2915 | 5694 | 1224 | 5750 | 2644 | 5804 | 916 |
| 5638 | 199 | 5695 | 1181 | 5751 a, b | 1023 | 5805 a | 2839 |
| 5639 | 314 | 5696 | 2146 | 5752 | 474 | 5805 b | 2887 |
| 5640 | 986 | 5697 | 1479 | 5753 | 890 | 5806 | 2961 |
| 5641 | 2609 | 5698 | 1192 | 5754 | 1577 | 5807 | 2894 |
| 5642 | 3013 | 5699 | 1454 | 5755 | 2267 | 5808 | 3018 |
| 5643 | 2350 | 5700 | 1779 | 5756 a, b | 2261 | 5809 | 2922 |
| 5644 | 310 | 5701 | 1424 | 5757 | 1796 | 5810 | 1670 |
| 5645 | 1742 | 5702 | 1452 | 5758 | 1653 | 5811 | 988 |
| 5646 | 1762 | 5703 | 1807 | 5759 | 3143 | 5812 | 317 |
| 5647 | 1666 | 5704 | 1868 | 5760 | 1760 | 5813 | 1500 |
| 5648 | 2248 | 5705 | 2153 | 5761 | 1179 | 5814 | 409 |
| 5649 | 1678 | 5706 | 2203 | 5762 | 1946 | 5815 | 1578 |
| 5650 | 1816 | 5707 | 2208 | 5763 | 1471 | 5816 | 852 |
| 5651 | 1758 | 5708 | 1255 | 5764 | 977 | 5817 | 894 |
| 5652 | 1756 | 5710 | 887 | 5765 | 2507 | 5818 | 879 |
| 5653 | 1867 | 5711 | 1789 | 5766 | 77 | 5819 a, b | 1026 |
| 5654 | 385 | 5712 | 1778 | 5767 | 72 | 5820 | 881 |
| 5655 | 2260 | 5713 | 2523 | 5768 | 23 | 5821 | 393 |
| 5656 | 2207 | 5714 | 413 | 5769 | 25 | 5822 | 863 |

| Inv. No. | Cat. No. | Inv. No. | Cat. No. | Inv. No. | Cat. No. | Inv. No. | Cat. No. |
|---|---|---|---|---|---|---|---|
| IP 5823 | 938 | IP 5878 | 1923 | IP 5934 | 2769 | IP 5987 | 3065 |
| 5824 | 389 | 5879 | 924 | 5935 | 1947 | 5988 | 1993 |
| 5825 | 448 | 5880 | 3170 | 5936 | 1938 | 5989 | 1395 |
| 5826 a, b | 1027 | 5881 | 2581 | 5937 | 1755 | 5991 | 2758 |
| 5827 | 926 | 5882 | 1918 | 5938 | 1225 | 5992 a | 1594 |
| 5828 | 917 | 5883 | 2463 | 5939 | 2264 | 5992 b | 1723 |
| 5829 | 2630 | 5884 | 2156 | 5940 a, b | 1034 | 5993 | 2026 |
| 5830 | 2692 | 5885 | 2165 | 5941 | 399 | 5994 | 1962 |
| 5831 | 1006 | 5886 | 196 | 5942 | 940 | 5995 | 1540 |
| 5832 | 927 | 5887 | 278 | 5943 | 995 | 5996 | 1381 |
| 5833 a, b | 468 | 5888 | 1476 | 5944 a, b | 1030 | 5997 | 1371 |
| 5834 | 3012 | 5889 | 1910 | 5945 a, b | 1029 | 5998 | 2321 |
| 5835 | 1101 | 5890 | 907 | 5946 a | 2594 | 5999 | 2325 |
| 5836 | 54 | 5891 | 146 | 5946 b | 2710 | 6000 | 1548 |
| 5837 | 2161 | 5892 a–c | 1028 | 5947 | 1729 | 6001 | 2332 |
| 5838 | 1378 | 5893 | 1010 | 5948 | 993 | 6002 | 2577 |
| 5839 | 1187 | 5894 | 64 | 5949 | 920 | 6003 | 2304 |
| 5840 | 1352 | 5895 | 3160 | 5950 | 967 | 6004 | 2298 |
| 5841 a | 1416 | 5896 | 71 | 5951 | 847 | 6005 | 1521 |
| 5841 b | 1952 | 5897 | 26 | 5952 | 400 | 6006 | 2028 |
| 5842 | 1229 | 5898 | 2168 | 5953 | 862 | 6007 | 2318 |
| 5843 | 1934 | 5899 | 2166 | 5954 | 366 | 6008 | 2667 |
| 5844 | 2180 | 5900 | 1448 | 5955 | 947 | 6009 | 3158 |
| 5845 | 912 | 5901 | 1435 | 5956 | 886 | 6010 | 2919 |
| 5846 | 2077 | 5902 | 2699 | 5957 a–c | 1037 | 6011 | 2726 |
| 5847 | 2170 | 5903 | 2443 A | 5958 a, b | 1031 | 6012 | 1063 |
| 5848 | 858 | 5904 | 936 | 5959 a, b | 458 | 6013 | 1072 |
| 5849 | 1919 | 5905 | 992 | 5960 a, b | 1038 | 6014 | 3167 |
| 5850 | 1559 | 5906 a, b | 465 | 5961 a | 2602 | 6015 | 3176 |
| 5851 a–c | 1025 | 5907 | 845 | 5961 b | 2411 | 6016 | 297 |
| 5852 | 2683 | 5908 | 446 | 5962 a, b | 2587 | 6017 | 294 |
| 5853 | 898 | 5909 | 906 | 5963 | 1219 | 6018 | 158 |
| 5854 | 1929 | 5910 | 443 | 5964 | 1652 | 6019 | 3162 |
| 5855 | 405 | 5911 | 401 | 5965 | 1842 | 6020 | 283 |
| 5856 | 1549 | 5912 | 2695 | 5966 | 1751 | 6021 | 2468 |
| 5857 | 1668 | 5913 | 2694 | 5967 | 2001 | 6022 | 2329 |
| 5858 | 913 | 5914 a, b | 1806 | 5968 | 2575 | 6023 | 2813 |
| 5859 | 2171 | 5915 | 99 | 5969 | 1991 | 6024 | 2812 |
| 5860 | 1955 | 5916 a, b | 454 | 5970 | 1391 | 6025 | 1496 |
| 5861 | 1657 | 5917 | 3138 | 5971 | 2874 | 6026 | 1695 |
| 5862 | 1562 | 5918 | 254 | 5972 | 2976 | 6027 a–g | 1990 |
| 5863 | 1691 | 5919 | 1447 | 5973 | 2882 | 6028 | 1047 |
| 5864 a, b | 1491 | 5920 | 1552 | 5974 | 1554 | 6029 | 1070 |
| 5865 | 1659 | 5921 | 1744 | 5975 | 2139 | 6030 | 1083 |
| 5866 | 2179 | 5922 | 1445 | 5976 | 3118 | 6031 | 1049 |
| 5867 | 1565 | 5923 | 1757 | 5977 | 2759 | 6032 | 386 |
| 5868 | 1658 | 5924 | 1754 | 5978 | 2501 | 6033 | 1059 |
| 5869 | 1654 | 5925 | 2078 | 5979 | 2320 | 6034 | 1060 |
| 5870 | 2735 | 5926 | 1437 | 5980 | 1503 | 6035 | 1104 |
| 5871 | 2162 | 5927 | 1840 | 5981 | 1363 | 6036 | 2393 |
| 5872 | 2135 | 5928 | 1605 | 5982 | 1697 | 6037 | 2576 |
| 5873 | 2144 | 5929 | 1444 | 5983 a | 1621 | 6038 | 1105 |
| 5874 | 2158 | 5930 | 1773 | 5983 b, c | 1638 | 6039 | 2394 |
| 5875 | 225 | 5931 | 963 | 5984 | 2308 | 6040 | 2352 |
| 5876 | 2164 | 5932 | 985 | 5985 | 2310 | 6041 | 2670 |
| 5877 | 871 | 5933 | 2573 | 5986 | 1992 | 6042 | 2424 |

| Inv. No. | Cat. No. | Inv. No. | Cat. No. | Inv. No. | Cat. No. | Inv. No. | Cat. No. |
|---|---|---|---|---|---|---|---|
| IP 6043 | 1201 | IP 6098 | 1366 | IP 6152 | 2560 | IP 6206 | 1369 |
| 6044 a | 1331 | 6099 | 1385 | 6153 | 2703 | 6207 | 1897 |
| 6044 b, c | 1865 | 6100 | 2712 | 6154 | 2498 | 6208 | 2189 |
| 6045 | 2182 | 6101 | 365 | 6155 | 2359 | 6209 | 1892 |
| 6046 | 309 | 6102 | 279 | 6156 | 2409 | 6210 | 2092 |
| 6047 | 2175 | 6103 | 1951 | 6157 a, b | 328 | 6211 | 2130 |
| 6048 | 2654 | 6104 | 255 | 6158 | 73 | 6212 | 1215 |
| 6049 | 3113 | 6105 | 247 | 6159 + IP 6057 | 87 | 6213 | 2719 |
| 6050 | 3169 | 6106 | 267 | 6160 | 331 | 6214 | 1347 |
| 6051 | 3105 | 6107 a, b | 329 | 6161 | 168 | 6215 | 1390 |
| 6052 | 2160 | 6108 | 186 | 6162 | 327 | 6216 | 2163 |
| 6053 | 1912 | 6109 | 111 | 6163 | 104 | 6217 | 2574 |
| 6054 | 1106 | 6110 | 52 | 6164 | 2176 | 6218 | 1252 |
| 6055 | 2512 | 6111 a, b | 270 | 6165 | 2091 | 6219 | 1542 |
| 6056 | 2875 | 6112 | 1086 | 6166 | 190 | 6220 | 1368 |
| 6057 + IP 6159 | 87 | 6113 | 284 | 6167 | 315 | 6221 a, b | 1539 |
| 6058 | 2137 | 6114 | 260 | 6168 | 277 | 6222 | 1081 |
| 6059 | 252 | 6115 | 144 | 6169 | 2617 | 6223 | 2152 |
| 6060 | 261 | 6116 | 2018 | 6170 | 1913 | 6224 | 1050 |
| 6061 | 209 | 6117 | 2562 | 6171 a, b | 1920 | 6225 | 1048 |
| 6062 | 145 | 6118 | 2631 | 6172 | 288 | 6226 | 383 |
| 6063 | 143 | 6119 | 2923 | 6173 | 271 | 6227 | 2571 |
| 6064 | 172 | 6120 a, b | 275 | 6174 | 268 | 6228 | 1085 |
| 6065 | 1093 | 6121 | 2940 | 6175 | 150 | 6229 | 2669 |
| 6066 | 1064 | 6122 | 96 | 6176 | 2099 | 6230 | 439 |
| 6067 | 433 | 6123 | 2532 | 6177 | 249 | 6231 | 2687 |
| 6068 | 1108 | 6124 | 2665 | 6178 a, b | 250 | 6232 | 2652 |
| 6069 | 1061 | 6125 | 1082 | 6179 | 222 | 6233 | 2535 |
| 6070 | 1094 | 6126 | 304 | 6180 | 269 | 6234 | 2364 |
| 6071 | 432 | 6127 | 160 | 6181 | 311 | 6235 | 2435 |
| 6072 | 1095 | 6128 | 2410 | 6182 | 324 | 6236 | 2561 |
| 6073 | 2702 | 6129 | 2550 | 6183 a–c | 273 | 6237 a, b | 2589 |
| 6074 | 2572 | 6130 | 118 | 6184 | 3114 | 6237 c | 2441 |
| 6075 | 1290 | 6131 | 264 | 6185 a | 164 | 6238 a, b | 2593 |
| 6076 | 1090 | 6132 | 148 | 6185 b | 318 | 6239 b | 2477 |
| 6077 | 2513 | 6133 a, b | 1043 | 6186 + IP 6139 | 88 | 6239 c–e | 2585 |
| 6078 | 1056 | 6134 | 149 | 6187 | 2349 | 6240 | 2186 |
| 6079 | 295 | 6135 | 175 | 6188 a, b | 2596 | 6241 | 321 |
| 6080 | 296 | 6136 a | 1421 | 6189 | 1228 | 6242 | 161 |
| 6081 | 169 | 6136 b | 1927 | 6190 a–c | 1227 | 6243 | 2731 |
| 6082 | 256 | 6137 a, b | 130 | 6191 | 210 | 6244 | 2674 |
| 6083 | 1600 | 6137 c | 291 | 6192 a | 259 | 6245 | 2412 |
| 6084 | 289 | 6138 | 298 | 6192 b | 272 | 6246 | 2739 |
| 6085 | 2693 | 6139 + IP 6186 | 88 | 6193 | 299 | 6247 | 2655 |
| 6086 | 1055 | 6140 | 2539 | 6194 | 253 | 6248 | 2414 |
| 6087 | 2177 | 6141 | 1088 | 6195 | 251 | 6249 | 2660 |
| 6088 | 2396 | 6142 | 2732 | 6196 | 1236 | 6250 | 2426 |
| 6089 | 192 | 6143 | 2755 | 6197 | 1921 | 6251 | 2447 |
| 6090 | 2651 | 6144 | 2747 | 6198 | 1893 | 6252 | 2392 |
| 6091 | 1089 | 6145 | 2546 | 6199 | 1585 | 6253 | 2451 |
| 6092 | 173 | 6146 | 2657 | 6200 | 2854 | 6254 | 2676 |
| 6093 | 257 | 6147 | 2436 | 6201 | 2770 | 6255 | 2384 |
| 6094 | 1579 | 6148 | 2419 | 6202 | 1232 | 6256 | 2453 |
| 6095 | 1066 | 6149 | 2425 | 6203 | 2408 | 6257 | 2511 |
| 6096 | 2169 | 6150 | 2622 | 6204 | 403 | 6258 | 3063 |
| 6097 | 2110 | 6151 | 2354 | 6205 | 1065 | 6259 | 2738 |

| Inv. No. | Cat. No. | Inv. No. | Cat. No. | Inv. No. | Cat. No. | Inv. No. | Cat. No. |
|---|---|---|---|---|---|---|---|
| IP 6260 | 2448 | IP 6287 | 1052 | IP 6313 | 1077 | IP 6337 | 2178 |
| 6261 | 2433 | 6288 | 1057 | 6314 | 2151 | 6338 | 1663 |
| 6262 | 2608 | 6289 | 1058 | 6315 | 1076 | 6339 | 1237 |
| 6263 | 2633 | 6290 | 1080 | 6316 | 1087 | 6340 | 1684 |
| 6264 | 2734 | 6291 | 1068 | 6317 | 1355 | 6341 | 1665 |
| 6265 a, b | 2590 | 6292 | 1084 | 6318 | 1185 | 6342 | 2309 |
| 6267 | 147 | 6293 | 421 | 6319 | 1969 | 6343 | 1152 |
| 6268 | 265 | 6294 | 1067 | 6320 | 1078 | 6344 | 1497 |
| 6269 | 263 | 6295 | 1079 | 6321 | 1062 | 6345 | 1692 |
| 6270 | 285 | 6296 a, b | 1042 | 6322 | 1071 | 6346 | 1350 |
| 6271 | 306 | 6297 | 1983 | 6323 | 2172 | 6347 | 1522 |
| 6272 | 281 | 6298 | 1916 | 6324 | 1966 | 6348 | 1649 |
| 6273 | 177 | 6299 | 1054 | 6325 | 1914 | 6349 | 1944 |
| 6274 | 248 | 6300 | 2183 | 6326 a, b | 1933 | 6350 a | 2102 |
| 6275 | 280 | 6301 | 1053 | 6327 a | 1420 | 6350 b | 1704 |
| 6276 | 159 | 6302 | 2157 | 6327 b, c | 1908 | 6351 | 2415 |
| 6277 | 167 | 6303 | 376 | 6327 d | 1932 | 6352 | 2786 |
| 6278 | 293 | 6304 | 1051 | 6328 | 1463 | 6353 | 2801 |
| 6279 | 1589 | 6305 | 1107 | 6329 | 1984 | 6354 | 3182 |
| 6280 | 300 | 6306 | 1091 | 6330 | 1922 | 6355 | 2994 |
| 6281 | 1354 | 6307 | 1073 | 6331 | 1404 | 6356 | 3024 |
| 6282 | 1909 | 6308 | 425 | 6332 | 1075 | 6357 | 3183 |
| 6283 | 1374 | 6309 | 1157 | 6333 a, b | 1044 | 6358 | 2962 |
| 6284 | 1382 | 6310 | 1372 | 6334 | 1074 | IM 2205 | 2341 A |
| 6285 | 382 | 6311 | 392 | 6335 | 1891 | | |
| 6286 | 1069 | 6312 | 1164 | 6336 a, b | 463 | | |

# INDEX

The index covers all the important items mentioned in the introductory paragraphs, the catalogue, and in the chapter on Provenance and Distribution of Types. Because the lamps are comparatively few, it has not seemed necessary to have separate indices for the subjects on the discus and for inscriptions. Discus representations are listed separately under that rubric, and similarly rim designs and neck designs. Signatures and other inscriptions are listed alphabetically in English with the Greek form that appears on the lamp following. References to the descriptions of the particular areas in the chapter on Provenance and Distribution of Types appear in italics in the index. All the numbers which appear in the index are page numbers.

PLATE 1

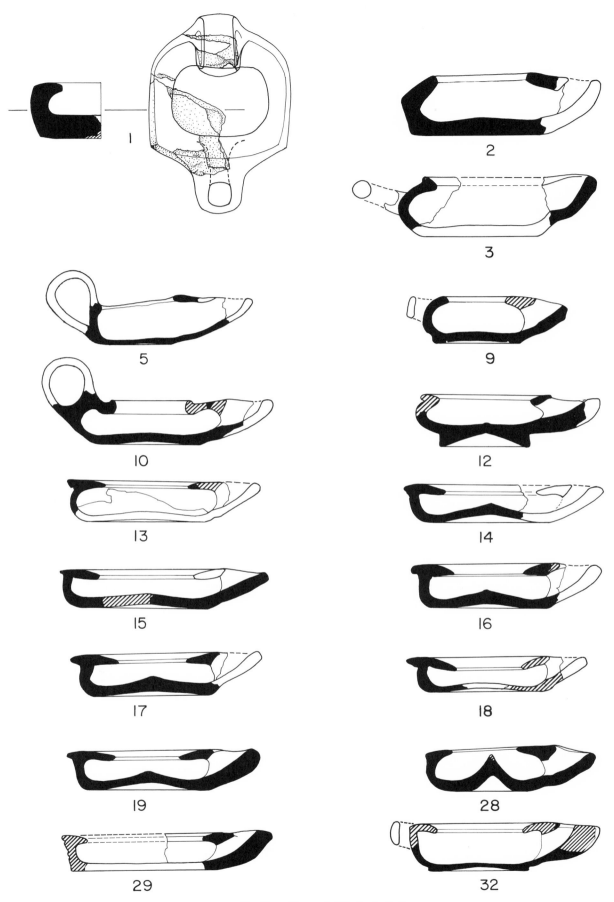

Profiles: Types I–III. Scale 1:2

PLATE 2

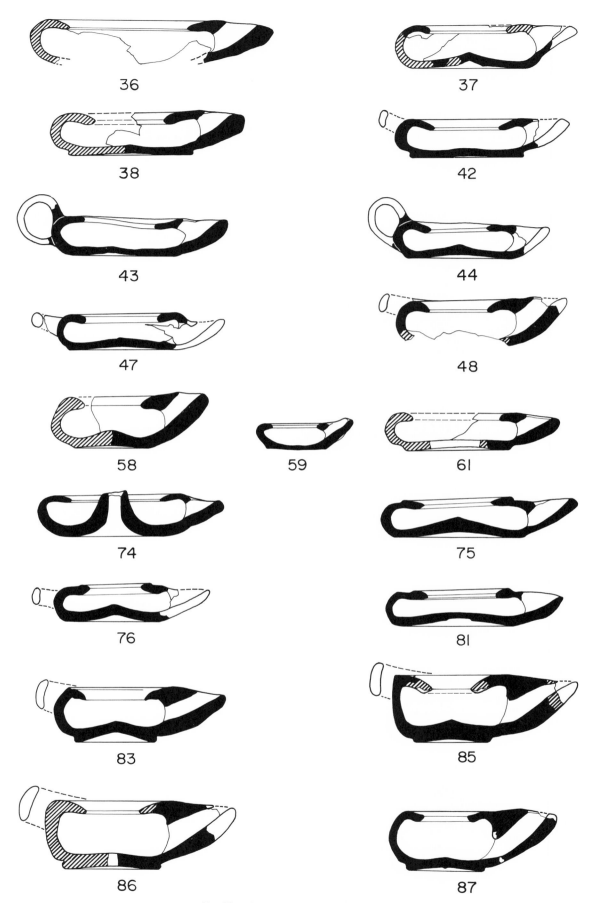

Profiles: Types IV–VI. Scale 1:2

PLATE 3

Profiles: Type VII A–F. Scale 1:2

PLATE 4

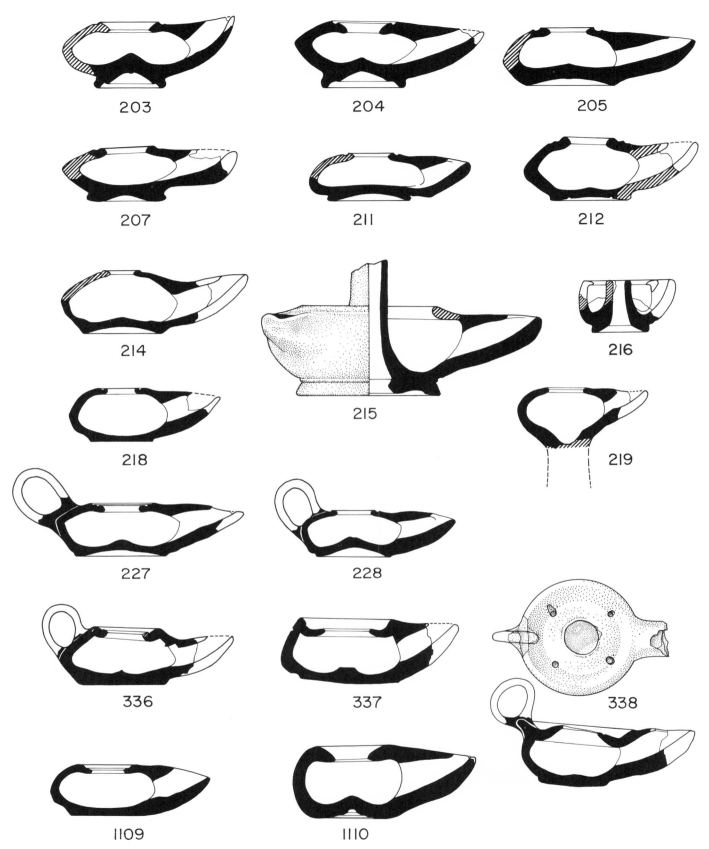

203

204

205

207

211

212

214

215

216

218

219

227

228

336

337

338

1109

1110

Profiles: Types IX–XII, XIV, XVII, and two unclassified Hellenistic. Scale 1:2

PLATE 5

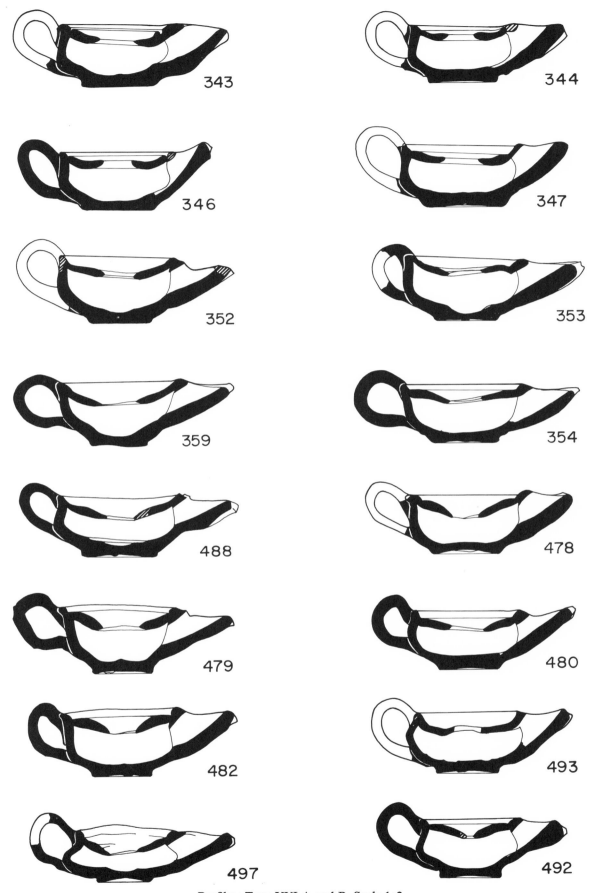

Profiles: Type XVI A and B. Scale 1:2

PLATE 6

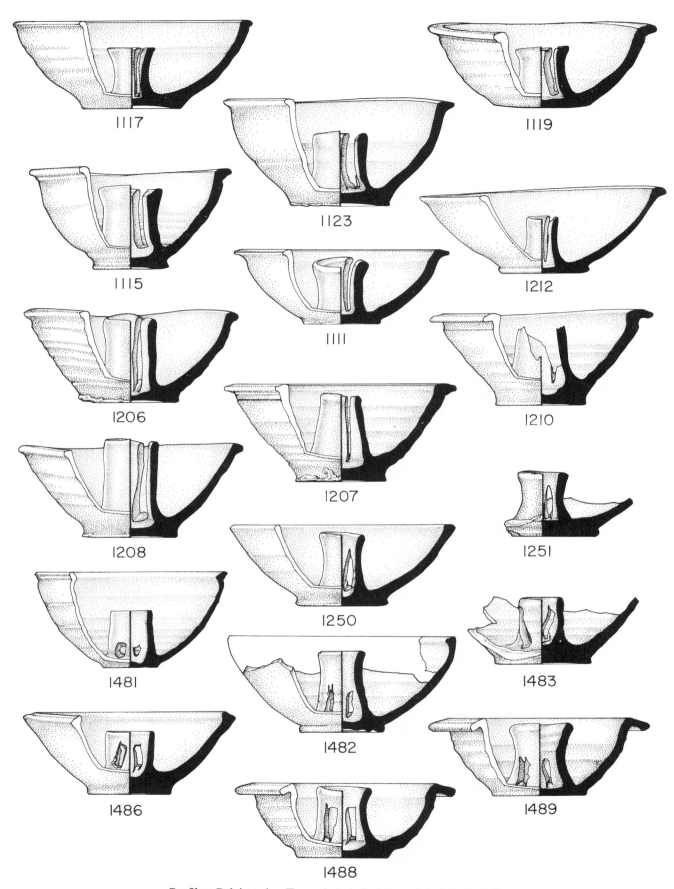

1117
1119
1123
1115
1212
1111
1206
1210
1208
1207
1251
1481
1250
1483
1486
1482
1489
1488

Profiles: Palaimonion Types A-1, A-2, A-3, and A-4. Scale 1:3

PLATE 7

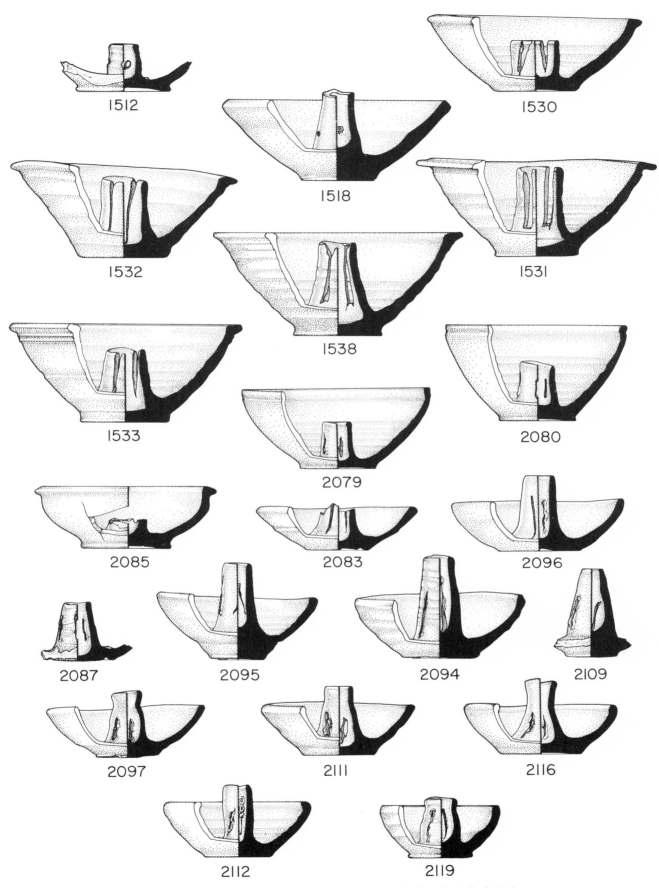

1512

1530

1518

1532

1531

1538

1533

2080

2079

2085

2083

2096

2087

2095

2094

2109

2097

2111

2116

2112

2119

Profiles: Palaimonion Types A-5, A-6, B-1, B-2, B-3, B-4. Scale 1:3

PLATE 8

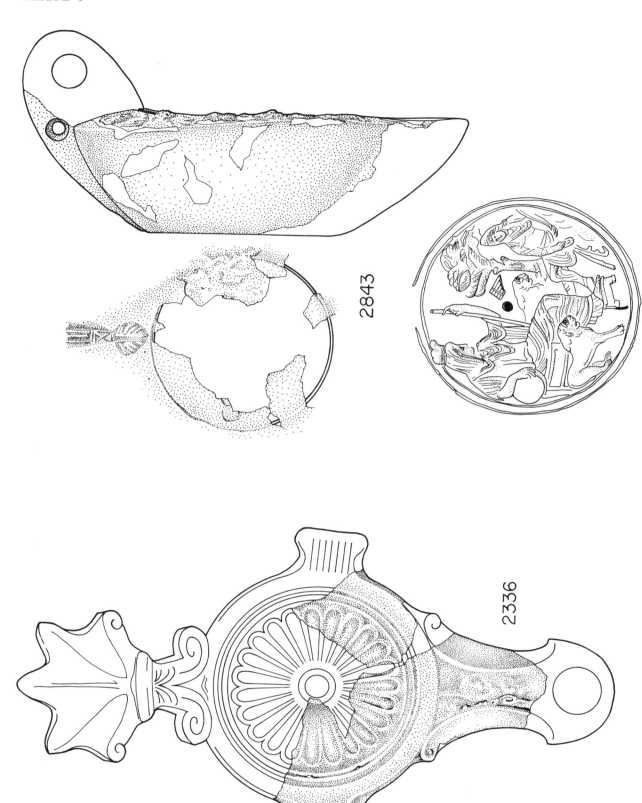

2843

2336

Two large lamps (Types XXI A and XXVII E). Scale 1:2

PLATE 9

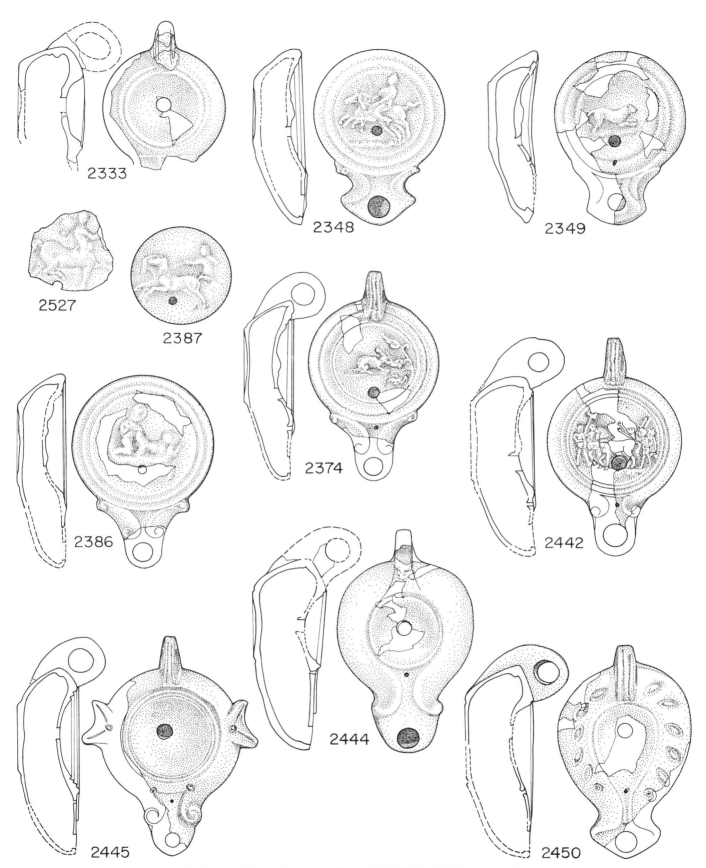

2333

2348

2349

2527

2387

2374

2386

2442

2445

2444

2450

Profiles and Face Drawings: Types XX, XXII–XXIV. Scale 1:2

PLATE 10

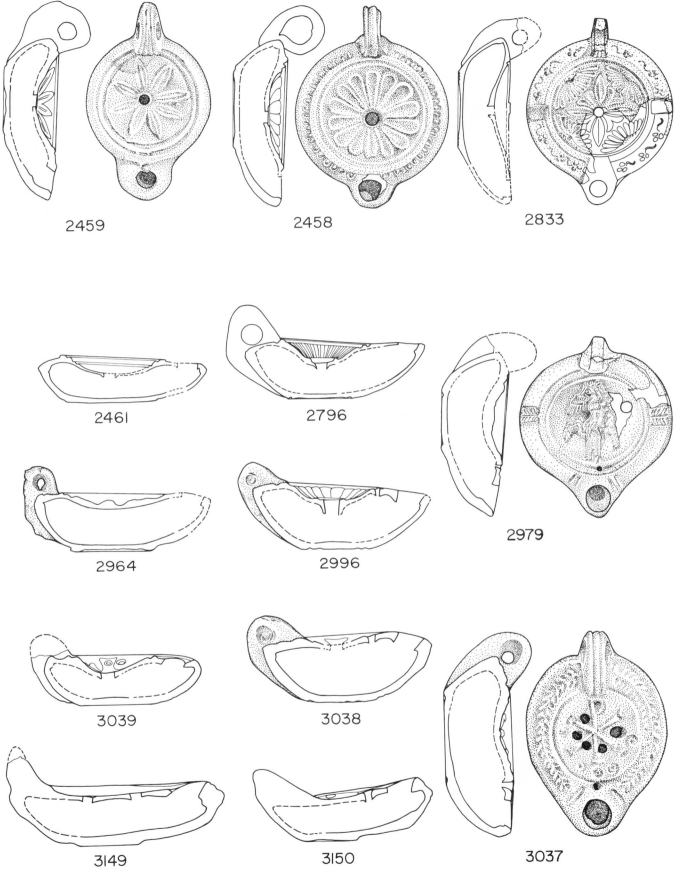

2459

2458

2833

2461

2796

2964

2996

2979

3039

3038

3149

3150

3037

Profiles and Face Drawings: Types XXV, XXVII, XXVIII, XXXI. Scale 1:2

PLATE 11

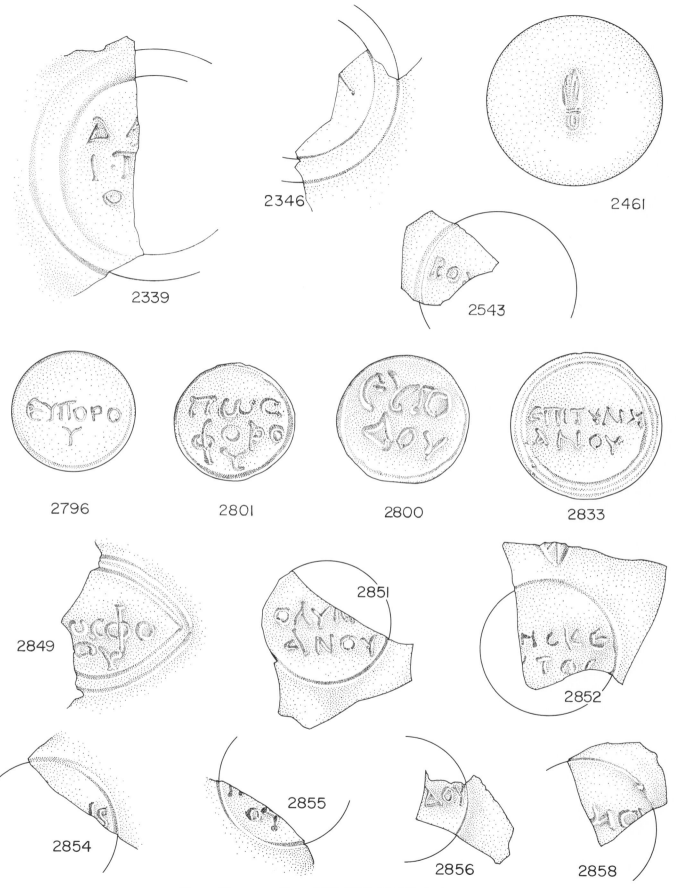

2339

2346

2461

2543

2796

2801

2800

2833

2849

2851

2852

2854

2855

2856

2858

Bases: Signatures, Types XXI–XXV, XXVII. Scale 1:1

PLATE 12

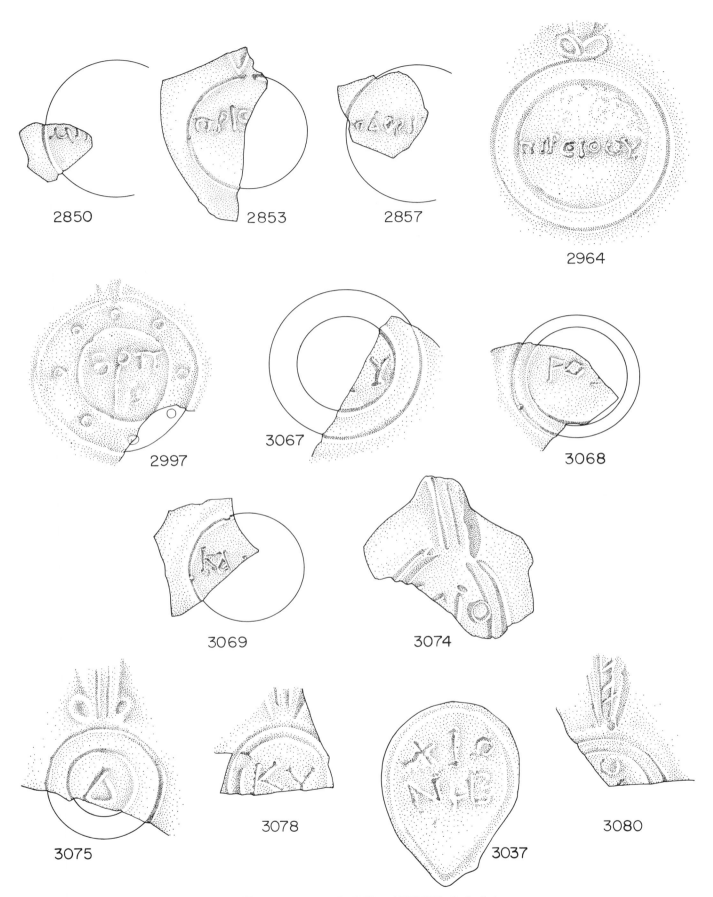

2850

2853

2857

2964

2997

3067

3068

3069

3074

3075

3078

3037

3080

Bases: Signatures, Types XXVII and XXVIII. Scale 1:1

PLATE 13

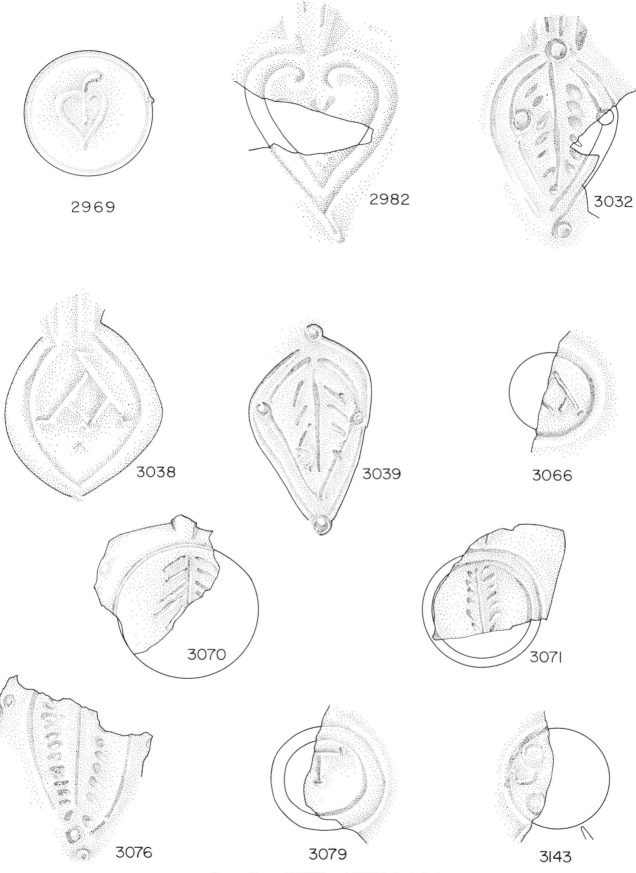

2969

2982

3032

3038

3039

3066

3070

3071

3076

3079

3143

Bases: Types XXVIII and XXIX. Scale 1:1

PLATE 14

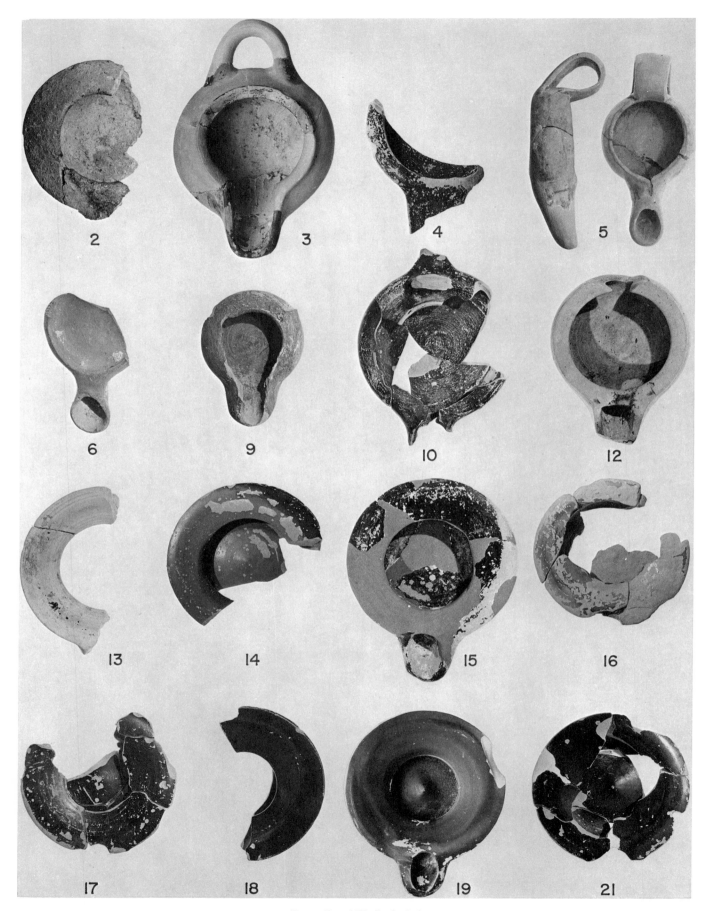

Types I and II. Scale 1:2

PLATE 15

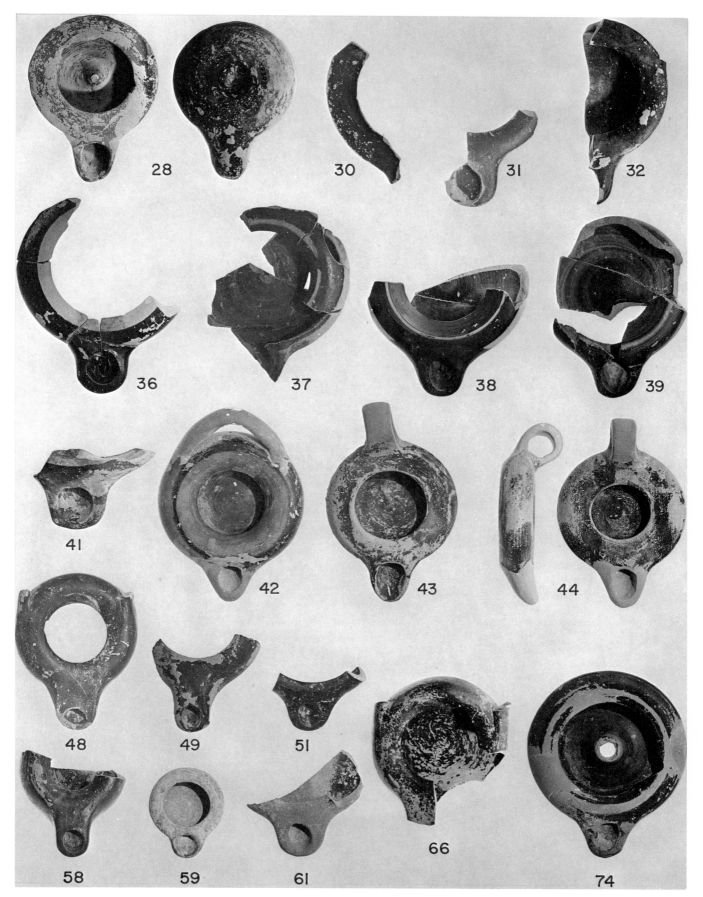

Types III and IV. Scale 1:2

PLATE 16

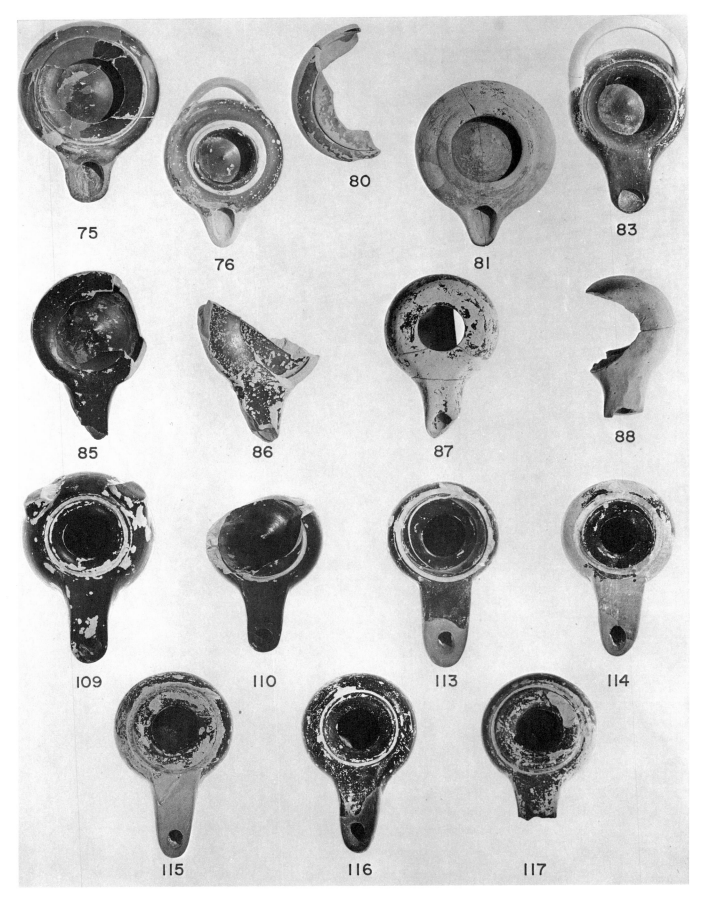

75
76
80
81
83

85
86
87
88

109
110
113
114

115
116
117

Types V–VII B. Scale 1:2

PLATE 17

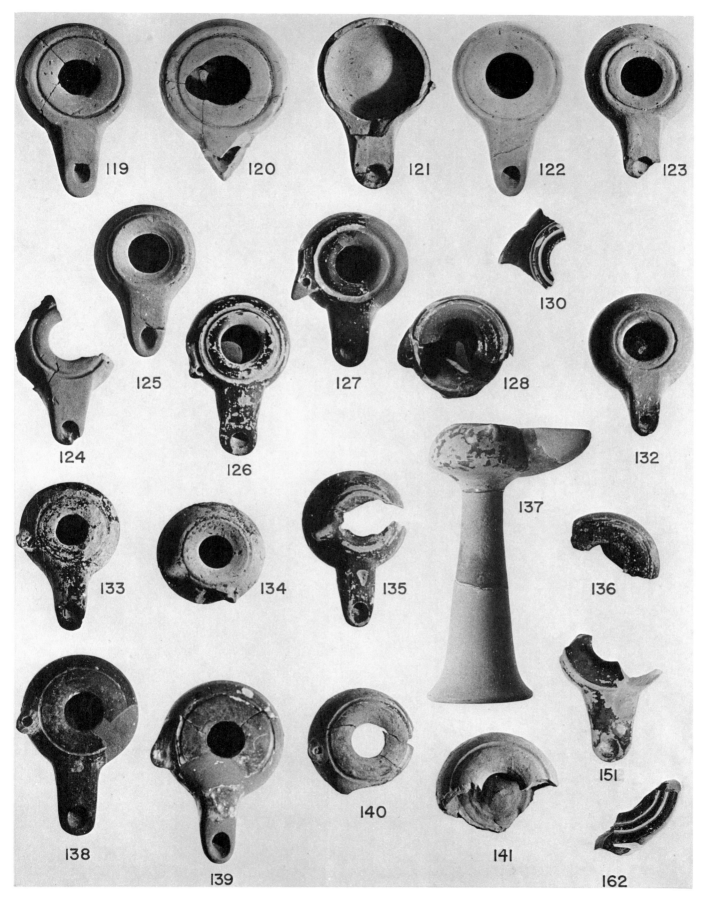

Type VII C–F. Scale 1:2

PLATE 18

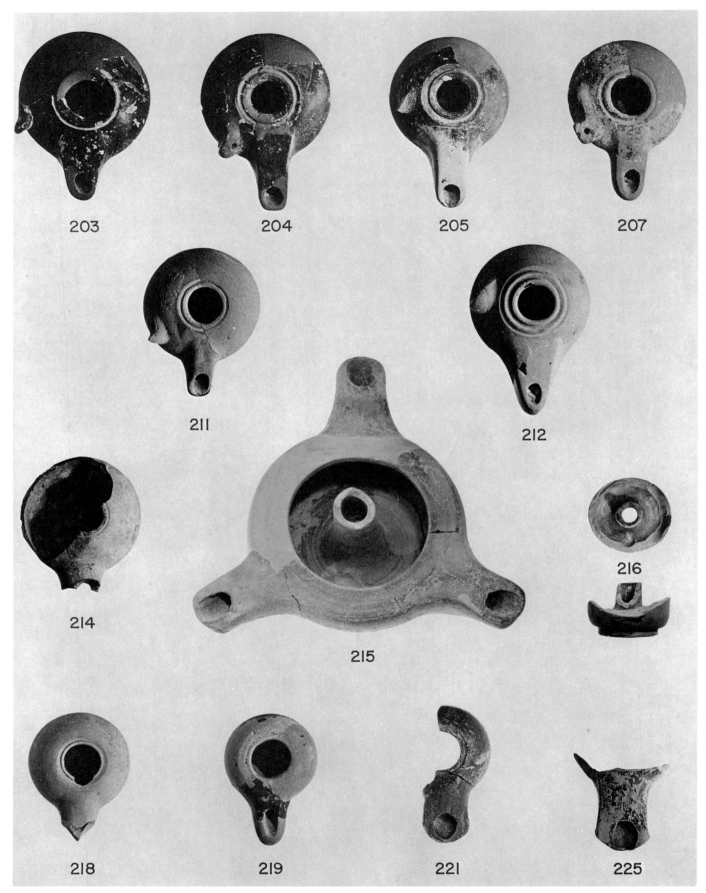

203 204 205 207

211 212

214 215 216

218 219 221 225

Types IX, X, and two unclassified Hellenistic. Scale 1:2

PLATE 19

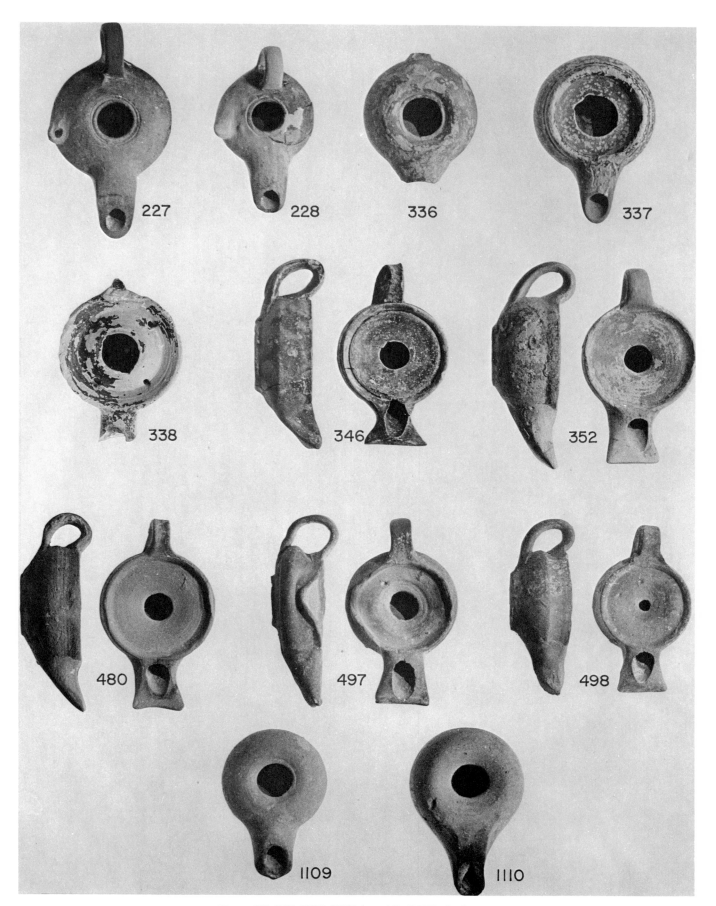

Types XI, XII, XIV, XVI A and B, XVII. Scale 1:2

PLATE 20

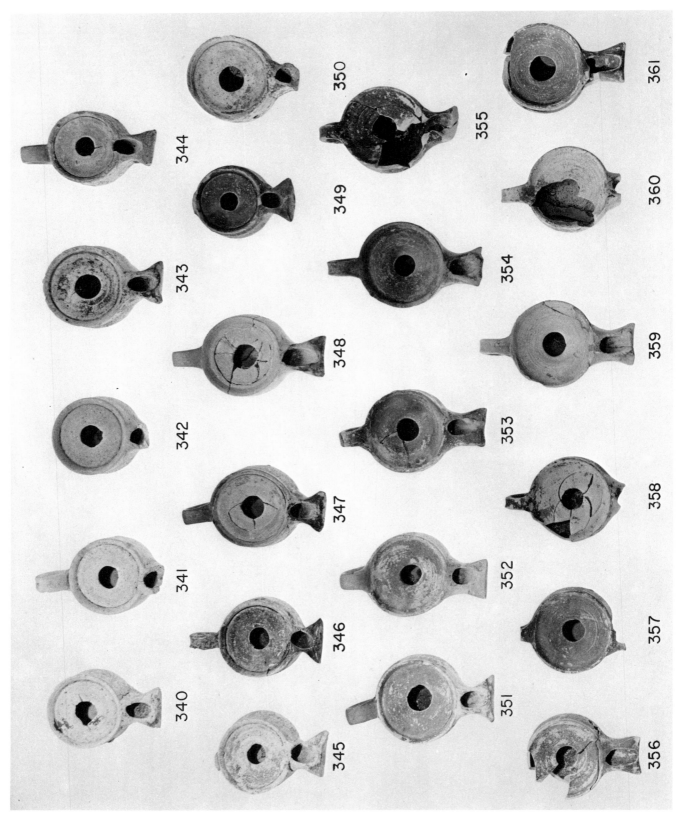

Type XVI A: top views. Scale *ca.* 1:3

PLATE 21

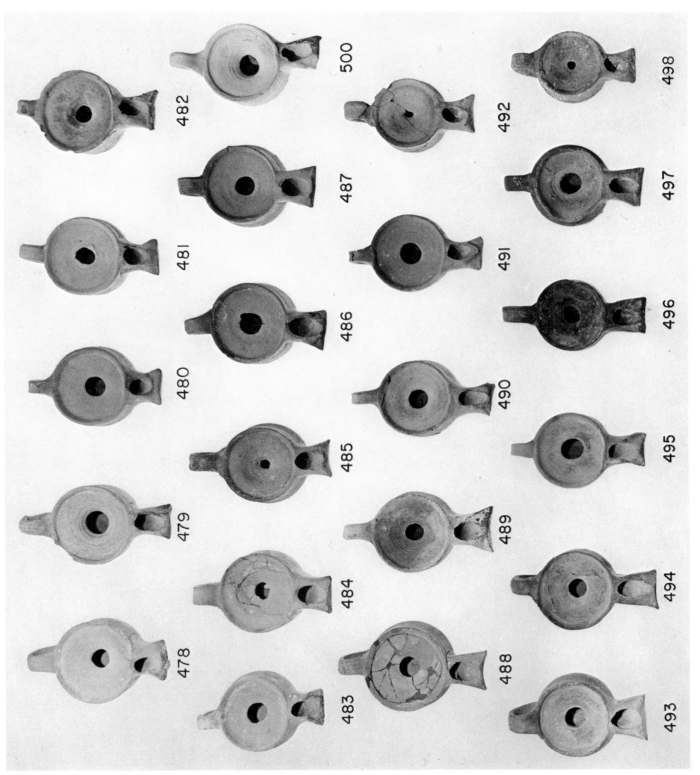

Type XVI B: top views. Scale *ca.* 1:3

PLATE 22

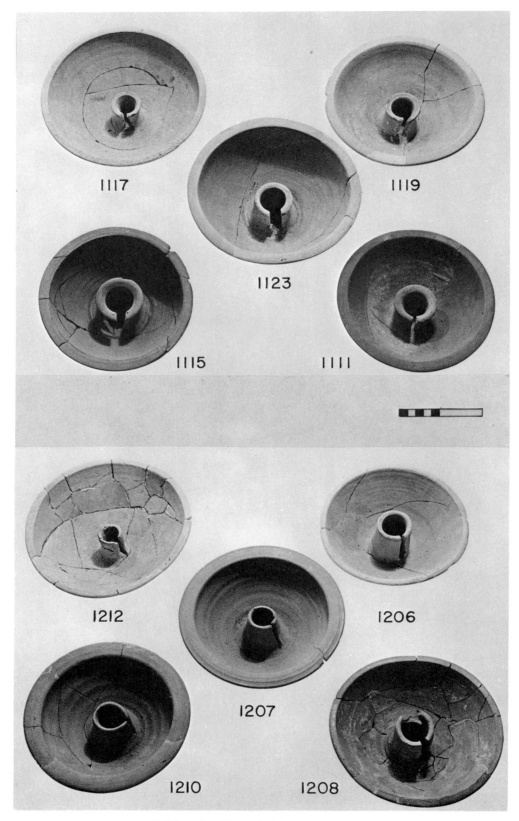

Palaimonion Types A-1, A-2: top views.

PLATE 23

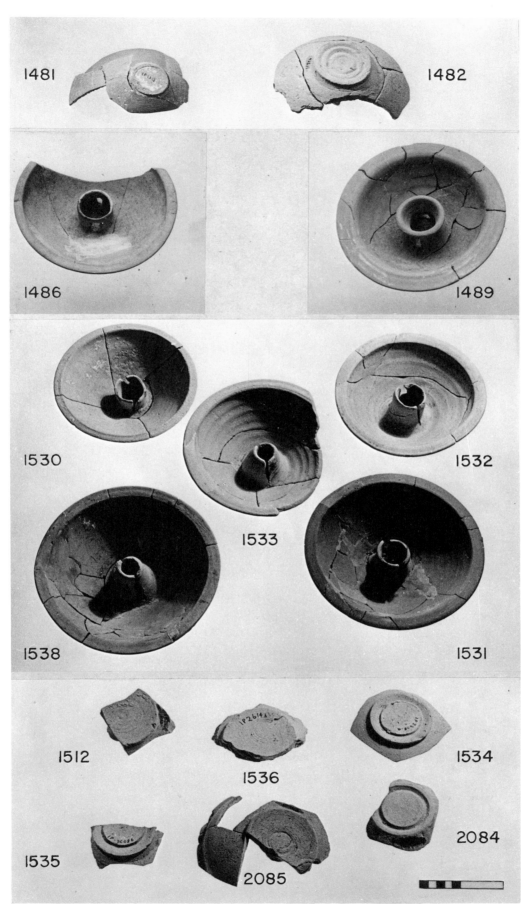

Palaimonion Types A-4, A-5a, A-6, B-2: bases and top views.

PLATE 24

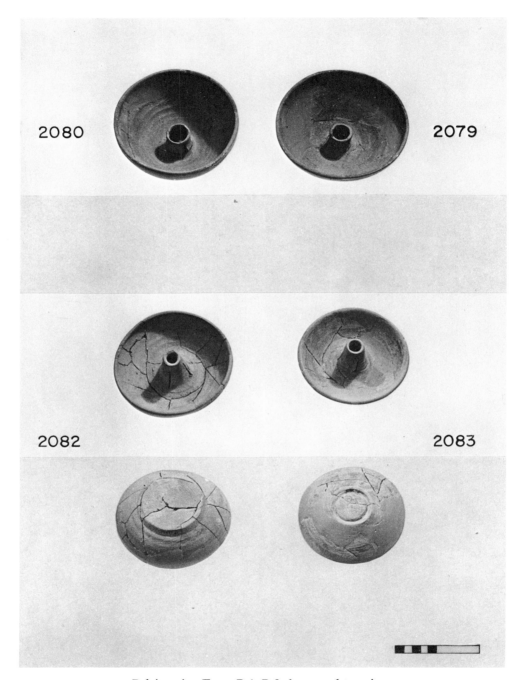

Palaimonion Types B-1, B-2: bases and top views.

PLATE 25

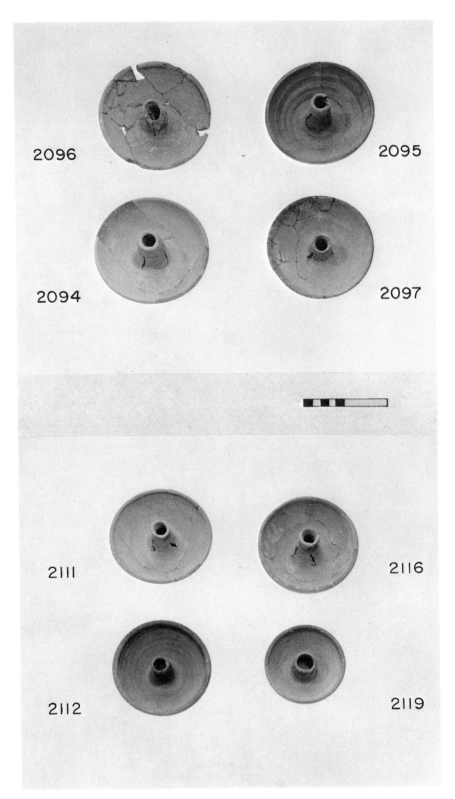

Palaimonion Types B-3, B-4: top views.

PLATE 26

1252      1253      1254

1495      1496      1497      1498      1511

1514      1517

1519      1520

2087      2100      2101      2109

Palaimonion Types A-3, A-4, A-5, B-2, B-3: sockets. Scale 1:2

PLATE 27

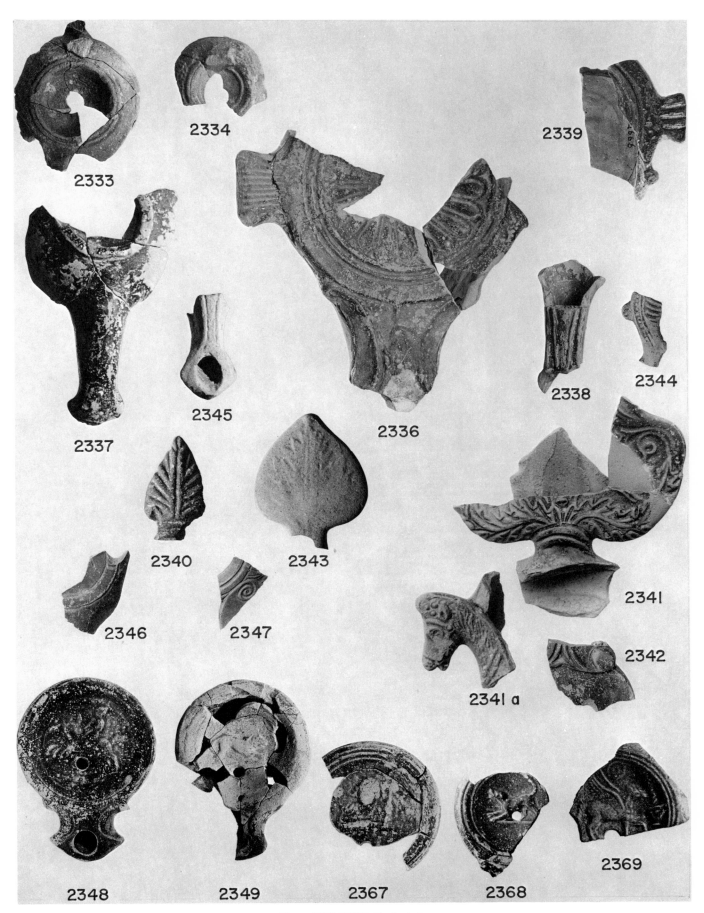

Types XX–XXII. Scale 1:2

PLATE 28

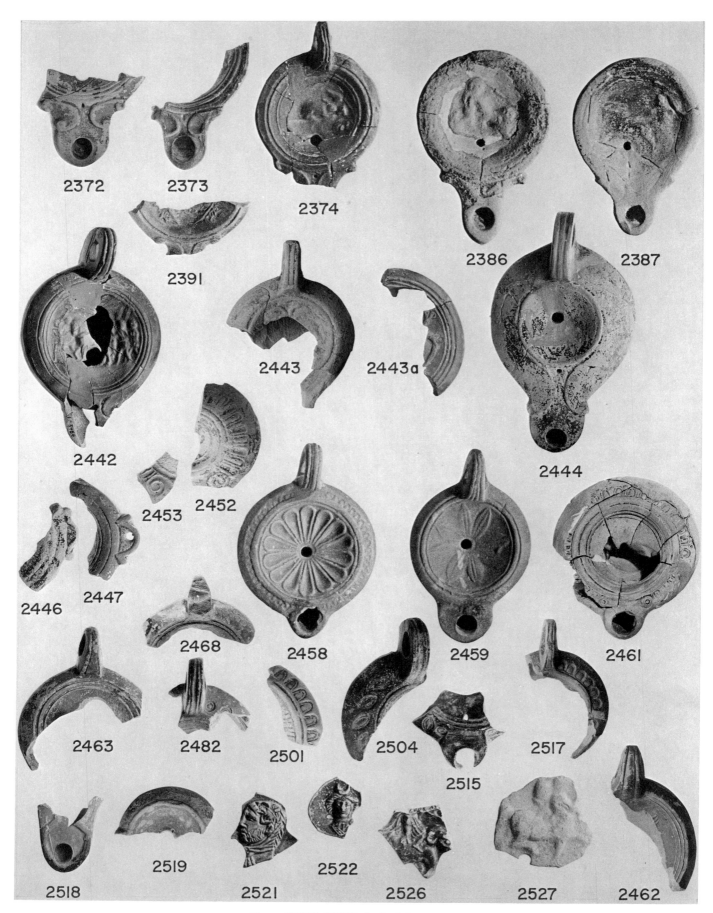

2372 2373 2374 2386 2387

2391

2442 2443 2443a 2444

2453 2452

2446 2447

2468 2458 2459 2461

2463 2482 2501 2504 2517

2515

2518 2519 2521 2522 2526 2527 2462

Types XXIII–XXVI. Scale 1:2

PLATE 29

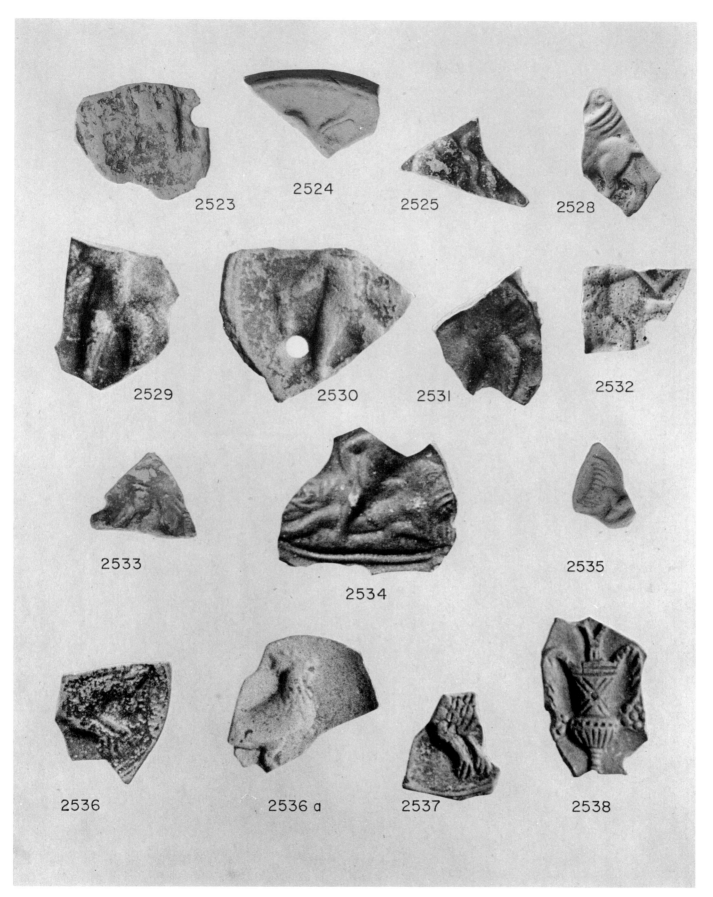

2523    2524    2525    2528

2529    2530    2531    2532

2533    2534    2535

2536    2536 a    2537    2538

Type XXII–XXVI: discus fragments.

PLATE 30

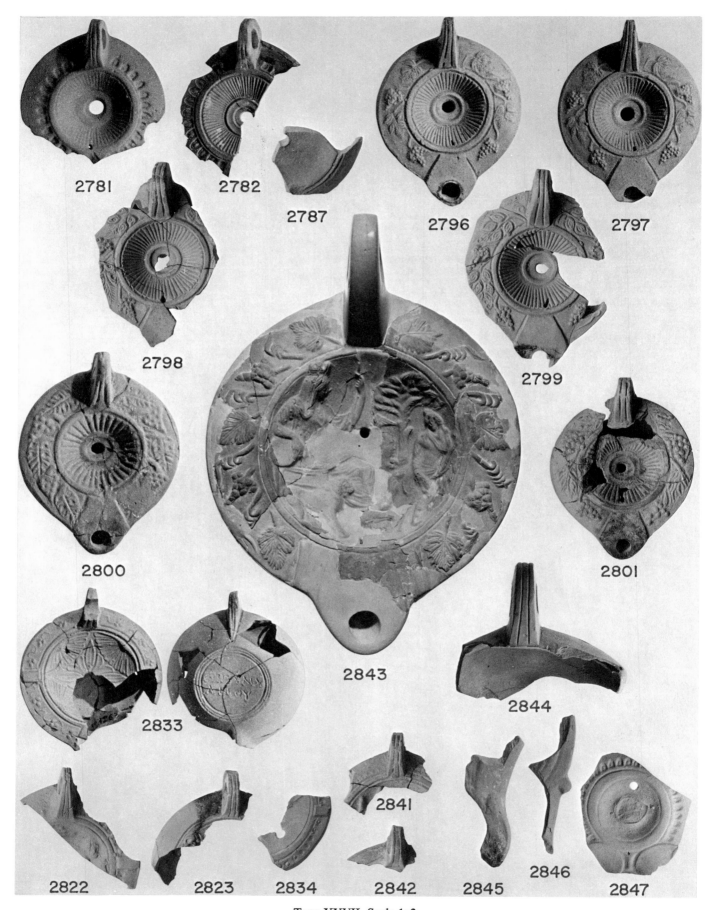

2781

2782

2787

2796

2797

2798

2799

2800

2801

2833

2843

2844

2822

2823

2834

2841

2842

2845

2846

2847

Type XXVII. Scale 1:2

PLATE 31

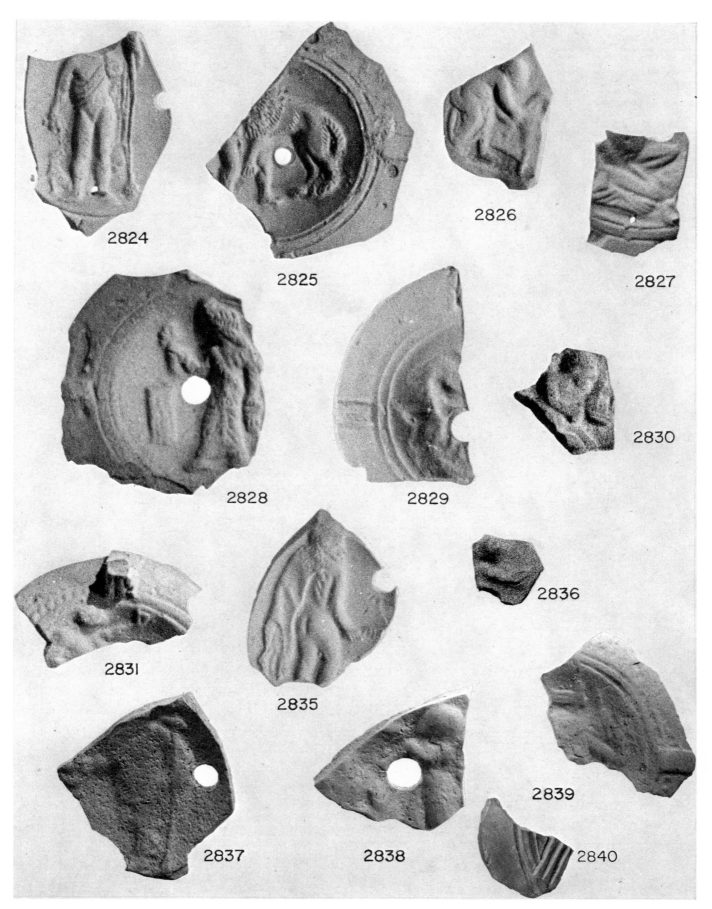

2824

2825

2826

2827

2828

2829

2830

2831

2835

2836

2837

2838

2839

2840

Type XXVII C: discus fragments.

PLATE 32

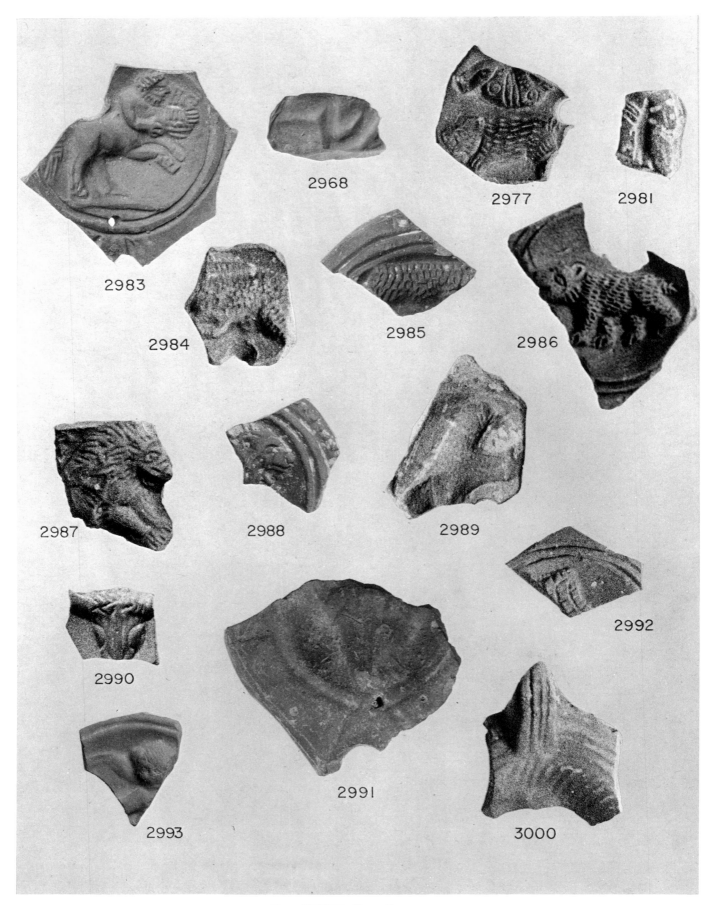

2983

2968

2977

2981

2984

2985

2986

2987

2988

2989

2990

2992

2993

2991

3000

Type XXVIII: discus fragments.

PLATE 33

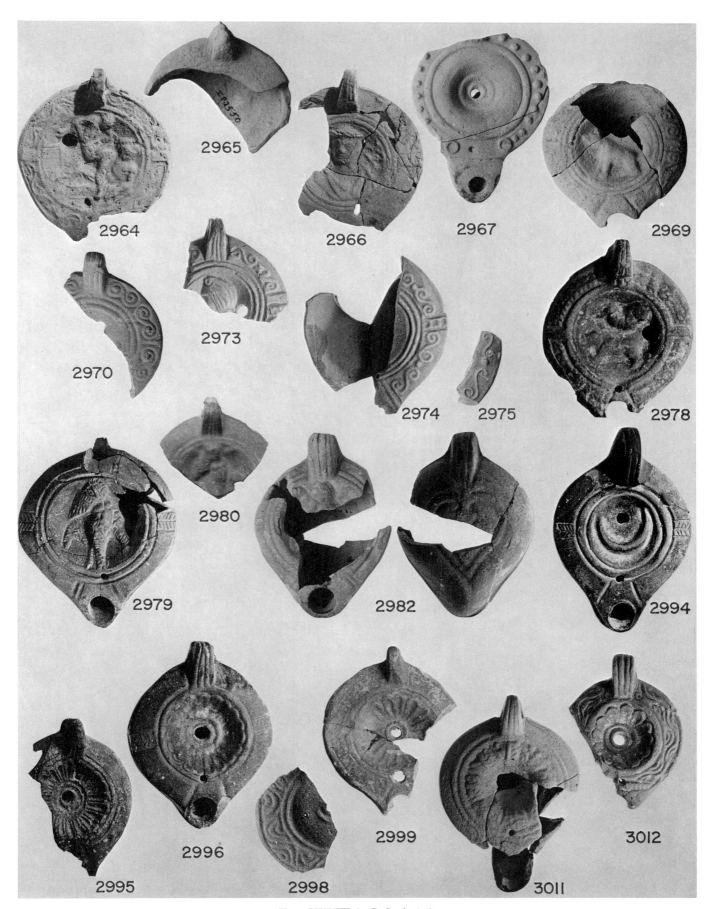

2965

2964

2966

2967

2969

2973

2970

2974    2975    2978

2980

2979    2982    2994

2995

2996

2998

2999

3011

3012

Type XXVIII A–C. Scale 1:2

PLATE 34

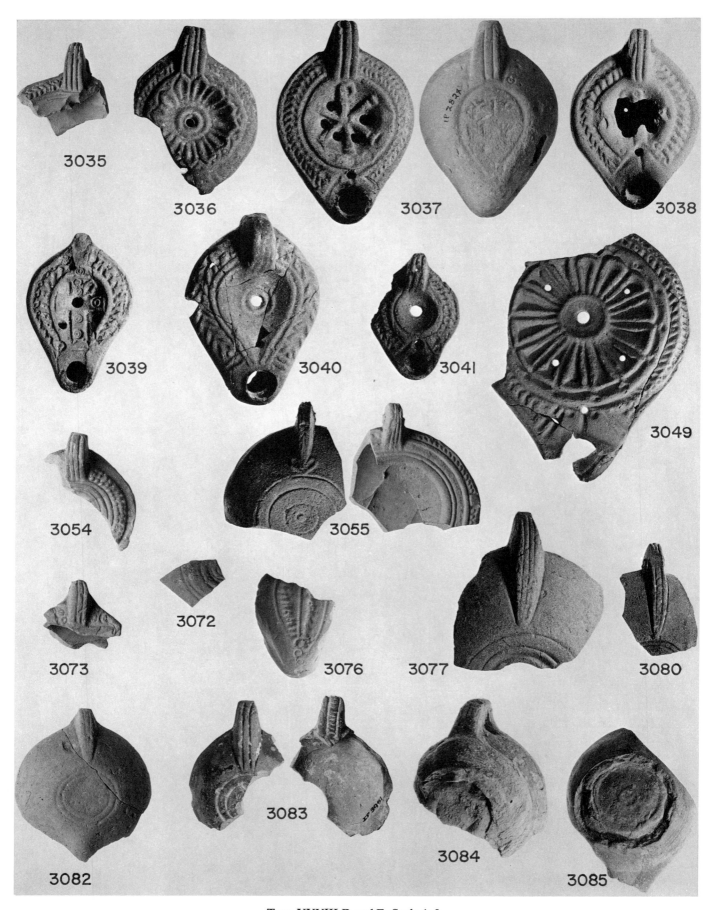

Type XXVIII D and E. Scale 1:2

PLATE 35

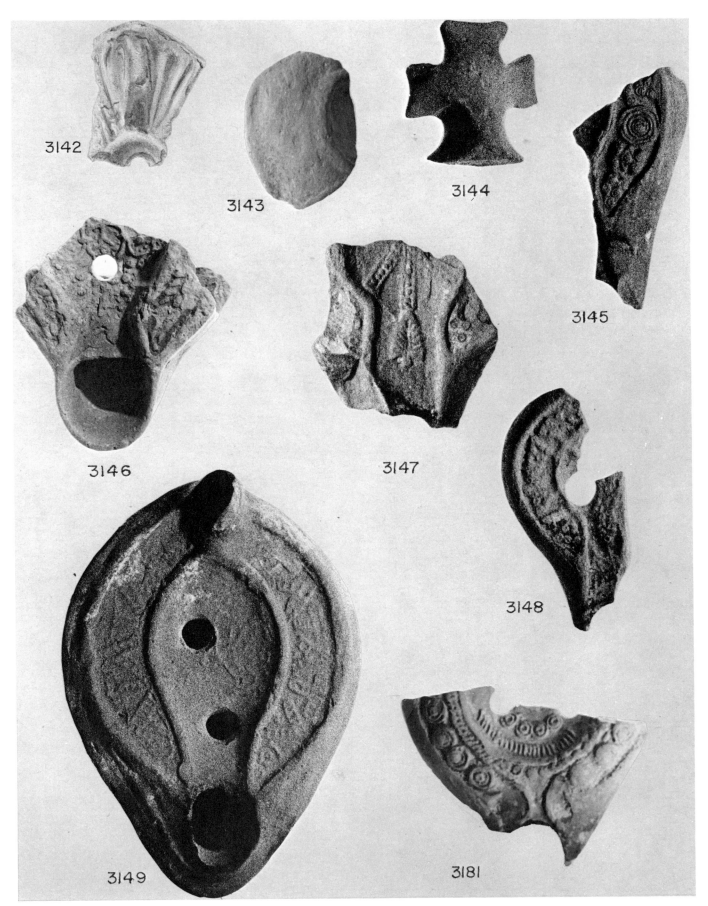

Types XXIX–XXXI, XXXIII. Scale 1:1

PLATE 36

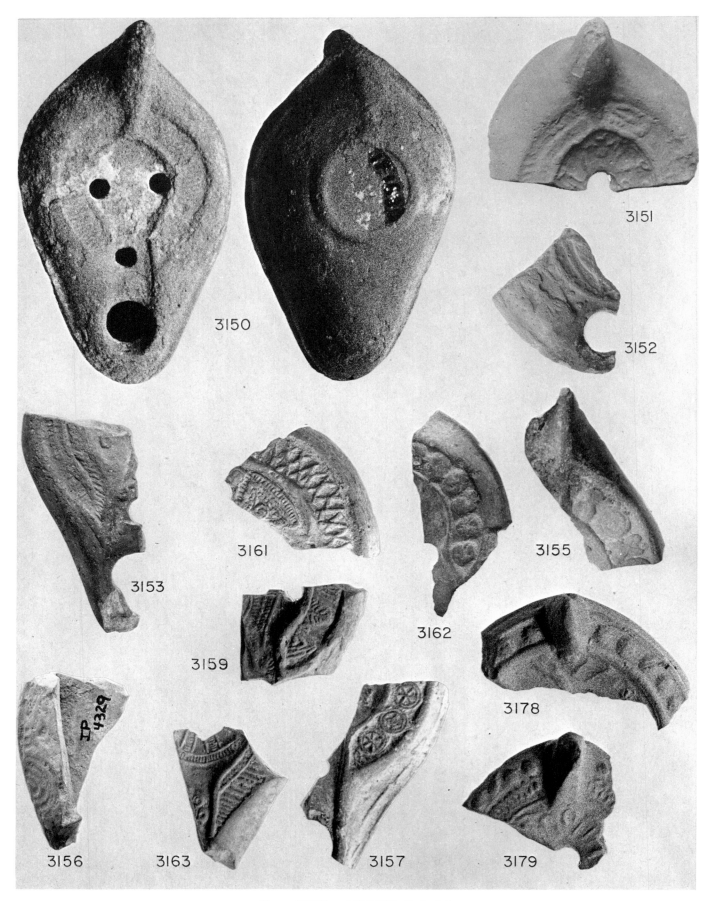

3151

3152

3150

3153

3161

3162

3155

3159

3178

3156

3163

3157

3179

Types XXXI and XXXIII. Scale 1:1

PLATE 37

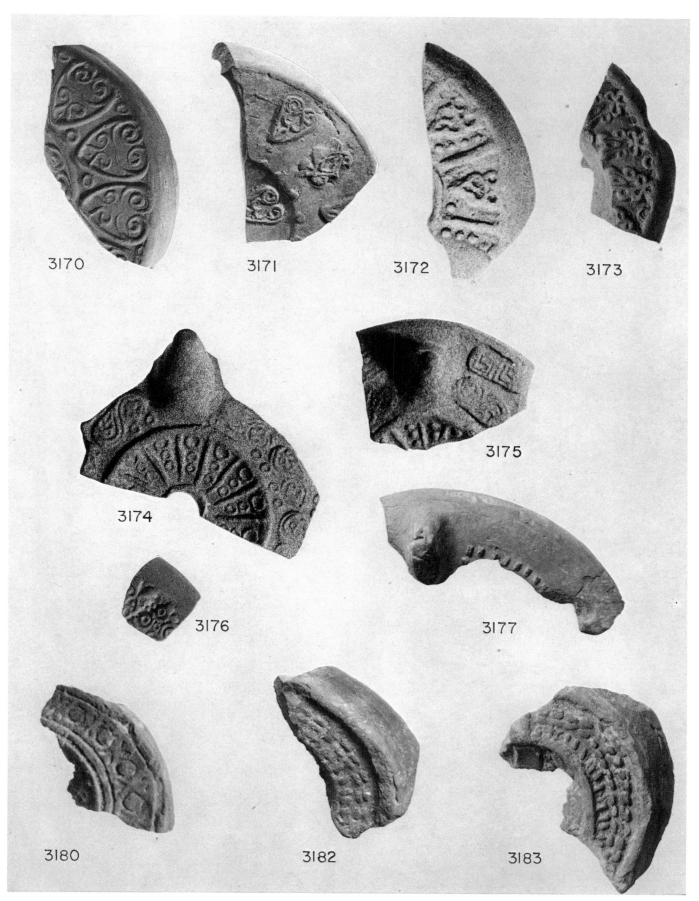

Types XXXII and XXXIII: rim and discus fragments. Scale 1:1

PLATE 38

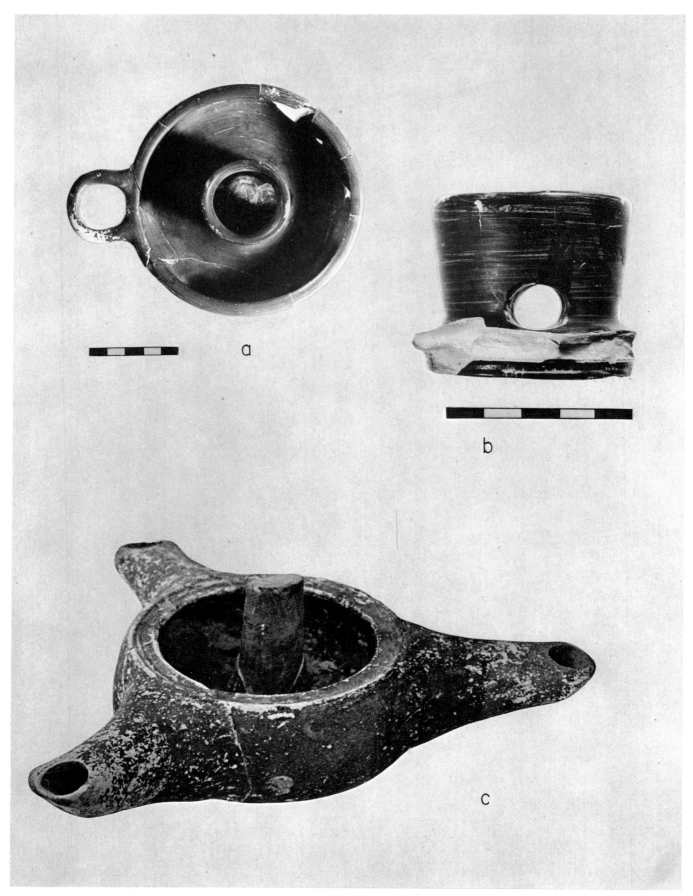

Comparative lamps from Athens and Ioannina

PLATE 39

Large Corinth lamp with horses' heads.

PLATE 40

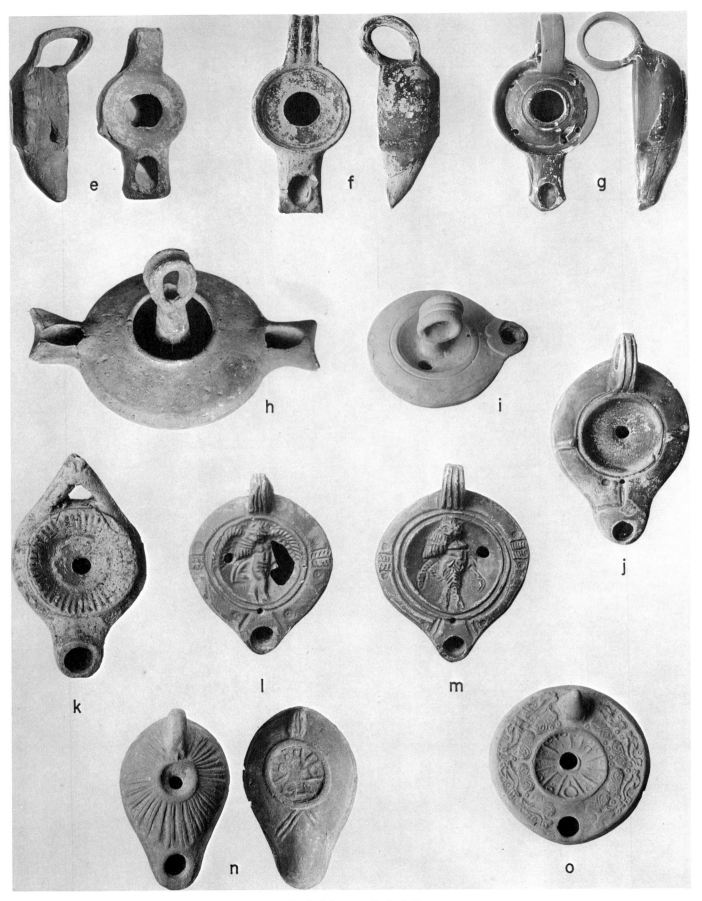

Corinth lamps. Scale 1:2

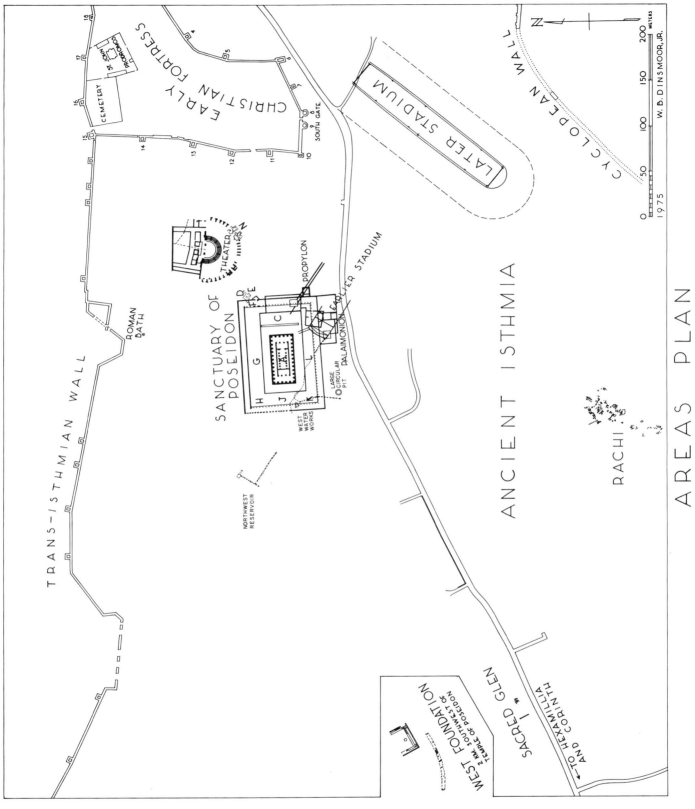

AREAS PLAN

ANCIENT ISTHMIA

W. B. DINSMOOR, JR.

1975